The Ninth King

The Last of the Celestial Empires
The Triumph of Christ over the Powers

WILLEM J. OUWENEEL

THE NINTH KING

The Last of the Celestial Empires
The Triumph of Christ over the Powers

WILLEM J. OUWENEEL

Based on the third Dutch edition

The Ninth King: The Last of the Celestial Empires: The Triumph of Christ over the Powers

This English edition is a publication of Paideia Press (P.O. Box 500, Jordan Station, Ontario, Canada L0R 1S0), a publishing imprint of the Cántaro Institute.

Book Design by: Michael Wagner

ISBN 978-1-998711-07-9

Printed in the United States of America

Table of Contents

Preface

THE HISTORY OF THIS WORLD has known a large number of "world-empires." These empires were governed by earthly rulers, but also by invisible, spiritual powers. The Bible localizes these powers in the "heavenly places," or, "celestial realms" (Eph. 6:12). Because of these invisible celestial rulers "behind" the earthly rulers, the earthly empires are "celestial empires" as well. In each world-empire, the greatest power is possessed by that angelic prince, who is venerated on earth as the chief god in that world-empire. This book deals with these world-empires, which followed one upon the other in world history, and which each had a particular (sometimes positive, often negative) relationship with the people of the God of gods.

The Ninth King is the heavenly as well as earthly Prince of the ninth and last world-empire, who destroys and replaces all previous empires, and who gives to God's people the place for which the God of gods chose it from the outset. This Ninth King is not only the prince of the last world-empire, but behind the screens of world history also governs the destiny of the previous empires. This book is about these nine world-empires, particularly viewed as celestial empires, and about the Ninth King, who has the supremacy in the celestial realms as well as on earth.

The inspiration for this work came from the late Dr. Frank

de Graaff (1918-1993), Reformed theologian and cultural philosopher, at the time pastor at the little town of Hattem (the Netherlands). I had the privilege of having many conversations with him, often with others at his home, sometimes privately in his study. He granted me deep insights behind the screens of world history and of our culture. Sometimes he reminded me of the nineteenth-century British pastor, Alexander Hislop (1807-1865), whose book, *The Two Babylons,* is quoted in this work. Both Hislop and de Graaff have often "seen" so far that I could not go along with them any further, and even definitely had to turn against them. In my view, at decisive points, de Graaff's faithfulness to the New Testament yields to his loyalty to Israel. However, perhaps we learn most from those thinkers with whom we disagree most. This, at least, was my experience with the unforgettable Dr. de Graaff.

I would like to express my warm thanks to those friends and colleagues who read the manuscript and made valuable remarks and criticisms. Among them are lawyer Henk P. Medema, whose book, *Europa 1992,* partly deals with the same subject matter, and Dr. Gerhard H. Kramer, whose book, *Ambrosius van Milaan en de geschiedenis* ("Ambrose of Milan and History"), also deals with a Christian view of history. Of course, for the final result I am responsible alone.

P.S.: Though strongly leaning on the English Standard Version, I have personally translated, directly from the Hebrew and the Greek and in an overly literal way, most of the Scriptures quoted in this book so as to approximate the original content and intention of the text as closely as possible.

Bible verses are quoted according to the numbering in the Hebrew Bible; especially in the Psalms many verses have a higher number than in common English Bibles.

Chapter 1
Light on the Other World

1.1. History and Metahistory

1.1.1. The Historical Pattern

SOME HISTORIANS AND PHILOSOPHERS OF HISTORY, such as Arthur Schopenhauer (1788-1860) or Herbert Fisher (1865-1940), did not believe that the course of history exhibits a certain pattern. However, they form a minority. Usually, historians do believe that the course of history does follow a pattern. They strongly differ, though, in their opinions about the nature as well as the extent of that pattern.[1] With regard to the latter point, some historians hold that we should not pursue historiography any further than describing the vicissitudes of the various nations and states. Others believe they can distinguish larger units in history. In that case, people speak of cultures, or civilizations, which comprise a number of nations or states.

Apart from this, an even more essential question has to be answered; I believe one of the most essential in historiography. That is the question as to how the various cultures are interrelated in space and time. A linear approach is possible, for which church father Augustine (354-430) opted, but also

1. I refer here to a simple introduction such as that of Harmsen (1968, part 3), in spite of his narrow-mindedness with regard to Christianity.

a cyclic one, which was defended in antiquity by Herodotus (c. 485-425 BC), Plato (429-347 BC), the Stoa, Cicero (106-43 BC), and in recent times still by historians such as Oswald Spengler (1880-1936) and Arnold Toynbee (1889-1975). In the present study, in characterizing the successive rising, flourishing, and declining world-empires we appear to follow a cyclic approach, but that is just seemingly the case. In the succession, the linear pattern clearly comes to light, especially in that this succession works its way to a definite climax.

Besides this matter of the *extent* of a historical pattern, the question as to the *nature* of this pattern is highly significant in historiography. For the answer to this question, it is decisive what "distance" one dares to take with regard to the course of history, or, to what "level of abstraction" one ventures to rise. I say, ventures, because all abstraction involves a certain measure of speculation. Those who just limit themselves to the "solid facts," such as those of a biological, psychoanalytical, social, economic, political, artistic, demographic, or technological nature, may count upon the benevolence of the modern historian. Those who, in addition to this, prefer an interpretation in terms of a worldview (idealism, materialism, [neo-] positivism, pragmatism, existentialism, postmodernism, etc.), have already left the domain of strict historiography and have entered into that of the philosophy of history. However, those who go even further and seek their explanatory approach in *transcendent* factors, particularly in spiritual powers "behind" history, will have to reckon today with the pity of the average modern historian.

The view that the course of history is governed by divine powers is surely the most ancient view in historiography. Yet, no modern historian "respecting himself" will dare to come up with it. Also, the average Christian historian does his job like any other historian, that is, factually as an agnostic, and will at best in his free time venture to express the conviction that, in history, in some way or another, "God's hand is working." He says this most carefully, and hardly dares to express himself in a more concrete way. Even less he would venture to include angels and demons in his view. Above all, he wishes not to be placed on one level with a Homer (eighth century BC?) or, to a lesser extent, with a Herodotus, who time and again saw the earthly vicissitudes of their heroes and nations influenced by the immoral, quarreling, intriguing gods of the Olympus.

It is self-evident that the Christian historian cannot view history in such a way. However, is he or she able today to view history at least in the way the church father Augustine did? Has the modern Christian still some knowledge of the kingdom of God with its heavenly angels and earthly believers, which, until the youngest day, will be entangled in a continuous struggle with the realm of Satan and his demons as well as his unbelievers (cf. Matt. 12:25-28)? Even though, in this way, certainly not every historical event can be interpreted right away, has the Christian at least still some notion of the fact that, in the most basic sense, history is precisely about this struggle?

The study that I offer here pretends no more and no less than to throw some light on this struggle. In other words, it unashamedly stands in the tradition of the oldest, that is, Augustinian, interpretation of history. This is the approach that sees "behind" history a *metahistory*, that is literally, a history "behind" history. The earthly events are a consequence of, as well as a reflection of, metahistorical events behind the scenes of world history. These events take place behind the boundaries that divide the immanent ("inner-worldly") realm from the transcendent ("outer-worldly") realm.

1.1.2. Metahistory and Responsibility

"Metahistory" is described as that which lies "behind" history, and actually determines and governs it. In this book, I defend the view that a study of metahistory to a large extent involves a penetration into the invisible realm of the "divine" powers. This higher realm remains hidden to most people.

We will only learn to discover this realm in the light of God's revelation. Only *from* the "outer-worldly" can there be light *about* the "outer-worldly." A truly Christian view of history and culture can only be developed in the light that divine revelation throws upon the cultures of the Middle-East and the West. The real "soul" or "spirit" of a culture, and of a history of culture, is "beyond" scholarly (causal-analytical) research, and lies at the "level" on which only God's Word can inform us.

In this study, I use Scripture as the most important source of knowledge. I do so on the standpoint of faith that Scripture indeed involves divine *revelation*. This means that Scriptural communications about spiritual powers are not based upon subjective human imagination and reflection, but on disclosures on God's behalf. Of course, I do not deny here that Scripture does describe examples of human imagination and reflection. Neither do I deny the value of exegesis, which, for instance, has to find out how far we, in a certain Scripture, have to do with a literal or a symbolical description of spiritual realities, what is the literary genre of that Scripture, etcetera. However, these distinctions do not diminish in any way the transcendent reality content of the descriptions given.

According to the Bible, history is governed by "forces" that belong to an "invisible realm." Of course, we primarily think here of the dominion, the providence of YHWH. It is the God of Jacob who leads, carries, steers, and drives the history of this world unto the end destined by him (cf., e.g., Isa. 46:9-13). Secondly, however, the Bible casts light, too, upon the "instruments" of which YHWH avails himself in world dominion. These are invisible powers in the celestial spheres as well as visible powers on earth. I hope to show that, according to the Bible, often very different, much higher, much more essential matters are involved than current historiography seems to realize.

In this book, strong emphasis will be laid upon the influence of higher powers. A measure of one-sidedness cannot be avoided here. While in the past so much one-sided emphasis was laid upon immanent forces in history, that is, upon human-responsible action, in this book the emphasis will shift to the transcendent forces. However, the great significance of human responsibility should not for a moment be lost sight of. We see this already in the story. How easy is it to ascribe the whole fall of man exclusively to the devil. But in Scriptures where the fall is evoked[2] not the devil but human responsibility takes the central place. And thus it is in the whole history of mankind. Unfortunately, the activity of the spiritual powers has been underestimated to a large extent. But where they were recognized, this sometimes took place at the cost of human responsibility.

The two "forces," the transcendent spiritual powers and the immanent human choices, should not be abused to cancel each another out but they complete each another. We may often understand by the "spirit" of a given culture a very concrete transcendent power. But the Dutch historian and politician Guillaume Groen van Prinsterer (1801-1876) was equally right when he, in speaking of the "spirit" of the French Revolution, did not think of the spiritual realm but primarily of the whole of human-apostate choices.[3] A "cultural force" can be a very concrete transcendent power; but at the same time, it is also *always* the power that consists of the free choices of responsible men. Calvin somewhere calls the human heart an *idolorum fabricam*; that is a "workshop of idols."[4] These idols can be very concrete demonic powers; but they can equally be the "idols" of our own pride and rebellion. Man submits to idolatrous powers outside him; but it is equally true that he *creates* idols in his own heart. The one thing needs to be

2. Particularly Rom. 5:12-21. Also, e.g., in 2 Cor. 11:3 and 1 Tim. 2:14 man's own responsibility always comes to the fore.
3. Groen van Prinsterer in his *Lectures on Unbelief and Revolution* (1847, trans. 1989).
4. *Institutes of the Christian Religion* (1559), 1.11.8 (cf. 1.5.12).

emphasized without neglecting the other.

Even when man "creates" his own idols for that matter, the objective "gods" outside him endeavor at the same time to make man the prisoner of his own "idols." And thus, man, creating "idols" according to his own free responsibility and submitting to them, is the prisoner of the "gods" outside him after all. Man never undergoes getting into the grip of the evil powers as a will-less tool but always as a consequence of his own free choice. His responsibility is never switched off. Therefore his excuse, "The serpent deceived me" (Gen. 3:13), is never valid for, even where this is true, it is always man who, of his own free choice, *had* himself deceived.

1.2. Biblical Historiography

1.2.1. God's People in the Centre

In speaking of Western culture, we realize that this culture is the spiritual heir of Hellenistic civilization and the culture of the (West-)Roman Empire. To this we have to add significant Celtic, Germanic, and Arabic influences. We find extensive prophecies about the antique cultures in the biblical book of Daniel. Later I will come back to them more extensively; at present I point to some significant starting points offered by Daniel. The book supplies us with a magnificent example of the various ways in which we can approach history.

Daniel views the world-empires at three "levels." The first "level" is found in Daniel 2. Here, the four ancient world-empires or world cultures are presented to the Babylonian king Nabu-kudurri-ussur (Nebuchadrezzar, c. 634-562 BC) in the form of an exceedingly impressive statue. In spite of modern, alternative approaches, I cannot doubt that the four parts of the image represent the (New-)Babylonian Empire, the Medo-Persian Empire, the Greek-Macedonian Empire including the Hellenistic culture resulting from this, and finally the Roman Empire.[5] However, the point that concerns me in particular now is that these four empires are presented to

5. See about this extensively Appendix 5.

the king in such an impressive manner. This is the way in which man without God has always viewed history: he sees "golden" and "silver," that is, mighty, impressive, empires and rulers, and he would hardly believe that history might be governed by anything else than by them. This is also the way in which history is taught at schools; there, we mainly hear about mighty statesmen and army generals.

In Daniel 7, however, the same four world-empires are viewed on a second, higher "level." They are presented in a dream, this time not to a pagan king, however, but to the prophet of YHWH, the God of Israel. And this man of God does not see a mighty statue, no empires represented by precious metals, but he sees four ignorant beasts, which do not know God but are only driven by their devilish-animal instincts. This is the true nature of cultures that do not submit to YHWH. Heathen kings have no notion of this nature – they cannot "see" such a dream – but the man of God does.

Moreover, something comes to light in Daniel 7 that did not yet come up in Daniel 2. In the chapter of the four beasts, the people of Israel turn out to take a central place in the history of the world-empires. Even more strongly, the little nation of Israel turns out to be the pivot around which, according to the counsel and the election of God, the whole of world history turns. Only the man of God is aware of this. He also knows that the world-empires without God will eventually perish, and that their judgment is the more severe the more they have oppressed Israel, whereas eventually the people of Israel will be delivered and will prevail. That is truly the pivotal center of history.

I would like to illustrate this central point a little further before we come to the third and highest "level" in Daniel. To this end, I mention some other examples that show what is the pivotal matter of biblical historiography. My first example comes from Genesis 14. Probably, before the episode described here many wars had already taken place on earth. However, the war of Genesis 14 is of great importance in salvational history, and worth mentioning, because God's elect, Lot and subsequently Abram, are all involved in it. The names of Amraphel and the other kings have only been preserved for later generations because they came into conflict with God's men.

A second, even more fascinating example is found in Isa. 44:24-45:8. Here a prediction is made concerning the rise of the Persian king Cyrus (Heb. Koresh, Gr. Kyros), who would conquer the New-Babylonian Empire and found the mighty Medo-Persian Empire. In Isa. 45:1-3 he is predicted to subdue nations before him, break in pieces doors of bronze. Indeed, Herodotus tells us about the hundred gates of bronze in the outer wall of the city of Babylon.[6] According to the prophecy, Cyrus was to conquer tremendous riches, which indeed he did, both in Babylon and in Lydia. In the latter country, he broke the power of the fabulously wealthy king Croesus.[7]

In v. 3-4, YHWH tells us why he would grant all this to Cyrus. He did it "for the sake of my servant Jacob, and Israel my chosen," and that Cyrus might know YHWH. It was Cyrus who allowed the Jews to return to their country and to rebuild the temple (Isa. 44:28; 45:13; Ezra 1:1-4). Therefore, God rewards him with a mighty empire. According to secular standards, this is absurd, but the prophet declares it here with great emphasis: Cyrus owes his whole gigantic empire to his benevolence with regard to the tiny nation of the Jews. To any thinking in terms of cause and effect, which is characteristic of common historiography, and understandably so, this is not only an unproven but also an extremely unlikely thesis. However, metahistory inevitably moves at a totally different "level." It counts with factors of which common historiography has no idea.

Let me give a third example. From secular history we know that the Persian king Xerxes I, or Ahasuerus, undertook an enormous expedition against Greece from the third to the

6. Herodotus, *History* 1,179.
7. Ibid. book 1.

sixth year of his government (cf. Dan. 11:2), which for the Persians ended in a terrible defeat.[8] If the expedition had ended in a different way, humanly speaking the history of Europe would have taken a different course. However, in the book of Esther this very expedition is quietly passed by. In Esther 1:3, we hear about a great feast of hundred and eighty days in the third year of the king. In fact, this cannot have been anything else than the preparation for the great war, but the Bible does not mention this. From this feast, we move immediately to the seventh year of Ahasuerus (Esther 2:16). Apparently, to JHWH it is far more important what happened to his people during this period. Therefore, the book of Esther is silent about the great war between the Greeks and the Persians, and it lays all the emphasis on the question as to how Israel went along in the period afterwards.

In Persian historiography it is precisely the reverse. There, all the light falls upon the war I mentioned, whereas Mordecai and Esther are entirely lacking (although some have wanted to equate Esther with queen Amestris[9]). To the world, the history of Israel at that time apparently had little value, but to God it is so important that he devoted a separate Bible book to it. For if Haman, the "enemy of the Jews" (Esther 3:10; 8:1; 9:10, 24), had had his way, all Israel would have been exterminated within the empire, including the Jews who had returned to Palestine, which at that time still belonged to the Medo-Persian Empire. In that case, the Messiah would never have been born. For the Western world, that would have been far more disastrous than if the Persians had won the war against the Greeks.

1.2.2. Invisible Powers

We now arrive at the third and highest "level" of consideration in Daniel, namely, in Daniel 10. In Daniel 7, we do get

---

8. Ibid. book 7.
9. Ibid. 7.61.114; 9.109-112; what we hear in this text about her character does not correspond with that of Esther, though.

a picture of the true nature of the godless cultures, but we are not yet given a real glance "behind the scenes." This only happens in Daniel 10. There, the prophet has an encounter with a celestial being, who reports to him about an encounter with the "prince of the kingdom of Persia" (or, the "prince of Persia"; v. 13, 20). He also speaks about the "prince of Greece" (v. 20), and in particular about "Michael, one of the chief princes," or, "Michael, your prince," "Michael, the great prince who has charge of your people," that is, the prince of Israel (10:13, 21; 12:1). It is obvious that Daniel 10 does not deal with earthly princes but with invisible powers in the spiritual realm, angelic powers, which turn out to be the steering forces behind the various empires. Not the earthly rulers but apparently these "celestial beings" are the actual potentates "behind the scenes," who dominate and manipulate the history of their respective empires and nations. We will extensively come back to that, for this point touches the actual theme of this study.

Another point is of great significance. These celestial beings turn out to be hostile towards the celestial messenger appearing to Daniel, and towards Michael, the "prince" of Israel, and thus towards Israel itself. Here we receive the deepest insight concerning the true nature of the four world cultures. They apparently are not just ignorant beasts as such, but are governed by invisible angelic powers. Moreover, these spiritual powers apparently do not primarily fight one another but first and foremost aim at Israel. In "common" history that which is going on first of all seems to be a war between Persia and Greece. But that is nothing but a chess match between two black kings. The *real* battle in history is fought between all black kings on one side and the great White King as well as his little white pawns on earth on the other side. In the cases of Cyrus and Ahasuerus we saw that it is not the mutual conflicts between the cultures which are of decisive significance in history, but their acceptance or rejection of Israel, and thus of YHWH. Israel is the pivot of world history, no matter how strange this may seem to the average historian.

In the following chapters we first want to investigate what Scripture has to tell us further about the invisible powers in the celestial realm, which, under God's universal dominion, determine world history.[10] In Hebrew the word for "prince" is *sar*. In Jewish tradition this is a well-known term for the angelic princes of the various nations, as we will see later. The same word is used many times for an earthly "prince," but a few times also for celestial "princes." Apart from Daniel 10:13, 20 and 12:1, this is the case in Joshua 5:14, where we hear about "the Prince of the army of YWHW," that is, a celestial prince, who as a commander is placed over a whole army of celestial beings. The war of Israel against Canaan was not only a battle between two earthly nations but in fact a spiritual conflict between two invisible powers: the army of YHWH and the evil spiritual army "behind" the Canaanite nations. A few times we receive a similar insight into God's army in the "higher world," in particular when people belonging to God get into a conflict situation, e.g., Jacob (Gen. 32:1-2) and Elisha (2 Kings 6:16-17; also compare 7:6).

In liberal, but also in conservative treatises about angels and demons, often a certain "development" in this subject matter is assumed, in comparing earlier with later Bible books. It is claimed that, at the outset, apparently the Bible writers only had a vague notion of angels and demons, which subsequently is supposed to have become more nuanced and differentiated. It is claimed that, for instance, the figure of Satan in the book of Job is "still" simply a common angel who plays the role of an "adversary" in a forensic sense before the throne of God, whereas this figure in 1 Chron. 21:1 has "developed" into the actual power of evil, the great adversary of God, as we also know him from the New Testament.

If the matter is presented in this way, I cannot agree with it. Here, the subjective element is strongly in the fore, and the danger exists that the whole view of angels and demons in

10. See also Appendix 1, in which some general remarks about angels are made.

the later Bible books is seen as nothing but a fully developed concept of pious imagination. The matter looks very different when we speak of a certain development in the *revelation* concerning angels and demons. This would then mean that Scripture gradually discloses more details concerning angels and demons, as it is the case with so many other topics in Scripture.

The subjective standpoint would gain force if it could be shown that the later Bible books not only give more details about the angelic realm, but that the ideas concerning the angelic realm change from the earlier to the later books. In my opinion, this is not the case. For instance, in the example concerning Satan it must be said that already in the book of Job this angelic prince is not only a forensic accuser but definitely an evil spirit, who aims at the destruction of Job. Or take, for instance, the fact that, in the Pentateuch, YHWH himself is still the Captain of his people,[11] whereas in Daniel 10-12 it is the archangel Michael who is Israel's prince. These are not necessarily two contradictory representations, but salvational-historical changes in the spiritual development of Israel, as we will see later.

There is yet another aspect which I would like to stress concerning the use of Scripture. Every angelological study endeavors to tell us as much as possible about these celestial beings, whereas it is striking how preciously little Scripture actually tells us about angels. Many questions could be asked about angels that have led to much speculation indeed, both by Jews and by Christians. But in Scripture these questions are simply not answered. I just mention questions such as: How were angels created? When were they created? Before the first day of creation? At the first day? At the second day of creation? What exactly are all their functions? How and when and why have certain groups of angels "fallen"? Did all the "fallen" angels "fall" at the same time, or was there more than

11. Compare Exod. 32:34; 33:2 with 33:12-17.

one fall among the angels? Are all fallen angels Satan's angels? To all these questions we receive no, or just a minimal, answer. We will therefore have to beware of any excessive speculation, that is, going beyond what Scripture tells us.

On the other hand, we are allowed to thoroughly examine, and fully "exploit," the few data that Scripture does supply us with. No fear of speculation should let us stay behind that which is actually revealed in Scripture, as has happened too often. In this regard, we will also have to consider that the limited data in the later books of the Old and in those of the New Testament cannot be severed from the Jewish literature, which tells us much more about angels. These writings are not inspired and certainly not free of speculation; they have even been written by men with the "veil" upon their heart, of which Paul speaks (2 Cor. 3:15). However, this does not mean that everything that is found in there is wrong. The Jews have been the first to do exegesis of the biblical texts concerned, and if at times they err, so do the later Christian expositors. Those who seriously take notice of these early Jewish views cannot deny that they form a useful source of data, which can help us to see the biblical data in a clearer perspective.

1.3. The Seven World-Empires

1.3.1. The Starting Point of Revelation 17

In the book of Revelation, ch. 17:7-9, John gives an explanation of the "beast," the eschatological world power, which is destroyed by Christ at his second coming. Later we will consider this beast more closely; we now give attention to one detail only. Verse 10 says that the seven heads of the beast are seven "kings." As is the case with each element in Revelation, there are many interpretations for this one. I myself prefer, with many expositors (Hengstenberg, Alford, Seiss, Ladd, Walvoord), to interpret these seven "kings" as seven personified kingdoms. These seven successive empires, leading to the "beastly" world power of the latter days, would then be: Egypt, Assyria, (New-)Babylonia, Medo-Persia, Macedonia-Greece, the Roman Empire, and a seventh empire to be identified later. Some interpreters (Greijdanus, Hendriksen) think of Old-Babylonia rather than of Egypt but, in my opinion, this empire lies outside the scope of Scripture.

The text of v. 10-14 can now be paraphrased as follows. The seven heads of the beast are seven kingdoms. Five of these empires, from the Egyptian to the Greek-Macedonian Empire, had already perished, the sixth (Roman) Empire still existed at the time of the author, the apostle John, the seventh empire had not yet come, and when it would come it would stay a short while. The beast itself is the eighth world-empire, as well as the head of that empire, but it is a revival of one of the previous seven empires. It ultimately will go to perdition, for it will perish by the hand of the Lamb, who is the King of kings. After the eight preceding kings, he is the Ninth King.

The fact that we have to do here symbolically with seven heads of the *one* beast, which itself is "the eighth," signifies that in the beast the continuity of the seven previous empires becomes manifest. They are the beast's heads because he comprises in himself all these previous empires. In the same way, the beast in Revelation 13 exhibits the features of three previous empires especially: the leopard, the bear, and the lion. According to Daniel 7:4-6, these are, in retrograde order, the Greek-Macedonian, the Medo-Persian, and the Babylonian Empire. The beast itself is the revived Roman Empire. This is the sense of the statement that the beast is itself "the eighth," but is "of the seven," namely, a revival of the sixth or Roman Empire.

Some interpreters have argued that "king" cannot mean "kingdom." However, in Daniel 7:17 the four "beasts" (i.e., empires) do carry the title of "kings." But perhaps we can meet this objection also in another way, namely, by thinking in Revelation 17 especially of the *angelic princes* who represent the successive empires, just as we found such princes in Dan. 10. In Scripture, the world-empires are usually particularly characterized by one special earthly prince. These are, respectively, the Pharaoh of the exodus (Egypt), Sennacherib (Assyria), Nebuchadrezzar (Babylonia), Cyrus, possibly Ahasuerus too (Persia), Alexander the Great (Macedonia), Augustus, possibly Nero too (Roman Empire), and the "beast" of Revelation.[12] Behind each of these earthly princes there is a spiritual power, an "angelic prince"; that is the topic that we will deal with first. If we just spoke of the "continuity" in the subsequent world-empires, we can now add that this involves the fact that behind the world-empires *one and the same* principal angelic power is hiding.

If John Adam Cramb (1862-1913) said that world-empires are "successive incarnations of the divine ideas",[13] I would like to put this in the following way: world-empires are successive "incarnations" of divine powers. And Britain's prime minister, Lord Rosebery (1847-1929), said of them, "not built by saints and angels, but the work of man's hands," but he adds, "human and yet not entirely human, for even the most unattentive and cynical must see the finger of the Divine."[14] I would like to put this as follows: world-empires are built by man's hands, which, however—without taking anything away from human responsibility (see § 1.1.2)—are steered by "divine" (read, angelic) powers, above which stands the God of gods.

The idea of seven world-empires is supported by the Jewish tradition saying that Israel in total has known six exiles.[15] These exiles were those in the Egyptian, the Assyrian, the Babylonian, the Medo-Persian, the Greek, and the "Edomite" (= Roman) Empire. Of course, there have been many more mighty empires in world history. Think, for instance, of

12. See my commentary on Revelation (1990:164-165). There, other interpretations of Rev. 17:7-10 are also dealt with. I have taken up all these matters again in Ouweneel (2012).
13. Quoted by Schulte Nordholt (1992:202).
14. Ibid.
15. Num. R. 10, 2 (see for a review of rabbinical literature and the meaning of the abbreviations used the Bibliography).

ancient China and India, the Inca empire, Mongolian and African empires, the Russian empire, etcetera. But the seven world-empires of which we speak here share one significant feature: they exhibited a close relationship with God's chosen people. That which in secular historiography is hardly of any importance is with God of the greatest importance: in his historiography, Israel is always the point of reference. We have already seen some examples of this.

Below, we will discover that there are certain parallels between the first empire (Egypt) and the eighth empire (Rome), and also between the third (Babylon) and the eighth empire (§ 4.1.3). Moreover, I will argue that the greatest catastrophes occur to Israel during the seventh and eighth empires. The seventh is the "Germanic" Empire, of which I hope to make it likely that its deepest point was German idolatrous national-socialism; that catastrophe is the holocaust. The eighth empire is that of Antichrist. The Ninth King is he who, a few verses further down in Revelation 17, in v. 14, is called "the Lamb" and "Lord of lords and King of kings." Only under him, all of Israel's exiles and tribulations will come to an end.

"(World-)empires" in the meaning here intended are not common countries or states, but a (world-)empire comprises a number of various countries, which each retain their own cultural character but have been brought together under one central ruler. We speak of a world-empire only if such an empire in the ("ancient") world forms a central power, which is supreme over other countries and empires. The idea that in history there are several such successive world-empires is deeply rooted in European history, as we will investigate extensively. Traditionally this phenomenon has been called the *translatio imperii*, the "transference of the world-empire."[16]

16. According to Van der Pot (1951:76), the idea of the transition of one empire to the other was, as far as can be ascertained, expressed first in a work ascribed to Demetrius of Phaleron (c. 300 BC). He presumes that the idea of *four* world-empires was first launched by Zenon of Rhodos, shortly after the battle of Magnesia (190 BC). Already then, the fourth empire would have

Such a *translatio* is precisely what Daniel presents to Nebuchadrezzar in Dan. 2: the power is transferred from the first to the second empire, etcetera.

Usually, it was believed in Europe that this transference moved from the East to the West: from Mesopotamia to Hellas, from Hellas to Rome, from Rome to Western Europe, from Europa to (North) America.[17] This thought certainly does not fit into the scheme of seven world-empires as we see it: from Egypt to Assyria is north-eastward, from Assyria to Babylon is southward, from Babylon to Susan is eastward. Only the movements from Susan to Macedonia (or, Athens in Greece), and from there to Rome, are westward. That also holds for the movement from Europa to America. The eighth empire, that of the beast, is indeed explicitly a revival of the ancient Roman Empire, but America, as co-heir of Rome, could be very well included in this (see chapter 9). However, the question whether the centre of power will be established in Rome (Brussels?) or in Washington cannot be answered with any certainty.

1.3.2. The Four Central Empires

In the summary given of the seven world-empires the Roman Empire is the sixth empire. In the summing-up of the four world-empires in Daniel 2 and 7 the Roman Empire is the fourth one. And in the German tradition, the Roman Empire lives on in the "First," the "Second" and the "Third Reich"; these are the Holy Roman Empire of the German nation, the German Empire of the Hohenzollern emperors, and the Nazi Empire, respectively. We therefore have to take care in numbering the empires (see the following scheme):

---

been the Roman one. Hartvelt (1977:56) claims that this pagan view was introduced by the church fathers into the interpretation of Dan. 2 and 7!

17. See concerning this extensively Schulte Nordholt (1992).

Numbering of the empires

1. Egypt
2. Assyria
3. = I. Babylon
4. = II. Medo-Persia
5. = III. Greece
6. = IV. Rome
   - i. Holy Roman Empire
   - ii. Little-German Empire
7. iii. "Third Reich"
8. = Empire of the Antichrist
9. = V. Empire of Messiah

Arabic ciphers: numbering of Revelation 17.
Large Roman ciphers: numbering of Daniel 2 and 7.
Small Roman ciphers: numbering of German history.

In the series of the seven world-empires together with "the eighth," the four empires standing exactly in the middle take up a special place. They are preceded by the Egyptian and the Assyrian Empire, and followed by the "seventh" ("Germanic") Empire and the eighth empire of the Antichrist. Today we also find other, liberal views of the identity of the four empires in Daniel 2 and 7 (see Appendix 5). However, for many centuries it was indisputable for both Jews and Christians that these four empires were the Babylonian, the Medo-Persian, the Greek, and the Roman Empire. As such, throughout the Christian era they have particularly stirred imagination.[18]

In this connection, time and again some key questions turned up. In Daniel 2 and 7, it is described how the fourth (Roman) Empire is immediately superseded by a new, a "fifth," empire, that of the Messiah. It could not be doubted that this, too, is an "inner-temporal" (immanent) empire, which as such is subsequent to the previous four empires in this world.[19] However, what is the nature of this fifth em-

18. See extensively Kocken (1935); Adamek (1938).
19. This "chiliast" or "millennialist" view was already held by church fathers

pire? Is it a Christian "empire" in Europe, which in numerous forms has existed since the fall of the West-Roman Empire? Or is it an empire that will only arrive at the second coming of Christ? How will the Messianic Empire seamlessly follow upon the fourth, the Roman Empire? Did this transition take place already under Constantine the Great? Or, after the fall of Rome (476), at the rise of the Carolingian Empire (eight century)? Or is it rather the case that, if the Messianic Empire only arrives after the second coming of Christ, it is precisely the Roman Empire which lives on in Europe in various forms until the present day? In brief: *do we live today in the fourth or in the fifth empire of Daniel?*

In this study, an unequivocal answer is given to this question. According to Daniel 7, in comparison with Daniel 2, it is none less than the Son of Man, the One who comes with the clouds of heaven, who puts the fourth empire to a *radical* and *sudden* end, and immediately after this empire erects the fifth and last inner-temporal empire. If we consider this, it must be crystal clear that the fourth empire has never been put to an end yet, and that the empire of the Son of Man will only arrive at his second coming.[20] We therefore live during the time of the fourth empire; more precisely: during the time between the apparent fall of the Roman Empire and its revival in the last days (see extensively chapters 9 and 10).

The Romans themselves, at the summit of their world power, viewed their empire, which really encompassed almost the entire world known at the time, as the last empire. They could hardly believe that their empire would ever perish and that another empire would take its place. In their opinion, the *translatio imperii* had come to an end in the Roman Empire, as the poet Virgil (70-19 BC), among others, expressed it in his

---

such as Irenaeus, Tertullian, Commodian, and Lactantius. Tuveson (1964:14) says that the doctrine of the millennial kingdom seems to have been very strong until late in the rule of Constantine.

20. This also was the view of all Greek and almost all Latin fathers, "even" Augustine (Kocken 1935:6-72; Adamek 1938:36-51).

pastoral poems. Jupiter was the god of that empire, and Virgil was his prophet, when he "received" the following words from Jupiter: *imperium sine fine dedi*, "I gave [you] an empire without end." It is striking that we find similar words in Daniel 2:44 and 7:14, 18, 27, but there the "empire without end" is not the fourth but the fifth empire! That is the kingdom of the Son of Man.

Of course, the Roman Christians knew about this fifth empire. But they had stayed sufficiently Roman so as to see the glory of Rome continue at least until the coming of that fifth empire. The famous Christian historiographer, Orosius (c. 375-418), pupil of Augustine, expressed it in this way: *Quando cadet Roma, cadet et mundus*, "when Rome falls, the world falls too." In some sense he was right. Even if in Revelation 17 there is a seventh and an eighth king after the sixth (Roman) king, that seventh and that eighth kingdom are nothing but revivals of the sixth empire, as said before. In this sense, the Christian knows that he lives in the "last" empire before the second coming of Christ. Therefore, the Christian lives *circa finem*, near the end of times, as the medieval Otto bishop of Freising (c. 1114-1158) put it because of the fact that the *translatio imperii*, the succession of the world-empires, was now completed (cf. 1 Cor. 10:11, us "on whom the end of ages has come").

The interpretation of John Calvin (1509-1564) was totally different. According to him, the four world-empires have found their end, not at the second, but at the first coming of Jesus Christ. Since that event we live in the "fifth" empire, the ecclesial empire of Jesus Christ, as he puts it.[21] It is no wonder that outside Calvinistic circles this interpretation has hardly received any following because of the exegetical mind-boggling involved. First, the stone in Daniel 2 destroys the Roman Empire in one strike, whereas at the birth or the ascension of Christ, or at the day of Pentecost (Acts 2), the Roman Empire

21. *Corpus Reformatorum* 40, 607.

did not fall at all. Secondly, the ideal of a "Roman" Empire in Europe never fully died out, also after it had turned Christian: it then simply became the Christian Roman Empire. Thirdly, in church history a true world-empire ruled according to the mind of Christ has never existed at all. Fourthly, even the West-Roman Empire was not destroyed by Christianity, but by pagan or Arian Germanic tribes. Fifthly, no matter how "heavenly" and "spiritual" the "fifth empire" of Christ may be, in the line of Daniel 2 and 7 it must be viewed, too, as an earthly, inner-temporal, political empire, and cannot be viewed as a "spiritual," religious, supratemporal empire *over against* the four earthly, inner-temporal, political empires. Sixthly, in Daniel 7 the Messianic Empire clearly arrives, not at the birth or ascension of the Messiah, but at his coming with the clouds.

Other Reformers have better understood that the "stone" of Daniel 2 up to their times had never become "a great mountain," and that the ideal of a "Roman" Empire in Europe had not yet died out at all. It is one of the very aims of this present study to throw light on this "Roman ideal." It lived on in the empire of the Carolingians, in the Holy Roman Empire (particularly with the Ottonians), in the world-empire of the Habsburger, Charles V, in the Renaissance "empires" of letters and scholars, in the Napoleonic Empire, and just the same in the Second (German imperial) and the Third "Reich," which were viewed as successors to the First (Holy Roman) Empire. Each time when the Roman ideal re-emerged people spoke of a renaissance, a "rebirth," namely *of antique (Roman) Man*: the Carolingian renaissance (c. 800), the Ottonian (c. 1000), the twelfth-century renaissance, and finally *the* Renaissance (since particularly the fifteenth century).

Philip Melanchthon (1497-1560) fully accepted and elaborated the idea of the four world-empires and that of the *translatio imperii*.[22] According to him, also after the fall of the

22. Ibid. 12, 718.

West-Roman Empire the "fourth empire" lived on in the Carolingian and the Ottonian empire, etcetera. It is significant that, in his opinion, the "fifth empire" in Daniel 2 and 7 is not a "Christian" empire in which we allegedly would live today, but that this empire will arrive at the youngest day, the second coming of Messiah, the resurrection of the dead and the end of times. In this connection, attention had to be given, of course, to the fragmentation of the empire and the rise of the national states. Melanchthon found the explanation for this in the Roman feet of the image of Dan. 2, which were partly of iron, partly of clay.[23]

Martin Luther (1483-1546) too speaks explicitly of the *translatio* of the Roman Empire, *von den Griechen auf die Deutschen,* from the "Greeks" (read, the East-Romans) to the "Germans" (read, the Carolingians and the Ottonians).[24] He applies the feet partly of iron, partly of clay, to the strong and the weak emperors. He expressly states that the Roman Empire is the last empire, and that Christ alone will break it down and replace it by his own empire.[25] On the basis of Daniel, the Turkish Empire rapidly rising in his days could not possibly form a fifth empire before the second coming of Christ and was only a forerunner of the anti-Christian empire of the last days.[26] Shortly after the empire of the Turks—that is in retrospect only at the end of the First World War (1917-18)!—the youngest day will arrive.[27]

Not all authors have viewed the empires after the fall of the West-Roman Empire as varieties of that Roman Empire. The "monk of St. Gall," an anonymous medieval chronicler (usually identified with Notker Balbulus, "the Stammerer," c. 840-912), saw, as it were, a new succession of empires arising after Rome. About the image which Nebuchadrezzar saw

23. Ibid. 13, 833.
24. *Weimar Ausgabe* 11, 2: 4, 20.
25. Ibid. 11, 2: 6, 3.
26. Ibid. 30, 2: 166, 12 and further.
27. Ibid. 30, 2: 170, 29-30.

(Dan. 2) he wrote,[28]

> When the Almighty, who governs all and determines the destiny of kingdoms and eras, had broken the feet of iron and clay of that wondrous image, that is, the Romans, he erected in the land of the Franks, by means of the renowned Charles, another, no less wondrous image with a head of gold.

Charlemagne (742-814) as a new golden head! But could a Christian such as this Sangallensic monk have wished to contradict Daniel 2? After the Roman Empire, the empire of the Son of Man arrives, that is certain from the outset. And thus, a new image of which Charlemagne would be the golden head is conceivable only *within* the framework of the Roman Empire as it survived in different (Christianized) varieties.

Many authors in all times of church history have preferred such a solution. Thus, Otto bishop of Freising, mentioned earlier, not only distinguishes the four world-empires, but also four eras in world history, in such a way that the four world-empires together form the first era of world history, the period up to the birth of Christ.[29] Since then, three eras allegedly have followed, of which the fourth and last was supposed to have begun with the emperor Theodosius I, who on November 8, 392, elevated Christianity to be the state religion of the Roman Empire and forbade all pagan worship.[30] However, these latter eras, too, in fact encompass stages of the Roman Empire. This empire in its fourth and last stage has become a "Christian" empire, which supposedly will last until the second coming of Christ.

Just as I had a question for the monk, I have one for the bishop. Will the "Christian" empire really last until the second coming? Is there not, just before the coming of Christ,

28. *Monachi Sangallensis de gestis Karoli Magni* (ed. Pertz, Hannover 1829), p. 731.
29. See A. A. van Schelven, "Otto, bisschop van Freising's denkbeelden over den zin der geschiedenis," in: Sneller (1944:94-95). Cf. Kocken (1935:112-116, 145-154).
30. *Codex Theodosianus* 16, 10, 10-12.

an anti-Christian empire on earth? And when will that *anti*-Christian empire begin, or did it even begin already? Could we not, with the same right, defend the thesis that this empire, so hostile to God, already began with the "Christianization" of the Roman Empire, the blending of church and state (to the detriment of the church)? This too is a question that is of essential significance for any Christian view of history and will be dealt with extensively.

Each time when, in European history, an important empire approached its end, this kind of eschatological question emerged. When in 1254 the house of the Staufen emperors died out with Conrad IV, many voices were raised in Germany warning that with the fall of the empire the empire of the Antichrist would arrive.[31] And just as it was believed that in the year 1000 history would come to its end and Christ would return, the same rumors arose everywhere in Christendom as it was facing the year 2000. We will see.

31. Cf. Grundmann (1984:424).

Chapter 2
Gods and Angels

2.1. God and the Gods

2.1.1. Gods: Concrete Celestial Beings

I HOPE IT HAS BECOME CLEAR from chapter 1 that a first means to receive biblical light upon a culture is to enter into the subject of the invisible realm of angels and demons. We deal here with those "princes" and powers of a spiritual nature that have been created by YHWH and, often against their will, are instruments in his hand and exert a decisive manipulating influence upon the cultures. In Daniel 10 we already briefly saw that each culture has its own "prince" (invisible celestial being). We will come back to this expression. At this moment we first state that Scripture usually does not speak of the "prince" (*sar*), but of the "god" (*elohim*) of a country, a nation, or a culture. We will therefore have to pay attention to the meaning of this word "god," and to the "gods" in general in Scripture.

At times Scripture speaks of the gods of the nations in a way that indicates that these gods are only "vanity," an illusion, that is, "nothing." But in fact, this always refers to the idols in the sense of idolatrous *images*.[1] Apart from these images, the gods are often spoken of as concrete, real powers. For instance, we read that YHWH executes judgment against

1. E.g., Isa. 44:9-20; 2 Kings 19:18; cf. Ps. 135:15-18.

the gods of Egypt[2] and the gods of the Philistines.[3] To be sure, it is said that there is no God except God,[4] but apparently this means: the way our God is, none other god is. Therefore, it is said elsewhere that YHWH is greater than all gods,[5] which implies that definitely there *are* other "gods." God is even called the "God of gods," which in Hebrew idiom can mean both "the God over all gods" and "the God pre-eminently."[6] In Deuteronomy 32:17 the reality of the "gods" is recognized, but it is added that they are only evil spirits,[7] not "gods" such as God is God. In Isaiah 26:13, the believing people of God recognize that "other lords" have ruled over Israel (cf. 1 Cor. 8:5), that is, again as a concrete reality, but that now they only worship the name of YHWH. In Deuteronomy 4:7, it is asked what nation there is that has the "gods" so near to it as YHWH is with regard to Israel; in Micah 4:5 we find something similar. So, there are concrete "gods," who are "near" to their respective nations, but none is so near to his people as YHWH. In Psalm 138:1, the psalmist says that he will sing praise to God "before the gods," and in Psalm 97:7 the "gods" are called upon to worship God.[8]

Who are these "gods," these "spirits," "lords"? In this connection, the most remarkable passage is Ps. 82, which begins as follows:

> God [is] standing in [or: presiding over] the assembly of the gods [el],

2. Exod. 12:12; 18:10-11; Num. 33:4; 2 Sam. 7:23.
3. 1 Sam. 6:5.
4. E.g., Deut. 4:35; 6:4; 32:39; Isa. 43:10; 46:9; Hos. 13:4.
5. E.g., Exod. 15:11; 18:11; 1 Chron. 16:25; 2 Chron. 2:5; Ps. 86:8; 95:3; 96:4; 135:5.
6. Deut. 10:17; Josh. 22:22; Ps. 50:1; 136:2; Dan. 2:47.
7. See further in § 2.3.
8. In 1 Sam. 28:13 we find a peculiar example of the reality of "gods." The medium of Endor sees *elohim* (lit. "gods"; possibly in the singular: "divine being") coming up from the earth; some translations say, "gods," others, "supernatural being," "a ghostly figure."

in the midst of [the] gods [elohim] he judges.

It has often been asserted that these "gods" would be the earthly judges. In the *application* this is not wrong, insofar as the earthly rulers are the visible "representatives" of the "gods." But in my opinion, this application does not really touch the heart of the matter. Usually, we are referred to Exodus 21:6; 22:8, 9, 28, where *elohim* supposedly means "judges," too, but that is not certain at all. In spite of the translation *theous* of the Septuagint one could very well translate "God" here. This holds in particular for 22:28, "*elohim* you shall not curse." The idea is, then, that the accused is brought "to God," that is, to the place of the *Shekhina*, the holy presence of God, where the judges pass sentences on behalf of God. In fact, there is no Scripture where it is certain that men are called *elohim*. Psalm 45:7-8 seems to be an exception, but that word is a prophetic reference to him who on earth is the Messiah, but who at the same time is an eternal, divine celestial being. By the way, this psalm throws some indirect light upon Psalm 82: there the *elohim* placed over the nations judge in an unrighteous way and are punished for it, but in Psalm 45 the Messiah is an *elohim* anointed over Israel and praised by all nations (v. 18), because he has loved righteousness and has hated wickedness.[9]

Comparing Scripture with Scripture, it seems more obvious that Psalm 82 does not speak of humans but, like everywhere else in Scripture, of celestial beings.[10] If we choose this interpretation, first the sense of v. 6-7 becomes clearer:

---

9. The only other place where the word *elohim* is applied to a man is Exod. 4:16; 7:1, but there it is not said of Moses in an absolute, but only in a relative sense.
10. One should honestly add to this that the older rabbinical literature does not mention this exegesis at all; Targum, Talmud and Midrash only think of the judges of Israel, or of the Israelites in general. The first to penetrate more deeply, in my opinion, is the great Jewish expositor, Abraham Ibn Ezra (1089-1164), who thinks of the celestial beings. In the nineteenth century, this exegesis was adopted by Hermann Hupfeld (1796-1866), and since then by many other expositors, both Jewish and Christian (see, e.g., the summary in Van der Ploeg 1974, in loco).

I have said, gods [are] you,
and sons of the Most-High all of you;
but like men [or, like a man; like Adam] you will die,
and as one of the princes [*sarim*] you will fall.

The latter sentence seems to support the assumption that the "gods" intended here originally were not men or (earthly) princes. What else they could be and how it is possible that they die will I try to explain below.

Secondly, the quotation in John 10:34 now becomes much clearer. The Jews blamed Jesus for making himself God. But he replied (in a free rendering) that Psalm 82 calls certain celestial beings "gods," too, so that he, as a person descended from heaven (v. 36!), even in this limited sense could be entitled "god." Of course, he was not just any celestial being, "a" god, but the highest of all, an uncreated, eternal celestial being, God the Son, one with the Father (v. 30). In my opinion, it can be far better understood that Jesus compares himself with other celestial beings than that he would only compare himself with the earthly judges of the Israelites in general.

I will come back later to the task of the "gods" in Psalm 82, that is, to judge the nations. First, I state that there are very good reasons to assume that the psalm in its actual sense speaks of the heavenly court of God. We see him here, presiding over the assembly of the "gods" (celestial beings). This exegesis is supported by many other Scriptures, as is indicated in Appendix 2.

2.1.2. Star-Gods

We now come to the essential question as to whether these biblical "gods," that is, angels or celestial beings, have anything to do with the "gods" that are worshipped by the nations. To answer this question, we first consider an expression found in 1 Kings 22:19, namely, the "host of heaven." The word for "host" (*tzaba*) often simply means "army," but it can also have a figurative meaning. The importance of this meaning is shown by one of the well-known names of God: *YHWH Tzebaot*, "LORD of hosts" (cf. Rom. 9:29, "Lord of Sabaoth"); *tzebaot* is the plural of *tzaba*. The expression *YHWH Tzebaot* can mean, "YHWH of the hosts of Israel," as in Exodus 7:4 and 12:41. It then refers to God's earthly army. However, the Bible also often speaks of the "host of heaven" in the sense of the whole of the celestial bodies: sun, moon and stars. Often the "host of heaven" is referred to as the realm of the celestial bodies that are worshipped by the pagans as gods.[11]

However, 1 Kings 22:19, and its parallel, 2 Chron. 18:18, show that the same expression, "host of heaven," can also be used for the household of God, that is, the angels.[12] The heavenly host can thus comprise both the stars and the angels (= "gods").[13] The celestial bodies worshipped by the pagans as gods are nothing but angels of God. Or perhaps we are allowed to say: the various celestial bodies have been "allotted" to various angels (see concerning this important "allotting," § 2.1.3). This thought is supported by Job 38:7, where the "morning stars" are also angels, "sons of God," and by Isa. 14:12, where a "morning star" is expelled from the "mount of the congregation."[14]

---

11. See Deut. 4:19; 17:3; 2 Kings 17:16; 21:3; 23:4-5; Jer. 8:2; 19:13; Zeph. 1:5.
12. Also in Ps. 103:20-21 and 148:2, "hosts" is parallel with "angels." In Josh. 5:14, the "prince of the host of YHWH" is mentioned, and this army of YHWH can consist of both stars (Judg. 5:20) and angels (2 Chron. 32:21).
13. See Wisd. 13:2, 5; Ep. Jer. 59; 1 Enoch 60:1; 80:6-7; 4 Ezra 6:3; 8:21; 2 Baruch 21:6; 48:10; 59:11 (the flaming angelic hosts; cf. Ps. 104:4).
14. Cf. Ps. 82:1 and the "holy mount of the gods" in Ezek. 28:14, 16. The idea of "stars" representing angels (fallen or not) frequently occurs in the pseudepigraphic book 1 Enoch (7:3; 18:12-15; 20:4; 21:1-6; 54:6; 86; 90:21-24; 102:2). In the Old Testament, Isa. 24:21-23 alludes to the judgment over these "star-gods." Possibly also the parallel between Job 4:18, 15:15 and 25:5 points to the connection of stars and angels. Job 38:31b, about loosening the bands of Orion, may point to such an association, which the Greeks have preserved in the myth of the strong giant Orion. This great hunter had offended the goddess of hunting and at his death was chained to the firmament. It is striking that this giant in Hebrew is referred to with a word that means "fool" (see Hartley 1988:172, 500).

    In the New Testament we may think of Rev. 9:1; 12:4a and of the "forces of

This connection between angels (= gods) and celestial bodies may seem strange to us because we have been influenced by modern astronomy, which can only own the physical-material aspect of the celestial bodies. The idea to connect stars with angelic powers may remind us of pagans who, for instance, saw the planets as animated and gave the names of their gods to them. To be sure, it is quite possible that pagans have held to some of the truth concerning the relationship between celestial bodies and "gods" (read, angelic princes). But first, their folly was that they honored these celestial bodies, or angelic princes, with divine worship in a way that only becomes the Most-High God. We will meet several "gods" whom we consider to be concrete spiritual powers and whose names are closely linked with the planets; we think in particular of Mercury (Greek, Hermes), Venus (Aphrodite), Mars (Ares), Jupiter (Zeus), and Saturn (Kronos). The most important "god" who has been associated with a celestial body is the "sun god," whom we will meet with several times: Osiris of the Egyptians, Bel or Nebo of the Babylonians, Mithra(s) of the Persians, Apollo of the Greeks.

Secondly, we do not care too much about what the pagans have asserted, but rather about what Scripture tells us concerning these things. Indeed, in the Bible not only the celestial bodies but also all kinds of other material things and natural phenomena are directly connected with angels. The clearest notions of the natural angels are found in the book of Revelation, where it is shown several times how the natural forces are supervised by angels. Thus, we read in chapter 7:1 about angels "holding the four winds of the earth," in 14:18 about an angel who "has authority over the fire,"[15] and in 16:5 about

heaven" in Matt. 24:29. The expression *YHWH Tzebaot* in the Septuagint is often translated with *kyrios tôn dynameôn*: "Lord of the forces"; cf. *dynameis* = "hosts" in Ps. 36:6; Isa. 34:4; Dan. 8:10; also cf. *dynam(e)is* in 1 Cor. 15:24; Eph. 1:21; 1 Pet. 3:22.

15. In Jewish tradition known as Yehuel, but sometimes as Gabriel; see Num.R. 12 (on Num. 7:1); cf. Pesakhim 118a; Jub. 2:2. In Midr.Ps. 117 §3 (240b), Gabriel is the angelic prince of fire, who in Dan. 3 made the fiery furnace

"the angel of the waters." At times natural forces and angels are even identified. In Psalm 104:4 we read,[16]

> He [is] making his messengers [or, angels] winds [*ruchot*],
> his servants flaming fire.

God has the highest power over the angels, and thus also over the elements, as we see, for instance, in Revelation 16:9. Therefore, the water-angel in v. 5 does not see God's judgment as an infringement into his domain but expresses his agreement with it.[17]

In examining the star-gods, one other Scripture deserves our attention. That is Amos 5:26, where YHWH says with regard to Israel's wilderness journey,

> ... and you have carried *sikkut* (of) your *mèlèch*,
> and *kiun* (of) your images,
> the star of your *elohim*, which you made to yourselves.

This is a very difficult Scripture, firstly because it is not clear whether the transcribed words have to be translated or have to be taken as personal names. I myself prefer translating as follows, "you have carried Sikkut, your king, and Kiun, your images...," as some translations also do.[18] If we accept

---

burning hot on the outside and cool on the inside, so that Daniel's three friends were saved.

16. Others translate conversely, "He makes winds his messengers [or, angels], flaming fire his servants," but in this way the meaning is lost. Heb. 1:7 sanctions the translation given in the text, which corroborates the notion that angels can have the form of wind or fire.
17. Another interesting Scripture is John 5:4, which is probably a gloss but may certainly go back upon a reliable tradition. Here again, we find a "water-angel," who descended at certain times and stirred the water of the pool of Bethesda. Jewish tradition also knows of the angelic prince of the Mediterranean Sea (Gen.R.10 [7d]) and the one of the sea of Tiberias (Pal. Sanhedrin 7, 25d, 18. 28. 43).
18. Other possibilities: (a) "you have carried the shrine of your king and the pedestal of your images..." (vgl. NIV); (b) "you have carried the shrine of your Melech [= Moloch] and the Kiun [= Kewan = Saturn], your images..." The quotation in Acts 7:43 (going back upon the Septuagint) sanctions (b), but reads the name Raiphan instead of Kiun. Presumably, this form is a de-

this translation, the word *sikkut* refers to Sakkut, a Babylonian name for the war and sun god, but also for the Roman god Saturn. This is quite likely, in particular because of the subsequent expression, "the star of your *elohim*." This can also be read as "your star-god," or "your star-gods," and that fits in very well with the planetary god Saturn. If this interpretation is correct, we have here a Scripture in which we directly find the expression "star-god(s)," namely, as a reference to gods identified or associated with stars or planets.

One peculiar topic is made up by the *stoicheia* in the New Testament.[19] This Greek term may refer to the celestial bodies, especially the twelve *stoicheia* (signs, constellations) of the Zodiac, as well as to the "elemental spirits": spirits (angels) associated with the elements or natural phenomena, such as the water-, wind-, and fire-angels mentioned before. If we take these two meanings together, the *stoicheia* are the star-gods (astral gods or spirits). In 2 Peter 3:10, 12, *stoicheia* means "elements," not in the modern-chemical sense but in the sense of the primordial components of matter according to the ancient view: earth, water, air, and fire. The Jewish thinker Philo (c. 20 BC-50 AD) tells us that these four *stoicheia*, called this way already by Plato, were deified by the Greeks, that is, identified respectively with Demeter (the Roman Ceres), the goddess of the fruits of the earth, Poseidon (Neptune), the god of the sea,

---

terioration of Kaiphan (the Hebrew letters R and K look alike), which in fact has the same consonants as Kiun (*k-i-u/v-n*). Many experts believe that the Masoretes replaced the vowel signs of the original Hebrew word, Kaiwan or Kewan, by those of the word *shiqquts*, "abomination (abominable image)." Thus, the original name would have been Kaiwan or Kewan. This word is closely related with the Akkadian word *kaiwanu*, a name for the planet (planetary god) Saturn.

19. I touched upon this topic in Ouweneel (1994:114-115 and 1997:245-248; see Dibelius 1909; Delling 1971:670-686, and the lexicons; also cf. Ouweneel 1988:342, 350). Also see Bruce (1984:97-100, 111-112) and Fung (1988:189-193) and the literature mentioned there. The basic meaning of *stoicheia* is "constituent parts of a series" (especially the sounds of the alphabet), and subsequently "first principles," the "ABC," e.g., of a certain doctrine (Heb. 5:12).

Hera (Juno), as the feminine *alter ego* of Zeus/Jupiter the chief goddess, and Hephaistos (Vulcan), the god of fire. In Wisdom 13:2, three of these four "elements" are summed up (fire, wind/air, water), and those who worship these "elements," or the stars, as gods are condemned:

> ... who have come to regard either the fire, or the wind, or the fast moving air,
> or the starry sky, or the impetuous water,
> or the lights of heaven
> as the rulers of the world [cf. 1 Cor. 2:6], as gods.

Most present-day expositors see these meaning(s) of *stoicheia* (elemental spirits, astral gods) also in Galatians 4:3 and Colossians 2:8, 20; some therefore translate "world spirits." In Galatians 4, the "gods" whom the Galatian Christians had worshipped before are associated with the "weak and poor world spirits" that these Christians were in danger of "returning to." Before, they had been submitted to the "gods" as slaves, now as Christians they wanted to submit to Sinaitic slavery (cf. 3:22-24). Paul calls this a "returning" to the *stoicheia*, for both the legalist and the idolator are slaves of the "world spirits." Elsewhere I have dwelt upon the relationship of the *stoicheia* to the law, now I emphasize the relationship with the celestial bodies. In Galatians 4:10, where Paul speaks of the ritual celebration of festivals determined by celestial bodies, the link between the "world spirits" and the celestial bodies is apparently presupposed. Also, in Colossians 2:16, such a connection between festivals and planetary gods is suggested. Compare v. 15, where the "rulers and authorities" have been "disarmed" on the cross, v. 18, where we hear about "worship of angels," and Galatians 3:19, where the law was given to Moses by "angels."

According to many, it therefore seems that also the New Testament notion of the *stoicheia* implies a reference to the realm of the spirits, possibly even to the "star-gods." In later literature, the singular *stoicheion* soon became a common reference to a spiritual being. In contemporary Greek, it still means "spirit" or "ghost."

In this section, we have seen that the notion of "star-gods" is not foreign to the Bible. This is of particular importance for our subject because the chief star-god is the sun god, whom we have met and will meet under various names among ancient nations. The "dragon" in the Bible is not only the angelic prince of an earthly kingdom but he is the "son of dawn" (Isa. 14:12), that is, the sun. He is a prince of cosmic significance, Lucifer, that is, "light-bearer." Among many nations, he has pretended to be the prince of the mightiest star, the sun. All the greater will be his fall when the Sun of righteousness will prevail over him (Mal. 4:2).

2.1.3. The Angels of the Nations

How could we describe the relationship between the celestial bodies and the angels (the *elohim* of God's household), or the "gods" (*elohim*) served by the pagans, more precisely? Let us look first at Deuteronomy 4:19-20,

> ... beware lest you raise your eyes to heaven and see the sun and the moon and the stars, all the host of heaven, and are drawn away and bow to them, and serve them that YHWH your God has allotted to all the peoples under the whole heaven. But YHWH has taken you and brought you out of the iron furnace, out of Egypt, to be to him a people of inheritance...

Here we see that God has "allotted" the celestial bodies to the nations. This is quite an obscure expression, but it becomes clearer if we connect the celestial bodies with "gods." To this end, we compare this same remarkable verb "allotting" with another verse, Deuteronomy 29:26, where Moses says,[20]

> ... and they went and served other gods (*elohim*), and bowed before them, gods whom they did not know, and [whom] he

20. Some translations try to get rid of the obvious meaning of the Heb. *khalaq*, which is "to divide, to allot, to destine," as in dividing an inheritance or a spoil (cf. Josh. 14:5; 18:2; 22:8; 1 Sam. 30:24; Prov. 17:2).

> had not allotted to them.

This word "allotting" in both chapter 4:19 and 29:26 is of great significance and deserves our full attention. For, when we connect these two verses it becomes immediately clear that God has "allotted" the *elohim* to the nations, that is, gave each nation its own *elohim*. This might sound strange to us, but in Jewish literature and among the church fathers this idea is perfectly familiar, as will be shown in the course of this study. Moreover, we read in Deuteronomy 32:8-9 (LXX),[21]

> When the Most-High divided [the] nations,
> when he dispersed [the] sons of Adam,
> He set [the] bounds of [the] nations
> according to [the] number of the angels of God;
> and [the] portion of the Lord [became] his people Jacob;
> [the] allotted portion of his inheritance [became] Israel.

These verses are generally understood in the following way: God in antiquity, not long after Noah's flood, divided the world into a number of nations, each with their own domain or "inheritance," and he allotted to each nation one of the "gods." He himself, however, received Israel as an inheritance. Thus, YHWH allotted the territories of the nations to the "gods," and conversely Deuteronomy 4:19 and 29:26 teach us that he allotted these "gods" to these nations.[22] In chapter 4:19-20 we find the same thought as in 32:8-9, namely, that God "allotted" to the other nations the "gods," but for himself he chose Israel as his "inheritance." An "inheritance" here is the portion that is allotted to someone when a whole inheritance is divided over the heirs; the "gods" each received their own nation, but YHWH received Israel.[23]

21. The reading, "angels of God," is supported by various other ancient versions (Symmachus, Vetus Latina, Syrohexaplaris), and also by a reading in a damaged Qumran manuscript (4Q), which says, *bené el...* Probably it said originally *bené elohim*, "sons of God" (that is, "gods," "angels"), instead of *bené yisrael*, "sons of Israel."
22. Cf. Jer. 16:19-20: each nation has a god as its inheritance.
23. We find the same idea in Sir. 17:17: "For when he divided the nations over

In Daniel 10, we see that each nation has its own "ruler" or "prince" (*sar*) in the sense of a *genius* (protective spirit or guardian angel). In contrast with Deuteronomy, we find in Daniel that Israel too has an "angelic prince" (see below).[24] As the prince of all angels, Michael has been placed over Israel, the nation of nations, until the end of the world. The victory of Michael (or the Man of v. 5) gained over the "princes" of Persia and Greece ushers in the victory of Israel over these nations, which it will gain in the last days through a "time of great tribulation" (12:1). The conflict between Israel and these earthly powers is basically this invisible battle in the "heavenly places" (celestial spheres) (cf. Eph. 6:12). That is an essential point, which plays in my present study a central role.[25]

In connection with the idea of "guardian angels," the remarkable word "watcher" in Daniel 4:13, 17, 23 is of importance, too. This term is here a synonym for "holy one," and

---

all the earth, he placed a ruler over each nation, but Israel is the portion of the Lord." This word, "ruler," reminds us of the word "lord" in Isa. 26:13 (and 1 Cor. 8:5) quoted before, and especially of Dan. 10:13, 20-21; 12:1, where celestial beings (*sarim*) are referred to as the "prince (of the kingdom) of the Persians," the "prince of Greece," and "Michael, one of the chief princes," or "your [= Israel's] prince Michael" (cf. Jude 9: the "archangel," i.e., chief angel, or, angelic prince).

24. In the same sense, 1 Enoch 20:5 says, "Michael, one of the holy angels, namely, he who was placed over the best part of mankind, over the nation" (= Israel).

25. With regard to the word "prince" (*sar*), also Dan. 8 is of importance. In v. 11, "the prince of the host" is the prince of the stars (v. 10), and in v. 25 God himself is called the "prince of princes." In Josh. 5:14 we hear of "the prince of the host of YHWH." Also the Greek word *archôn* ("prince, ruler, archont") can mean "star-god" ("planetary god"). This word, also occurring in Dan. 10:13 (LXX) and in 10:13, 20-21; 12:1 (Theodotion), is found in the New Testament in some significant meanings. In 1 Cor. 2:6,8, some exegetes explain the "princes [or, rulers] of this age" (to be taken as an objective, not a temporal genitive) as the angelic princes (archonts) of the various nations. A special place is taken up by Satan, the archont of the cosmos (John 12:31; 14:30; 16:11; cf. Exod.R. 17, 4 [on Exod. 12:23]). This expression can be connected with the expression "prince of the demons" (Beelzebul) (Matt. 12:24; Mark 3:22; Luke 11:15) and the expression "prince of the power of the air" in Eph. 2:2.

thus also means "angel" (as the Septuagint indeed translates it).[26] They are the star-angels, who as radiant "eyes" watch while people are sleeping. One could also think here of the cherubs, or the living beings, full of eyes in Ezekiel 10:12 and Revelation 4:8. Thus, either stars "are" living beings—perhaps this is intended in 1 Cor. 15:40-41—or living beings (angels) rule over, or represent, stars, or in some other way are associated with stars.[27]

After Israel has worshipped the golden calf, YHWH at first does not want to move at the head of the nation anymore. Instead of going himself, he wants to send an "angel" before them.[28] According to a Jewish tradition, this also refers to Michael. This could explain why so many Scriptures as well as pseudepigraphic works state that YHWH himself is a "watcher" or "prince" over his people, and no angel, whereas in Daniel all at once the archangel Michael turns out to be the "prince" of Israel. Apparently, a time has come in that YHWH has placed Israel, which before stood directly under

---

26. Cf. Isa. 62:6 and many places in 1 Enoch, such as 61:12, the "never sleeping ones."
27. 1 Baruch 3:34 says, "the stars shine in their watch houses...," where angels (again represented as stars) are also seen as watchers. Some would also interpret in this fashion the "angels" representing the seven churches in Rev. 2 and 3 (as the national gods represent the nations) and in their turn represented by "stars" (1:20).

    In Jub. 15:31 we read, "there are many nations and many peoples, and they are all his, and he gave the spirits power over them, in order that they would lead them away from him. But over Israel he did not give power to any angel or spirit, for he alone watches over them [note here again the idea of the "watcher". WJO], and demands them of the hand of his angels and his spirits, and of the hand of all his powers, in order that he would watch over them and bless them, and that they would be his, and he theirs, from now on until eternity."

    According to 1 Enoch 89:59-60, the angelic princes (called "shepherds") of the gentile nations on God's command rule over Israel as long as the Jews are under the dominion of the gentiles (cf. again Isa. 26:13); but these angels themselves depart from God's will and are judged for that at the end of the days.
28. Exod. 33:2-3, 14-15; 34:9; also cf. already 23:20-21.

him, under "prince" Michael. For when the Israelites consistently worshipped the idols, they were placed under a guardian angel just like the nations. This was exactly what YHWH had threatened to do to them already in Exodus 32:34-33:3,

> ... my angel shall go before you...
> I will send an angel before thee...
> for I will not go up in your midst; for you [are] a stiffnecked people,

and thus the prayer of Moses in v. 15, "If your presence [is] not going with [me], do not let us go up from here."[29] When, centuries later, Israel does worship the idols continuously, this very moment that Moses had feared arrives: God himself does not go before his people anymore, but "his angel goes before them." In this way, Israel in a certain sense has become Lo-Ammi ("not-my-people") (Hos. 1:9). Jeremiah 25:11-18 (cf. 1:5) simply calls Israel one of the *goyyim*; for, if it has consistently served the "gods" of the *goyyim*, it is itself not more than one of them after all. Therefore, it receives an angelic prince, as had the other *goyyim*. However, by God's grace

29. Apparently, Test.Levi 5 also refers to Michael in speaking of "the angel who prayingly sets free the generation of Israel, lest Beliar [i.e. Belial; see 2 Cor. 6:15 Gr.] trample them, for every evil spirit storms against them." The Armenian text says, "I am the guardian of the generation of Israel, lest they perish to the utmost." 1 Enoch 89-90 speaks of an archangel, one of the seven "wise" (90:22; cf. Rev. 8:2), who is appointed by God as an overseer over the seventy "shepherds" ruling over Israel (see above) and who also intercedes for Israel (89:76; cf. Jude 9). This intercession is necessary because the great "adversary" (Heb. *satan*) among the angels accuses Job and the high priest Joshua before God (Job 1:6-12; 2:1-7; Zech. 3:1-3). God's throne hall is like a very emotional court of justice, which helps us to understand Bildad's word, "him who makes peace [= executes judgment] in his high heavens," that is, among the heavenly beings (Job 25:2). This fits in directly with the following rabbinical statement (Pesiqta K. 176a; cf. Rev. 12:10b): "May it be your will, o Lord, our God, to make peace in the heavenly family [i.e., the guardian angels of the various nations?] and in the earthly family," i.e., the nations of the earth? Rashi explains this as the heavenly council and the earthly congregation of the wise (the rabbis), respectively, according to a footnote in the Soncino edition.

Israel's "prince" is one of the mightiest, if not the mightiest. Therefore, the people always remain miraculously protected. Moreover, this angelic prince is not God's last word. Eventually, after all its distress, Israel is again restored, and YHWH himself becomes their "prince" again (cf. Dan. 8:11, 25).

2.1.4. The Ruling of the Nations

YHWH is the God of history. He leads the history of his people, but also of all other nations on earth. Although he made his covenant with Israel alone (cf. Amos 3:2), when it comes to God's world government there is no intrinsic difference between Israel and the other nations. On the contrary, there are striking correspondences. For instance, YHWH also led other nations out of the land of their origin and brought them into their own inheritance; for instance (Am. 9:7),

> [Are] you not as the sons of [the] Cushites to Me, sons of Israel?
> [is] the saying of YHWH.
> Have I not brought up Israel out of the land of Egypt,
> and [the] Philistines from Caphtor,
> and Aram [= the Syrians] from Kir?

At later stages too, YHWH time and again intervenes in the history of other nations. For instance, YHWH arranges that Hazael becomes the successor to Benhadad as king over Aram.[30] Assyria is the rod of God's anger against Israel and other nations, but is judged itself by God when it rises against him (Isa. 10:5-19). Later, the very same thing becomes true of the "Chaldeans," that is, the Babylonians (Hab. 1 and 2). Cyrus, the first prince of the Medo-Persian Empire after the fall of Babylon, has been "raised up" by YHWH himself. To him, he delivers the nations, him he calls his shepherd and his anointed, whose right hand he has taken to subdue nations before him.[31] YHWH has messages sent to the neighboring nations to tell them that he will subdue them to Nebuchadrezzar,

30. 1 Kings 19:15-17; cf. 2 Kings 8:7-15.
31. Isa. 41:2-4; 44:28; 45:1-4.

the king of Babylon (Jer. 27:3ff.). YHWH uses Necho as a rod against king Josiah, sending the former with strong words,

> ... God commanded me to make haste; refrain from [meddling with] God, who [is] with me, lest he destroy you (2 Chron. 35:21).

Scripture confirms that Necho simply spoke the truth: "Josiah ... did not heed the words of Necho from the mouth of God" (v. 22). To these examples many others could be added, all showing that God's dealings with Israel always take the pivotal place in his dealings with other nations. They even show that exceptionally it may be the gentiles who play the positive, and Israel that plays the negative role.

On the other hand, Scripture also mentions that God let all nations walk in their own ways (Acts 14:16), that is, away from God. It is these nations' own gods (read, angelic princes) who determine the history of these nations, be it always under God's supreme dominion. Of this, too, we give some examples. Numbers 21:29 quotes an ancient saying in which Moab after its angelic prince is called "people of Chamosh," and where is said directly of this prince,

> he gave his sons [up as] escaped,
> and his daughters as the prisoner to the king of the Amorites, Sihon.

Here, Chamosh has a similar relationship with the Moabites as YHWH has with the Israelites, namely, that of a father with his children.[32] Moreover, it is Chamosh here who leads the history of his people by (in this case) not caring for his children but by delivering them into the hands of Sihon, and thus into those of the angelic prince of the Amorites. In Judges 11 we find something similar. Judge Jephthah, negotiating with the king of the Ammonites, who claims parts of the land beyond Jordan, uses the following argument (vs. 23-24),[33]

32. Cf. Num. 11:12; Deut. 14:1.

33. The inner coherence of the verse is underlined in that all six times the same

> and now, YHWH, the God of Israel, dispossessed the Amorite from before his people Israel; and you want to dispossess it [= Israel]? Will you not take to possess what Chamosh, your god, gave you to possess? And we will take to possess whatsoever YWHW, our God, gives us to possess.

It seems as if Jephthah places YHWH and Chamosh on one level: YHWH is the *elohim* of Israel and has allotted a certain possession to Israel, while Chamosh is the *elohim* of Ammon[34] and has allotted a certain possession to Ammon. Here again, the *elohim*, the angelic prince of a nation, functions as the ruler of its history. For Jephthah, this does not mean at all that YHWH would not be the almighty Supreme Ruler of all nations. On the contrary, in v. 27 he argues that, if Ammon would not be prepared to give in, YHWH as the great Judge would judge between Israel and Ammon. YHWH is not only the *elohim* of Israel, but also the Judge over all *elohim*, and that is precisely what we learned from Psalm 82, where *elohim* (God) judges in the midst of the *elohim* (gods, celestial beings, angelic princes).

2.2. Gods and Demons

2.2.1. What Are Demons?

The last points in § 2.1 referred to the relationship between the angelic princes whom God has placed over the nations and the "gods" who are worshipped by the nations. These points remind us again of Psalm 82, in which God blames the angelic princes for not having executed good government. Each angelic prince is like a vicegerent placed over a country and a nation. Like a judge in the book of Judges he has to do justice to his people both outwardly and inwardly. Outwardly, each will probably have taken more or less good care of the affairs of his people, for YHWH does not speak of that. He

---

verb is used, in ever changing nuances.

34. Elsewhere he is called the god of the brother-nation Moab, whereas Milkom is normally viewed as the god of Ammon (see 1 Kings 11:5, 33; 2 Kings 23:13).

speaks of their failure with regard to social justice at home. In their territories, they have tolerated wickedness, oppression, and injustice. They did not help the weak over against the oppressor but often placed themselves on the side of the mighty (v. 2-4). In v. 3-4, the *elohim* receive another chance, but they do not use it; not so much because of rebellion but rather because of a lack of understanding (v. 5):

> Nothing they know, and nothing they understand,
> in darkness they walk about;
> all [the] foundations of [the] earth totter.

Then follows judgment (v. 6):

> *I* have said, gods [are] you,
> and sons of the Most-High[35] [are] all of you;
> but like men [or, like a man, like Adam] you shall die,
> and like one of the [earthly] princes [*sarim*] you shall fall.

Like men, fallen angels will eventually end up in the "second death," that is, the lake of fire.[36] One day, YHWH will put an end to the rule of the gods' "intermediate realm" and to all flimsy vice-royalty of angelic princes, and in Christ himself he will take up again non-mediatorial world government (v. 8):

> Arise, o God, judge [= rule] the earth,
> for you possess all nations.

This word "possess" is quite remarkable. It also means "inherit" or "receive as a possession (inheritance)." Not only Israel, which became God's peculiar possession or inheritance but, under the coming world government, all nations will be the inheritance, not any longer of angelic princes, but of YHWH himself (cf., e.g., Isa. 19:23-25).

In that the *elohim* of the nations led the nations into idolatry,

35. "Sons of God," celestial beings, angelic princes.
36. Rev. 19:20; 20:6, 10, 14; cf. 2 Pet. 2:4; Jude 6. Also cf. the "perishing" of the false gods in Jer. 10:11 (the only verse in Aramaic in Jer., thus connecting it with the Aramaic parts in Daniel, in which the decline of the world-empires and the restoration of Israel is announced).

they became false gods, or "demons." The Greek word *daimôn* originally means "god, deity," in particular "lower deity." Thus, we find the related word daimonion still in Acts 17:18: the Athenians believed that the apostle Paul taught strange *daimonia,* for he preached Jesus and the resurrection.[37] Then *daimôn* also means "guardian deity" (cf. guardian angel), "intermediate being" (between a higher god, or gods, and men), but then also a higher being that can bring mischief, an "evil spirit." These meanings, "lower deity," "guardian angel" on the one hand, "evil spirit" on the other, fit well into what we saw with regard to the "gods" in the Old Testament.[38]

Deuteronomy 32:17 (LXX) reads, "they sacrificed to [the] demons and not to God." The Masoretic text reads, "they sacrificed to the demons,[39] not to God,[40] [to] gods [whom] they did not know." Psalm 96:5 (LXX) reads, "all the gods of the nations [are] demons" (Heb., "idols"). Psalm 106:37 (LXX) reads, "they sacrificed their sons and their daughters to the demons" (Heb. *sedim*).[41] Isaiah 65:11 (LXX) reads, "preparing for the demon a table" (Heb., *Gad,* the goddess of fortune).[42] In Hosea 4:12 and 5:4 it is a "spirit of fornication" that leads Israel astray.[43] We find the same notion in the New Testament,

37. Perhaps, as for instance Chrysostom believed, "Jesus and Anastasis," on the assumption that the Athenians believed resurrection (Gr. *anastasis*) to be a goddess.
38. We have to leave aside here a secondary correspondence, namely, that both *daimôn* and *elohim* may also refer to the spirit of a dead person—in itself an interesting subject (see 1 Sam. 28:13; cf. Isa. 8:19).
39. Heb., *sedim* (this term too originally referred to good spirits!).
40. Or, "[who are] no gods," or "not God."
41. The Targum uses here another word for "evil spirits."
42. Targum, "idol"; cf. 1 Cor. 10:21! Also in the pseudepigrapha, the demons are mentioned several times, e.g., 1 Baruch 4:7: "You have irritated him who made you in sacrificing to demons and not to God." 1 Enoch 19:1: "...the angels who mixed with the women [Gen. 6:1-4], and their spirits, assuming many forms, defile the people and seduce them to sacrifice to the demons as to gods." Jub. 22:17 says: "the nations... worship the demons" (cf. 19:28); according to Jub. 11:3-4, Mastema (that is Satan, the prince of the evil spirits) is the moving spirit of idolatry.
43. Also, according to 1 Enoch 15-16 and 99:7 idolatry is worship of demons.

especially in 1 Corinthians 10:20-21 ("what [the nations] sacrifice, to demons and not to God they <sacrifice> it") and Revelation 9:20: "the people... did not repent... that they should not worship the demons and the idols of gold, and silver, and brass, and stone, and wood." Revelation 16:14 speaks of "spirits of demons" seducing the kings of the earth and of the whole world.

In the New Testament, the word *daimonion* received the fixed meaning of "evil spirit." In some translations the word is rendered this way, not only because it is more familiar but also because demons in the Greek sometimes are literally called "evil spirits" (*pneumata ponèra*).[44] This brings us nearer to the question as to what demons precisely are.[45] I leave aside the view that demons are just a superstitious reference to all kinds of natural mischief, or that they represent the spirits of wicked dead people. Neither do I enter into the view sometimes heard in Christian circles that demons would be the disembodied spirits of the inhabitants of some pre-Adamitic earth, or the monstrous offspring of angels and women. The latter refers to Genesis 6:1-4, where the *bené ha-elohim* are almost certainly angels, but there is not the slightest indication that their bastard children became demons.

There is one biblical explanation for the origin and the identity of demons that obviously fits best: demons are fallen angels. The Bible speaks of Satan and his angels (Matt. 25:41; Rev. 12:7). Satan is also called "Beelzebul, the prince of the demons," and these demons are called his "kingdom" (Matt. 12:24, 26).[46] For a more extensive treatment of what demons in

44. In Luke 8:2a we *find pneumata ponèra*, in v. 26 *daimonia*.

45. See Ouweneel (1988a:117).

46. However, we should not confuse these fallen angels with other angels who, in contrast with the former, are not free but bound, because God, "having thrown them into the Tartarus, has delivered them to chains [other reading, holes] of darkness to be reserved unto judgment" (2 Pet. 2:4). These are "angels who did not keep their origin [= original or elevated state] but left their own habitation," of whom we read that God "has reserved [them] unto [the] judgment of [the] great day with everlasting chains under darkness" (Jude

the Bible precisely are, I refer to Appendix 1.

2.2.2. Chief Angelic Powers

The Septuagint and the New Testament know various names for higher angelic powers, which throw some more light upon our subject. According to Colossians 1:16, God in Christ created all things which are in the heavens and which are on earth, the visible and the invisible, thrones (*thronoi*), dominions (*kyriotètes*), principalities (*archai*), and authorities (*exousiai*). In Ephesians 1:20-21, Christ is placed in the heavenly realms above all principality (*archè*), authority (*exousia*), power (*dynamis*), dominion (*kyriotès*), and every name. Ephesians 3:10 speaks of *archai* and *exousiai*, Romans 8:38 of angels, *archai*, and *dynameis*, and 1 Peter 3:22 of angels, *exousiai*, and *dynameis*. Apparently, these are distinct angelic categories, which corresponds with Jewish opinion.[47]

According to Daniel 7:27 (Theodotion), one day "all *archai*" will be submitted to the people of the saints of the Most High, that is, Israel. The text does refer to earthly kingdoms, but because of their connection with national angelic princes (Dan. 10) one may, here too, think of the submission of these angelic princes.

---

6). These chained angels are to be distinguished from Satan and his demons in that the latter have freedom of movement in the "heavenly realms" (Eph. 6:12). The fall of Satan and his angels must have taken place at least before the fall of man, whereas many interpreters connect the group of chained angels with Gen. 6:1-4. Other expositors believe that the actual demons, too, are not all free, but that many of them are chained in the "abyss" (Gr. *abyssos*), a kind of temporary prison for evil spirits, from which they will be set free in the last terrible phase of wicked rebellion on earth (Luke 8:31; Rev. 9:1-2, 10).

47. See Test.Levi 3. The members of these categories are also referred to as "angels of power," "angels of dominion" (1 Enoch 61:10). 2 Enoch 20-21 speaks of "fiery hosts of great archangels, bodyless forces and dominions, principalities and powers, cherubim and seraphim, thrones and many-eyed" (cf. for the latter the "watchers" in § 2.1.2). 2 Enoch 20-21 and Test.Levi 3 render it likely that the five powers mentioned in the text represent the highest angelic categories, which belong to the highest heaven, in the direct presence of God.

With the (probable) exception of Titus 3:1,[48] Paul means by *archai* always "principalities" in the sense of angelic powers, both good and evil. The latter are at least implied, if not exclusively intended, in Romans 8:38; Ephesians 1:21; 3:20; Colossians 1:16, and certainly intended in Ephesians 6:12 (see below). Through Christ's work on the cross, the *archai* and *exousiai* have been disarmed and denounced (Col. 2:15); he submitted them to himself (Eph. 1:21; 1 Pet. 3:22) and placed himself as Head over them (Col. 2:15), so that they could not threaten the believers any longer (Rom. 8:38). Their final perdition is described in 1 Corinthians 15:24.

Of course, Ephesians 6:12 is of special interest. Paul points out here that the actual conflict of God's people is not with visible powers of flesh and blood, but with invisible powers in the heavenly realms: the [evil] *archai*, the *exousiai*, the *kosmokratores* ("world rulers") of this darkness—read, the "angelic princes of this dark world"—and the *pneumatika* ('spiritual powers") of wickedness.

Especially the word *kosmokratôr* is of interest. Originally, it could refer to a planet or planetary god, or in a wider sense, to a ruler (cf. *kratos* = "force") of a certain celestial (cosmic) sphere, and then also to the rulers of the universe, who determine the fate of people (cf. astrology!). Later, the term was used for the gods in the Greek world. The word does not occur in the Septuagint, but it does as a loanword in the rabbinical writings. In Ephesians 6:12, it is one of the terms for demonic powers. It is not impossible that something of the notion of (evil) angelic princes is still retained in it: princes who each have a certain territory of the cosmos under them, allotted to each one of them by their "prince," Satan (cf. Eph. 2:2).[49] I

48. Unless the intention is that our deepest respect for "authorities" is based on the fact that their authority goes back upon angelic princes, so that in fact we are subject to the latter. Cf. *exousiai* in Rom. 13:1 and cf. v. 4: *theou diakonos* ('servant of God").

49. According to a Midrash (Lev.R. 18, 3 [on Exod. 24:7]; see also Exod.R. 51, 8), God told the angel of death, i.e., Satan (cf. Heb. 2:14), that he, though set by God to be *kosmokratôr* over all people, was not allowed to have anything

already mentioned the "rulers (archonts) of this age" (*aiôn*) in 1 Corinthians 2:6, 8, where we possibly find the same meaning.

So far, we several times came across the name Satan. The Hebrew word *satan* means "enemy" or "adversary." It corresponds with the Greek word *diábolos* (in English corrupted into "devil"), which means "slanderer,"[50] but also "tempter,"[51] "cause of division," "adversary." Sometimes the word is literally translated this way (Num. 22:22; Ps. 109:9). According to Job 1:6 and 2:1, Satan is one of the *bené ha-elohim*, the angelic princes. In these Scriptures we see how YHWH at times receives the celestial beings and executes judgment. Satan is here the accuser, the mouthpiece of the law, as the angel of YHWH in Zech. 3 is the defender, the mouthpiece of grace. But he is more: even as an accuser, Satan is always an evil power, who aims at the fall of Job and who drives David to sin (1 Chron. 21:1); he accuses because of sins he himself has caused.

For our subject, it is important that Satan is called the "god of this age" (2 Cor. 4:4), an expression related to the "princes (rulers) of this age" in 1 Corinthians 2:6, 8, a passage just mentioned. He is therefore a "god," an *elohim*, an angelic prince, namely, in the evil sense; he is the greatest prince known in the present "age," that is, the world with its present *zeitgeist*, which is foreign to God.[52] This fits in well with the expression mentioned, "prince (*archôn*) of this world."[53] Satan is the head of all apostate national angelic princes, for he can, to a certain extent truly, say that he has power over all kingdoms of the world, as he does in Luke 4:5-6. Actually, we do not find the

---

to do with the Israelites, for the latter were his children (cf. Deut. 14:1).

50. Cf. Job 1:9-11; 2:4-5; Zech. 3:1; Rev. 12:10, although the word *katègôr*, "accuser," is used there.
51. Cf. Matt. 4:3; 1 Thess. 3:5, although *peirazôn*, "tempter," is used there; also see 1 Chron. 21:1.
52. The word *zeitgeist* (ESV, "course") adequately expresses the sense of *aiôn* in Eph. 2:2.
53. John 12:31; 14:30; 16:11.

word *cosmos* here, like in Matthew 4:8, but *oikoumenè*, "inhabited earth," which in Luke always refers to the Roman Empire (see 2:1; Acts 11:28; 17:9; 19:27; 24:5). Later in this study, this will turn out to be a point of great importance, for according to later Jewish tradition, Samael, that is, Satan, is the angelic prince of the Roman people and empire. The conflict between Christ and Satan is the conflict between God's people on the one hand and "Roman" (Western) culture on the other.

One of the names of Satan in the New Testament is *Beelzebul*.[54] The Syrian and other Eastern manuscripts speak of *Beelzebub*. This is a corruption of the Hebrew *Baal-Zebub*, which means "lord of the flies." According to 2 Kings 1:2-3, 6, 16, this was the god of the Philistine city of Ekron. The actual name was *Baal-Zebul*, "lord of the height," and was presumably corrupted by the Israelites into *Baal-Zebub* in order to ridicule the name. The fact that the name of this idol was transferred to Satan, confirms again that behind the idols real spiritual powers hide themselves.

Something similar we see in the name *Belial*. The Hebrew word *beliyyal* literally means "worthlessness"; "men (or sons) of Belial" are "worthless men." The idea is more or less, "one plotting vileness." In 2 Corinthians 6:15, however, Paul uses the word *belial* as another name for Satan. Possibly the name is linked with the Babylonian goddess of vegetation, who presumably was also the goddess of the underworld. The word may therefore indeed be a term for the "underworld," or the world of the demons. In Psalm 18:5 (= 2 Sam. 22:5), the "floods of Belial" are parallel with the "bonds of death," and mean as much as "floods of perdition," "floods of the underworld."[55]

That which I refer to in this section concerning Satan is only a brief introduction. We will encounter him again in

54. Matt. 10:25; 12:24, 27; Mark 3:22; Luke 11:15, 18-19.
55. Already in the pseudepigraphic literature of the Old Testament, Belial is a name for the devil; see Asc.Isa. (passim), Jub. 1:20 (15:33?), Test. XII, in the form Beliar, which also occurs in 2 Cor. 6:15 according to the main manuscripts.

several sections, particularly in chapter 4, which deals with the angelic prince of the Roman Empire, the "dragon" in the book of Revelation, and in chapters 9 and 10. There we will also examine the remarkable passages in Isaiah 14 and Ezekiel 28, which have been taken to refer to the fall of Satan.

Chapter 3
The First Five World-Empires

3.1. Egypt

3.1.1. The Gods of Egypt

IN § 1.2 WE HAVE, ON THE BASIS of Revelation 17, decided on a succession of seven world-empires: Egypt, Assyria, Babylonia, Medo-Persia, Macedonia-Greece, the Roman Empire, and a seventh, "Germanic," Empire to be further defined later. Then follows the eighth, that is, the eschatological world-empire of the Antichrist. The series is concluded with the Ninth King, the Son of Man, who erects an everlasting kingdom (Dan. 7).

Let us now look first at Egypt, at the metahistorically most important moment of its history: the exodus of Israel from Egypt. Exodus 12:12b states that YHWH joins battle with the "gods" of Egypt.[1] The plagues of Egypt actually entailed a judgment over the various "gods" (angelic powers) of Egypt. God speaks of these gods as concrete powers, and announces their perdition. The Egyptians themselves associated their "gods" with natural phenomena. For instance, Hapi was the Nile-god of flood, and Osiris the god of fertility; the plagues that aimed at the Nile and the harvest were therefore aimed at these two gods. The frogs were associated with Heqt, a form of

1. Also see Exod. 18:10f.; Num. 33:4; 2 Sam. 7:23.

Hathor, the most important goddess of Egypt; the frog plague thus showed the superiority of Israel's God over Hathor. The midge and fly plagues were a blow in the face of Isis, the wife of Osiris. The murrain and boil plagues were directed against Ptah (or Apis), the god of Memphis (represented as a bull[2]), and against other gods, represented as a cow, a ram, a goat, etcetera. The locust plague was aimed at the god Serapis, the god protecting against locusts, and the plague of the three days of darkness was aimed at the sun god, Amon-Ra or -Re, or at Osiris again.

What we are concerned with here is not simply some primitive superstition of the Egyptians, which we could quietly lay aside. On the contrary, God does take these "gods," which after all are nothing but angelic powers subjected to him, very seriously indeed. But he shows them also his majesty by triumphing over them. Moreover, we will also meet with the sun god in the next world-empires. The Egyptian god Osiris will then turn out to be identical with the Babylonian god Bel or Nebo, the Persian Mithra(s), and the Greek Apollo, all names for one and the same angelic prince. This is the prince who in *all* world-empires until the kingdom of Christ has the highest control over the angelic powers: Samael, or Satan.

Later in this book we will also see that this sun god is the great, false imitator of Christus: it is quite striking that this god is often presented as the divine child of the mother-virgin. Osiris is not only the husband of the goddess Isis, but also her son, and in this form is identical with Horus. The myth dealing with this matter[3] tells us how Osiris, because of his good gifts and readiness to help people, was beloved by all. This stirred the jealousy of his brother Seth (also called Typhon), who laid a plot against him with seventy-two other conspirators. They persuaded Osiris to lie down in a marvel-

---

2. Actually, the calf Apis was another representation of Osiris, the chief Egyptian godhead. It was this deity that the Israelites depicted when at Sinai they constructed the golden calf and worshipped it (Exod. 32).
3. Comte (1994:201-204).

ous coffin, which fitted him exactly, and then quickly closed the lid. In procession they carried him to the river, submerged the coffin in the water, and this carried him to the sea. Under the most difficult circumstances, the body was traced by the broken-hearted Isis, and taken back to Egypt. However, Seth again got hold of the body, cut it into pieces, and distributed them over all Egypt. But Isis collected the pieces and put them together. She even managed to have (the dead? living?) Osiris beget a son with her, Horus, who in fact was a reanimation, a "reincarnation" of Osiris himself. One of the titles of Osiris is therefore, "Husband of the Mother." His death and resurrection symbolize the alternation of summer and winter, but also the hope for a life after this life.

In an analogous way, Apollo, as the son of Zeus and Leto, is the "Child of the Sun," but also himself the sun god.[4] We will see that Zeus/Apollo is identical with Osiris/Horus. As with Osiris and Horus, the characteristics of Zeus and Apollo often merge. Thus, with the Romans, the equivalent of Zeus, the supreme god Jupiter, was also worshipped as *Jupiter-puer*, the boy, son of Fortuna.

In the plague of the three days of darkness in Egypt, YHWH struck the sun god in the heart. But there is also another way in which he hit him. In antiquity, the sun was often symbolically represented by a serpent. Therefore, the sun god in Egypt was often depicted as a disc with a serpent around it. There are reasons to believe that in antiquity the worship of the sun was closely linked with the worship of the serpent as a holy, divine animal.[5] This fact throws special light on the meaning of the miracle which Aaron performed, when he changed his staff into a serpent. The sorcerers of Egypt clearly showed that they were not simple illusionists, but that they stood in direct contact with the "gods" of Egypt. They proved their "divine" power by changing their staffs into serpents as well. However, the God of Moses and Aaron, as the God of

4. Comte (1994:63-68).
5. Compare the "creeping animals" worshipped as gods (Rom. 1:23).

gods, demonstrated his supreme power by swallowing the staffs of the magicians (Exod. 7:10-12).

3.1.2. The Chaos Powers

It is extremely important to see that the crossing of the Red Sea, too, was a divine war against angelic powers (cf. Appendix 4). In order to see this, we have to pay attention to the meaning of the name *Rahab*. This is primarily the name of the chaos-angel, the angelic prince of the worldwide, turbulent "deep," or "flood." The word *Rahab* literally means "impetuous" or "reckless." We meet the Rahab for instance in Job 26:12 (cf. 9:13), where the word is parallel with the sea, and apparently can be identified with this. Talmud and Midrash[6] conclude, also on the basis of this verse, that Rahab is the name of the angelic prince of the sea or the primordial ocean. In Psalm 89:11 and Isaiah 51:9, Rahab may be thought to refer to the primordial ocean (see Gen. 1:2), but also to the Red Sea.[7] Besides its general meaning as angelic prince of the primordial ocean, Rahab also turns out to have a more limited meaning, which regards Egypt.

We should not think of the Rahab as a prehistoric or legendary monster, in spite of the language in Ezekiel 29:3; 32:2. It is the monstrous angelic prince, be it in the wider sense of the oceans, or in the narrower sense of Egypt's prince. Usually, Rahab is described as originally referring to the feminine chaos monster, comparable with the chaos monster Tiamat of Babylonian mythology. This name Tiamat presumably resounds in the Hebrew *tehôm*, "primordial ocean, (water)flood, deep."[8] Rahab, then, is the chaos angel, the angelic prince of the original state of emptiness and void, and particularly of the worldwide, impetuous "flood" (Gen. 1:2). This angelic

6. Baba Bathra 74b; Num.R. 18 (185a).
7. Cf. Pesakhim 118b and Arakhin 15a, which speak of the angelic prince of the Red Sea; also cf. Ps. 74:13.
8. See Gen. 1:2; 7:11; 8:2; 49:25; Deut. 33:13; Job 28:14; 38:16, 30; 41:23; Ps. 36:7; 42:8; 104:6; Prov. 8:27-28; Isa. 51:10; Ez. 26:19; Am. 7:4; Jon. 2:6; Hab. 3:10.

prince stands under the control of God's power, as is shown by Job 26:12. In Job 38:8-11, too, we clearly see how God has subdued the angelic prince of chaos.

It is especially modern form criticism that has paid much attention to the "monster" (angelic prince) of the primordial chaos, or ocean. However, it uses such reflections to refer Genesis 1 to the realm of (ahistorical) mythology (see more extensively Appendix 3). This is the reason why many conservative Bible interpreters shrink away from such views. We should not, however, throw out the baby with the bathwater. If the Old Testament indeed refers here to the chaos powers, which played a role at God's creative work, we should not suppress these data, but do justice to them. We have to use them, not in order to "dehistorize" or "demythologize" Genesis 1, but to draw attention to the spiritual warfare in the heavenly realms, which presumably played a role already in the creation story (see again more extensively Appendix 4).

3.1.3. The Red Sea

Psalm 89:11 may refer to the creation story (cf. v. 10-13), but presumably we (also) find here an allusion to the exodus from Egypt. This is much clearer in Isaiah 51:9-10:

> Awake! awake! put on strength,
> o arm of YHWH,
> awake as in ancient days,
> [in] the generations of old.
> [Were] you not he who has cut down Rahab,
> who pierced the dragon [or, serpent, monster]?
> [Were] you not he who has dried the sea,
> the waters of the great flood [or, deep; *tehôm*],
> who has made the depths of the sea a way
> for the ransomed to pass through?

This is in many ways a remarkable passage. The cutting down of the Rahab is placed here "in ancient days," in primitive time, as is also clear from the reference to the *tehôm*, the primordial ocean. But this great water flood is then immediately linked with the Red Sea. This is because the drying of a way through the sea, for the ransomed of YHWH to pass through (cf. v. 11), can only refer to the passage through the Red Sea. Here, too, the chaos powers of the time of creation are identified with the angelic powers that withstood YHWH at the exodus of his people from Egypt. A similar passage is Psalm 74:13:

> You divided the sea by your strength,
> You broke the heads of the dragon[9] in the waters.

This is presumably another reference to the exodus of Israel (also cf. v. 15b, 16). Perhaps Scripture wants to say, here too, that the chaos powers of Genesis 1:2, once subdued by God, at the redemption of God's own people again raised their monstrous heads as it were, just to be cut down anew. This chaos power of the Red Sea is nothing but the angelic prince of Egypt. Sometimes the name Rahab simply refers to the land of Egypt (Ps. 87:4; Isa. 30:7). Ezekiel 29:3 refers to the Pharaoh of Egypt in the following way:

> Thus says the Lord YHWH:
> Lo, I am against you, Pharaoh, king of Egypt,
> you great dragon [or, serpent, monster], lying between your streams.

In the same way, it is said in Ezekiel 32:2 to the Pharaoh of

9. Actually, "dragons," but perhaps with a singular meaning. The Hebrew word is *tannin*, the Greek equivalent is *drakôn*. In antiquity, the "dragon" was among all nations the embodiment of a power hostile towards the gods or the chief god. Originally, God also created the "dragons" (*tanninim*) (Gen. 1:21; Job 7:12; Ps. 74:13; 148:7; Isa. 27:1; 51:9; Jer. 51:34; Ez. 29:3; 32:2). Insofar as these "dragons" are symbolic representations of angelic powers they have turned against their Creator. Thus, the "dragon" can become a reference to the angelic prince of Egypt (see the text) or to that of Babylon (Jer. 51:34). Elsewhere, *tannin* simply means "serpent"; but here too, in the word is clearly reverberating the power of a dark angelic prince, who enslaves (Exod. 7:9, 12) and poisons (Deut. 32:33) God's people, but who is subdued by the faithful (Exod. 7:9,12 and Ps. 91:13; cf. Rom. 16:20).

Egypt,

> You are like a lion [among] the nations,
> and you [are] as a dragon in the seas,
> and you toss around in your rivers,
> and trouble the waters with your feet,
> and mud their streams.

This is a very lively picture of a great monster moving around in the river, fiercely stirring the water with its feet and tossing up the mud. Again, this is clearly a figurative language rising far above the earthly prince of Egypt. Just as the dragon in the book of Revelation is the evil angelic prince of the Roman Empire, rising above "the beast" of Revelation 13 (the earthly prince of that empire), so the dragon is, here in Ezekiel, particularly the monstrous angelic prince of Egypt. However, Pharaoh is the earthly "incorporation" of this angelic prince, and therefore, at the same time both Pharaoh and his angelic prince can be addressed. This takes place more or less in the same way as in Isaiah 14 and Ezekiel 28, where behind the earthly princes of Babylon and Tyre clearly looms up the angelic prince of Babylon and the one of Tyre, respectively, of whom the earthly prince is only the "incorporation."

The way we have to imagine the "incorporation" of the angelic prince and his earthly regent is an important, but also a difficult question. Henri Frankfort expresses it as follows:[10]

> Pharaoh was no mortal being, but a god. This was the fundamental concept of Egyptian kingship, that Pharaoh was of divine substance, an incarnated god; and this view can be followed back as far as texts and symbols lead us. It is wrong to speak of a deification of the Pharaoh. His divinity was not proclaimed at a certain moment, in a way comparable with the *consecratio* of the dead emperor by the Roman senate. His

10. Frankfort (1948:5); by the way, the Assyrians and Babylonians did see the king as a man, be it in close relationship with the realm of the gods (p. 6). See the extensive explanation in Frankfort (1948): vol. 1 (about Egypt) and vol. 2 (about Mesopotamia).

> coronation was no apotheosis [elevation to godhead. WJO], but an epiphany [appearance as godhead. WJO].

Pharaoh is often called after the god Horus or the god Re. According to Egyptian thinking, he *is* Horus or Re, the sun god, even though we cannot go as far as speaking of an "incarnation," like the incarnation of Christ, the Son of God. But the quotation of Frankfort does underscore, in our terminology, that Pharaoh as it were "embodies" the angelic prince, the "god." Pharaoh is not the "incarnation" of Egypt's angelic prince in the sense of an absolute identification of this angelic prince with the spirit of Pharaoh. But in him, the "god" is embodied in a unique way insofar as the king's acts are in fact those of the angelic prince. Therefore, the fall of Pharaoh is also the fall of Egypt (king and nation are one), as well as the fall of the angelic prince.

At the crossing of the Red Sea, the angelic prince of Egypt grabs his last chance against Israel and attempts to stop the people, and even devour them. But YHWH is mightier than this angelic prince. The divine irony of the story is that it is the very Pharaoh and his army that are devoured by the chaos waters of the Red Sea. It is indeed the "chaos waters" we find here, as is clear from Exodus 15:5, 8. There we find the expression *tehomot*; this is the plural of *tehôm*, which, as said before, refers to the "primordial ocean," the "great flood."

How important it is to read the story in this way. "Scientific" explanations concerning the crossing of the Red Sea are of no avail here. For instance, one might point out that the drying of the Red Sea, though brought about by God, was a "natural" phenomenon after all, for it was caused by a "strong east wind" (Exod. 14:21). But if we speak like this, we overlook the fact that the same word *ruach* ("wind, spirit, breath") is used here as in Exodus 15:8, where we literally read, "through the *ruach* of your nostrils the waters were heaped up." And in v. 10 we find, "You blew with your *ruach*, the sea covered them." That is the pivotal point. We cannot discard such statements by claiming that this is "just" poetical language. Israel was not saved by an "air displacement from a high pression area to a low pression area" sent by YHWH, but by his *ruach*. We can take this to be his "breath," for v. 8 speaks of God's nostrils and v. 10 of his blowing, but we can also understand it to be his Spirit that was sent out by Him. It is here like in Genesis 1:2, where the Spirit (*ruach*) of God is "hovering" over the chaos powers and withstands them by creating order in the chaos.[11]

Very important is Exodus 15:11: "Who [is] like you among the *elim* [mighty ones, gods], YHWH?" The *ruach* of YHWH has prevailed over the gods of Egypt (see again 12:12), not only by means of the plagues, but also at the Red Sea. Now we can also understand what YHWH says in Exodus 14:14: "YHWH shall *fight* for you, and you shall be still." At the Red Sea, we have not to do with just a miracle, the miracle of the drying and the flowing back of the waters, but with *fighting*. Verse 25 shows that the Egyptians themselves realized very well that they met not just with a miracle but with battle: "...YHWH [is] fighting for them against Egypt." Note, not against "us," neither against "the army," but against *Egypt*. In the deepest sense this means: against the angelic prince of Egypt. In what other sense would YHWH "fight" against Egypt, if the only thing he did was having the waters flow back over the army of Egypt? He fought against the angelic prince of Egypt, who had the power over the chaos waters of the Red Sea. He deprived that angelic prince of his power, made the waters depart from the people of Israel, and made these same chaos waters flow back over the Egyptians.

In this case again, we find a confirmation in Jewish tradition. The Talmud repeatedly speaks of the angelic prince

11. Similarly, we read in Ps. 104:4 that God makes his angels *ruchot* ('spirits" or "winds"), again in connection with, among other things, the *tehôm* in vs. 6-7, which fled away before God's rebuke.

of the Red Sea.[12] The Midrash[13] points to Exodus 15:1c: "the horse and its rider [singular!] has he thrown into the sea." The Midrash thinks here of the falling down of the angelic prince of Egypt, which allegedly took place in a visible way before the eyes of Israel. And then something striking follows. The Midrash says that thus all world-empires are to be destroyed, in that their angelic prince is cut down. Here, a principle is formulated that for our study is of the greatest importance: each world-empire will be defeated by the God of Israel, and each time a world-empire will perish in that the angelic prince of each empire is slain by YHWH.

The Midrash referred to explains this by means of some Scriptures that partly will be dealt with later in this study. First, there is Isaiah 14:12, where it is the angelic prince of Babylon who is cut down at the fall of Babylon. Secondly, I mention Isaiah 24:21-23, where judgment comes over "the host of the hight in the hight," that is, the angelic prince(s) and his/their army. Thirdly, Isaiah 34:5, where the Midrash reads, "my sword has got drunk at the heavenly prince," namely, the angelic prince of Edom. We can also think here again of Isaiah 51:9-10, which literally speaks of the "cutting down" of Rahab, the angelic prince of Egypt, whereby the Red Sea was dried and Egypt was defeated.

For a further study of the important subject of the chaos powers I refer again to Appendix 4.

3.2. Assyria

3.2.1. The Gods of Assyria

In the series of the seven world-empires, Asshur or Assyria is the second empire. Direct biblical statements concerning the angelic prince of Assyria are rare, but perhaps there is a simple reason for this. The Assyrian king was viewed as the earthly viceroy for the national god, who carried the same name as people and country: Asshur. This means that, where Scrip-

12. See note 7.

13. Mekhilta Exod. 15:1 (43b).

ture speaks of "Asshur," in many cases the angelic prince of Assyria will have been included. The main temple of Asshur stood in the capital, Asshur, while other gods were the guardians of the other cities of the Assyrians: Anu and Adad also in Asshur, Ishtar (Astarte) in Nineveh and Erbil, Nabu (cf. Nebo in Babylon) in Nineveh and Kalah, etcetera.

The god Nisroch, in whose temple Sennacherib was murdered (2 Kings 19:37), is called in the LXX Esorach, and is possibly the same as Asshur; some, however, have thought of a (mocking?) corruption of Marduk. Marduk is viewed as a Babylonian deity, but in general the religion of the Assyrians can be said to be very similar to that of the Babylonians. After the conquest of their empire by Babylon, the Assyrians themselves identified Marduk with Asshur.[14] Asshur's wife, Ninlil ("lady of the storm"), was originally the wife of the Sumerian god Enlil, the storm-god ("lord of the storm"), who in Akkadian is called Bel. Bel, too, is a Babylonian deity, whom we will meet later. If therefore we would acquire further understanding of the angelic prince(s) of Assyria, we will also have to refer to the next chapter, in which we will deal with Babylonia. The connection between these two empires goes so far that, where the Bible unmistakably refers to the Babylonian Empire, sometimes still the old name Asshur is used.[15]

The significance of the chief god Asshur was great. As I said, the Assyrian king stood in a close relation with him; this sometimes came to expression in the royal names. For instance, Asshurbanipal means, "Asshur has made a son,"[16] and Esarhaddon means, "Asshur has given a brother." Other kings were called after other gods: Sennacherib after the moon god Sin, and Shalmaneser after the god Shulmanu.

The Assyrian king regularly reported his activities to the chief god, Asshur. The campaigns of the Assyrians were

---

14. See extensively Dhorme (1949:156-164).
15. Ezra 6:22; Jer. 2:18; also in Sanhedrin 22a.
16. Presumably, this king is identical with the "great and noble Asnappar" in Ezra 4:10.

therefore viewed as holy wars against all those who refused to acknowledge Asshur's supremacy. This clearly resounds in 2 Kings 18 (= Isa. 36), where Sennacherib sent his marshal (the Rabshakeh) to Jerusalem in order to induce the people to surrender to him. In so doing, the marshal uses this argument (v. 33-35):

> Has any of the gods of the nations at all been able to deliver his land out of the hand of the king of Assyria? Where [are] the gods of Hamath and Arpad, where the gods of Sepharvaim, Hena, and Ivah [cf. 17:30-31]? Have they delivered Samaria out of my hand? Who [were there] among all the gods of the countries that have delivered their country out of my hand, that YHWH could deliver Jerusalem out of my hand?

In 2 Kings 19:10-13 (= Isa. 37:10-13), Sennacherib uses the same argument over against Hezekiah. Here, the *gods* of the other nations are compared with the *king* of Assyria. To the mind of the heathen, such a comparison was justified only if the king of Assyria is viewed here as closely associated with his "god," that is, his angelic prince. Moreover, because of the identity of the names, "the king of Assyria" does not only refer to the king of the city (or the kingdom) of Assyria, but also to the king who belongs to Asshur and represents him. The fundamental error of Sennacherib is that he places the God of Israel on one level with the gods of other nations, and views them all as inferior to his god. The history of his fall proves that he has to do with the God *of gods*, over against whom the "gods," who are only angelic princes, possess no more power than he allows them.

Remarkable are the harsh words that the prophet Isaiah addresses to the king of Assyria (Isa. 37:22-29). Even more remarkable is the fact that the war of Israel's God against the king of Assyria, and therefore against the god Asshur, is fought on the "level" of the spiritual powers. It is none less than "the Angel of YHWH" who at night kills 185,000 men in the army of Assyria, and in this way strikes Asshur himself.

The Greek chronicler, Herodotus, described this event such as if a plague of mice came over the Assyrian army at Pelusium, at the border of the Egyptian delta.[17] Because this place is notorious for its sickening climate, and mice are a symbol of pestilence (cf. 1 Sam. 6:4), it has been presumed that the ancient Egyptian legend to which Herodotus refers here means that the army of Sennacherib died of bubonic plague.

The king himself seems to escape—as Isaiah (37:29, 34) had predicted—but that is only an illusion. It is quite striking that YHWH let this Sennacherib escape in order to strike him at his most sensitive spot: in the temple of his own god Nisroch, who, as said before, is possibly Asshur (37:38). Not in Judeah, but in the direct "domain" of his god (his angelic prince) Sennacherib is killed. We know that this happened only some twenty years later, yet the text implies that he fell into the hands of the God of Israel. When Hezekiah prayed to his God, he was delivered from his enemies (37:14-20); when Sennacherib prayed to his god, he was murdered by his own sons. In this was the hand of YHWH.[18]

3.2.2. The Fall of Assyria

In his actual prophecies, Isaiah tells us some other things about the fall of Assyria, which seem to throw further light upon the spiritual powers involved. This is a fall that goes far beyond the defeat of Sennacherib. We have to do here with the final destruction of the Assyrian world-power, primarily by means of the Babylonians, and ultimately with the destruction of "Assyria" as an eschatological world-power. In order

17. *History* 2,141: "When the opponents [of the Egyptians, viz., the Assyrian army of Sennacherib] had arrived there [in Pèlousion] too, at night a troop of field mice was poured out over them, and these consumed their quivers and bows and the carrying-straps of their shields, so that the next day they took to their heels unarmed, and many of them perished" (1978:132). Footnote by Damsté: "Mice are often the symbol of epidemies."

18. Sanhedrin 95b,96a states that YHWH appeared to Sennacherib at his old age, and also that Sennacherib promised to sacrifice his sons, but was overheard by them and killed by them himself.

to get some insight into the spiritual powers behind Assyria, we consider some striking Scriptures; but at the outset it must be said that the data are scarcer than in the case of the other world-empires.

In Isaiah 10:5, we hear about Assyria as "the rod of God's anger," that is, as the instrument in his hand to chastise Judah. It is striking that Sennacherib's marshal himself also claims to have been sent by YHWH against Judah, although at the same time he presents YHWH as an adversary (36:10, 20). This is not just a matter of mockery by the Rabshakeh, for he simply spoke the truth. YHWH and Asshur are adversaries, but at the same time the Assyrians are entirely at the disposal of YHWH because he is mightier than Asshur. Assyria, however, does not recognize this and boasts, "Are not my princes altogether kings?" (v. 8). It is easy to interpret this as if Sennacherib refers here to his "princes" (generals) as "kings,"[19] but in the literal sense the text does not speak of him at all. It is "Asshur" who speaks in this way. One could say, Assyria is personified here; one could also say, the god Asshur *is* the personification of Assyria, and it is he who speaks here of "his" princes as kings. Only in v. 12, "the king of Assyria" is mentioned, and here too we cannot sever him for a moment from his angelic prince.

Another significant but also difficult verse is Isaiah 30:33. Both the translations and the interpretations of this verse rather differ. In my view, what it says is more or less the following:

> For Tophet [or, the stake] [is] ready since yesterday [i.e., of old];
> it too [or, yea, it] has been prepared for the king;
> He has made deep [and] large his fire-hearth,
> fire and wood are abundant;
> the breath of YHWH like a stream of brimstone kindles it.

The pivotal questions are: (a) what is Tophet, or, what stake

19. Cf. Ezek. 26:7, where Nebuchadrezzar is called "the king of Babylon, the king of kings."

is intended here? and (b) who is "the king"? The first question is the least important. For, whether one thinks of a literal or a figurative stake, of the temporal defeat of Assyria or of its eternal perdition, at any rate it is certain that it is Assyria's fall that is referred to. But who is here "the king"? Some would, on the basis of 2 Kings 23:10 and Jeremiah 7:31-32, interpret the Hebrew *mèlech* ("king") as the Moloch; thus the word is rendered in some translations of Isaiah 57:9. But this change of vowels is not accounted for. Also, the idea that the text refers to the eschatological prince of the unbelieving Israel (that is, in some interpretations, the Antichrist) is hardly likely, because he does not fit into the context. It seems more obvious to think here of the ruler of Assyria. And precisely because eternal damnation is at least also implied here, we should think not only of the earthly king of Assyria but also of his angelic prince. We have to do here with *Asshur* who is frightened by the voice of YHWH when he smites with the rod (v. 31). Asshur is the "king," who is ultimately relegated to the everlasting fire. Compare here Isaiah 31:8,

> Asshur shall fall by the sword of him who is no man;
> and the sword of him who is no human shall devour it.

This refers not only to his king but to "Asshur himself." We learn here about a *superhuman* battle, as the expressions "no man" and "no human" indicate. Ultimately, the angelic prince of Assyria, who is more than the king, his earthly viceroy, will be defeated by him who is more than a man or a human. Note here the remarkable v. 9,

> his rock will perish of fear,
> and his frightened princes will leave the banner.

Many interpretations have been given of this "rock," but the best ones seem to be those who understand it either as the king of Assyria, or as his "god," his angelic prince Asshur. Samuel R. Driver mentions Arabic examples indicating that "rock" can also mean "prince." In my opinion, "his rock" is then the angelic prince in whom the king of Assyria put his confidence, and "his princes" are his earthly viceroys. Quite interesting is the parallel with the Messiah following directly afterwards. Of him it is said that he, and each of his "princes," will be "as the shadow of a mighty rock in a thirsty land" (32:1-2). As the Messiah-God is like a rock for the people of Israel, so is Asshur like a rock for the people of Assyria. The latter will perish from fear by the power of the former. When YHWH, or the Messiah, appears (cf. 31:4-5), the angelic prince of Assyria with all his princes will perish, and the Messiah with all his princes will assume the dominion and erect the kingdom of peace. The rock of Assyria makes place for the rock of Israel.

A similar parallel is found in Joel 2:20-21, if we assume that the expression "those of the north" indeed refers to Assyria, as many expositors believe. This northern enemy "has done great things" (v. 20), but of YHWH too, who removes and destroys him, it is said, "YHWH has done great things" (v. 21). Here too, a man cannot be simply compared with YHWH: it is the god, the angelic prince of Assyria, who can be compared to some extent with the God of gods, YHWH. Here is a god who has done great things, but he is far surpassed by YHWH, who has done great things.

3.2.3. Nimrod

We find some further important references to Asshur in the books of the minor prophets. Having mentioned Joel, I now refer to Micah (this section) and Nahum (§ 3.2.4).

In Micah 5:4-5, we are astonished to find the land of Assyria referred to as the "land of Nimrod." The text speaks of the coming Messiah, who will bring judgment over the land of Assyria. As in Isaiah, Assyria turns out to have an eschatological meaning as a reference to the evil world power which will oppress Israel in the last days. The remarkable fact is now that Nimrod appears here who, except for Genesis 10:8-12 (and 1 Chron. 1:10), nowhere else occurs in the whole Bible. Is it just a poetic description, a Hebrew parallelism for Assyria? Or is there more to it? According to Flavius Josephus,[20] Nimrod, or, as he calls him, Nebrodes, was

> the one who led [the people] in thus despising God. He, not less brave than bold, made them believe that they owed all their good fortune only to their bravery, and not to God. And because he strived for tyranny, and tried to induce them to choosing him as their Captain and leaving God, he presented himself so as to protect them against YHWH, since he threatened the earth with a new flood, and to build to this end a tower so high that not only the waters would not be able to rise above it, but that he would also revenge the death of their fathers.

If this is a proper rendering of the reason why the tower of Babylon was built, then Nimrod is surely someone with a strong *genius* or angelic prince. Nimrod has been linked with Nimurta (or Nimurd[a], Ninurta), the Sumerian god of hunting and of war. Of this name, Israel supposedly had made the name "Nimrod," which in Hebrew means as much as, "we will be rebellious." If we may believe Josephus, Nimrod is the instigator of the building of the tower of Babel; but in any case, he is the founder of both Babel and Asshur[21] (Gen. 10:10-11). The city of Kalah mentioned too was later called Nimrud. The Biblical Nimrod is either a "divine" being, like the giants and the mighty men in Genesis 6:1-4, or a mortal man who, as the first one in the Bible, may be considered to be closely associated with a mighty angelic prince. As says 1 Chronicles 1:10, "Nimrod was the first who became mighty on the earth" (compare Gen.10:8: "the first mighty man on the

20. *Jewish Antiquities* I, 4, 2.
21. Here the translation is important. Some read, "From that land [Shinar] he [Nimrod] went to Asshur and built Nineveh," etcetera. Others read, "From that land [Shinear] Asshur went out, and built Nineveh", etcetera. In the first case, Asshur is a land where Nimrod comes to power, in the second case, Asshur is a mighty man like Nimrod. If the latter is correct, and Asshur is a deity afterwards, then presumably Nimrod, too, is a deity, going back upon a historical figure.

earth"). Might is here not simply a political notion but indicates power "by the grace of god" (note the small g): power as a "quantity of divine mandate." Abel, Abraham, Isaac, Jacob, Joseph, Moses and David are shepherds, men who care for the animals; Nimrod is a hunter, a killer of animals, a violent man—but under the supervision of the God of gods (Gen. 10:9). Shem, Heber ("passing through"), the patriarchs, are men of tents, strangers and pilgrims on the earth (Heb. 11:9, 13). Cain (Gen. 4:17) and Nimrod are builders of cities, which figuratively stand for centers of power and protection.

Nimrod is possibly some ancient king of Assyria. People have thought either of Ninus, or Sargon, or Tukulti-Ninurta I, or a king of Akkad, such as Naram-Sin. Words like Ninus, Ninurta or Naram may be etymologically related with Nimrod. Others think of Gilgamesh, the hero of the Gilgamesh epos and king of the first dynasty of Urukh (Erekh in Gen. 10:10).[22] Gilgamesh, in the tradition a semi-divine figure, was a descendant of the hero of the Babylonian flood story, Ut-napishtim, like Nimrod via Cush was a descendant of Noah. But whoever Nimrod may have been, as the very embodiment of a mighty god he seems to be the founder of the land of Shinar, of the old Asshur, from where the lines run to the Assyria and the Babylon in the time of Israel's kings.

From antiquity, as embedded in pagan legends from which emerges the vague figure of Nimrod, the lines are drawn even to the last days, when Messiah himself will subdue the land of Nimrod. Presumably, this is the most important reason why Nimrod with his Assyrian/Babylonian kingdom is mentioned already in Genesis 10. The pedigree of the nations in that chapter is centered around Israel. The meaning of Nimrod is that his kingdom, the first mighty empire within the scope of the Old Testament, metahistorically continues until the mighty world-empire of the last days. Nimrod is a mighty man, but the God of gods keeps an eye on him. From the start

22. Cf. Gispen (1974:328).

to the end of world history, this mighty man stands "before YHWH." He cannot get out in any way, and at the end he is terminated. The child of Bethlehem will be a ruler in Israel, and from Israel unto the ends of the earth. To reach this goal, also Nimrod must give in (Micah 5:1-5). Nimrod himself may be dead a long time; but the angelic princes who gave him his power will continue to the end, when the dragon of Assyria/Babylon-Rome will be thrown in the lake of fire (Rev. 20:10).

Some of the most significant reflections on Nimrod possibly come from theologian Alexander Hislop (1807-1865) in his famous work *The Two Babylons*. He identifies Nimrod with figures from very different mythologies, which, in his opinion, go back upon the same "deity," or angelic prince. Thus, he furnishes impressive arguments that Nimrod is identical, or related, with the Egyptian deity Osiris, with the Babylonian deity Marduk (Nimrod and Marduk allegedly come from the same ground-form *mered*, "rebel"), with the Greek god Kronos and the latter's Roman equivalent, Saturn, but also with Tammuz,[23] that is Dionysus/Bacchus, with Ares/Mars, with Phaeton, etcetera. All these deities from different Eastern traditions, and even deities within the same tradition, allegedly go back upon the figure of Nimrod. Even if Hislop has "found" (far) too many identifications, his arguments do underscore that we find in Nimrod not only a historical figure but also the deity behind him, the angelic prince whose embodiment he was.

3.2.4. Belial

One of the most significant prophecies concerning the ultimate fall of Assyria is found in the book of Nahum. The king, or the angelic prince, of Assyria is directly addressed in Nahum 1:11,

> [One] has come out of you who imagines evil against YHWH, he who counsels *beliyyal* [or, a *beliyyal* counseller; see also 2:1].

23. Mentioned in Ezek. 8:14.

In § 2.2.2, the word *beliyyal* was already mentioned. It literally means "worthlessness." The "men of Belial" in the Authorized Version mean so much as "men plotting vileness." The theologian Thomas K. Cheyne (1841-1915) links the name with the Babylonian goddess of vegetation, who presumably was also the goddess of the underworld. Therefore, as said before the word may be a term for the "underworld," or the realm of the demons.

In Nahum 1:11, the intention seems to be that out of "you," that is, Nineveh, the capital of the Assyrian Empire, a prince has come out who entertains "underworld thoughts" against YHWH. He is a companion of Belial, that is Satan (cf. 2 Cor. 6:15); he is not just the earthly king of Assyria, but Asshur, the angelic prince. This interpretation is supported by the fact that apparently the prince described here cannot be associated with one particular Assyrian king. Of course, he who imagined evil against YHWH seems to be primarily Sennacherib (2 Kings 18:32-35), but at the time of Nahum the latter was dead already a long time. In his commentary on Nahum, O. Palmer Robertson therefore correctly states that *all* kings of Assyria who rose against God's people exhibited the characteristics of this prince. But then it is only one step to say that this is a description of this prince himself, that is, of the one angelic prince, Asshur, who hid behind *all* wicked kings of Assyria. And thus, Robertson concluded, also in the light of the term "belial":[24]

> An ominous figure stands behind the ruler from Nineveh, prodding him on in his wicked determinations. But one stands against him, the divine counterpart to his position of power. It is "the Christ," the anointed king who rules for the Lord throughout the ages. These two persons and the kingdoms they represent remain in conflict with one another until their struggle is finally resolved.

In v. 14 follows:

24. Robertson (1990:76).

Against you YHWH has commanded:
of your name no more will be sown;
out of the house of your god(s) I will cut off
the graven images and the molten images;
I will make your grave,
for you have become worthless.

The first of these prophecies means that Asshurbanipal, the last king of Assyria, would have no son anymore who would carry on his royal name. There is a famous inscription of Asshurbanipal,[25] in which he prays that his son who would succeed him would honor and preserve his name in the inscriptions which he had placed on his buildings to his own honor. The king also warns that all those who would venture to remove his name would be judged by Asshur and the other Assyrian gods. The God of gods, however, does not fear the god Asshur and has cut off the memory of Asshurbanipal, even the memory of his angelic prince, Asshur himself. Therefore, this god is also mentioned: out of the house of Asshur, the god of the king, the idolatrous images would be taken away and destroyed, by which the god himself would be dishonored. Yes, when a grave is prepared for the last king of Assyria, his angelic prince himself is cast down into the underworld, as we see this so strikingly in the case of Babylon's king in Isaiah 14. I have referred before to the connection between the pantheon of Assyria and that of Babylon. Of the king of Babylon we will speak now.

3.3. Babylonia

3.3.1. Introduction: the Four World-Empires

On the basis of a certain interpretation of Revelation 17:10, we have previously distinguished seven world-empires. We have given brief attention to the spiritual powers behind the first two of them, the Egyptian and the Assyrian Empire. The four empires to which we come now form a unity in themselves, because they exist during the time that Israel is formal-

25. Nr. 838 in the well-known collection of Daniel D. Luckenbill (1881-1927).

ly (though not intrinsically) "Lo-Ammi," *Not My People*, as Hosea 1:9 puts it. This period encompasses the "many days" that the Israelites

> shall abide without a king and without a prince,
> and without a sacrifice and without an image,
> and without an ephod and [without] *teraphim* (3:4).

This is the time after the last Judean king, Zedekiah, until the coming of Messiah (3:5), in brief, the "times of the *goyyim*" (cf. Luke 21:24).

In salvational history as it is described in the Bible, the history of these four world-empires, in relation to the history of God's covenant people of Israel, plays an essential role. We find the four empires particularly in the book of Daniel, especially in chapters 2 and 7, but also in Zechariah and Revelation. Because of modern historical criticism of the Bible, today unfortunately it is necessary to argue more in detail what the precise identity of these four world-empires is. Attention to this is given in Appendix 5.

In particular, we will try to get some more insight into the angelic princes who have ruled successively over the four world-empires. The main direct indication for this we find, as said before, in Daniel 10, where we are presented with the angelic princes of the Medo-Persian and the Greek world-empires. The Man of Daniel 10:5 comes to Daniel especially with a prophecy concerning the Medo-Persian Empire, its conquest by Alexander the Great, the division of the Greek Empire after Alexander's death, and the further history of the Seleucid and the Ptolemaean Empires (Dan. 11). It is self-evident, therefore, that in Daniel 10 only the angelic princes of the Persian and the Greek Empires appear. However, it is equally obvious that the Babylonian and the Roman Empire have their own angelic princes. Indeed, we find these in the Bible without any difficulty.

3.3.2. Bel/Nebo/Marduk

With regard to the angelic prince of the Babylonian Empire, Scripture as well as Babylonian tradition supply us with fascinating materials. It is quite striking, and actually unique, that the fall of Babylon in the Bible is so explicitly associated with the fall of the *gods* of Babylon: Bel and Nebo. Both the prophet Isaiah and the prophet Jeremiah make this connection. When Isaiah thinks of the future fall of Babylon, caused by the Medes, he says (46:1),

> Bel sinks down,
> Nebo bows down.

That is, they have to recognize that they have been defeated. Jeremiah says of this (50:2; 51:44):

> Babylon is taken,
> Bel is put to shame,
> Merodach [= Marduk] is frightened.
>
> I will punish Bel in Babylon,
> and make [him] spit out of his mouth that which he has swallowed up [= Israel].

Note here the fact that the prophets primarily speak of the fall of the city of Babylon and of the king of Babylon. However, this king is the embodiment of his angelic prince. This becomes obvious if we read Jeremiah 51:44 (about the god) in comparison with v. 34 (about the king):

> Nebuchadrezzar, king of Babylon, has devoured me,
> he has frightened me,
> he has made me an empty vessel,
> he has swallowed me up like a dragon [or, serpent],
> he has filled his belly with my delicates,
> he has cast me out.

Nebuchadrezzar is compared here to a dragon (Heb. *tannin*), but this dragon is actually his angelic prince, called Bel. That which Nebuchadrezzar has swallowed (v. 34) is spat out by Bel (v. 44). Such a way of speaking is only possible if king and god are strongly identified.

In Isaiah 51:9-10, the deliverance of Judah out of Babylon is compared with the victory over Rahab, the "dragon" of Egypt, at the exodus of Israel out of that land. In Revelation 12 and 13, the "dragon" is the angelic prince of the Roman Empire. "Dragon" is the usual name for the angelic prince of a certain world-empire, whether this is Egypt, Babylon or Rome. Therefore, the decline of a world-empire involves the decline of the "dragon," the angelic prince of that empire.[26] Thus, the prophets associate the fall of Nebuchadrezzar with that of the "gods" of Babylon, specifically Bel, Nebo, and Marduk. As Dhorme puts it,[27]

> the close link between the god and his city is clearly witnessed in this passage from Jeremiah concerning the fall of Babylon: "Babylon is taken, Bel is put to shame, Merodach is frightened" (50:2). Bel-Marduk, split into Bel and Marduk, undergoes the fate of Babylonia.

The victory of the Persians over Babylon is a victory of the angelic prince of Persia over the angelic prince of Babylon, be it only according to the will and under the allowance of YHWH, the God of gods. Therefore, it is he in Isaiah and Jeremiah who gains the actual victory over the "gods" (= the angelic princes) of Babylon, even if he does so by means of the angelic

26. Several exegetes (Paul Kleinert, Thomas K. Cheyne), who, to my mind correctly so, view the history of Jonah as a prophetic representation of the history of Israel, refer to Jer. 51:34, 44. Just as Jonah went to the sea (a picture of the impetuous mass of the nations, Isa. 17:12; Rev. 17:15) and landed in the belly of the fish, so Judah went the way of the *goyyim* and landed in the belly of the "dragon," Babylon. But YHWH, who commanded the fish to spit out Jonah, took Judah out of the belly of the "dragon," in order that it would continue its calling to be a witness among the nations (cf. Jonah 3:1; Isa. 42:4-7; 49:3, 6; 52:10, 15; Rom. 2:19-20). Only the Messiah has completely fulfilled this task (Rom. 15:8-9; Eph. 2:17), just as he, as the true Jonah, is the true "Israel" (Matt. 12:39-41). See on the "dragon" also § 3.1, note 7.
27. Dhorme (1949:144); see extensively p. 138-156.

prince of the Persians.

Who precisely are Bel, Nebo (or Nabu) and Marduk? In the Babylonian pantheon, as often in ancient Eastern mythologies, the relationships between such gods are vague. Bel was the Babylonian chief god. His name is identical with the name Baal, well-known from the Bible, and means "lord." He is the same as the Sumerian god Enlil already mentioned, the "lord of the storm," one of the three Sumerian chief gods, together with Anu and Enki (or Ea). The name Bel has also been linked with the Semitic root *b-l-l* (or *b-l-*[c]), which means, "to mix up, confuse." This verb is used in Genesis 11:7, 9 for the "confusion" of the language and linked directly with the name "Babel," which thus means "confusion." Because of the meta-historical as well as (popular?) etymological link between Babel and its angelic prince Bel, the name Bel therefore also means "confuser."

Bel occurs in the well-known apocryphal story of Daniel and the image of Bel, which is "unmasked" by the prophet (in Roman-Catholic Bibles, Dan. 14). Bel was identified with Marduk, and Nebo was therefore called both son of Bel and son of Marduk. The symbol of Marduk was the horned dragon (cf. Jer. 51:34). At the time of the New-Babylonian Empire, a certain tendency to monotheism originated, in which the other gods were only considered to be aspects of the nature of Marduk. In fact, the names Bel/Marduk and Nebo always refer to one and the same "divine substance." In other words, behind these names one and the same angelic prince is hidden. Perhaps this is even suggested by the poetical parallelism in Isaiah 46:1; the Bel who sinks down, is then the Nebo who bows down.

The name Nebo (or, Nab[i]u) has sometimes been derived from the Hebrew word *nibba* (the niphal form of the Semitic root *n-b-'*), which means as much as "to pass on an oracle," "prophesize." It would thus be closely related to the Hebrew word *nabi*, "prophet."[28] In this way, Nebo fits into a whole complex of ancient Eastern deities of whom the same characteristic is reported. The best known of them is the Greek god Hermes, the messenger as well as interpreter of the gods. His name is related to *hermeneuô*, "to interpret" (cf. the word hermeneutics). Among the Romans he is known as Mercury. In antiquity Hermes was called the origin of religious rites through which people had access to their gods. The Roman author Hyginus (64-17 BC)[29] says that in former days the people all spoke one language, but after Mercury had "set out (set apart?)" the languages of the people—therefore, says Hyginus, an interpreter is called a *hermeneutès*—he also divided the nations, with which the disharmony started. Hermes is therefore identical with Nebo as well as with Bel, both interpreter and confuser. The "interpretations" of the false gods are only "confusions." Bel/Nebo is a "false prophet."

Now Hermes in his turn is identical with the Egyptian god Horus; in the root *h-r* perhaps even an etymological relationship may be discovered, as the Egyptologist Christian C.J. (von) Bunsen (1791-1860) suggested. We have seen that Horus is often identified with his father, Osiris, who is called both the husband and the son of Isis. Sometimes, Horus is called a new "incarnation" of Osiris after the latter's death, in order to revenge this death. In this way, we can pursue the line from the previous chapters: in Osiris/Horus (Egypt), Asshur (Assyria), Bel/Nebo/Marduk (Babylon), and Hermes (Greece) we meet with one and the same spiritual power. Either they are distinct but closely related angelic princes, which can be subsumed under the same power, or they are different names for one and the same great angelic prince.

As to the Greek and Roman gods, still other lines have been

28. See the Hebrew lexicon of Gesenius, s.v.; Dhorme (1949:151) translates Nebo as "radiant," and points out that, as Nebo is identified with the planet Mercury (= Hermes) (see the text!), the Greeks called this god *Stilbôn*, "radiant."

29. Hyginus, *Fabulae*, 143; quoted by Hislop (1959:26).

drawn to Bel/Nebo/Marduk. In the Greek-Roman pantheon, too, all kinds of gods are in fact nothing but hypostasized attributes of one and the same deity. Marduk for one has been linked with Mars, and this not just because of the resemblance in the names. As said before, Marduk may have been derived from the Semitical root *m-r-d,* "to rebel," as Mars is the "rebel" among the Roman gods. The goddess who is thought to be the sister as well as the wife of Mars is Bellona, which in Akkadian means, "the lamenter of Bel." In an analogous way, Isis, the sister and wife of Osiris, is presented as the "lamenter" of her murdered husband.

Another example of a "divine" couple that beside husband and wife was brother and sister is the Greek couple of Kronos and Rhea (among the Romans, Kronos was called Saturn). According to Theophilus of Antioch (second century AD), Kronos was worshipped in the East under the name Bel.[30] And Eusebius of Caesarea (c. 300) tells us that the first Assyrian "king," whose name was Belus—that is the god Bel, called Bèlos by the Greeks—was also called Kronos.[31] Kronos means "horned one" (cf. Gr. *keras,* "horn"); do we find here a link with the horned dragon, the symbol of Marduk? And is there a connection with the fact that in antiquity the devil was also depicted with horns? The epithet "horned" (*karneios*) was also applied to Apollo; the *Hymn to Apollo* (in the ancient Orphic Hymns) calls him the two-horned god. Apollo too, the sun god, the son of Zeus, belongs to this pantheon, for both Osiris and Bel were worshipped as the sun god. Herodotus identifies Bèlos with Zeus by speaking of the "sanctuary of Zeus Bèlos" in Babylon.[32]

One of the most striking associations, which will be elaborated later, is the connection with the Roman god Janus, the "god of gods," the "origin" (*principium*) of all gods. The

30. Clericus, *De Philosophia Orientali* 1,2,37; quoted by Hislop (1959:32).
31. Eusebius, *Chronicon* (Venice 1818), p. 6; quoted by Hislop (1959:32).
32. Herodotus, *History* 1,181; 3,158.

ancient name of Janus was Chaos, as Latin poet Ovid states.[33] He is therefore the god of "confusion," which links him with Bel. The symbol of Janus was the club, to which Jeremiah 50:23 and 51:20 seem to allude, where it is said of Babylon, or of his angelic prince,

> How is the hammer of the whole earth broken down and dispersed,
> how has Babylon become a desolation among the nations!
>
> You [are] to me a battle axe,
> [You are my] weapons of war,
> with you I will smash the nations,
> and with you I will destroy kingdoms.

Bel, who has broken and dispersed so much (Gen. 11), is now dispersed himself (cf. 50:2). Now, if Janus is identical with Bel, and Bel with Kronos/Saturn (see above), then Janus is identical with Kronos/Saturn. Saturn is the "hidden" god, the god of the mysteries, just as is Hermes (who is identical with Bel/Nebo), as well as Janus. The name of the Egyptian chief god, Amon—in fact the same as the Egyptian god Osiris—means "hidden god." And Horus, son of Osiris, but often identical with him, has two faces as Janus has. Janus is the "key god," the mediator and interpreter, who gives access to the realm of the gods. In the course of our investigation, this figure will be shown to be of great significance, because in Christianized Rome he turned up in quite a peculiar form.

In summing up, it looks very much as if, under all kinds of different ancient Eastern names, we time and again meet with one and the same spiritual reality. There is quite a striking continuity between the angelic princes of Egypt, Assyria, Babylon, Greece, and Rome. We should not be deceived by apparent differences. For instance, Hermes is called an "incarnation" of the Egyptian god Thoth, who is the counselor

33. *Fasti* 1,104; quoted by Hislop (1959:26).

of Osiris.[34] In this way, he seems to be distinguished from Osiris, as Hermes, the messenger of the gods, is distinct from Zeus (cf. Acts 14:12). But in other respects, their attributes coincide again, just as we saw that father and son—Osiris and Horus, Bel/Marduk and Nebo, Kronos and Zeus, Zeus and Apollo—often "coincide."

It appears very strongly as if one and the same angelic power, even though various angelic figures may be discerned in it, dominates the history of the seven world-empires. At times these empires are opposed to one another; when one succeeds to another, the former subdues the latter. In that case, apparently one angelic prince turns against the other. However, Daniel 10 makes it clear that in reality the angelic princes form one combined power, whose most real and actual adversary is never one specific other empire, but the people of God, and the God of gods who stands behind those people. Perhaps, Osiris/Horus, Bel/Nebo/Marduk, Kronos/Zeus/Apollo, Saturn/Jupiter/Janus, are distinct angelic princes. But their attributes blend so strongly that they often present themselves as one and the same power. We only have to do here with different appearances of the same diabolic power, which stands over against YHWH and his people.

3.3.3. Nebuchadrezzar[35]

Like the Egyptian and the Assyrian Empire, the Babylonian Empire was a typically monolithic culture, which was totally "comprised" in its (earthly) prince. In Daniel 2, the golden head in the image of Nebuchadrezzar was on the one hand a representation of the Babylonian Empire, on the other hand a representation of the absolute head of that empire, Nebuchadrezzar himself (v. 37-38). With more right than the French king, Louis XIV (1638-1715), Nebuchadrezzar could

34. Hislop (1959:56, 209, 227).
35. We use the more correct spelling "Nebuchadrezzar," as it also occurs in Jeremiah, whereas Daniel reads "Nebuchadnezzar." The Babylonian form of the name is "Nabu-kudurri-ussur," which supports the reading with "r."

say, *L'État c'est moi* ("The state that's me"). He *was* the empire; for this purpose, YHWH had given him absolute power over the empire (Dan. 2:37-38; 5:18-19). At the same time, by this gift YHWH demonstrated that he is the God of gods; Nebuchadrezzar is only his "servant" (Jer. 27:6). In Daniel 7:4, where the Babylonian Empire is represented as a lion, we seem to have an allusion to Daniel 4:16, the history of the humiliation of Nebuchadrezzar, who behaves like a lion. In this way, the empire again seems to be identified with its king.

As with the Assyrian kings, the close association of the invisible angelic prince of a world-empire with the visible earthly prince of that empire comes to light in the names of the New-Babylonian Empire's kings. Nebuchadrezzar is called after the god Nebo; his name means presumably, "Nebo has protected the succession rights." His son's name, Evil-Merodach, that is Amel-Marduk, means, "The man is Marduk" (2 Kings 25:27; Jer. 52:31). This almost seems to imply an identification of the man with his god. His grandson, Belshazzar (Dan. 5), is called after Bel; the name means, "Bel has protected the king (or, the kinghood)." One of Nebuchadrezzar's predecessors, Merodach-Baladan (Isa. 39:1), is also called after Marduk.

Dutch philosopher Klaas J. Popma (1903-1986), whose thoughts I follow, extending them strongly, has called attention to the important fact that it is the king himself who receives the illustrious dream in Daniel 2.[36] Even if he cannot interpret the dream, he is a prophet, as is Daniel who receives dreams. In this way he honors his name, for he is called after the god Nebo, whose name probably means "prophet." It is YHWH who grants him the dream, but he does so in a form with which Nebuchadrezzar's angelic prince can be content. For the king sees himself in his dream as he liked to see himself in everyday life: as the golden head. This gold forms a sacral-symbolical reference to the light of the sun. Here again

36. Popma (1945:124 etc.).

we find a correspondence with Louis XIV: Nebuchadrezzar is the *roi soleil*, the sun king. But even far more important: he is the sun god, or rather, the earthly-human embodiment of the sun god. Nebuchadrezzar has the courage to present himself as such; that is obvious from the golden image which he erects for himself in Daniel 3.[37] His god breathes this thought into him, but also the God of gods, who gives the final shape to the dream, allows him to do that.

Long before the time of Nebuchadrezzar, people were familiar with the idea of golden, silver, brazen, and iron ages (of course, not meant in the archeological sense!). Afterwards, this idea was worked out extensively by the Greek poet, Hesiod (c. 700 BC), and the Roman poet, Ovid (43 BC-17/18 AD). Normally, the golden age was associated with the paradise-like primitive state of mankind. One of the rivers of the garden of Eden flows around a land "where [is] the gold, and the gold of that land [is] good" (Gen. 2:11-12). Now, the peculiar thing in Daniel 2 is that the gold is not applied to the paradise-like primitive state, but to the empire of Nebuchadrezzar. It is a pseudo-empire, a kingdom of the "golden" angel, who was in the garden of Eden too (cf. Ezek. 28:13-14). In a proper rendering of Isaiah 14:4, the king of Babylon is called "the golden one"; that is literally, the "one making [something] gold," thus, "he who brings the golden age."[38] This refers especially to the golden angelic prince behind the

37. Note that the image in Dan. 2 only has a golden head, whereas the image of Dan. 3 is entirely of gold. It is as if Nebuchadrezzar rejects the idea that his empire, his "golden age," would be succeeded by silver, brazen, and iron empires or ages. The demand to worship the image underscores the identification of the state, the king, and the angelic prince.

38. To be sure, the translation of that word "golden" (Heb. *mad-heba*) is uncertain. Translations that have "oppression," or a similar word, read *mar-heba* and in this way follow the Dead Sea scrolls and some ancient versions. Older translators deduced the unknown word mad-heba from the Aramaic root *d-h-b*, which means "gold." The form *mad-heba* is then a feminine form of a hiphil participle, which could be translated as "she who turns [things] into gold." Babylon would then be the world power "which introduces the golden age."

king of Babylon. Indeed, Isaiah 14 is an extremely significant Scripture with regard to the angelic prince of Babylon, especially v. 12-15:

> How have you fallen from heaven,
> o morning star, son of the dawn!
> You have been cut down to the ground,
> you who [before] overpowered the nations!
> You have said in your heart,
> "I will ascend into heaven,
> above the stars of God will I erect my throne,
> and I will sit upon the mount of the congregation,
> far in the north.[39]
> I will ascend above the heights of the clouds,
> I will make myself like the Most High."
> On the contrary, in *hades* you shall be cut down,
> deep into[40] the pit.

---

39. This could also be the proper name Zaphon, referring to a mountain in North-Syria (cf. Josh. 13:27; Judg. 12:1 in the various translations; possibly, along with Tabor and Hermon, also in Ps. 89:13). Thus, in Isa. 14, it would be the name for the holy mountain where the gods abide, or meet (cf. Ezek. 28:16). However, the term can also mean that the mount of the gods has to be localized in "the north" in a figurative sense. In Job 37:22 (see notes 17-19) and Ezek. 1:4, the glory of YHWH also comes out of "the north," as it were from this mount of the gods. But "the north" is also a reference to the kings of the world-empires, since their armies penetrate into Palestine from the north; for instance, Asshur (Zeph. 2:13), Babylon (Isa. 14:31; Jer. 1:14 etc.; Zech. 2:6; 6:6, 8). Persia in its turn is "the north" for Babylon (Jer. 50:3, 9, 41); in a general sense see Jer. 25:26; Ezek. 32:30; Joel 2:20. Perhaps the conclusion should be that the world-empires in "the north" are the empires of which the angelic princes meet together on the "mount of the congregation" in "the north." Herodotus (*History* 4,13 and 22ff.) and other Greeks tell us of the "Hyperboreans," that is, those living "beyond the north," with whom Apollo liked to stay.
40. Actually "at the sides of"; this comes to mean, "within" (e.g., Ps. 128:3; so here: "within," i.e., "deep in" the grave; cf. Judg. 19:1: "deep in the mountains"), or "far in" the north (vs. 13; Ps. 48:3; Ezek. 38:6), or "at the far end(s) of" the earth (Jer. 6:22). If we have to read here "Zaphon" (see note 14), the meaning may also be, "on the top of the Zaphon"; possibly: "on the top(s) in the north."

After all we have discussed concerning angelic princes, we now can easily see looming up behind the king of Babylon his (diabolic) angelic prince. For instance, already the Jewish exegete, Abarbanel (1437-1508), saw it this way. Some church fathers (Tertullian, c. 200; Jerome, c. 400) thought here of the fall of Satan (cf. Luke 10:18; Rev. 12:8). This is correct insofar as there is a close link between the angelic prince of Babylon and that of Rome, as will be shown below. In Revelation, the angelic prince of Rome is indeed Satan. In any case, it is crystal clear that we see here a higher, spiritual power, but one that is directly associated, if not identified, with the earthly king of Babylon. It is no wonder, therefore, that the boundaries between the verses in Isaiah 14 dealing with the earthly king of Babylon and those dealing with his celestial angelic prince can hardly be drawn.

It is certain that we find the latter at any case in v. 12-15, where the angelic prince of Babylon is called a "morning star" and a "son of the dawn" (v. 12). The "morning star" was worshipped by the Babylonians as Ishtar (Astarte), the goddess of love (Venus). In Job 38:7 too, angelic princes are referred to as "morning stars." Next, the angelic prince is a "son of the dawn"; that is either a person characterized by the dawn, the rising sun, or he that is born as a son of the dawn, i.e., the sun (god). Thus, here again, the king of Babylon is the golden sun god; he is the Greek and Latin Apollo, whom we will meet later in connection with the Roman emperor. This is a new link with Rome; and to add yet another one: Rome, too, has been called, for instance by Alcuin of York (c. 800), Charlemagne's court scholar, *caput mundi, mundi decus, aurea Roma*, "the world's head, the world's ornament, the *golden* Rome."

It is striking that Isaiah 14 speaks of both a goddess, Ishtar, and a male god, the sun god. Similarly, in v. 4 the "driver" (viz., of the "bucks of the earth"; v. 9) is male, and "the golden one" is female.[41] Although the English does not show this,

41. The angelic prince seems to be a kind of androgynous (male-female) figure, possibly a foreshadow of the combination of the great whore (Ishtar is the

the Hebrew does. Both the morning star and the sun are the proclaimers of the new day, which is here a new time, the golden age. The angelic prince pretends to bring a (pseudo-) Messianic age, to return the gold of paradise to the earth. Precisely in Isaiah, this pretension stands in a sharp contrast with the real Messianic age, which indeed clearly reminds us of paradise (cf. Isa. 11, especially v. 6-8, and 65:17-25). The angelic prince of Babylon, closely related, if not identical, with Satan, is here the great usurper, who as the angelic prince of the Antichrist will soon proclaim his most beautiful and most false pretensions of a millennial kingdom of peace.

In fact, we may say that, since Nebuchadrezzar, each world-empire has carried such a pretension of introducing the golden Messianic age. Two examples that will be dealt with later are, first, the Christianized Roman Empire, which was viewed by various church fathers since Augustine as the fulfillment of the millennial promise. Secondly, Adolf Hitler had the pretension that his empire, being the Third Reich, would likewise be the last, the millennial empire. However, it is only YHWH who, out of his own glory, will bring the "gold" of the "sun" upon the earth at the dawn of the Messianic age. Compare here the peculiar text in Job 37:21-22,

> ... [sometimes] one [can] not see the sun [lit., the light],
> though radiant in/behind[42] the clouds,
> but [then] the wind passes and wipes the clouds away.[43]
> [Thus] the gold comes out of the north,
> with God [is] awesome majesty.[44]

---

goddess of erotic love!) and the beast (the sun god is the angelic prince of Rome!) (Rev. 17). Interestingly, the "you" in Ezek. 28:14, addressing the angelic prince of Tyre, is also in the feminine form.

42. or, "... while darkened by the clouds."
43. or, "one [can] not look at the sun, [for] radiantly she [stands] at the sky, when the wind passes and wipes it clean."
44. That is either, "out of the north comes the gold, but God is covered with awesome majesty," or, "out of the north it [= the sun] comes (in) gold(en splendor)," or, "out of the north comes God (in) gold(en splendor), he is covered with majesty." If we take this and the previous notes together, the

Just like Isaiah 14, this text speaks of that remarkable "north" from where the glory of YHWH appears in golden splendor.[45] In Isaiah 14:13, the angelic prince of Babylon takes up his place on "the mount of the congregation far in the north," a common expression for the "mount of the gods," the place of God's throne and his celestial household. A similar expression is found in Ezekiel 28:14, which speaks of "the holy mount of God" (or, "of the gods").[46] Usually, a connection is seen here with mount Casius or Aralu, the holy mountain on which, according to the Canaanite, Babylonian, and other mythologies, the gods meet together (cf. the Olympus in Greek mythology). This does not mean that the Bible adopts a piece of mythology here, but rather that the Bible refers here to a spiritual reality, described in figurative language, which was also known to pagan nations, and which *they* described in corrupted, mythological language (see Appendix 3).

---

text presumably means: (a) as the sun appears radiantly at the cleaned sky, so radiantly is the golden splendor of God's appearing majesty; or, (b) as the sun for a time is behind the clouds, but then reappears radiantly, so also appears the golden splendor of God's awesome majesty; or, (c) the sun is for a time behind the clouds but then reappears radiantly, and also the gold can be brought forth from the north; but God hides himself in his awesome majesty. Because the idea that the gold comes out of the north (see [c]) is foreign to Scripture, I prefer (a) or (b).

45. Also cf. Job 26:7: "stretching [the] north over desolation, hanging [the] earth over that-which-is-nothing." The "north" is parallel with the "earth" and refers to the heavens (see a similar expression in 9:8; Isa. 40:22), presumably in the sense of God's dwelling-place, the "mount of the gods" (see the text). At the same time, it is "heaven" in the sense of the sky above the "desolation" (*tohu*; Gen.1:2), the desolated state of the earth before God's creative work of the six days. The "north" is here an indication of hight, the highest heavens, as standing over against the "underworld" in v. 6: *Sheol* ("hades") and *Abaddon* ("perdition" = death; see 31:12; cf. Ps. 88:12; Rev. 9:11).

46. Also cf. Ps. 46:3, where the localization of mount Zion "in the far north" is an allusion to the "mount of the gods." The idea is that Zion now is the "mount of God," where the throne of God is found and where he lives in the midst of his people. The ancient Jewish expositors, Rashi, Ibn Ezra and Kimchi, believed that also in Isa. 14:13 mount Zion is intended.

3.4. Medo-Persia

3.4.1. Cyrus and Xerxes

The fall of the angelic prince of Babylon is brought about by the angelic prince of the Medes and the Persians, but here too this angelic prince is strongly associated with an earthly prince, Cyrus (in the Bible called Koresh). To be sure, the power of Cyrus was less absolute than that of Nebuchadrezzar, for the Medo-Persian kings were bound to the "laws of the Medes and Persians" (Esther 1; Dan. 6), whereas the Babylonian kings were virtually bound to no law whatsoever. I presume that this is why the empire of Cyrus is only silver, and not gold (Dan. 2:39). Yet, the Medo-Persian Empire is still strongly monolithic. Here again, the earthly prince is as it were the visible "expression" of the invisible angelic prince, who in his turn is only a servant of YHWH, even if Cyrus, or his angelic prince, usually does not care about that.

Quite strikingly, Cyrus, though an idolator, is called the "shepherd" and "anointed" of YHWH (Isa. 44:28; 45:1), just as Nebuchadrezzar, too, was called the servant of YHWH (Jer. 27:6). To assess the extent to which they were truly servants, shepherds and anointed of YHWH, it is of decisive importance to consider their attitude towards Israel, or the God of Israel. In deporting Israel into exile, Nebuchadrezzar did nothing but carry out God's orders (Jer. 27 and 28), and three times he, and in him his angelic prince (!), recognized YHWH as the "God of gods" (!) and the "Lord of kings" (Dan. 2:47), as the "most high *èlahah*" (3:26; Aramaic for *elohim*) and the Most High (4:34). However, his grandson Belshazzar mocked the God of Israel and was cut down, and with him the empire.[47]

We find the same for the Medo-Persian kings. Cyrus, or the Persian angelic prince, is an obedient servant of YHWH in executing judgment over the Babylonian angelic prince.[48] Jeremiah 51:11 speaks of the "spirit" of the kings of Media, which could point to the angelic prince, the "spirit" which

47. Dan. 5, especially vs. 18-28; cf. Jer. 25:11-14; 50 and 51.

48. Cf. Isa. 13:17; 21:2; Jer. 25:14; 27:7; 51:11, 28; Dan. 5:30; 6:1; Zech. 6:8.

operated in the kings of Medië. Conversely, Zechariah 6:8 says,

> those going out [= Medes and Persians] toward [the] north country [= Babylon] quiet my Spirit in the north country.

The Persian angelic prince, or Cyrus, is also God's servant in letting the Jews return to their land.[49] Therefore, in Isaiah 48:14 he is even called, "he whom YHWH loves." True, his successor, Xerxes I, the Ahasuerus in the book of Esther, is a weaker figure, more open, namely, to being influenced by the "enemy of the Jews" (!), Haman. Ultimately, he does turn out to stand on God's side (Esther 7-10). Eventually, however, the Medo-Persian angelic prince did not continue to submit to YHWH either. The following words about the Medo-Persian "ram" in Daniel 8:4 are significant: "he did according to his pleasure, and made himself great." Therefore, he is destroyed by the "hairy he-goat," the Greek Empire, with its "notable horn between its eyes" (v. 5), Alexander the Great, "the first king" (v. 21).

3.4.2. Zoroaster

In order to get a better view, as far as possible, of the angelic prince of Persia, we first have to look at the oldest Indo-Iranian religion. Among the gods or *daivas* (literally, "heavenlies") there was a highest category of deities, the so-called *asuras* or "lords," among whom Mithra, or Mithras, must be mentioned in particular. The title "lord" connects him with Baal ("lord") and Bel (= Enlil, "lord of the storm"), but also with the Semitic word *adon*, "lord," which we find in ancient Eastern names of deities such as Athon or Athan, Adonis and, as Hislop[50] suggests, possibly even Athena (the goddess that gave Athens its name). The names Adon or Adonis were also given to Tammuz, the husband as well as the son of the Sumerian goddess, Ishtar (Astarte), who is mentioned in Ezekiel 8:14, where the

49. 2 Chron. 36:22-23; Ezra 1:1-4.
50. Hislop (1959:20).

women are "weeping" for Tammuz. We have also met Bel and Osiris as gods who are lamented because of their death, and there is no doubt that Tammuz corresponds with Osiris (as Plato already suggested), and also with Adonis, who is lamented because of his death.

Again, we meet here the whole complex of more or less identical gods, to which also belongs Mithra. According to Greek-Roman historian Plutarch (c. 100 AD),[51] Mithra is the "mediator," which is only one feature in which he imitates Christ. The correspondence was so strong that the early church chose the name day of Mithra, December 25, as the birthday of Christ, although everybody knew that at night, in the middle of the winter, the shepherds of Bethlehem did not stay outdoors with their sheep. Tertullian[52] tells us that a water sprinkling ceremony formed the rite for the initiation into the mysteries of Isis and of Mithra. The priests of Mithra also knew the tonsure, and these are just some of the practices that the early Roman Catholic church apparently adopted from the Mithra cult, and possibly other pagan cults. Even in 398, a synod at Carthage forbade the shaving of beard and hair, because else the Christians would resemble too much the pagan priests. But in the sixth century, the tonsure became common in Christendom as a sign of mourning. In the Torah, such a shaving as a sign of mourning is forbidden (Deut. 14:1). Catholics have linked the circular tonsure with Christ's crown of thorns, but that seems to be a typical afterthought.

In the sixth to the eighth century BC—estimations rather vary—a prophet appeared in Persia, called Zoroaster or Zarathustra. He introduced a monotheism, in which the traditional gods of the older Indo-Iranian religion merged into one *asura* (or *ahura*), which he referred to as Ahura Mazda; in modern Persian, Ormuzd or Ormazd, the "wise lord." This was the great god of the Persian king, Darius I the Great (c. 500 BC). This is the Darius who allowed the Jews that had

51. Plutarchs, *De Iside.*
52. Tertullian, *De Baptismo.*

returned to Palestine to rebuild the temple (Ezra 4:5; Hagg. 1:1; Zech. 1:1). Ahura Mazda is elevated above the older gods such as Mithra, whilst at the same time the attributes of these gods blend with those of Ahura Mazda.

Christian missionary John Wilson (1804-1875) at Bombay, in his work on the "Parsi" religion,[53] or Parsiism (a word derived from "Persian"), another name for Zoroastrism or Mazdeism, writes that there was a Zoroaster long before the Zoroaster who founded Mazdeism. Those who normally speak of Zoroaster mean the latter, Zoroaster of Bactria, but the first was a much older Assyrian or Babylonian, who supposedly was the founder of the Babylonian religion. It is striking that this Zoroaster allegedly died a violent death, for in this, he corresponds with Mithra, the lamented god, and thus with Adonis, Tammuz, Bel, Osiris and Bacchus. Here, too, we have to do with one complex of deities, presupposing one and the same angelic power.

Hislop explains the name Zoroaster—also written as Zeroastes—as the Akkadian "Zero-ashta," that is, "woman's seed" (*zero* = "seed," *ashta* = "woman").[54] Compare, for instance, the name Zerubbabel, *zeru-Babili*, "seed of Babel," in the Greek (LXX) corrupted into Zorobabel. Similarly, he explains Isis as *H'isha*, "the woman (or, lady)," and Osiris as *He-siri*, "the seed." But why would such Persian and Egyptian names have to be derived from a Semitic language? Today, the name Zarathustra is usually thought to come from the Middle Persian word *ustra*, "camel."

The rites of Zoroaster were intended for the sun god, and in this regard his cult is connected again with that of Osiris, Bel, Apollo, etcetera. The older Zoroaster was the head of the fire worshippers, and the great fire is the sun. Folk etymology connects the name Zarathustra with *ustra*, "light." In this way, the identity of the Osiris/Horus-Tammuz-Adonis-Bacchus-Bel/Nebo-Kronos/Zeus/Apollo-complex becomes a little

53. Bombay 1843.

54. Hislop (1959:59); compare, respectively, the Hebrew *zèra* and *isha*.

clearer. In Revelation 12:3 we meet with the "fire-red dragon," that is Satan (v. 9); "fire-red" is *pyrros*, derived from *pyr*, "fire"; we might also read, "fire-dragon."[55] In Ezekiel 28:14, we find the angelic prince of Tyre, who is closely related with Satan (cf. v. 13!), in the midst of "stones of fire." This angelic prince is the Moloch, that is, "king." He is the false king, who demands of his worshippers that they make their children to pass through the fire as sacrifices (2 Kings 23:10). Jeremiah 19:5 and 32:35 show that he is identical with Baal.

In summary: also in the chief figures of the Persian pantheon, Mithra and the older Zoroaster, we clearly recognize the features of that spiritual power which we found in all the previous empires. Even if the angelic princes of the successive empires differ, basically it is the one power that we meet with in these empires. Time and again, this power turns against God's people, but once in a while it does good to this nation, and in this respect it has to own the God of gods as its superior. We are now going to meet a striking example of this in the person of Alexander the Great.

3.5. Hellas

3.5.1. Alexander the Great

One could hardly imagine a closer association between an earthly prince and an angelic prince, even an embodiment of an angelic prince in the sense defined before, than in the case of Alexander the Great (356-323 BC). He is the "mighty king" who "shall rule with great dominion, and do as he wills" (Dan. 11:3). He is just as much a servant of YHWH as Nebuchadrezzar and Cyrus, even if Scripture does not explicitly say so in his case. First, he executes divine judgment on the Medo-Persian Empire (Dan. 8). Secondly, he has shown a remarkable respect for the God of Israel, as we will see shortly.

The association of Alexander with the Greek angelic prince finds a peculiar expression in the many Alexander legends, which have made a god of him. As said before, in

55. Cf. the tradition of the "fire-spitting dragons" (Job 41:10).

a certain sense he was that: an embodiment of the Greek angelic prince. In Egypt, he was hailed by the priest of Am(m)on as a son of this god (essentially the same as Osiris), which obviously was because, shortly before, Alexander had been crowned as Pharaoh in Memphis. On golden medals and silver coins he is sometimes depicted with the so-called Amon horns. The Egyptian god Am(m)on was sometimes depicted with a ram's head, and these are the ram's horns we see on Alexander's head. According to Greek tradition, the gods are founders of cultures, and according to Alexander himself, the conqueror and new ruler of the former Persian Empire necessarily had to be a god. Therefore, in 327 he wanted to introduce the Persian custom of the *proskynèsis* (the falling down before the king to render him homage), which certainly for the Greeks and Macedonians must have implied divine worship. They therefore refused. Alexander did consider himself as the god of the new world-empire. In 324, he asked the Greek cities of the Corinthian League for recognition of his divinity, this time successfully.[56]

As said before, Amon is essentially Osiris/Horus, the sun god, that is, Zeus/Apollo. Olympias, Alexander's own mother, claimed that he did not stem from her husband, king Philip, but from Zeus, who had begotten him in the form of a serpent. It is quite striking that, whereas in the Bible the "seed of the serpent" refers to Satan and his spiritual offspring (Gen. 3:15; cf. John 8:44), in antiquity each prince of a world-empire who was worshipped as a god necessarily had to be the "seed of a serpent." The emperor Augustus, too, who claimed to be the son of the sun god Apollo, asserted that this god had

56. Cf. Tarn (1948,I:77-82,113-115; II:347-374), who, by the way, is convinced that Alexander did not really considered himself to be a god (son of Zeus or Ammon). However, Callisthenes (see Plutarch, *Alexander* XXXIII) claimed that Alexander on one occasion called himself "son of Zeus." And it is a fact that in 324 he had himself deified by the cities of the Corinthian League. Many believe that, when Aristotle, Alexander's teacher, declared that the chief ruler, when he would come, would be "like a god among the people" (*Politics* III,13), he thought of his great pupil.

assumed the form of a serpent in order to beget him.[57]

When Alexander referred to the inner "divine" urge that led him, he spoke of his *póthos,* which means as much as an "inner longing for someone or something," often connected with a feeling of missing. Many great world leaders have witnessed of this inner, indeterminate drive, up to Napoleon, Lenin and Hitler. Each of them thus expressed in his own way the truth that they were "driven" ones, pushed along by forces that they did not know, but without which they would have been nothing. Alexander's teacher, the Greek philosopher Aristotle, perhaps found the right word when he described happiness as *eudaimonia,* "having a good demon or spirit." And Socrates, the teacher of Aristotle's teacher, Plato (and thus Alexander's spiritual "great-grandfather"), knew himself to have been propelled by his *daimonion*. In both cases, the *daimon(ion)* still had the positive meaning of a "(lower) deity"; the great ones knew themselves to be driven by the "gods."

Rabbinical literature has in its own way preserved Alexander's peculiar metahistorical significance. Let me first give a negative example. The Talmud[58] has handed down conversations between Alexander and the Jewish sages, in which at some moment Alexander asks the question, "Why do you resist me?" This was because the Jews held on to their own religion. The sages answered, "The Satan is too powerful." This is an ambiguous reply. The superficial meaning is, Satan prevents us from giving up our religion and accepting yours. But the deeper meaning is, you have received your power from Satan, and it was only given to you in order to test us.[59] If this interpretation is correct, this tradition views the angelic prince of Alexander as something negative, which, of course, is no wonder given the further history of Israel and the Greek Empire.

57. Cf. Suetonius, *Vita Augusti* 94,4.
58. Tamid 31b-32b; more specifically, 32a.
59. See the note in the Soncino-ed.

However, there is also a positive and very striking tradition, which was handed down in various versions. The Samaritans once asked Alexander whether he would allow them to destroy the temple at Jerusalem. This was reported to the high priest, Simeon the Just, who put on his priestly garments and, with a great following, travelled to Alexander in Antipatris (between Jerusalem and Caesarea):[60]

> When he [= Alexander the Macedonian] saw Simeon the Just, he descended from his carriage and bowed down before him. They said to him, "A great king like yourself should bow down before this Jew?" He answered, "His image it is which wins for me in all my battles."[61]

That is, Alexander's "god" (angelic prince) receives help from Simeon's God. According to other sources,[62] Alexander, when seeing Simeon, stood up for him and said, "Praised be the God of Simeon the Just!"[63] And to his suite he said, "When [or, As] I went to the battle, I saw a form which resembled his, and gained the victory."

Historically, these traditions are open to criticism; Simeon the Just for one was not high priest at all at the time of Alexander. However, also Flavius Josephus knows this tradition, but relocates it in the time of the high priest Yadduah, the real contemporary of Alexander the Great.[64] He tells us how Alexander in great anger marched against the Jews at Jerusalem, how the high priest with all the people cried to God for deliverance, and how YHWH commanded him in a dream to ornament the city with flowers, open all the gates, clothe the priests and all the inhabitants in white, and go out to meet Alexander without fear. At the approach of the king, Yadduah went out to meet him with great pomp and circumstance.

60. Yoma 69a; also cf. Megillat Taanit 9.
61. Meg. Taan. 9: "I saw his image, when I went out to war and gained the victory."
62. Pesiqta K. 4,9; Pesiqta R. 14,15.
63. Cf. Lev.R. 13,5.
64. *Jewish Antiquities* 11,8.

When Alexander saw this multitude and the magnificently dressed high priest, he approached him, worshipped the holy Name that was written on the golden plate on his forehead, and saluted the high priest, to the great astonishment of his following. His great favorite, Parmenio, asked him why he, who was worshipped by the world, worshipped the high priest of the Jews. The king answered:

> "It is not the high priest I worship, but the God whose servant he is; for when I was still at Dio in Macedonia and considered how I could overpower Asia, he appeared to me in a dream in this same garment, exhorted me to fear nothing, commanded me to undauntedly pass over the strait of the Hellespont, and assured me that he would guide my army and would make me conquer the empire of the Persians. Therefore, because I have never before seen anyone with such a garment as this one who appeared to me in my dream, I cannot doubt that it is divine providence that made me undertake this war, and that I will overcome Darius, will destroy the empire of the Persians, and that I will succeed in all as I wish."

Thereupon Alexander embraced the high priest and the other priests, entered with them into Jerusalem, where he went up to the temple, and sacrificed to God at the directions of the high priest. Yadduah even showed him from the book of Daniel (8:1-26; cf. 11:3) how it had been prophesized that a Greek prince would destroy the Persian Empire, about which Alexander rejoiced much. After this, he granted the Jews many favors.

Apart from possible embellishments in the story, it is, if we take the book of Daniel historically seriously, certainly not impossible to assume that the story, in its various readings, goes back upon a historical kernel. Alexander is only another "Nebuchadrezzar" who, or, whose angelic prince (!), had to recognize the power of YHWH as the Chief Ruler of all *elohim.*

3.5.2. The Angelic Prince of Alexander

Quite remarkable is a tradition in the Palestinian Talmud:[65]

> Rabbi Jonah [c. 350] said, "When Alexander the Macedonian wanted to ascend on high, he ascended further and further on high, until he saw the world [under him] as a ball, and the sea as a saucer. Therefore, people depict him with a ball in the hand...."

Of course, in a dream Alexander can ascend as high as he wants, but perhaps his angelic prince is intended here. This idea is indirectly supported by a footnote in the ed. Hengel, which notes that such a picture of Alexander is not known, but that it is quite common on Roman coins at the time of the tetrarchy (from 286 AD) and the Constantinian time. Now, the interesting thing is that these coins show a picture of the imperial *genius* (!), holding a ball, with an inscription like GENIO AVGVSTI ("To the *genius* of Augustus") or something similar. (A *genius* is the guiding spirit or patron deity, in this case of the emperor.)

If there is indeed a parallel, we have here a direct hint at the angelic prince of Alexander, that is, the angelic prince of the Greek Empire, who abides in higher spheres. The ball, as a reference to the earth globe, is a presumable indication that Alexander's empire, like that of the Roman emperors, possessed the status of a "world-empire." Further remarks by rabbi Jona (ibid.) show that the ball in the picture of Alexander signified that he ruled over the "earth" as it was then known. He did not rule over the sea, however; therefore, there is no saucer in his hand.

The most important reason why I believe we have to see in Alexander a (compelled) servant of YHWH, is found in the establishment of a rather uniform empire, with Greek as its unifying language and with the high Greek civilization, be it mixed with many Asian elements; we speak here of the

65. Aboda Zara 3, 42c, 47; also see Num.R. 13,14.

Hellenistic culture. This empire has become the important preparation for the establishment and expansion of Christianity. The Greek language became so important that even the Tenach (our Old Testament) had been translated into that language (the so-called Septuagint, abridged LXX). Thus, when Christianity came up, the Old Testament was already available in the cultural language of the time, the New Testament was added in that very language, and the unity of the empire allowed a rapid extension of Christianity.

In fact, by that time the empire had since long been absorbed by the Roman Empire. Also, the Greek Empire has provoked the anger of YHWH. We see this in Daniel 8 and 11: after Alexander's death and the war of the Diadochi, the empire was split into four kingdoms, two of which receive great attention in Scripture because of their significance for Israel. These are the kingdom of the Seleucids ("the king of the north") and the kingdom of the Ptolemaeans ("the king of the south," of course viewed from the geographic position of Israel). At the outset, Palestina lay within the Ptolemaean sphere of influence, afterwards it passed into that of the Seleucids. The latter, king Antioch IV Epiphanes in particular, provoked the anger of YHWH because of their crimes with regard to the people of YHWH.[66] Therefore, also the power of the Hellenistic kingdoms, like the power of all empires which rise against YHWH and his people, had to come to an end, as this indeed occurred through the Romans.

The latter are mentioned on one occasion already in Daniel 11, namely, in v. 30. Although the Seleucid kingdom had by no means reached its end, it is significant that already the wicked Antioch collided with the irresistible power of the Romans. The "ships of Kittim (or, the Kittites, or [NIV], the western coastlands)" mentioned there are ships of the Romans, who in 168 BC intervened in a campaign of Antioch against Egypt. The Romans had just subdued Macedonia in the

66. See Dan. 8:22-25; 11:21-35; 1 and 2 Macc.

battle at Pydna; a great battle directed against the center of the former Greek-Macedonian Empire. They then rapidly moved their ships to Egypt to intervene in the threatening battle between the kings of the "north" and the "south." The Roman envoy, Gaius Popillius Laenas, came with an ultimatum of the Roman Senate to Antioch, and out of fear for the mighty Rome, the latter gave up the conquered lands, and departed from Egypt. A new power was rising: the fourth and last of the four world-empires, that of Rome.

Even a long time after Alexander's empire had collapsed, his fame lived on. Gerhard C. Aalders (1880-1961) gives some striking examples of this.[67] The later Macedonian king, Cassander, who certainly was not tender-hearted, still shivered when, many years after Alexander's death, he had to pass the latter's statue in Delphi, as Plutarch reports. In the ancient Bactria in East-Persia (now in Afghanistan), on the slopes of the Hindu-Cush, noble families even into the twentieth century derived their descent from Alexander. Even among the Beduins, the memory of Alexander lived on. When they saw Napoleon, they believed that Alexander had risen from the dead. What an acute idea, if we begin to sense what metahistorical lines run from Alexander to Napoleon (§ 8.2)!

3.5.3. The Greek Pantheon

Those who venture to investigate the Greek pantheon, are in the danger of drowning in this *mer à boire*. We will have to limit ourselves to the absolute essentials. In previous chapters and sections, we already met with several Greek gods: Kronos, Zeus, Apollo, and his half-brothers Bacchus (or, Dionysus), Hermes, and Ares. In the current representation, the "family relationships" are as follows. Zeus is the son of Kronos and Rhea, he himself is the father of Ares (by Hera[68]), Apollo (by Leto), Bacchus (by Semele), and Hermes (by Maia). However,

67. Aalders (1954:84).
68. Strictly speaking, Zeus is only Ares's "legal" father, because the latter's conception did not involve any male sperm (cf. Comte 1994:134-135).

in fact many of the attributes merge in such a way that the figures coincide to a large extent. Or their attributes complete each other, form one another's complement, like in the case of Apollo and Bacchus, so that together they supply us with a balanced picture of the angelic power which they represent. Thus, the devil has an Apollonian and a Dionysian side: he is like an angel of light (2 Cor. 11:14; cf. Isa. 14:12) as well as the prince of darkness (Luke 22:53; 2 Cor. 6:14-15; Eph. 6:12), like a meek lamb (Rev. 13:11) as well as a roaring lion (1 Pet. 5:8); seemingly worthy and noble on the one hand, infamous and destructive on the other.

Alexander the Great ornamented himself with the horns of Amon, that is, Apollo. But of course, he also associated himself with the chief god, Zeus, whose features overlap with those of his son, Apollo. Zeus is the god of light(ning), Apollo the god of the (sun)light. Zeus and Apollo are threatened directly at their birth: Zeus has to fight the Giants, Apollo the Python. Zeus is the storm god, and is thus identical with the Sumerian Enlil, that is, the Babylonian Bel; but the latter is identical with the sun god, and thus identical with Apollo. Apollo is also the oracling, prophesizing god, and as such associated with Bel/Nebo, with Hermes and Janus, and with Osiris/Horus. Apollo is the serpent killer as is Horus; therefore, Herodotus does not hesitate to identify the two, but adds that Osiris equals Dionysus.[69]

Now, Osiris and Horus on the one hand and Apollo and Dionysus on the other are each other's complement. Therefore, we may associate Apollo with Osiris too. Apollo is the sun god as is Osiris/Horus. Apollo is the oracling god as is Osiris, represented by Horus. Apollo was threatened at his

69. Herodote, *History*, 2, 144 (1978:134): "[before, the Pharaohs] would have been the gods, who ruled in Egypt, namely, as living together with the people, and of them, always one had the supremacy; Horus, the son of Osiris, had been the last king over the land, who was called by the Greeks Apollo. After having driven Typhon from the throne, he supposedly was the last god-king of Egypt. Osiris is the Greek Dionysus."

birth by enemies just like Horus, the reborn Osiris, was. Both therefore had to fight a serpent: Apollo fought Python, Horus fought Typhon.[70] In one tradition, Horus is cut to pieces as was his father, Osiris. Also in Greek tradition, it is sometimes claimed that Apollo died a violent death. Horus is a war god as is Apollo.

These things may show with what power Alexander the Great had covenanted. According to its spiritual essence, it was the same power that had dominated Egypt as well as Assyria, Babylon, and Persia. Although the gods may represent distinct angelic figures, they do after all represent one single power, the "dragon," which is fundamentally directed against YHWH and his people. But as in Nebuchadrezzar and Cyrus, we find in Alexander the Great a striking example of a potentate through whose person the angelic prince acknowledges his superior in the God of gods, whose compelled servant he is.

---

70. Note the correspondence between the names Python and Typhon: an obvious case of (phonetic) metathesis, that is, exchange of letters.

Chapter 4
The Roman Empire

4.1. The Roman Angelic Prince
4.1.1. Introduction

AT THE END OF THE PREVIOUS CHAPTER, we arrived at the sixth—in Daniel's summing up: fourth—world-empire in salvational history: the Roman Empire. Here again, we will have to ask for the identity of the angelic prince. Since, for the history of the West, the Roman Empire is of the greatest importance, a more thorough investigation than in the case of the previous empires is necessary. This investigation will also be more complicated than in the case of the other world-empires, because the Roman Empire was a far less monolithic empire than, particularly, Nebuchadrezzar's "golden" empire. This clearly follows from Daniel's interpretation of Nebuchadrezzar's dream (v. 41-43):

> [something] of the hardness of the iron shall be in it, just as you saw the iron mixed with miry clay, and the toes of the feet partly of iron, and partly of clay; that kingdom shall be partly hard, and [a part] of it shall be fragile. And that you saw iron mixed with miry clay [means,] they will be a mixture through [the] seed of men [i.e., marriage], but not remain adhering to one another, just as iron does not mix with clay.

Viewed from a despotic standpoint, the Roman Empire was of a far lesser substance than the previous empires of gold, silver and bronze. The silver was less than the gold because the Persian kings ruled within the limits of the laws of the Medes and Persians, and the bronze was less than the silver because Greek political tradition was more republican than that of the Medo-Persian Empire. The Roman Empire was the most republican of all, even to a certain extent "democratic"; the authorities ruled by the grace of the *vox populi* (the "voice of the people"). But at the same time, the iron was the most useful to smash hostile powers. Macedonia was annexed by Rome in 168 BC, Greece forever subdued in 146 BC, the territory of the Seleucids west of the Tigris was annexed by Pompeius in 63 BC, and Egypt became a Roman province after the battle at Actium in 31 BC. Thus, Rome showed its iron fist, a stone-hard, reckless hand, which, during the rule of Traian (98-117 AD), brought the most extensive mass of territories under the sway of Rome.

Daniel 2:33 seems to imply a two phase structure in the history of the fourth empire. The first phase is represented by the legs of iron, the second by the feet partly of iron, partly of clay. The image is a giant on fragile feet, but with iron legs. The great hardness of the empire is characteristic for its former phase, but in the latter phase we find along with the hardness of the iron also the fragility of the clay. Verse 43 makes it clear that this is not just a matter of distinct "characteristics" of the empire, but of national "components," which are foreign to one another, even if they mix through marriage.

In order to understand to which this might refer, it is most important to consider the ultimate fate of the fourth empire. As we saw before, an accurate comparison of Daniel 2 and 7 makes it clear that the fourth empire will only come to its end by the appearance of the Son of Man with the clouds of heaven and the erection of his everlasting kingdom. In my opinion, no thorough expositor could deny this, and it was also the conviction of by far the most church fathers[1] and of Jewish tradition, as we will see further down. This means that we cannot simply discard the problem by stating that the (West-)Roman Empire came to its end in 476 with the fall of Rome. First, we will see that also the Carolingian empire and the Holy Roman Empire were, in the opinion of the medieval expositors,[2] forms of the Roman Empire, and even the Napoleonic empire and the "Third Reich" were unmistakably revivals of the Roman Empire as far as the political aspect and their extension was concerned.

Secondly, during the Middle Ages, after the fall of the West-Roman Empire, the European unity was guaranteed by the Roman (!) church, which added a spiritual dimension by turning the *imperium Romanum* ("Roman Empire") into an *imperium christianum* ("Christian Empire"), at least according to its outer profession. In reality, another "spirit" dominated this empire. Therefore, when in the New Time the European unity became rather guaranteed by Renaissance and Enlightenment, this was a far less drastic contrast with the previous period than it might seem at first sight. This will all be discussed in later chapters. Now we only want to show how the history of the Roman Empire in fact runs parallel with the history of Western culture to this day. This is no *eisegesis* of ours; medieval thinkers, and even some of the Reformers, felt that the Roman Empire *had to* remain in existence because, according to prophecy, at the end of the Roman Empire also the end of the present world will come.[3]

Let us now return to our question as to which may be the national "components" which are presented by the iron and the clay. It seems that in the iron we have to do with the original, Roman element, and that the clay refers to the barbarian, Germanic hordes that in the later phase invaded the empire, overthrew Rome, and by decrees divided the empire into a

1. Kocken (1935:10-69).
2. Kocken (1935:69-119); Adamek (1938:53-127).
3. Adamek (1938:1-19).

number of separate, independent states, once the pride and the power of the imperial Rome had been broken. As said before, this did not stop the later generations from trying to revive the ancient Roman Empire, as in the empire of the Carolingians, but it was never more than a mixture of the hardness of the original Roman iron and the fragility of the Germanic clay.

No doubt, this heterogeneity of the later West implies that in the case of the fourth empire we cannot simply speak of "a" or "the" angelic prince of Rome. So to say, there is not only the hardness of "the" (original) angelic prince, but also the fragility of the Germanic element, which brought along its own "gods." The passage in Daniel 2 clearly seems to point to the "polylithic" character of Western culture. We have to assume that a plurality of angelic powers has dominated the history of the West. On the other hand, Scripture makes it equally clear that one specific angelic prince, surely in the "end time" of Western cultural history, prevails in the West. That is the "dragon" of the book of Revelation.

Actually, we should not draw the borderline between the Roman and the Germanic gods too tightly. The Germanic chief god Wodan or Odin exhibits too many features of the Greek-Roman pantheon. The name Wodan/Odin has been linked with a whole group of names mentioned before: Adon, Athon, Athan, Adonis, but this is unlikely: the latter names have a Semitic origin (*adon* = "lord"; cf. *Adonai*), whereas Wodan/Odin has a Germanic origin: it is probably related to German *Wut* (Dutch *woede*), "fury" (Adam of Bremen, eleventh century, described Wodan as *furor*, "the furious"). In another sense, there *is* a relationship with the mentioned gods from antiquity: besides the dead and "lamented" gods Adonis, Tammuz (i.e., Adon), Bacchus, and Osiris, also Wodan/Odin has a son who is murdered and lamented: Balder. And here too, father and son merge, as in the case of Osiris/Horus and Zeus/Apollo. Balder is therefore a "side" of Odin himself.

There are more remarkable things to be noted. For instance, it is striking that, as Adon has a son Thouros, Odin has a son Thor (Donar).[4] Another son of Odin is Tyr (or Tiwaz, Teiwas, Old German: Ziu), a name related to that of the Greek Zeus. Tyr was the god of war and justice. Among the continental Teutons his name was Thincsus, i.e., god of the "thing" (the Germanic people's meeting). From him, our Tuesday got its name, which in French is called *mardi*, derived from *dies martis*, "day of Mars," the Roman war-god. But also Thor resembles Mars. In the case of Wodan we meet again with striking imitations of Christ. Wodan was the god of wisdom and poetry, who obtained magic and mantic knowledge by hanging at a tree for nine days and nine nights, pierced with his own spear (Gungnir); hence his name *Hangagud*, the "hanging god."[5]

Considering these data, we may wonder whether in Wodan (Odin) too we meet with the very same angelic power that misleads all the nations, and sets them against God's people. At any rate, there is a closer relationship between the Roman and the Germanic gods than may seem at first sight. It is rather shocking that national-socialism in Germany so eagerly reverted to its Germanic roots, even to the Germanic pantheon, which before had been so strongly glorified by Richard Wagner in his opera cycle, *Der Ring des Nibelungen*. When "Wodan" gets the upper hand in Adolf Hitler, this is basically the same diabolic angelic power as that which, in many earlier forms, has oppressed and destroyed God's people.[6]

4.1.2. The Satanic Angelic Prince of Rome

Let us first have a closer look at the satanic element in the Roman Empire as we find this clearly in Daniel 7. The fourth

4. Hislop (1959:312).
5. Cf. De Vries (1980:5-18); Jung (1984:46); Weiler (1989:23).
6. See the article by Jung (1984:45-58) concerning Wodan, particularly as to the German *Volksgeist* (national spirit) and national-socialism.

beast is

> dreadful and terrible, and exceedingly strong; and it had huge teeth of iron [!]: it [was] devouring and grinding, and trampling the residue with its feet (v. 7; cf. v. 19, 23).

In Daniel 7, this empire is depicted particularly as one rising in the end time against the "people of [the] saints of the Most High[7]" (Israel), even against the Most High himself (v. 27; cf. v. 18, 21-22, 25). As we have seen, this aggression against Israel, and thus against the God of Israel, led to the fall of each previous empire, and that is what occurred to the Roman/Western Empire. Also, the West will eventually perish because of its aggression against Israel and the God of Israel.

This in itself suffices to bring out the satanic character of the (chief) angelic prince of Rome (in brief, "the" angelic prince). But this comes to expression even more clearly in the book of Revelation, as will be discussed more extensively later. Here again we find the four world-empires, briefly touched upon in chapter 13:2. We find here the "beast out of the sea," that is, "the first beast," or in short, "the beast," as it is called afterwards in Revelation. In this "beast" we find, in a retrograde way, the characteristics of the Greek Empire (the leopard), the Medo-Persian Empire (the bear), and the Babylonian Empire (the lion) (cf. Dan. 7:4-6). This beast itself is the fourth animal in Daniel 7:7, the Roman Empire of the days of the apostle John. It is an empire that John identifies for us by declaring that the seven heads of the beast are "seven mountains." These are unmistakably the seven hills of Rome, the *urbs septicollis* ("city of the seven hills," 17:9).

That which concerns us right now is this. Revelation does not only depict "the beast," the visible Roman Empire itself as well as its head, but also the invisible spiritual power concealed behind this empire, that is, "the dragon." It is this dragon that gives the beast its strength, its throne and

7. An Aramaic word; in fact a double plural, with a singular meaning (cf. Heb. *elohim*).

great power (13:2). Even more remarkably, when the dragon itself is described, it turns out to exhibit the features of the beast, that is, of the Roman Empire or its head, namely, the seven heads and the ten horns, and on the heads seven crowns (cf. 12:3 with 13:1-2). The dragon is the invisible personification, or the angelic prince, the "god," of the Roman Empire, as, conversely, the beast (the head of that empire) is the "incorporation" of the dragon. Among the church fathers it was perhaps Hippolytus, the bishop of Rome around the year 200, who expressed this in the clearest way: he called the Roman Empire in its essence satanic;[8] other church fathers (Justin Martyr, Melito), however, have completely misjudged the true state of affairs.

When the Roman Empire tried to devour the newborn son of Revelation 12:5, it was in fact the "god" of that empire, who is the "god of this age" (*aiôn;* 2 Cor. 4:4), who attempted to destroy Christ. It was Herod the Edomite (! see below) who tried to kill the child Jesus, and later it was the prefect, Pontius Pilate, representative of the Roman Empire, who ratified and executed the death sentence on Christ. In this way he was, though unconsciously, nothing but an instrument of the dragon, be it under God's allowance, as Jesus himself declared (John 19:11). Revelation 12:9 and 20:2 tell us who this dragon is: he is the old serpent, called the Devil and Satan, the deceiver of the whole world. The serpent in the garden of Eden (Gen. 3) was the embodiment of Satan. It is quite striking that this angelic prince of the Roman Empire is cast down from heaven by none less than Michael, the angelic prince of Israel (Dan. 10:21) – a foreboding of the Roman Empire's fall through the Messiah of Israel (19:11-21). The conflict between Michael and the dragon finds its counterpart in the conflict between Israel and the Roman Empire (Rev. 12 and 13).

The word for "world" in Revelation 12:9 is the Greek word *oikoumenè*, which means as much as the "inhabited part

8. In his *Commentary on Daniël*, IV, 9, 2.

of the world" (unfortunately, English versions which translate "world," obscure the specific meaning of this "technical" term). In Luke 2:1 this rather general term is a clear reference to the then known inhabited world, that is, the Roman Empire, the territory of the Roman emperor, Augustus. A few pages further, however, in Luke 4:5, the devil is called the actual ruler of the *oikoumenè*, that is, its angelic prince. Also in Acts 11:28 and 24:5, and in Revelation 3:10, the *oikoumenè* is obviously the Roman Empire. In Acts 17:6-7, Paul brings the *oikoumenè* in turmoil by preaching that there is a "different king" over it—different from the Roman emperor, and even from the Greek and Roman gods—Jesus. One day, at his coming again, He will judge the *oikoumenè* in righteousness (v. 31; cf. Dan. 7!).

Jewish tradition knows perfectly well that Satan (or Samael, or Mastema, as he is also called in rabbinical literature) is the angelic prince of the Roman Empire. But before we enter into this, we first have to point out another, quite remarkable point in Jewish tradition, which is closely related with the previous one. Numerous times in rabbinical literature, the Roman Empire is referred to as "Edom" or "Esau"—Edom was the nation descending from Esau (Gen. 36:1)—while the angelic prince of the Roman Empire is identified with the angelic prince of Esau/Edom. This fits in with the close link between the Edomite Herod and the Roman Empire, which I just indicated. Moreover, also great Christian exegetes were familiar with this interpretation, for instance, the church father Jerome (c. 400).[9]

This may be the explanation for the fact that, according to the prophets, Edom turns out to play a main role in the last days; at times no doubt in the literal meaning (Isa. 11:14; Ez. 25:12-14; Dan. 11:41), but sometimes apparently in a much

9. See his *Commentary on Isaiah*, on chapter 21:11-12; also Idem on *Malachi*, on chapter 1:4-5 (Kocken 1935:7). The Jews also believed that many Edomites had travelled westward, and had put a strong demographic stamp on the population of the Roman Empire (Martin 1993:163 etc.).

farther reaching sense, as in Isaiah 34 and 63, and in the book of Obadiah. Isaiah 34:10 and 63:2 for one may be compared directly with Revelation 14:11, 19 and 19:13, 15, where we find the judgment on the Roman beast. Thus, the relationship between Edom and Rome is obviously implied by Scripture as well. Further down in this chapter, we will find some other relationships between prophecies concerning Edom on the one hand and the Roman Empire on the other.

Of course, the enormous significance of the identification of Edom with Rome, including their angelic princes, is immediately obvious. Through this identification, Jewish religious understanding has acutely brought to light that the whole history of Western culture circles around the conflict between the Roman Empire and the people of Israel. This fits in entirely with Daniel 7 and Revelation 12 and 13. The conflict between Rome and Israel finds its origin in, or is typologically represented by, the ancient conflict between Esau and Jacob. In other words, the great eschatological conflict between the angelic prince of the Roman Empire and the Messiah of Israel is foreshadowed by the conflict between the angelic prince of Esau on the one hand (who is believed to be identical with the angelic prince of the Roman Empire) and (the God of) Jacob, the progenitor of Israel, on the other hand. In § 4.2 this will be further examined in the book of Genesis. First, we briefly deal with some other relationships, not only between Rome and Edom, but also between Rome and Egypt, and between Rome and Babylon.

4.1.3. Egypt, Babylon, and Rome

Not only Edom (see Appendix 6 and 7) but sometimes also Babylon is a symbol for Rome, like in the book of Revelation (see Appendix 10). This is understandable in so far as the Babylonian and the Roman Empire, as the first and the last of the four world-empires, stand in a close relationship.[10] This

10. The early Christian authors, Orosius and Augustine, already pointed to this close link between Babylon and Rome (Kocken 1935:64-65).

connection between Babylon and Rome is quite important for the understanding of Isaiah 14:4-21. This Scripture describes the king of Babylon, but in v. 12-15 we clearly see a higher, spiritual power rising behind him, which, because of its identification with the king of Babylon, can be none other than the angelic prince of Babylon (see § 3.3.3). We will see that this angelic prince exhibits features that are found back in the angelic prince of Rome.

There is an equally important parallel between the Egyptian and the Roman Empire. In Appendix 10, this is explained by means of the plagues in Exodus as compared with those in Revelation.

In Revelation 12, we even find a reason to directly relate all three of these empires, Egypt, Babylon and Rome, when it comes to this important point: the deliverance of Israel out of the grip of these empires. The significance of the comparison lies in the fact that, throughout the history of all seven empires, one and the same continuous hostile higher power is aiming at Israel, God's people. The seven subsequent world-empires form one continuous history of conflict between the higher powers and the God of Israel, a conflict that is ultimately resolved to the advantage of the God of gods. The parallel between the three empires mentioned separately reveals moreover by whose hand the final victory is to be gained. These are the most significant parallels:

(a) The actual captain of the spiritual powers is the "dragon," the Devil and Satan. Earlier, we have referred to Isaiah 51:9-10, which tells us that YHWH at the exodus out of Egypt cut down "Rahab, the dragon," that is the angelic prince of Egypt. In Isaiah 51 this is quoted as a direct parallel with the exodus of Israel out of Babylon (cf. 43:14; 48:14, 20; 52:11-12). In Jer. 51:34, Babylon, or Nebuchadrezzar, is called a "dragon" that has devoured Israel, but later has to spit it out again, that is to say, it is his angelic prince, Bel, who is urged to do so (cf. v. 44). Also, in Revelation 12 it is the dragon, Rome's angelic prince, who is the great enemy of Israel, God's people. Both Exodus (14:8) and Revelation (12:13) speak of God's people being persecuted by the enemy.

(b) At the outset of the three deliverances always a peculiar birth of the redeemer is mentioned. At the beginning of Exodus this is Moses, in the second part of Isaiah this is the well-known Servant of YHWH, and in Revelation 12 it is the "male son" that is born and will redeem his people, that is, the Messiah. The parallels between Moses and Jesus are so striking that Appendix 8 is devoted to them. Also, in the case of the Servant of YHWH, birth and youth are emphasized (Isa. 49:1; 50:4; 53:2). Even pre-Christian Jewish tradition often applied the prophecies concerning the Servant of YHWH to the Messiah, although their first meaning might also involve some post-exilic figure such as Zerubbabel or Cyrus (cf. Isa. 44:27-45:1).[11] At least, Zerubbabel can be called a type (foreshadow) of the Messiah; each Scripture foretelling or describing his appearance also points to the coming of Messiah (see, for instance, Hagg. 2:21-24; Zech. 4).

(c) In all three redemptions, the people of God are delivered from the claws of the respective world-empires. However, they are not immediately carried to their full deliverance but first led through the threatening waters. After the exodus

---

11. The traditional Jewish interpretation sees in the Servant of YHWH either the suffering people of Israel, or the prophet himself, or in some verses the people and in other verses a certain person (that is, either a pre-exilic person such as Moses, Uzziah, Hezekiah, Isaiah, Josiah, Jehoiachin, Jeremiah, Ezekiel, or a post-exilic person such as Zerubbabel or Cyrus), or the Messiah. Ibn Ezra, Rashi, Abarbanel and other Jews, who themselves had given up this interpretation, admitted that this was the oldest Jewish interpretation. Hengstenberg in his *Christology* (1854-58) gives detailed proofs from the antique Jewish writings. In the books of Enoch, 4 Ezra, and the Syrian Baruch apocalypse, the description of the Messiah seems to contain clear allusions to Isa. 53. Rabbinical Judaism applied Isa. 53 more than once to "the godly one" (Berakh. 5a; Sanhedrin 39a; Mo'ed Qatan 28a; cf. Strack-Billerbeck 1922, I:484), which refers pre-eminently to the Messiah. The references to Isa. 53 are few, however. Dalman states (1887:2), "the rabbinical tradition concerning the suffering Messiah almost without exception appeals to Isa. 53."

out of Egypt, Israel passes through the Red Sea (Exod. 13-15). In Isaiah 43:16-17 and 51:9-10, a parallel is drawn between this passage and the exodus out of Babylon, and Israel also receives the promise, "When you pass through the waters, I am with you" (43:2). In Revelation 12, too, the "woman" (Israel) comes into contact with the threatening waters: the dragon sends a stream of water to her to have her dragged away by the stream, but the waters are swallowed by the earth (v. 15-16).

(d) After the waters, God's people are led into the wilderness. In all three cases it looks like a kind of "flight" (cf. Exod. 13:18; Isa. 48:20; Rev. 12:6). After the exodus out of Egypt, Israel is led through the wilderness in order to be put to the test (Deut. 8:2-4), but by God's providential faithfulness it is supplied with water (Exod. 15:27; 17:1-7; Num. 20:2-13; 21:16-18). After the exodus out of Babylon, Judah is also led through the wilderness (Isa. 40:3; 43:19; also cf. 35:8-10 with 51:11, and further Jer. 31:1-6; Ez. 20:8-10, 33-38; Hos. 2:13-14), and supplied with water as well (Isa. 41:18; 43:19-20; 48:21; 50:2). Also, the "woman" in Revelation 12:6 is led into the wilderness to be nourished there and to be protected against the dragon (compare again the parallel with Isa. 51:9-11).

(e) The two wings of the great eagle, with which the woman in Revelation 12:14 escapes, remind us of God himself, who compares himself to an eagle, which on its wings carried the people out of Egypt and protected them (Exod. 19:4; Deut. 32:11). Also, in Isaiah (40:31), it is said of God's people that they "mount up with wings as eagles."

(f) The most important and interesting parallel is this one: in each of the three deliverances, God's "pawn," God's "trump-card" against the great, mighty dragon is a little, tiny animal, the lamb. *Here lies the essence of world history: the conflict between the lamb and the dragon.* The exodus out of Egypt is not primarily based on violence and display of power, but on the blood of the lamb, behind which Israel was allowed to take refuge. It is striking that, as an argument for the Passover, YHWH states that he will execute judgment against the "gods" of Egypt (Exod. 12:12), that is the "dragon" of Isaiah 51:9-10. Again at the exodus out of Babylon, the little, weak lamb is central: the suffering Servant of YHWH, by whom alone this exodus can be realized, is as a lamb brought to the slaughter (Isa. 53:7; also cf. 50:6).[12] And in Revelation 5-19 it is the Lamb who challenges the dragon, who by his blood makes his people overcome the dragon (12:11), and who ultimately himself gains the final victory over him (17:14; 19:11-20:10).

4.2. Jacob and Esau[13]

4.2.1. Birth and conflict

We have seen that world history is basically determined by the conflict between the Lamb and the dragon. The Lamb is the Messiah of Israel, the dragon is the angelic prince of the Roman Empire, that is, according to Jewish tradition, Esau/Edom. In other words, world history revolves around Jacob/Israel on the one hand and Esau/Edom on the other; or, around the God and the Messiah of Israel on the one hand and the angelic prince of Edom on the other. Genesis 32 is the

12. Isa. 53 clearly follows the Levitical sacrificial system, in which the innocent sacrificial animal dies atoningly and substitutionally for the people; see, for instance, what is said of the lamb in v. 7 and the trespass-offering in v. 10, and a technical term such as "bearing" (*naça*) in v. 4 and 12. If the continuous lesson of Leviticus is that time and again Israel needs a propitiating sacrifice that "bears" (expiates, blots out) the sins of the people, it is the lesson of Isa. 53 that the ultimate atonement of Israel depends on a perfect and definitive propitiating sacrifice. This, for instance, is also the message of Dan. 9:24, where the seventy year-weeks eschatologically end in the atonement of Israel. Again, this is the message of Ps. 40:7-11, where the true David (type of the Messiah) becomes the true sacrifice, peace-offering, burnt offering, and sin offering. Not Israel dies the atoning death for the nations, as the usual Jewish interpretation of Isa. 53 has it, but the Messiah dies the atoning death for the believers among Israel as well as for those among the nations.
13. Cf. for the following paragraphs De Graaff (1982), though I give far more extensive evidence from the Jewish sources (see Appendix 6 and 7), and I do not always agree with De Graaff's exegeses, certainly not with regard to the alleged "device of Jacob" in the Gospels.

chapter where, according to an ancient rabbinical tradition, we meet with this angelic prince of Esau. We will take a closer look at this Scripture; but for the light that Jewish tradition throws upon it we refer emphatically to Appendix 6 and 7.

Let us imagine the situation. Esau and Jacob were twins out of Isaac and Rebecca. YHWH announced to Rebecca before their birth (Gen. 25:23),

> Two peoples [are] in your womb,
> and two nations shall separate themselves from your inner parts;
> and [the one] nation shall be stronger than [the other] nation,
> and [the] great [= elder] shall serve the little [= younger].

When the boys are born, first Esau comes out, immediately followed by Jacob, whose hand holds Esau's heel (25:26). The name Esau means "hairy, shaggy," and Jacob means "heel-holder," and then, in the negative meaning, "supplanter, deceiver," but also, "taking the place of another."[14] The holding of Esau's heel at birth is therefore on the one hand a hint to Jacob's deceiving character. On the other hand, it also refers to Jacob's justified claims: the fact that he holds the heel of Esau implies that, according to divine right, he will take Esau's place.

We know the further history of the two brothers. By ignoble intrigues, Jacob brings upon himself much misery. He has to flee from his brother's wrath, and has to dwell for twenty years outside that very land that had fallen to him as a promise through Isaac's blessing. After this exile, at God's command Jacob returns to Canaan, but in great fear for Esau. Therefore, the former tries to soothe the latter with enormous gifts. When he finally meets him, Jacob says to Esau (Gen. 33:10),

---

14. Heb. *ᶜaqêv*, "heel"; *ᶜaqav*, "grab at the heel," and hence also, "deceive" (Jer. 9:4; cf. Hos. 12:4). Since *ᶜaqeev* in the derived sense also means "footsteps" (see Ps. 77:20; 89:52; S.o.Sol. 1:8), for *ᶜaqav* the meaning, "tread in someone's footsteps," is also conceivable, that is, "take someone's place."

> "... for therefore I have seen your face, as one sees the face of *elohim* [lit., as the seeing of the face of *elohim*], and you have taken pleasure in me."

For our subject, this is a key verse. Usually, this statement is discarded as flattery on the part of Jacob, but in the opinion I represent here, much more is involved. Jacob notes here that Esau has accepted his, Jacob's, "face," that is, his person. But, Jacob adds, he himself had seen the face of Esau "corresponding with his seeing of the face of *elohim*"! What do these enigmatic words mean? What "correspondence" is involved here? And when did he see the face of *elohim*? Who is this *elohim*? And what link is there between the face of this *elohim* and the face of Esau? The simple answer that suggests itself is: this *elohim* is the angelic prince of Esau; his face corresponds with the face of Esau himself,[15] and Jacob saw this face when he wrestled with the *elohim* of Esau at the Jabbok.

Thus we arrive at that significant event in Jacob's life, which is described in Genesis 32:24-31. The great majority of Christian expositors saw in the Man wrestling with Jacob a good angel, an (or, the) angel of YHWH, or YHWH himself, or the pre-incarnate Christ. In Appendix 6, objections are adduced against this exegesis, and it is extensively argued that we have to do here with the angelic prince of Esau (that is, Rome).

> And he [Jacob] took them [= his family], and made them pass over the brook [= the Jabbok]; and he made pass what he had. And Jacob was left alone; and a man wrestled with him until the breaking of the day (Gen. 32:23-24).

Why does the guardian angel of Esau come to wrestle with Jacob? The reason for this is to be sought in the blessing that father Isaac, after having given the actual great patriarchal blessing to Jacob, granted to Esau:

15. Cf. Acts 12:15 for the notion that a person's face corresponds with that of his guardian angel.

> Behold, your dwelling shall be away from the fatnesses of the earth,
> and away from the dew of heaven from above;
> and by your sword you shall live,
> and you shall serve your brother;
> and it shall be, when you rove around [or, if you obtain the dominion],
> that you shall break his yoke from your neck (Gen. 27:39-40).

Isaac points out that the blessing of the firstborn, which includes the blessing of the coming Messiah and of the ultimate kingdom of God, lies with Jacob. For Esau this implies that he, apart from Jacob, will always be deprived of this blessing. Therefore, there are only two ways open to Esau. He may either own Jacob's birthright, and thus, in and through him, share in the great blessing after all. Or he may continually dispute the birthright with him and attempt to abolish his priority: "break Jacob's yoke from his neck." Here we encounter one of the principal features of all world history, especially when we keep in mind that, in Jewish opinion, Esau/Edom represents Rome or the Roman Empire. God had already told Abraham (Gen. 12:3; cf. 18:18; 22:18; 26:4),

> I will bless those who bless you,
> and curse him who curses you,
> and in you all families of the earth shall be blessed.

Isaac, and also YHWH, repeated this to Jacob (27:29; 28:14). This promise has a universal bearing. It holds for all families of the earth that he who blesses Abraham/Jacob/Israel, in him will be blessed himself. "Blessing" Israel means, wishing Israel the best, seeking the good of Israel, but also, recognizing Israel's divine blessing, and thus its priority, and thus sharing in this blessing. This was the way of blessing that Esau could have chosen.

Also, for Western culture as a whole, only two options are open, which apparently dominate its history: either to seek the blessing with, and to own it from, the God of Israel, or to reject Israel, and therewith his God, deny its priority, "break its yoke from the neck." As the destiny of the previous three world-empires depended on their attitude towards the God of Israel, and towards Israel itself, this will also be the case for the Roman Empire. Therefore, the holocaust is one of the signs of the utter decline of Western culture, and there will be salvation only for those who, in and through Christ, have a personal relationship with the God of Israel.

In Genesis 32, we see how Esau's angelic prince chooses the second option, and comes to fight Jacob. In the solitude of the night, Jacob is attacked. But Jacob is strong, for a whole army of angels, given to accompany and protect him (32:2-3), is with him. Esau's guardian angel sees that he will not manage to throw off Jacob's yoke, even less to prevail over him. This is a general rule: never will Edom/Rome gain the victory over Jacob/Israel, because the latter has YHWH on his side. But Edom/Rome does have the ability to terribly strike Israel, and has done so many times in world history.[16] We see this here too. Esau's angelic prince inflicts grievous harm on Jacob by smiting the socket of his hip. This is no arbitrary injury. In Scripture, the hip (Heb., *ᶜarêk*) is primarily connected with procreation: Jacob's sixty-six descendants came forth from this very "hip."[17] When Esau's guardian angel cannot prevail over Jacob himself, he tries to touch him in his offspring. That is exactly what is happening to Israel since almost two thousand five hundred years now, from the time that his newborn sons were thrown into the Nile until the time that his sons and daughters died in the gas chambers of Auschwitz.

How, in his turn, does Jacob fight the battle with the angel? In v. 26, we get the impression that Jacob does not flee from the angel, but does not strike him either; even less is he trying to destroy him. He himself therefore does not aim at Esau's perdition. He limits himself to taking his opponent in

16. See extensively Ouweneel (2014a).
17. Gen. 46:26; Exod.1:5; also cf. Judg. 8:30.

an iron grip, from which the latter cannot free himself. This evil angel shuns the daylight. Therefore, when dawn appears, he appeals to Jacob to let him go. According to an important interpretation of Hosea 12 (see Appendix 6), he even weepingly begs for Jacob's grace. But Jacob does not let him go; he even tells the angel, "I will not let you go unless you bless me" (v. 26).

At first sight, this seems to be one of the strongest indications that the angel is a representative of YHWH himself; whom else would Jacob ask for a blessing? However, we should not forget that Jacob has no need whatsoever to ask God for the blessing, because he already possesses the great blessing. Therefore, quite a different interpretation is possible, namely, that Jacob expresses his great desire that Esau, too, will "bless" Jacob, so that God's blessing can be granted to him (Esau). We have seen before, and Jacob knows this, that Esau will only find blessing if he owns Jacob's birthright, that is, the latter's blessing. Jacob says as it were to (the angelic prince of) Esau, "If you bless me, you will be blessed yourself." This is exactly the way the great Jewish expositor, Rashi (Rabbi Shlomo Yitschaqi, 1140-1205), interpreted the passage: "unless you bless me" means, "unless you own my title to my father's blessings." Only in this, lies the blessing for Esau/Edom/Rome.

Thus even today, until the dawn of the new world, "Jacob" (Israel) still embraces the empire of the *goyyim*, "Rome" in particular, the Western world. Israel does so because it knows that the blessing for the world will only arrive when the latter will own the birthright of Israel. The world has to seek its blessing there, namely, with the God and the Messiah of Israel. This is the blessing that Jacob wrings out of the angel; for if the latter will bless him, Esau (Rome, the Western world) will be blessed. Therefore, Jacob does not let the angel go. This is not out of self-defense, for he only has to let loose the angel, and the latter will flee before the dawn. No, he does not let the angel go out of love. This is no longer the deceiving Jacob, the supplanter, but a princely man, not primarily alive to his own victory, but to Esau's wellbeing. Therefore, the angel says (v. 28),

> Your name shall no longer be called Jacob, but Israel[18],
> for you have behaved princely with *elohim* and with men[19], and have prevailed.

Rashi explains this verse as follows:

> No longer will there be said that the name Jacob fits you because you have obtained the blessing by deceit [cf. 27:36], but because [now] you have obtained it by open battle and victory.

Jacob clasps the angel until the latter cannot do but bless him (v. 29). Jacob, who had so strongly been occupied with Esau's face (v. 20), says of that place (v. 30),

> I have seen *elohim* face to face,
> and my soul [= my life] has been preserved.

That is the result of the wrestling: Jacob has not lost his life, on the contrary, he has gained the victory, be it at the prize of a serious injury, which hurts him in his offspring and threatens the fulfillment of God's promises. But all that misery cannot throw any doubt on Israel's ultimate victory. When the sun of God's new kingdom will rise one day (cf. v. 31), Israel will be victor, and Edom will be blessed because, and insofar as, it has blessed Israel. More precisely, Edom/Rome as a whole, with its angelic prince, will necessarily go and meet its final judgment, but there will be everlasting blessing for every "Edomite" who has "blessed" Israel, that is, has accepted the "salvation out of the Jews" (John 4:22).

4.2.2. Jacob/Israel and Edom/Rome

In Genesis 33, all these things must find some fulfillment in

18. That is, "he who fights with *el*," "he who behaves princely towards *el*," or, "prince of *el*." Hence the verb "behave princely" ("behave as a *sar*") in this verse.
19. This refers back to the word "man" in v. 24.

the actual encounter between Jacob and Esau. After the victory that Jacob had gained over Esau's guardian angel, Esau comes with four hundred men to meet Jacob. Yet, he can do nothing but "accept" Jacob's "face," that is, be reconciled to him. For a moment, things seem to go wrong when Esau refuses the blessing that Jacob wants to give him. This cannot be, for it is of vital importance for Esau that he accepts this blessing; apart from Jacob, there never can be any blessing for him! Then we hear the very significant words of Jacob, in which he does not say directly, "You will have to accept this, for I have prevailed over your *elohim,*" but expresses himself in a much more subtle and modest way (v. 10-11):

> "If I have now found favor in your sight,[20] then receive my present from my hand; for therefore I have seen your face, as the seeing of the face of [your] *elohim,* and you have taken pleasure in me. Please, take my blessing that is brought to you, for God has been gracious to me [or, God has granted them to me graciously]."

Jacob says as it were, I have seen your *elohim*, I have wrestled with him, and then not: I have prevailed over him, but: he has—be it as a consequence of my victory!—taken pleasure in me, as is evident from the fact that he has blessed me. Jacob means to say that Esau is bound to that blessing. He, that is, his guardian angel, has blessed Jacob, and therefore he must now accept the blessing of Jacob: "blessed [be] he who blesses you." Esau is now being blessed by Jacob, that is, by YHWH, for, as his words show, the blessing that Jacob gave him came from YHWH himself. As Jacob clasped the angel until he blessed him, so now he insists that Esau will accept Jacob's blessing (v. 11b).

After this, the two men separate. Esau with his four hundred men and Jacob with his children and his herds cannot go together. They form two totally different worlds. But they do

20. Rashi reads here, "the sight of your face is by me equally highly esteemed as the sight of your guardian angel whom I have seen."

not separate forever; on the contrary, they only go two different ways which lead to the same goal. Jacob announces that, in his own time and manner, he will arrive at Esau in Seir (the mountains of Edom) (v. 14). This too has been interpreted as a pretext by Jacob, but why not accept that he means it literally? The great Jewish expositor, Rashi, asks, "When will Jacob arrive in Seir?" and referring to Obadiah 21 he answers,

> In the days of the Messiah, for it has been said, "And saviors shall come up on mount Zion to judge the mount of Esau."

The important question as to how we have to read Hosea 12:4-6 is dealt with separately in Appendix 6. It is now time to pick up our main subject again, and to ask ourselves what these things tell us about the history of Western culture. I have noted that in the rabbinical writings the name Edom, the popular name for the descendants of Esau, is the common reference to Rome. Numerous times this can be corroborated from the Targumim, the Midrashim, and the Talmud. For the correctness of this identification, Jewish tradition finds an important proof in Numbers 24:17-19: one day, a Star will come out of Jacob, and a Scepter rise out of Israel. This refers to the coming of the Messiah and the arrival of the kingdom of God:

> And Edom shall be conquered (or, dispossessed),
> and Seir shall be conquered (or, dispossessed), his [= Israel's] enemy;
> and Israel shall do valiantly,
> and [one] from Jacob shall rule.

In the light of Daniel 2 and 7, it is understandable that the dispersed Jews understood "Edom" to signify here the fourth, Roman Empire, which would be destroyed at the coming of the Messiah (the "[one]" of v. 19) (see again extensively Appendix 7). Viewed from a metahistorical standpoint, the history of Western culture exhibits as one of its main features the deep-lying conflict between Jacob and Esau. That is the conflict between Israel with the God of Israel on the one hand and

Edom/Rome with Satan, its angelic prince, on the other. The outcome of this conflict is prophetically certain: Western culture will be brought to its end by nothing but the coming of the Messiah of Israel and the erection of God's kingdom. But before reaching its end, this culture time and again reveals the following main features:

(a) Esau continually attempts to break off his neck the yoke of Jacob. Western history is almost one long pogrom, with as its horrible climax, so shortly before the end time, the holocaust. Esau has struck Jacob terribly on his hip: he has killed Jacob's children, has tried to ruin his expectations.

(b) Israel has never given up on Edom. It has never deserted Western culture, particularly Europe, on the contrary: it occupies crucial posts in Western culture to this day. It entwines Esau and will not let loose until dawn, no matter how it has been beaten by Esau. It holds Edom, not to destroy it, but in order that Edom will acknowledge the birthright of Israel and will convert to the God of Israel. "Salvation is from the Jews" (John 4:22).

(c) Of course, here lies a discrepancy, for there is no hope for Samael himself, the angelic prince of Rome, as Scripture makes clear: his end is in the lake of fire and sulfur (Revelation 20:10). For Western culture as such there is no hope either: the beast undergoes the same fate as the dragon that deceived him (ibid.). But the blessing that the angel gives to Jacob does imply that *within* Western culture there are those who, in the end time, will own Israel as God's people and God as the God of Israel. As Zechariah 8:23 puts it,

> In those days [it will be], that ten men from all languages of the nations shall grasp, yes, grasp the sleeve of a Jewish man, saying, "Let us go with you, for we have heard [that] God [is] with you."

4.2.3. Israel and Rome in the Gospels[21]

It is quite fascinating to follow the conflict between Jacob/Israel and Edom/Rome in the Gospels, because the true "Israel," that is, the Messiah, opposes the whole diabolic power of the Roman Empire. In Matthew's Gospel, this conflict between Christ and Rome becomes visible in the clearest way.

We have seen that, when the Roman Empire tried to devour the newborn Christ (Revelation 12:5), it was in fact the "god" of that empire who attempted this. The Herod who tried to kill the child Jesus (Matt. 2:16-18) was an Edomite! Later, it was the Roman prefect, Pilate, who condemned Christ to death. The Edomite and the Roman belong together, for the Edomite is nothing but a vassal and a straw-man of the Romans. In Revelation 12:9 we read that the dragon, the *genius* (guardian angel) of the Roman Empire, deceives the whole "world"; that is in Greek the *oikoumenè*. As we have seen, in Luke 4:5 the devil is called the ruler of the *oikoumenè*, that is, the Roman Empire (cf. 2:1). In this way, a peculiar light is thrown upon the temptation in the wilderness. The encounter between Christ and Satan, the angelic prince of Rome, is in fact a new confrontation of Jacob and Esau. Esau's angelic prince wrestles again with Christ, the true "Israel," to prevail over him (see Matt. 4:1-11).

Again, the central question is, who will ultimately receive Jacob's blessing; who will be the ultimate "god" of the *oikoumenè*, Christ or Satan?[22] Edom/Rome sees a menacing rival in Christ, for Rome, too, wants to bring peace and salvation to the world: the *pax Romana* ("Roman peace"). In the first temptation, Satan challenges Christ, if he is the Son of God, to turn stones into bread. Satan himself is a "son [i.e., member of the guild] of the gods," one of the *bené ha-elohim* (Job 1 and 2), and by means of Rome he supplies the people with *panis et circenses*, "bread and games." Satan acts in a cunning way; he tries

21. Cf. for the next paragraph De Graaff (1989), again with the restrictions mentioned in note 1.
22. Cf. Ibid. (1987:214-228).

to draw Christ down to his own level and thus to make him superfluous. But in spite of his hunger, Jesus sticks to the way of God: the true subject of his empire, does not live by bread alone, but by every word that comes from the mouth of God.

Then Satan takes Jesus to the pinnacle of the temple. That is the place where Jewish tradition expects that Messiah will reveal himself one day.[23] Again, Satan acts cunningly: he tries to replace the true kingdom of God by some imitation. By having Christ casting himself down from the temple he suggests a pseudo-Messianic appearance. Imagine if Jesus with such a jump would descend triumphantly in the temple court. What an impression would that make on the Jews in the temple! The Messianic kingdom could start right away. Here again, Edom/Rome wants to draw the Messiah down to his own level; for the Roman prince himself always seeks the way of popularity, the favor of the people, to retain his grip on the masses. Christ, however, does not primarily seek the favor of the people, but of the Father: he waits for the proper hour that the Father has determined.[24] In this way alone the true blessing of the Messianic Empire can come to the people.

Again, in the third temptation, Satan offers Christ an easy way to kinghood, or, in fact, emperorhood. As said before, he speaks here as the angelic prince of the Roman Empire, and says to Christ as it were, Own the supremacy of Rome, and you will be my highest vassal; I will make you emperor of Rome. What a temptation! What a blessing could Jesus, as emperor of Rome, not bring over Israel! In fact, many Christians, including Protestants, have claimed that this is precisely what Christ did: become "god" and "king" of the "Christianized" Roman Empire, the *imperium christianum*, from the fourth century onward. If that were true, in fact he would have abandoned his people of Israel. Then the Church would have taken the place of Israel as God's people on earth: *the*

23. Pesiqta R.36 (162a): "When the King, the Messiah, reveals himself, he comes and stands on the roof of the sanctuary."

24. Cf. Luke 22:53; John 2:4; 7:30; 8:20; 12:23; 13:1; 17:1.

birthright would have moved to Esau after all! However, there can be no question of this. Therefore, Jesus says that he holds without restraint to "YHWH your God," that is the God of Israel. He never gives up Israel for Rome; that is the error of Augustinian "supersessionism." As the Servant of this God, as the Messiah of Israel, he will not bow down before Rome and his angelic prince, but will triumph over them, he will subject Rome to the God of Israel. In the Messianic kingdom, Israel will be the center, not Rome. On the contrary, Esau will only be able to arrive at the blessing through Jacob.

Another "confrontation," but now on a very different level, we find in Matthew 8:5-12, where the son of the Roman centurion is healed. In extreme distress, the Roman soldier calls Jesus for help; that is, Esau asks Jacob's help! When he himself is at the end of his wits he recognizes that true life can only be found in the true "Jacob." But Jesus does not grant the request right away. "Me? Should I come to heal him?" Should Jacob now all of a sudden be ready to render labor services to Esau? Rome has at its disposal all the priests and all the healers of all the nations in its empire; does it in the same way have the Messiah of Israel at its disposal? With that question, Jesus invites the centurion to own the true relationship between Esau and Jacob. Jacob can only bless Esau if Esau first blesses Jacob.

This is precisely what the centurion does by owning the word-power of Jesus. In this way he makes it clear that he has freed himself from the power of Rome's angelic prince. Therefore, Jesus should not come under his "roof"; he does not have to enter with the Roman to give the Messianic blessing. On the contrary, ultimately the Roman must come under the "roof" of Israel—the "tents of Shem" (Gen. 9:27)—even if this is not expressed here. The centurion recognizes that he stands under *exousia*, that is, under the supremacy of Rome, that is basically, Rome's angelic prince. And he himself can apply this *exousia* to others. If this authority is so strong, how much more the authority of the King of Israel, which even extends over the domain of death, and thus certainly over Rome! Here, the *exousia* of Rome fails, and Esau has to own his superior in Jacob. Only the word of the Messiah can save Rome, and thus it has been throughout history for every "Roman" who recognized the supremacy of Christ and the power of his word. By the way, vv. 10-12 make it clear that for the Jew, too, the blessing is only possible in this manner: the way of faith in the Messiah. The Messianic kingdom is only available for the "remnant" of Israel, which has learned to accept the Messiah.[25]

The next great confrontation with Rome is Jesus's encounter with the Roman prefect, Pontius Pilate.[26] Much could be said here, but I limit myself to some significant points. Jesus is the prisoner of Pilate, and the latter is a man of little scruples. Yet he tries to get rid of the problem-Jesus. The angelic prince of Rome is conscious of the terrible consequences if he has Jesus crucified. He feels entwined by Jesus, as once Esau by Jacob, and cannot get away from him without blessing him. What the centurion manages to do, Pilate cannot work himself up to. He is placed before the choice: either bless Jacob (this also involves owning him as his superior), and thus be blessed himself, or kill Jacob, and thus "maintain" himself, but consequently, paradoxically enough, perish.

It is remarkable that in Matthew (27:19) Pilate's wife is involved in this conflict. Through a dream, the *genius* of Esau/Rome tries to wring himself out of the entwining by Jacob/Christ. The woman "sees" in her dream that Jesus is the Righteous one, and what will be the consequences if he is killed by Rome. By getting this picture of the terrible effects, she *suffers* "many things," as the text says. The angelic prince "sees" very far, and shares some of the resulting misery with the woman. In her suffering, the whole of Rome suffers, for the angelic

25. This is one of those essential points in which I seriously differ from De Graaff; he says beautiful things about the centurion, but he completely distorts v. 11-12 (1989:140-144).
26. Cf. Ibid. (1989:468-484).

prince realizes that Jesus's death means the ultimate triumph of Jesus and Israel, and the fall of Rome. But the woman's dream does not help. Pilate washes his hands in "innocence," but in fact he consciously chooses, and through him the angelic prince, the other way which Isaac had pointed out (Gen. 27:39-40),

> ... and by your sword you shall live,
> and you shall serve your brother;
> and it shall be, when you rove around [or, obtain the dominion],
> that you shall break his yoke from your neck.

Rome wants to prevail. It wishes to live by its sword for many more centuries, also after its "Christianization" as we will see, and even to obtain the dominion over "brother" Israel. The fall of Jerusalem in 70 AD seems to ensure Rome's triumph: Edom has broken Jacob's yoke from its neck. What a self-deceit! Rome even believes it can take the liberty to scornfully deal with the King of the Jews. Roman soldiers mock him (27:27-31). Has not Rome all power? It can take the liberty to sneer at the pretensions of Jacob's birthright. It not only rejects Jacob, but it mocks him, beats him, spits on him. And this is what Rome has done throughout the centuries, *not the least "Christianized" Rome.*

Thank God, many in Rome have sought and found the other way: to bless Jacob, to own Jacob's Messiah, and thus to find the way of peace and salvation. We see this in a remarkable way in the testimony of the Roman centurion at the cross (also see Appendix 9).[27] When Jesus dies, it appears as if Rome has gained the ultimate victory over him; but that is only seemingly so. Right at the moment that Jesus enters death, his power reveals itself in an impressive way: the veil of the temple is torn in two from top to bottom, the earth shakes, the rocks are split, and many deceased saints are raised. The centurion with his men, who had to guard Jesus, have well

27. Cf. Ibid. (1989:500-501).

fulfilled their task. But then they see something of the glory of this seemingly pitiful, crucified man. They observe the tremendous natural phenomena. And then we read, "they were filled with awe" (Matt. 27:54). A Roman troop that is afraid of a dead man on a cross! That is unheard of. They submit to the crucified Jew, and this even after he has died. In Matthew's Gospel, it is the whole group of soldiers that speaks the words of capitulation, "Truly this was the Son of God!"

This is a striking confession. These hardened soldiers are of below, of Edom/Rome, of the earth. But here they stand eye to eye with a truly divine person. Above his head it is written, "This is Jesus, the King of the Jews" (v. 37). Before this divine king, the Roman bows down; Esau bows before Jacob! Edom blesses Jacob by blessing the true "Jacob," the King of the Jews. This is the very first victory of the crucified Jesus over the angelic prince of Rome. The first Roman troop is withdrawn from the power of Rome's *genius* and brought under the supremacy of the King of the Jews. Thus, Esau is blessed because he blesses Jacob. That is one of the most essential elements of world history.

Chapter 5
The "Christianization" of the Roman Empire

5.1. The "God" of Christendom

5.1.1. Christian Intermediate Beings?

IN PREVIOUS CHAPTERS, we have drawn the attention to the "mixed" character of Western culture. In this culture, the first we have to do with is the *Satan* ("adversary"), Samael, the angelic prince of the Roman Empire. He represents the purely "pagan" element in Western culture, as this comes to light within this culture ever more clearly, particularly since the Renaissance. But on the other hand, something special is the matter with Western culture, which did not hold for the previous empires or cultures. This is the fact that in the fourth century this culture has become a "Christian" culture.

As to Israel, there is no difference in this regard: all four empires had to do with Israel and have been judged, or will be judged, on this very point (Dan. 7; Rev. 13 and 19). However, with regard to Christendom there is a difference. The previous empires or cultures never knew such a thing as Christianity: a religion which on the one hand calls itself after the God of Jacob and after the Messiah of Israel, and on the other hand has committed the greatest crimes of all history over against Israel, and has denied the true Christ of the Scriptures in all conceivable ways.[1]

Of course, we have to make a clear distinction here. We do not speak of true, biblical Christianity, but of the Christendom of history, the established nominal Christendom of Western culture. This is the official Christendom of the Roman Empire since Constantine the Great, which had become the *imperium Romanum christianum*. Christianity is here pre-eminently the "Roman religion," especially since the fall of the (West-)Roman Empire, with still the same capital Rome. It is the religion with still a *pontifex maximus* at its head, as Rome's pagan chief priest and the emperor had been before the pope, with a corresponding hierarchical structure as the ancient Roman Empire possessed, and full of other ancient Roman institutions, offices and traditions. In this way, Western culture since the fourth century has indeed pre-eminently become a "Christian" culture. But if, as I claimed, this is not the true, biblical Christendom, what then is the nature of this "Christendom"? We have previously seen that the questions concerning the essence of a culture particularly involve the questions concerning the angelic prince of that culture. If the Christ of the Scriptures is not the Lord of Christian culture as a whole, but only the Lord of believers faithful to the Scriptures, we have to ask who is the "lord," or who are the "lords" of Western, Christian culture.

In this regard, the early Christian writers give us a striking answer. Of course, they were quite familiar with the existence of national angelic princes. Pseudo-Clemens[2] (second-fourth century?) for one says that God divided the nations of the earth into seventy-two parts, and placed an angel over each of them, but over Israel he placed the greatest among the arch-

1. This has been described in a striking way in the story of the high inquisitor in Dostoevsky's magistral analysis of Christian culture: *The Brothers Karamazov* (see Ouweneel 2003).
2. *Recognitiones* (of Pseudo-Clemens) 2,42; thus too the Syrian church father, Ephraem.

angels. According to Clemens of Alexandria (c. 200),[3] God set angels over nations and states; elsewhere[4] he apparently alludes to Deuteronomy 32:8-9, namely, to the probably correct reading of Qumran and the antique versions of it ("sons of God" instead of "sons of Israel") (see § 2.1.3). Origen (early third century), too, often speaks of national angels on the basis of Deuteronomy 32:8-9.

That which interests us now is that the church fathers not only knew of national angels in general, but also of such an angelic prince for Christendom. They mention this in line with the doctrine crept in at an early stage involving that the Christian church would have taken over the position, the blessings and the promises of Israel ("supersessionism"). In this view, the church is the "spiritual Israel." Along with this, also Michael, the angelic prince of Israel, was annexed by the church fathers. Thus we read,[5] "Michael... who has the authority over this nation and rules over them." Of course, the expression "this nation" originally refers to the Jews, but is applied here to Christendom. Elsewhere we find the view that, just before the destruction of Jerusalem in 70 AD, the angels had left the rejected people, with them Michael too, and these would then have "deserted" to the Christianized gentiles.[6] Of course, we emphatically reject this idea of Michael's desertion, for Daniel 12 and Revelation 12 point out that Michael remains Israel's advocate, if not angelic prince, until the second coming of Christ. My point is now only to show that the early church was familiar with the notion of national angelic princes, and even with the idea of an angelic prince of Christendom, even if they erred as to the latter's identity.

By the way, this error shows that the church fathers intuitively sensed a parallel between Israel and Christendom.

---

3. *Stromateis* 6,157 (Dind. 3,241).
4. *Stromateis* 7,6 (Dind. 3,255).
5. *Pastor of Hermas* 8.3,3.
6. Vgl. Flavius Josephus, *De Bello Judaico* VI,298/9 (V,3), Eusebius, *Historia Ecclesiastica* III.8,5.6.

As long as Israel went its way with YHWH, it was his direct inheritance, and there was no question of the intervention of an angelic prince. But, as discussed before, Israel departed from YHWH and entered upon the way of the gentiles. Finally, it was even led into exile among the gentiles. In a certain sense, it never really "returned" from this exile because, from Zerubbabel to the fall of Jerusalem in 70 AD, the Jews in Palestine remained a part of the respective world-empires, and were therefore factual exiles in their own land (cf. Neh. 9:37). From Israel's idolatry and the subsequent exile onward, Israel too was placed under the supervision of an angelic prince. To be sure, this was Michael, the chief of the angelic princes, but he was still an "intermediate being" between YHWH and Israel (Dan. 10:21; 12:1).

Christendom, as far as it departed from God, has been placed under such an angelic prince, too. However, this is not a good angel like Michael. In the book of Revelation, the "great whore" is nominal Christendom as centered in Rome, riding on the "beast," the Roman Empire. Like two wings, a religious and a political one, they form one power, standing under the supervision of the "dragon," the angelic prince of the Roman Empire. A distorted, syncretistic "Christendom" conquered the previously pagan Roman Empire. Within that Christendom, there were many true Christians, who as martyrs gave their lives for their heavenly Lord. But the system of which they were a part stood under the power and the influence of Samael, the angelic prince of Rome. Especially after the "Christianization" of the empire under Constantine and his successors, the mass of the "Christians" lost the personal, vital link with the God of Jacob. As a consequence, it became possible that, here too, "intermediate beings," but then diabolical powers, placed themselves between the God of gods and the Christianized West, the "people of the Christians."

Throughout the centuries, a "remnant" of faithful believers preserved the living communion with Christ. Often, this "remnant" placed itself beside the main road, that is, kept aloof of all the main events as they occurred in the heart of Christendom, as we will see. But the mass of Christendom did, and does, not know this vital link. It does not know the personal communion with Israel's God; it only knows the angelic princes, the intermediate beings, who factually have taken the place of Christ and in his stead have become an object of worship and service (cf. Col. 2:18).

Of course, in this view it is of vital importance that these angelic princes venerated by (the mass of) Christendom are viewed as Christ himself or, as we will see, as his apostles, Peter in particular. If one accepts this viewpoint, a totally new light is thrown upon the history of Christendom, or Western culture. The "Peter" venerated in the church of Rome only exhibits a vague likeness with the apostle Peter of the New Testament. And the "Christ" worshipped by the mass of the Christians—Catholic, Orthodox, Protestant— only exhibits a vague likeness with the Christ of the Scriptures. The latter is only known to the narrow line of those believers faithful to the Scriptures—within the Catholic, Orthodox, and Protestant churches—a line running through the whole of church history.[7] After all, even that which in the Reformation was truly a great work of God remained only a narrow line in church history. Within Protestantism, too, on the whole only a "remnant" has known the communion with the Christ of the Scriptures.

It is not at all strange to assume the worship of false "christs" in church history. Our Lord himself warned (Matt. 24:24; cf. Mark 13:22),

> ... false christs [Gr. *pseudochristoi*] and false prophets will arise and perform great signs and wonders, so as to lead astray, if possible, even the elect.

Usually, it is assumed that by these "pseudochrists" earthly

7. A church-historical work like that by Broadbent (1931) intends to throw light upon these Christians "beside the main road," who throughout the centuries have pursued the line of biblical Christianity.

people are meant, and this may certainly be the primary intention of the text. But would there be real imitation-messiah's on earth without spiritual pseudochrists "behind" them? These do make use of human instruments, but they themselves are angelic powers. Paul clearly states that our spiritual warfare is not primarily against people of flesh and blood, but against the powers behind them: the "world-rulers [or, cosmic powers] of this darkness," the "spiritual [forces] of evil" in the heavenly regions (Eph. 6:12). Also think of 2 Cor. 11:4, where Paul speaks of "another [Gr. *allos*] Jesus," that is a "Jesus" besides the Lord Jesus of the Scriptures, in a direct parallel with "a different [Gr. *heteros*] spirit." We have to do here with spiritual powers, which sometimes even adorn themselves with the name "Jesus." This also occurs with certain people who have come under the occult influence of such "Jesus" spirits.[8] Now, if we have evidence that indeed there are spirits that present themselves as Christ, it is not strange that whole multitudes would worship such "pseudochrists," "pseudoprophets" (e.g., 2 Pet. 2:1; 1 John 4:1 Gr.), and "pseudapostles" (see 2 Cor. 11:13 Gr.), that is, spiritual angelic powers.

The view presented here implies that the history of Western culture, or of Christendom, exhibits at least the following lines. First, the line of *Samael*, the angelic prince of ancient, pagan Rome, which over against the Christians behaved like a "roaring lion" (1 Pet. 5:8).[9] In the fourth century, the activity of Satan as a roaring lion seems to have been rather suppressed by the Christianization of the Roman Empire. The power of this lion, however, remained perceptible and, particularly since the Renaissance, increased enormously. In general, the Enlightenment sharply turned itself against Christianity, not the least against the Roman church. That

8. See Ouweneel (1988a:271-273).
9. The name "lion," which people like to associate with Christ (cf. Rev. 5:5), seems strange with regard to Satan. In Semitical thought, however, the lion was sometimes associated with the serpent or dragon, as in Ps. 91:13. On the temple of Marduk in Nippur stood a monster, which exhibited features of both the lion and the serpent.

was certainly no camouflage, but real hatred.

Secondly, there is the line of the pseudochrists, who along with the Christianization of the Roman Empire came to ever increasing power. Here, Satan transformed himself into an "angel of light" (2 Cor. 11:14). It cannot be denied that this historical phase also brought a certain (outward) cultural blessing upon the West. Our Western culture not only rests upon the ancient components of Hellenistic and Roman, and also Celtic, Germanic and Islamic culture, but in particular on Christianity. However, we have to remember here that this "Christianity" does not primarily refer to the influence of the biblical Christ, but to the influence of the pseudochrists, the angelic princes, or "gods," of Christendom. Further down, we will more closely investigate the identity of these "gods."

There is yet another good reason to clearly distinguish these two forms of Samael, the "roaring lion" and the "angel of light." Since the Christianization of Europe, Satan reveals himself to the Christians as an "angel of light." But for the Jews he generally remained the "roaring lion." As said before, one of the keys to understanding Western cultural history lies in the conflict between Jacob and Esau, between Israel and Edom, between the Jews and the Roman Empire. Unfortunately, with regard to *this* conflict the question whether we have to do with a pagan or a Christianized Roman Empire makes no difference. Also, after the Christianization of the empire, in Europe alternately cultural powers (read, angelic princes) dominated that either bowed down before the God of Jacob, or, under their "Christian" cloak, fiercely fought against the God of Jacob. When we are now to consider the Christianization of the empire under Constantine the Great, this fact may peculiarly strike us.

5.1.2. The Roman Empire Before Christianization

The metamorphosis of Samael, the ancient angelic prince of Rome, from a roaring lion into an angel of light, took place at the Christianization of the Roman Empire. This Christianization made a start under the great emperor, Constantine (306-337). Let us first briefly look at the developments preceding this Christianization.

Around 200 AD, the Roman Empire had finally become a great cosmopolitan whole, in which one could truly speak of one general civilization. In this empire, Latin or Greek was understood by every civilized person. This unity in culture and language had been prepared by the providence of God in order to enable the general extension of Christianity in the whole empire. The Roman philosopher and politician Cicero (106-43 BC) wrote, "We have overcome all the nations of the world because we have realized that the world is directed and governed by the will of the gods."[10] It was the "gods" who had decided that Rome was to rule the world.

The gods were experienced in Rome as a *reality*: Romans only worshipped gods insofar as these had clearly manifested themselves through miraculous signs. One example of this is the way in which the Etruscan goddess, Juno, was brought to Rome.[11] People were aware of the spiritual powers that had made this world-empire so great. Romulus was the founder of Rome, and was considered to be the son of Mars, the impetuous war-god, one of the oldest and most venerated gods of the Italic peninsula, progenitor of the Romans. However, it is his father, Jupiter, literally the "Godfather," who became the supreme lord of the Roman Empire. As an angelic prince he too was a reality; emperor Augustus, the earthly embodiment of the angelic prince, even claimed to behold him in his dreams.

Over against such divine powers, the conflict with the new "god," whom the Christians preached in an exclusive manner, was all the more acute. Like Judaism, but other than the pagan religions, Christianity was absolute in the sense that it pretended to preach the sole and only truth. It is important to see this so as to understand why, during the third century, the

10. *De Haruspicum Responsis* 19.

11. Comte (1994:27).

Roman emperors so fiercely persecuted this very Christianity. Within the empire, numerous religions and philosophies were competing, and they were all tolerated by the Roman authorities. The council of priests in Rome, under the direction of the chief priest, the *pontifex maximus*, was never reluctant to add a new deity to their Pantheon (cf. Acts 17:16,18,23). Because of their pragmatic nature, the Romans realized that gods and religions could better be incorporated than persecuted. However, the point was that Christianity declined being incorporated because it claimed to know the truth alone, at the exclusion of all other religions and philosophies.

Moreover, there was another serious matter. The Roman emperors united more functions in themselves than any world-ruler before them, and this made them to some extent superhuman. A person enjoying so much the favor of the gods was considered to be divine himself. As the many heterogeneous nations and races within the empire found their unity in the central imperial government, also all the religions within the empire had to find their unity in the emperor, who was worshipped as a god. Since Julius Caesar, this central figure not only held the office of *pontifex maximus*, but from Augustus onward, each emperor at his death was declared a deity by the Senate. The totally corrupted Gaius Caligula (37-41) asserted, already during his life, that he was a god, and wanted to erect a statue for himself—in the temple of Jerusalem of all places. The emperor Domitian (81-96), who ruled as a tyrant, demanded of his subjects that they address him as "Lord and God." He persecuted the Jews and the Christians, who refused the demanded worship. Adherents of no matter what religion or philosophy were tolerated by the Romans on the condition that they would pay the emperor divine homage. Precisely the Jews and the Christians, with their exclusive pretensions, could not possibly bring themselves to do this. Here lies the main reason for the horrible persecutions that were organized against the Christians in the first and the second, and particularly the third century.

It is quite understandable why the Romans were so wroth with the Christians. The latter reserved titles as *kyrios* ("lord") and *sotèr* ("savior") exclusively for God and for Christ. Their refusal to address the emperor in this way was considered by the Romans not only as sacrilege, but also as high treason. Those who refused to pay the homage to the emperor that was due to him were not good patriots, or even more strongly, were enemies of the state. The worship of the emperor greatly contributed to the unity and harmony of the empire; it was the binding factor in the plurality of religions and nations. This was the reason why the Christians were so heavily blamed for being spoilsports. Remarkably enough, it was particularly the "good" emperors who persecuted the Christians, such as the famous Stoic "soldiers' emperor" Marc Aurelius (161-180). These were the very emperors who strived for the unity of the empire and fought the inner corruption as best they could. They considered the Christians to be troublesome obstructors in the realization of these, in themselves noble, ends. Of course, the Christians strongly resisted these accusations with the argument that they too desired the unity and the peace of the empire, and in their prayers for the emperor wished nothing but the best for him, as was argued by the great Christian Apologist Tertullian in his famous *Apologeticum*.

We should not commit the error of rejecting the claims of the Roman emperors too quickly. In the previous chapters we saw that the mightier a ruler is, the closer he is associated with the angelic prince of the empire, up to the point that we may almost speak of an embodiment ("incorporation"). The Roman mind was quite conscious of this association, as is clear from the deification of the emperor; after all, the angelic prince is a "deity"! It is also clear from the notion of the *genius*, mentioned before. This Latin word, derived from *gigno* (old Latin, *geno*, "to beget, to generate"), literally means "begetter, generator." It refers to a divine being representing the procreative power of the father, accompanying a man as a guardian spirit throughout life, governing his fate, and sharing in his joys and sorrows. Every person, but also each city and every land, had such a *genius*. The *genius* (angelic prince!) of the Roman Empire is the *genius* of the emperor. The divine claims of the emperor were therefore far more "true" than people are usually aware of. But this makes it the more understandable why the Christians could not worship the emperor as *kyrios* and *theos*. They knew the angelic prince of Rome only too well (Rev. 12:9). If they would have paid divine homage to the emperor, they would have fallen into the temptation which Satan placed before Christ, when showing him all the kingdoms of the (Roman) *oikoumenè* and saying (Luke 4:6-8):

> "All this power I will give you, and their glory; for [this] has been delivered to me [cf. John 19:11!], and to whom I will I give it. You therefore, if you will worship before me, it will all be yours." And Jesus answering said to him, "It is written, You shall worship the Lord [*Kyrios*!] your God [*Theos*!], and him only shall you serve."

By the end of the third century, after a time of great chaos and anarchy in the empire, the emperor Diocletian came to power (284-305). This son of a slave founded an absolutistic monarchy, in which the inhabitants of the empire were no citizens anymore but subjects, even forced laborers. As a *kyrios kai theos* (Latin, *dominus et deus*), titles which he, as said before, demanded for himself already during his life, the emperor stood at the head of the officials, not appointed by the people but by himself. Perhaps in no Roman emperor the features of the dragon, certainly with regard to the Christians, came more clearly to light than in Diocletian. It was he who released the heaviest of all persecutions of Christians in Roman history, which lasted from 303 to 311. Samael, the angelic prince of "Edom," the god of the *oikoumenè*, presented himself as the "roaring lion" and openly fought all Christian worshippers of the God of Jacob.

However, it belongs to the miraculous enigmas of

history that this cruel emperor did not touch "Jacob" himself, the Jews! In 286, he issued an edict in which all nations were obliged to sacrifice to the Roman gods, with the exception of the Jews. True, they still were not allowed to enter Jerusalem, but in their public religious meetings they were protected by the Roman authorities. In general, we can state that each power persecuting the Jews is an *evil* power, but that powers favoring the Jews are therefore not necessarily *good* powers.

Usually, we only see one side of the really tremendous turn which, so shortly after, the God of Jacob brought about in the history of the Roman Empire. It is this side: within a lifetime, Christianity changed from a cruelly persecuted religion into the official state religion of the Roman Empire. But historically and metahistorically, the other side of the "great turn" is equally important. The Jews had long been protected by the Roman emperors, but "thanks" to Christianity, within a short time they got into a position in which they gradually lost all rights which they had enjoyed under the "dragon." At the moment when for Christendom the day broke, for the Western Jews a night was closing in, which, apart from some lighter periods, was to last until far into the twentieth century.

The instrument for the "great turn" was Constantine. In order to understand how he got the supremacy we must know that Diocletian used the governmental system of the "tetrarchy." That is, while he himself as *augustus* ruled over the eastern part of the empire, he appointed a *co-augustus* over the western part. Under each *augustus* stood a *caesar*, who was to succeed his *augustus*. In 305, Diocletian forced his *co-augustus* Maximian to abdicate "voluntarily" with him; they were succeeded as *augusti* by their two *caesars*. The one of the West was Constantius Chlorus, a wise and moderate man; the one of the East was Galerius. It is remarkable that Constantius hardly, or not at all, carried out the edicts against the Christians in his part of the empire, possibly out of sympathy with Christianity. Eusebius[12] calls him "very pious and virtuous," and refers to him as an adherent of "monotheism," which worshipped the *summus deus* (the supreme god).[13] Even more remarkable is that the convinced polytheist, Galerius, with his co-rulers Constantine and Licinius (see the next sections), by means of an edict in 311 put an end to the persecutions of the Christians. These were the forebodings of the "great turn."

5.2. Constantine the Great

5.2.1. Past History

When Constantius served as a soldier in Upper Musia (now Serbia), he was illegitimately married to a *stabularia* (inn-keeper), called (Flavia) Helena, a woman with an excellent character. In that region, in the town Naissus (today Niš, in South-Servia), around 280, a son was born of this relationship called Flavius Valerius Aurelius Constantinus, the later emperor Constantine I the Great. When, in 293, Constantius was appointed *caesar* in the West, he brushed Helena aside and married Theodora, the stepdaughter of the emperor Maximian. At the instigation of her son, Helena later became a very pious Christian, who was afterwards canonized by the church. At a high age, she made a pilgrimage to the Holy Land, where, as tradition records, she discovered the cross of Christ and founded the Church of the Holy Sepulchre. It was on the island with her name that Napoleon spent the last year of his life.

Constantine spent his early youth in the service of the emperor Diocletian in the latter's residence Nicomedeia in Bithynia. In 305, when his father became *augustus* in the West, Constantine was passed over at the choice of the new *caesar* in favor of Severus. He fled from Nicomedeia and joined his father in the campaign against the Picts in Britannia. When, already the next year at York, his father died, Constantine was immediately appointed *augustus* by his troops instead of

12. *Historia Ecclesiastica* 9,9.
13. *Vita Constantini* 3,37.

Severus. Shortly after, the latter was eliminated by Maxentius, the son of Maximian, who in 305 had been passed over too. Now a time of great confusion began, in which at a certain moment there were even six rivalling *augusti*. In 307, Constantine married Fausta, the daughter of the still living Maximian, who in spite of his (forced) abdication was his greatest rival, but with whom from now on he kept a certain peace. In 310, however, Maximian rebelled against Constantine and was executed.

Already in this period, Constantine was much occupied with religious questions because of the unmistakable calling he felt with regard to the entire empire. He ascribed this calling to the sun god, the *Sol Invictus* ("invincible sun"), as is shown by coin effigies of 310, after the fall of Maximian. This sun god is the god of the whole empire, as had already been announced by the emperor Aurelian (270-275). In our view, this god therefore is none other than Samael, the "dragon," the god of the *oikoumenè*. This is the same god as Bel, the Babylonian chief god.[14] He is identical with Apollo, the son of the chief god Zeus, and concerned with the wellbeing of suffering mankind. As such he is the counterpart of Christ, the Son of God, the Savior of the world (see further about the important parallel between Apollo and Christ in Appendix 9).

In the views held at that time, the emperor who placed himself under Apollo's protection was called to determine the fate of the whole empire, as is shown in the *panegyricus* (laudatory oration) which in 310 was held in Trier in honor of Constantine.[15] Here his claim to power is not founded upon his participation in the tetrarchy anymore, but upon his imperial descent. The god Apollo, who in Gallia was worshipped as the sun god, was, according to this panegyric, the *genius* of this dynasty, and of Constantine in particular. In a Gallic temple of Apollo, Constantine allegedly had seen this god, accompanied by Victoria, the goddess of victory. These two

14. See § 9.3 note 7.

15. See *Panegyric* 7 with Galletier.

gods granted him a laurel-wreath with the number XXX, and thus promised him the victory and a long life.[16] This connection with Apollo always remained; even in 315, Constantine's profile is depicted against that of Apollo on a medal coined in Pavia.

In 311, the emperor of the East, Galerius, died a few days after his edict of tolerance. This left the empire with four *augusti*: in the West, Constantine contra Maxentius, and in the East, Licinius (who in 308 had become *augustus* and had been a convinced co-signatory of the tolerance-edict) contra Maximinus Daia (since 305 *caesar* of Galerius and a fierce persecutor of the Christians). Constantine managed to associate himself with Licinius by promising him his sister Constantia as wife. Then he marched against his rival Maxentius and managed to inflict a crushing defeat upon him at the Milvian Bridge on October 28, 312, which cost Maxentius his power and his life. In this way, Constantine obtained undivided dominion in the whole European West and in North Africa. In February 313, he held a conference with Licinius in Milan, where in the famous convention of Milan the two emperors agreed upon freedom of religion for the whole empire. Later that year, Licinius defeated his own rival, Maximinus Daia. The two remaining *augusti* and brothers-in-law ruled together in alternating friendship and war until 324, when Constantine invaded the eastern part of the empire. After several victories, he forced Licinius to abdication, and shortly after had him executed, in spite of a promise of safe-conduct. From 324 until his death in 337, Constantine the Great was thus the sole and supreme ruler of the empire. By then the "great turn" had already taken place.

The actual "turn" began during the conflict between Constantine and Maxentius. In the time of that conflict, Constantine, though no persecutor of the Christians, was himself still a representative of the "dragon," whereas Maxentius, in the

16. Ibid. 7,21.

first part of 312, had attempted to gain the favor of the Christians by giving back to the church in Rome its confiscated goods. However, these were not the factors that determined the outcome of the conflict, but totally new events, which occurred entirely unexpectedly. Against the advice of his officers, Constantine with extreme speed crossed the Alps, occupied a number of cities in the north of Italy, and led his army in hot haste to Rome, which his numerically stronger rival wanted to defend as his last bulwark. During this campaign, the decisive turn in the life of Constantine took place, which eventually would lead to the great turn in the whole empire.

5.2.2. The "Great Turn"

It is important to carefully study the sources with regard to this turn. The first report of it is supplied by Lactantius,[17] who around 318, that is only six years later, tells us the following:[18]

> During his sleep, Constantine was exhorted to place the heavenly sign of God on the [soldiers'] shields, and thus enter into combat. He did as he had been commanded and put on [a sign for] "Christ" [in the form of] a transverse letter X with a curved upper part.

Apparently, Lactantius refers here to the *crux monogrammatica* (the monogram cross), consisting of a transverse x, that is, +, of which the upper part was bent to the right. This yields a Christ monogram, as the sign consisting of X and P, better known to us.

Here we have the tradition in its soberest form. A "simple" dream, which demanded a rather simple action, but one with tremendous consequences. For the first time in history, a Roman emperor with a Roman army went to battle, not under a pagan, idolatrous banner, but under the protection of the

17. *De mortibus persecutorum* 44.
18. *Commonitus est in quiete Constantinus, ut caeleste signum dei notaret in scutis atque ita proelium committeret. Facit ut iussus est et trans versa littera X summo capite circumflexo Christum notat.*

"god of the Christians" (the reader will be able to presume why I write "god" with a small letter here). Therefore, when Constantine gained a sensational victory, this necessarily had to be ascribed to the "god of the Christians." It was this god who henceforth had to be worshipped as the guardian god of both emperor and empire.

The tradition had grown quite considerably by the time bishop Eusebius of Caesarea, a personal friend of the emperor, describes the story a quarter of a century later in his *Vita Constantini* ("Life of Constantine"). According to him, Constantine wanted to undertake the campaign against Maxentius under the protection of the god of his father. He therefore asked this god to reveal himself to him and to grant him his help. Immediately after this, in the late afternoon, he and his army saw "at the sky, above the sun, the victory sign of the cross of light," along with the Greek words: *toutôi nika*, that is, "be victorious by this," or "be victorious through this [sign]."[19] In the following night, Christ appeared to him with the cross, and commanded him to make a copy of it and carry it in his campaign as an amulet. Thereupon, the emperor had an imperial standard made according to his indications, consisting of a long rod with a transverse rod and at the top a circle, within which the Christ monogram was put. This was the monogram that Constantine later also carried on his helmet. At the transverse rod a square flag was hung, and above this, on the longitudinal rod, the busts of Constantine and his sons were placed. This imperial standard was later called *labarum*.

People have attempted to discard this report by Eusebius as a later addition in his biography of Constantine, the more so because he does not mention the story in his *Church History* written around 324. What he does mention in this work[20] is a prayer by Constantine before he marched to Rome, in which

19. Cf. the Latin version: *in hoc [signo] vince*. In the text I implicitly reject explanations as those by Jones (1978:85ff.), who suggests that Constantine only observed a "halo phenomenon."

20. *Historia Ecclesiastica* 9,9.

he called upon "the God of heaven, and his Son and Word, our Lord Jesus Christ, the Savior of all." But at any rate we know that Eusebius certainly knew himself the story of the sign of the cross, for he clearly alludes to it in his panegyric at the governmental jubilee of the emperor in 335.[21] Nevertheless, we may be pretty sure that by the time Eusebius heard it the tradition had already been richly embellished. This does not stop us from maintaining the unmistakably historical kernel. This kernel is that Constantine was convinced that, at the beginning of his campaign against Maxentius, the sign of the cross of Christ had been revealed to him, and that with the latter's help he had gained the victory over his opponents, who still trusted in the power of the pagan gods.

It is equally undeniable that Constantine, by the latter part of 312, had accepted "Christ" as his guardian god. This is shown by all kinds of historical details, like the words of the pagan *panegyrist*, who in the autumn of 313 at Trier hailed the victory by Constantine over Maxentius.[22] It is remarkable that he did not give a name to the god who had granted him the victory, but only reported that Constantine, in conjunction with the god who was with him, had entered into combat. He had done so against the fears of his officers, because this god, with whom he was connected through a deep secret, had promised him the victory. It is even more remarkable that the panegyrist in his description of the emperor's triumphant entry into Rome did not speak of the victor's traditional trip to the Capitol and of the usual sacrifice to Jupiter. Apparently, Constantine skipped this. The panegyrist did oppose Maxentius's pagan practice of predicting the future by inspecting entrails, whereas Constantine had put his trust in the instructions of his god.

After Constantine's victory, the Roman Senate devoted to him a triumphal arch completed in 315 at Rome, which of course mainly reflected the idolatrous views of the pagan

21. *Tricennial Orations* 6.
22. *Panegyric* 9.

senators. Therefore, they had the emperor depicted with the attributes and the attitude of the *Sol Invictus*, but remarkably enough the inscription does not mention the name of the sun god, but ascribes the victory only to an "inspiration by the godhead" (*instinctu divinitatis*) (which may be understood as the neo-Platonic supreme being but also in a Christian way) and to the "mental power" (*mentis magnitudine*) of Constantine. By the way, also the tolerance-edict of Milan (313) had spoken of the deity in very general words: *summa divinitas cuius religioni liberis mentibus obsequimur* ("the highest deity whom we worship each according to his understanding"), or even vaguer: *quidquid divinitatis in sede caelesti* ("whatever deity may reside in heaven"). This was something every pagan could live with.

Another memorial of the victory was the statue of the emperor on the Forum Romanum. Eusebius writes about this,[23]

> [Constantine], according to the piety deeply implanted in him, neither triumphing over the shouts raised [at his entry], nor delighted by the acclamations rendered to him, rather noticing the help which he had received of God, immediately commanded that a trophy of the Savior's suffering be placed in the hand of his own statue. And when they had erected his statue, which thus held the saving sign of the cross in its right hand, at the most public square of Rome, he commanded that the following inscription be written on it in the Roman language, as follows: "By this saving sign, the true ornament of bravery, I have saved your city and delivered it from the yoke of the tyrant. Moreover, I have restored both the Senate and the Roman people in their old dignity and splendor."

In the Greek style of this inscription, we can still see some traces of the Latin original. This quotation clearly refers to the "heavenly sign of God" mentioned by Lactantius, the Christian cross, probably in monogrammatic form. Through this unusual statue, Constantine wanted to openly confess his

23. *Historia Ecclesiastica* 9,9.

attachment to the Christian cross over against the people of Rome. After these events, the Christ monogram was therefore to appear more and more often on Roman coins.

By the end of that same year 312, Constantine writes to Maximinus that the persecutions of the Christians in the eastern part of the empire have to be stopped immediately.[24] To the prefect Anulinus in North-Africa he writes that the confiscated goods of the church have to be given back. To the Catholic bishop Caecilian of Carthage, he sends in a letter a rather large sum for the clergy "of the legitimate and most-holy Catholic worship." In another letter to Anulinus, the clergy of the church of Carthage is exempted from public services, so that they can fully devote themselves to the accurate and worthy performance of the clerical service, to which Constantine apparently attaches great value.[25] Also the mentioned convention of Milan (February 313) shows the new attitude of Constantine. Thus, an imperial decree explicitly going back upon the Milan convention, expresses the conviction that, through the new favors bestowed upon Christianity,

> the divine favor towards us, which we have already experienced at many occasions, may continue in a stable and lasting way for all times.[26]

5.3. Metahistorical Meaning of the "Great Turn"

5.3.1. Who Appeared to Constantine?

It can hardly be doubted that the "conversion" of Constantine entailed a tremendous revolution in the cultural history of Europe and of Christendom, even an event of world-historical meaning. However, with regard to the cause and the meaning of this turn the opinions strongly divert. Already Edward Gibbon (1737-1794), in his famous *The History of the Decline and Fall of the Roman Empire* (1776-88), did not discern

24. Lactantius, *De mort. pers.* 37,1.
25. Eusebius, *Historia Ecclesiastica* 10,5, 10,6 and 10,7.
26. Ibid. 10,5; cf. Lactantius 48,11.

anything else in it than a victory of Christian syncretism over the antique world that had become decadent. The Marxists, but also Arnold J. Toynbee (1889-1975) for one, only saw a class-war, a revolution of the proletarians, against the upper class that had ruled until that moment. It does not have to be denied that such factors, and others, may have played a role in the "great turn." An example of these is the high moral character of most Christians, that had so clearly manifested itself during the heavy persecutions. However, what is still lacking here, in my opinion, is insight into the decisive meta-historical factors. To get some more light in this respect we will ask ourselves: (1) what exactly happened at Constantine's "conversion," and (2) what did the "great turn" mean for the Roman Empire and for the Christian church?

Concerning the first question: I have argued already that the historical facts undeniably show that Constantine, at the beginning of his campaign against Maxentius, really became convinced that the sign of the cross had been revealed to him. But then immediately the question arises: of what nature was this transcendent experience? For the answer to this question there seem to be only two possibilities: either it was a diabolical one, or it really was an appearance of Christ (or of a good angel of God). What was it?

At first sight, it seems rather difficult to think of a satanic appearance, or an appearance of a direct servant of Satan. So far, Constantine had been a servant of the "dragon," and after his "conversion" he turned his back to the "dragon," at least seemingly. Can this be the intention of a satanic appearance? Or was this a satanic ruse? Was this not precisely a proof that Satan had laid down his form of a "roaring lion," and had now taken on the form of an "angel of light"? It is to be noted here that, if we may believe the tradition, the "imperial sun god" and the goddess Victoria, that is, Samael with his consorts, had promised him the victory and a long life. In this way, possibly anticipating the important turn of Constantine, they had enforced themselves on him as his guardian gods.

Has Constantine rejected them by choosing their greatest enemy, the god of the Christians, as his guardian god? Is the situation not rather that he *kept* serving his old gods, be it now in the new form of an "angel of light"? Is not precisely the *sun god* the very form of Satan as an angel of *light*, as the "son of the dawn" (Isa. 14:12)?

In any case, the statue that Constantine had erected for himself in 330, in the newly founded Constantinople ("city of Constantine") as always depicts him in the attitude and the garment of the sun god, Apollo (Greek, Helios)! The statue was put in place by soldiers with candles in their hands, along with the burning of incense, and the pouring out of wine, exactly as it had always been done for the divine hero who had become founder and name-giver of a city. Constantine also remained the *pontifex maximus* of pagan religion in Rome until his death, as in fact he also was for the Catholic church—though not for the other Christian churches and communities, that he did not want to know, or even persecuted.

We should not be deceived by the tremendous blessing that Constantine's religious choice meant for the church: freedom of faith, possibilities for theological and pastoral development, free preaching of the gospel, extensive spreading. After all, this is a blessing of the God of gods, not thanks to, but in spite of, Satan. In the many new, beneficial laws that Constantine enacted this divine blessing clearly comes to light: he abolished the death penalty by crucifixion, the branding of a runaway slave's face ("because he is an image-bearer of God"), as well as the cruel gladiators' fights. Thus, the barbarism of paganism gradually gave way to a humanization of society. That is all a blessing of God, beyond all work of Satan. But at the same time, it is also an enormous camouflage, a great vanishing-trick of Satan, who gives the impression of having been banished through the front door and coming in again through the back door, now as a "good spirit," who wishes the best for the Christians.

At any rate, I find it very hard to assume that it was Christ, or an angel of Christ, who appeared to Constantine. Does Scripture give us a reason to suppose that Christ would appear to unbelieving generals? That he would take sides in a secular military conflict? That he would refer to the cross or the Christ monogram as a field-ensign? Is this idea not just as foolish and objectionable as the *Gott mit uns* ("God with us") written on the belts of the Prussian soldiers?

Other objections could be mentioned. For instance, if Christ had appeared to Constantine as genuinely as he did to Saul of Tarsus, one would expect this to have exerted an equally large effect on him. But this is precisely the point: it is doubtful whether Constantine ever became a true Christian. During his whole reign, he kept bearing the title of *pontifex maximus,* that was the title of the pagan head of the Roman state religion (and that, by the way, the pope still bears today). He may have entertained a deep interest for Christianity, but he committed crimes that are in absolute conflict with the Christian faith, like the jealous murdering of his son, Crispus, and his wife, Fausta. True, he regularly attended church services, but he only had himself baptized on his death-bed, because of the pagan idea of entering eternity with as few sins as possible. This baptism was carried out by an Arian, someone adhering to the denial of the Father's and the Son's equality in being. On the church in Constantinople, where he was buried, there was no cross, but a star—in fact the sign of Apollo.

A third group of objections refers to the consequences of the "great turn" for the church, consequences that definitely were not all positive. I mention in particular *caesaropapism*: the system that renders the church subservient to the state, and the church leaders subservient to the emperor. Constantine differed in no way from his predecessors in his longing for one strong and uniform state religion, which furthered the unity of the empire, and thus the power of the emperor. Constantine wanted to turn the church into a Roman imperial church, that is, a Roman-Catholic church, in which

"Catholic" refers to the universality of the empire. Of this church, he demanded to be the factual leader. Therefore, it was he who called together the episcopal synods, particularly the Council of Nicea (325), presided over them personally or through representatives, and also in other ways intervened in church affairs. A probably not born-again emperor, and afterwards each of his successors, thus became the factual head of Christendom. It was this head that appointed and dismissed bishops, even the bishop of Rome. It was he who at times favored the orthodox and persecuted the heretics, but at other times did the reverse. Later, this system characterized especially the eastern part of the empire. It became known there as "byzantinism"; but also in the West it had long after-effects.

Could that have been the intention of Christ, if indeed it was he who had appeared to Constantine? Caesaropapism, or byzantinism, is in flagrant contradiction with the New Testament, with the words of Christ himself. True, Constantine was no longer *dominus et deus*, but he did remain the only and direct representative and embodiment of the heavenly *dominus et deus*—and strictly speaking the earlier emperors had never been anything else. In this respect, really not much had changed, except that Constantine in name was the representative of a different *deus* than his predecessors had been.

The assertion that Christ did appear to the emperor, but that the latter did not act in his spirit, does not hold water. Constantine's actions were not in conflict with the appearance, but agreed with it. The god did not appear to a church leader to promise him the victory over the imperial persecutors, but appeared to the emperor himself, as the leader of the empire, who subsequently became the highest representative of "Christ" on earth, and thus automatically the highest authority within the church. This was not because he was a Christian with exceptional qualities but because he was the emperor. The power that the emperor in the church drew to himself was in absolute contradiction with Scripture—but in perfect agreement with the nature of the appearance.

Therefore, in my opinion this cannot possibly have been an appearance of Christ. It must have been a different *elohim*, a different celestial being, a "different Jesus," a *pseudochrist*, who places himself above Christendom, above the Christianized Roman Empire. As soon as we take this view, the difficulties mentioned disappear. We then can maintain that Constantine really had a supernatural appearance; that this appearance seemingly forced the "roaring lion" out of his position within the Roman Empire, even that this god became the new *genius* of the Roman emperor, and of most of his successors. We can maintain that this "light-angel" thus became the new god of the empire, even of a Christian empire, of Christendom, or, that he was the same *genius* in a new appearance. We can maintain that this god intentionally assumed many features of Christ, but to those who perceive more deeply he turns out to differ fundamentally from Him. We can maintain that this god nevertheless, especially at the outset, brought with him much (outward) blessing upon Christendom, but along with it much corruption. I even suggest that the supremacy of this new god in fact implied the "Fall of Christendom," as says the title of Gerrit J. Heering's (1879-1955) illustrious book.

Apart from the tremendous changes, it is particularly striking that so much remained the same. The new god was still the *genius* of the emperor. The bloody sacrifices were abolished, but instead, Christian *flamines* appeared, which is the name for the priests who were consecrated to a certain deity. In the cities, the children, led by their teachers, each day proclaimed the divine glory of the emperor just like before. No wonder; in the deeds of the "Christian" emperor the deeds of God, or the god, manifested themselves.

In chapter 6, we will attempt to further identify the new "god" of Rome.

5.3.2. The Consequences of the Appearance

By consenting to become a servant of the emperor, the church largely lost the possibilities and credibility of its divine mission to be a salt and a light in this world (Matt. 5:13-14). By placing itself under the protection of the emperor, it became an enormous, secular, even carnal power. This power ensured its position by privileges from the political authorities, and henceforth strived for dominion over all cultural areas, which as such are foreign to its nature. It even strived for absolute power over the bodies as well as the souls of the people (cf. Rev. 18:13). There was no lack of people: once Christianity had become the state religion of the Roman Empire, thousands flocked to the church, very often not because of a spiritual conviction, but only because of the social and economic advantages. Illustrious Christians of that time (fourth century), such as Ambrose[27] and Prudentius, saw in the Christianized empire the fulfillment of Christ's kingship, and the foreboding of his coming again. For those taking notice only of the outward consequences of the "great turn," which seem to be only blessed ones, this negative side is perhaps difficult to accept. But we should learn to give heed to metahistorical consequences.

At a superficial look, one might even think that, if it was not Christ who appeared to Constantine, at least it was an *elohim* (guardian angel) of the God of Jacob, and that the "conversion" of Constantine therefore implied the great prostration of Edom/Rome before the God of Jacob, and thus to Jacob himself. The prefect Pontius Pilate, once the representative of the emperor of Rome in Judea, rejected Christ and referred him to the cross. Now, an emperor of that same Rome bows down before the god of the Christians and turns the cross into a mark of honor of the empire. Edom blesses Jacob; this has entailed much blessing for Edom, for he who blesses Jacob, is blessed himself (Gen. 27:29).

However, here lies a very serious problem. Constantine blesses the god of the Christians, or what he holds to be their god, but certainly not the God of Jacob. How often have Chris-

27. See Kramer (1983:ch.5, particularly p. 140ff.).

tians, in their euphoria about the "great turn," neglected to pay attention to Constantine's attitude towards "Jacob," the Jews. The angelic prince of Constantine blesses the Christians, but curses the Jews. Only if we take Constantine's attitude towards the Jews into consideration, the "great turn" receives a more proper perspective. Heinrich Graetz (1817-1891), the great pioneer of Jewish historiography—he wrote between 1853 and 1875 eleven volumes *History of the Jews from the Oldest Times until Today*—already remarked,[28]

> Who can, in the astonishing event that a Jewish child from Nazareth could subdue thrones and empires to himself, overlook the fact that the development, necessary from a historical viewpoint, was to carry the old, worn out world to its grave and let arise a new one? Jewry might have rejoiced over this triumph of the spirit over violence rattling with the weapons, if triumphant Christendom had followed the gentleness of its founder. But its dominion, which in world history involves a decisive turn, only brought new, heavy and long-lasting trials over Jewry.

The convention of Milan (313), which promised freedom of conscience to all inhabitants of the Roman Empire, also held for the Jews. They kept the same rights that henceforth were also granted to the Christians. This freedom only lasted two years—but how significant are these years, in that Christians and Jews together enjoyed absolute freedom of religion within Western culture. And how terrible is it that it was the newly established Christendom, as soon as it had come to power and esteem, which took the Jews in an iron grip. In 315, the first decree against the Jews was promulgated. In this it was forbidden to assault Jews who converted to Christianity; neither were they allowed to convert non-Jews to Judaism. In all these cases, the persons concerned would be burned alive.[29] In this decree, the Jews are called a "pernicious sect" (*feralem sectam*) and a "wicked (criminal) sect" (*nefariam sectam*).

28. Graetz (repr. 1985).
29. *Codex Theodosianus* 16,8,I.

Other decrees against the Jews followed. They did not just come from a government that was still half pagan, as is perfectly clear from the Council of Nicea (325). This Council at least accomplished one good thing: it confirmed Athanasius's Scriptural doctrine of the deity of Christ and his equality in being with the Father over against the heresy of Arius. However, it at least did two bad things. First, it factually allowed the (probably not born again) emperor to demand and obtain the primacy within the church. Secondly, it assumed a very anti-Semitic attitude. The Christian Easter feast, which so far had always been celebrated together with the Jewish Passover feast, was severed from the latter. The reason was, as argued the emperor, and thus also the church, that[30]

> it would be unworthy, that at this holy feast we would follow the custom of the Jews, who defiled their hands with the most horrible crime and remained spiritually blind. In future, we no longer wish to have anything in common with the hostile people of the Jews, for our Savior pointed to us a different way.

A new imperial decree in 335 forbade the Jews again to bother their previous co-religionists who had become Christians. Neither were they allowed any attempts to win outsiders for their faith; they were not even allowed to convert or circumcise their own slaves, Christian or pagan. These were really imperial decrees, but it seems inconceivable that Constantine, who as such was a tolerant man and only interested in the unity and tranquility of the empire, would have promulgated them without the consent or even the insistence of the church.

Things were not different under Constantine's son and successor, Constantius (337-361), who aggravated some extant edicts and added new decrees, such as the prohibition to the Jews to buy or to possess Christian and even pagan slaves. Whereas elsewhere slavery was simply left intact, and even was accepted by the church, the descendants of those who had crucified the Son of God, as Eusebius put it, were not

30. Eusebius, *Vita Constantini*.

allowed to be master over the slaves freed by him. In economical respect, this prohibition struck the Jews very heavily, since at that time the entire economic life was based upon slaves' work. Henceforth, agriculture, the shipping-trade, and all kinds of handicraft had virtually become impossible for them. The ancient angelic prince of the Roman Empire had persecuted the Christians, but had often protected the Jews. The new angelic prince, however, granted secular power to the Christians and started for the Jews a long, heavy persecution under Christian dominion.

It is striking that the very emperor who returned to paganism, Julian the Apostate (361-363), again stood up for the Jews. In a famous letter, he asked the Jews to pray for his imperial office, so that, he says,[31]

> when I will have successfully finished the war with Persia, I may rebuild through my own efforts the holy city of Jerusalem, which for so many years you have desired to see inhabited, and may bring there immigrants, and together with you may glorify there the Most High God.

Very striking! Do we really have to assume that the angelic prince of this pagan emperor is nearer to the God of Israel than the angelic prince of the "Christian" emperors?

Metahistorically even more important is the fact that indeed, at the order of the emperor, the temple territory in Jerusalem was leveled and a beginning was made with the construction of a Third Temple. This was reported in the *Church History* of Salamanius Hermias Sozomenus (c. 450). This man, a born Palestinian, who claims to base his story on reports of eye-witnesses, tells us that an earthquake combined with fire put an end to the work. It was still far from God's time for the Third Temple. Moreover, Julian died shortly after, and when the power again got into the hands of "Christian" emperors, the chance for a restoration of the temple was entirely lost.

---

31. Goldberg (1976:224); also see Aalders (1983:109-112).

For the West as having turned Christian, it was to be a question of vital importance whether it would ever learn to bless Jacob—though of course this does not necessarily have to occur in the form of a rebuilding of the temple. However, the question does arise whether in the history of the Roman Empire a cultural power (read, an angelic prince) has been able to manifest itself that has maintained "Christendom" but precisely as a "Christian" power has blessed Jacob, in order to be blessed itself. On the whole, it was "Christendom" that throughout the centuries has placed upon itself a tremendous guilt over against Israel.

5.3.3. The "Roman-Catholic" Angelic Prince(s)

In § 4.2 I gave arguments for the thesis that the angelic prince who, from the "great turn" under Constantine the Great, dominates the Christian (that is, Roman-Catholic) Western world, cannot be Christ or an angel of Christ. However, at a superficial look it seems difficult to assume that he might be an angel of Satan. The greatest difficulty of such an interpretation is of course that people do not see a third possibility. Usually, we divide the realm of the angels in two great "blocks": "good" angels, who have remained faithful to God, and "evil" angels, who are servants of Satan. If this sharp division were correct, it is impossible to think of an angelic prince who would neither be an angel of God or Christ, nor an angel of Satan. The great question is, however, does Scripture indeed teach such a sharp division? My answer is that on the whole it does, but a division less sharp than is usually assumed.

First, we have seen that indeed there is a category that may be described as "angels of Satan,"[32] but that does not prove that all evil spirits are under his direct dominion. For instance, in 2 Peter 2:4-5 and Jude v. 6 we found a category of fallen angels who are evil spirits, but enclosed in the Tartarus. They thus seem to be clearly distinct from what we call demons in the usual sense, namely, the non-bound angels of

32. Matt. 25:41; Rev. 12:9.

Satan, freely roving around. As said before, these bound angels have often been linked with Genesis 6:1-4. Whatever may be thought of these difficult verses, he who, like me, strongly prefers to think here of the *bené ha-elohim* as angels, cannot get around the assumption that possibly also after the fall of Satan (that was before Gen. 3) angels have departed. Not all fallen angels fell at the fall of Satan.

Secondly, in chapter 2 we got an idea of what Scripture teaches about the so-called national angels, the guardian angels of the various nations. These national angels seem originally to be good angels, who nevertheless have often cared badly for their nations. They did not maintain justice among these nations, and they allowed themselves to be idolatrously worshipped by these nations as "gods." This is the reason why in Psalm 82, and for instance in Psalm 58:2, they are called by God to account for their deeds. These are angels who could hardly have been involved in the fall of Satan and his angels. They rather seem to be angels who after the fall of Satan were still angels faithful to God, but who have failed in their function of national angels, and who, through their idolatrous worship, have actually become rebels against the God of gods. It is possible that such departures are intended in Scriptures such as Job 4:18 and 15:15:

> Behold, in his [heavenly] servants he puts no trust,
> and he charges his angels with error.
>
> Behold, in his [heavenly] saints he puts no trust,
> and the heaven[lie]s are not pure in his sight.

Such Scriptures cannot be discarded as references to the fall of Satan, or as errors made by Elifaz. They seem to indicate that God at times did, or does, find error and impurity among the angels. This may involve direct rebellion, as in the insurrection of Lucifer, and also in Genesis 6:1-4. This leads to repudiation, to a deep fall, and everlasting damnation. However, apparently it may also be a departure that can be met by exhortation. In principle, such an error may be corrected; but it is quite possible that angels, once departed, eventually all land in the company of Satan and his angels. In that sense, I have no problems with the ultimate division of the angels into two parties. It may be that eventually all departed angels do have to be characterized as angels of Satan. But this is not sure. We will have to avoid any cheap schematization, where Scripture appears to know more nuances.

For our subject, this is not of decisive importance for the following reason. The angelic prince of Constantine the Great was either (a) definitely an angel of Satan, but then disguised as an angel of light, an angel who seemingly challenged the dragon but in fact was his agent; or (b) he was a (rather) "good spirit," with noble intentions, who ultimately still got into the wake of Satan. In both cases, the West did ultimately fall into the hands of the dragon after all. For what happened to the angelic prince(s) who since Constantine dominated the Roman-Catholic West? To this question Scripture gives a clear answer: the great Babylon of Revelation 17 and 18, that is, false nominal Christendom, especially as centered in Rome,[33] is the "great whore," riding on "the beast," the Roman world-empire. The Roman church dominates the Roman Empire. Thus it was in the fourth century, thus it is in the end time. But this Roman Empire of the end time stands under the control of the dragon, that is, the Devil and Satan. In the end time, Satan is again entirely the angelic prince of the Roman Empire.

However, if the "great whore" appears to exert such a tremendous power in that empire, she herself—the *system* she represents—must necessarily be under the control of the dragon. Whatever (relatively) "good spirit" may have animated Constantine the Great, ultimately such spirits turn out to be evil spirits, or to gradually have become evil spirits. In the days of Constantine, other, more positive spirits seemed

33. See Ouweneel (1990 and 2012) on Rev. 17. This does not alter the fact that there are many faithful souls in Rome; we speak of the *system* here.

to push the dragon out of his power. A tremendous contrast seemed to exist between the dragon of the pagan Roman Empire and the spirits dominating the Christianized Empire. But in the end time, the dragon turns out to be supremely powerful again, both in the restored empire and in the "church" of that empire.

How could it be otherwise! In his great standard work, *The Two Babylons,* Alexander Hislop adduced many arguments for the thesis that the great Babylon of Revelation, that is, the Roman church, is very literally "Babylon" in the sense that the essential character of its religion, the great objects of its worship, its feasts, its doctrine, its rites and ceremonies, its priesthood and its orders, were all to some extent—that is, apart from the biblical elements in it—derived from the apostate religion of ancient Babylon. It is quite likely that Hislop wanted to prove too much and overplayed his hand. But in any case, it cannot historically be denied that Roman-Catholicism, wherever it set its foot, was able to establish its doctrine through syncretism, that is, through adoption, Christianization and incorporation of the local religions or religious customs. And we have seen how much of the ancient religions go back upon the religion of (Egypt and) Babylonia.

It is no use to sum up the many idols, insofar as this would be at all possible, that from the outset were annexed by the Roman church. At any rate, the figure of Mary is important, which was gradually equipped with many attributes and titles adopted from paganism. One of her main titles is *Regina Coeli,* "queen of heaven," a title originally borne by the Semitic chief goddess, in Assyrian called Ishtar and in Phoenician Astarte.[34] In Mesopotamia, she was known as *sharrat shamé,* "queen of heaven." In Jeremiah,[35] we read how the people of Jerusalem made cakes for her, bearing her image and burning

34. Heb. *Ashtarót* (Judg. 2:13; 10:6; 1 Sam. 7:3-4; 12:10; 31:10) or *Ashtóret* (1 Kings 11:5, 33; 2 Kings 23:13); the form *Astartè* is the Greek transcription of the name. See extensively Ouweneel (1998).

35. Jer. 7:18; 44:17-19, 25.

incense for her.

With regard to the notion of "national angels," it is of interest to point out the fact that certain Christian nations and countries know a certain "saint" as their patron. A well-known example is St. George, the patron saint of England. In the same way, cities too can have a patron saint; thus, St. Dionys(i)us (*Saint Denys*) is the patron saint of Paris (and France), St. Joseph of Berlin, and St. Nicholas of Amsterdam. In this idea of a patron saint or guardian saint, the pagan notion of a *genius* lives on, a "divine" power taking a certain nation, country, or city into its special protection against other powers. Such patron saints again show that the "saints" of the Roman Church go back upon idols. Of course, that does not change the fact that, for instance, George or Nicholas (may) have been genuinely existing people, who afterwards were "canonized." The Roman calendar of saints knows many names of historical persons. But that does in no way change the fact that behind the idea of guardian saints the pagan (and Christianized) notion of "divine" *genii* (guardian angels) is hidden.

Thus the ancient, still half pagan England made St. George its guardian saint because of the religious conviction that a certain *genius* leads and protects the English nation as well as, or better than, the pagan godhead did before. What a lovely *genius*, by the way: one who was victorious over a *dragon*! Perhaps there is more behind this than a simple myth or legend. There may be a, strongly inflated, historical kernel behind it: a Christian hero defeating some monstrous animal, which in religious imagination grew into a dragon. But it may also be founded in some deeply metahistorical notion: that of the warfare in the heavenly regions.

This does not mean that England really possesses a *genius* called George (Geourgios); *geourgios* means "tiller of the ground," that is an unusual occupation in the heavenly regions. Moreover, it was England's free choice to appoint, of all saints, St. George to be its guardian saint. And when people were not pleased with a patron saint anymore, he could be simply exchanged. For instance, St. Martin of Tours was for centuries the patron saint of the Dutch city of Arnhem, which concretely means that the main church of the city, like everywhere, was consecrated to this "saint." However, around the middle of the fifteenth century, for some reason he did not "satisfy" the people anymore. Therefore, the newly built church was consecrated to a newly chosen guardian saint: the second-century martyr St. Eusebius. For this purpose, even the relics of this saint, residing in the ancient Carolingian abby of Prüm, were taken to Arnhem, so that together with Eusebius's bones his spirit would more easily feel at home in the city. In reality, however, not the historical Eusebius was, or is, the *genius* of Arnhem. People, cities, and nations serving the idols place themselves under the protection, not of historical persons but, of the "divine" powers in the heavenly regions.

5.3.4. "Pergamus"

The official church of the Roman Empire—I repeat: I mean the system, that is, apart from the many faithful within that church—has become a pantheon of many pagan gods. Behind these idols, concrete demonic powers are hidden.[36] This means concretely that the "great Babylon" of the end time is, as it has been since a long time, "a habitation of demons and a prison for every foul spirit" (Rev. 18:2). We do not have to wonder whether these "demons" and "foul spirits" are angels of Satan or not, for the whore rides on the beast, which is closely associated with the dragon. At the end of the Roman Empire's history, both empire and church will be dominated by Samael, the angelic prince of Edom/Rome. Thus, the scenario of the end time is fixed: it involves the great cosmic conflict between Samael, the angelic prince of Edom, and Jesus Christ, the Messiah of Israel, that is, between Esau and Jacob, between the dragon and the Lamb. We will extensively come

36. Deut. 32:17; 1 Cor. 10:20; Rev. 9:20.

back to this.

The reader inclined to the view that the angel who appeared to Constantine was a camouflaged angel of Satan can find support for this in Revelation 2. In one of my dogmatic volumes, I have defended the view that in Revelation 2 and 3 we find a prophetic survey of church history, from the departure of the apostles until the second coming of Christ.[37] The letter to Pergamus says in 2:13, "I know (...) where you dwell, where Satan's throne [is]." Presumably this refers to the fact that Pergamus was the official centre of Asia for the emperor's worship; there stood the temple for the "god" (emperor) Augustus and the "goddess" Rome. Later, also a temple for the emperor Trajan was built there, so that the city received the title "double temple guardian." This link between Satan and the Roman emperor—the latter was worshipped as a god—fits in with Revelation 12:3 and 13:1-4, where a direct link is made between the dragon (Satan) and the beast (the head of the Roman Empire).

Now, if the prophetic interpretation of Revelation 2 and 3, which I represent, is correct, the letter to Pergamus refers to the period from Constantine the Great until the Middle Ages. The church put itself under the protection of the emperor, and thus under the protection of the dragon. In this way, the church obtained its "dwelling-place" in the territory where the dragon exerts his power, or, where "Satan's throne" stands. The faithful in Pergamus could not help it that they had gotten into this territory, having been dragged along with the new developments. But the mass of the church, as well as the system as such, had effectively become servants of Satan. It is this church that prophetically "debouches" on Thyatira, the Roman church of the Middle Ages, with its extensive fornication and idolatry, and with its alleged knowledge of the "depths of Satan" (Rev. 2:24), that is, the mystical occultism in the Roman church (§ 7.1.2). It is this Thyatira that ultimately

37. Ouweneel (2011, ch. 2).

"debouches" on the great Babylon of Revelation 17 and 18, a dwelling-place of demons and foul spirits. It is this great Babylon that eventually is fully destroyed by God.

5.4 Disastrous Consequences

5.4.1 Healing Ministry

In summary, one can say that, since the "great turn," that is, the Constantinian revolution, the consequences of the "fall of Christianity,"[38] that is, the pseudo-Christianizing of the Roman Empire, have been tremendous. This "fall" has led to at least five catastrophes. I already mentioned two of them, I mention briefly a third one here, and to the others I will pay attention in the next sections:

(1) *Caesaropapism:* the church was made subservient to the state, and the church leaders were made subservient to the emperor (later to other heads of state).

(2) The rising *persecution of the Jews:* the end of the persecution of the Christians implied the start of the persecution of the Jews, because the latter did not want to join the Christian church.

(3) *Healing miracles*: after several centuries in which the New Testament healing ministry had still blossomed powerfully, it decreased rapidly after the "great turn" as a consequence of the spiritual weakening of the church and the mixture of the healing ministry with pagan elements.[39] Many church fathers have witnessed of miraculous healings and deliverances, such as the Apologists, Justin Martyr (c. 100-165) and Irenaeus († 180), the great church father Tertullian (160-220), also Origen († c. 253). At the same time, the church fathers already were aware of the fact that, in their time, the miraculous gifts were decreasing. Lactantius (c. 300) warned that the church would keep its power to heal "as long as there is peace among the people of God."[40]

38. Cf. Heering (1928).
39. Ouweneel (2003:ch.2).
40. *Institutiones Divinae* V,22.

Even after the "great turn," the healing miracles did not stop right away. Athanasius of Alexandria (357), John Chrysostom (386/87) in Antioch, the three great "Cappadocians" (Basil of Caesarea, Gregory of Nazianzus, Gregory of Nyssa, second half fourth century), and even church father Augustine (354-430) witnessed of healing miracles. Whereas the anti-millennialist (see § 5.4.2) Augustine, in his earlier writings, still claimed that Christians should not expect a continuation of the gift of healing, he stated, especially against the end of his life, that in his time miracles still occurred.[41] At the same time, unfortunately, he wrote about healings at which relics of the saints were used. Thus, "even" he allowed paganism to penetrate.

John Chrysostom (end of the fourth century) warned the believers against seeking their refuge with unbelieving healers—a wise word in that post-Constantinian time as thousands of pagans joined the church without having been purified from their pagan customs. Even some church fathers began to adopt superstitious, if not pagan, customs in the healing ministry, such as Ambrose (end of the fourth century), who used relics of martyrs when laying hands on the possessed. The mixture of Christianity and paganism from the fourth century was a devastating blow to the biblical healing ministry.

Interestingly, it was nothing less than a token of gratitude for being healed from a serious disease that the emperor Theodosius in 380 made Christianity the state religion of the Roman Empire. However, this hardly led to a Christianization of the world, but rather to a further secularization of the church, and to bloody persecution of Christians not belonging to the official state church.

5.4.2 Anti-Millennialism

The idea of a "Christian" empire made the perspective of the Messianic kingdom to perish: this kingdom allegedly is

41. *De Civitate Dei* XXII, VIII.

realized here and now in the "Christian" Roman Empire. The church was taking a lead in politics, and in the wars of this world, and recognized the emperor as its head and as the chairman of its meetings, not because he (supposedly) was a Christian but because he was the emperor. Such a church will necessarily develop totally new prophetic views. Before that time, the *pagan* empire had been viewed as the great adversary of the church, and thus as *the* instrument of Satan. Since the "great turn," the empire had changed its character one hundred and eighty degrees: it had now become the ally of the church, and thus an instrument of God in the development of a new, "Christian" empire.

The church fathers saw in the image of Nebuchadrezzar (Dan. 2) the four *pagan* empires, of which the Roman Empire was the last one. From 324 AD, however, there was no more any pagan world empire; the last one had been followed by a "Christian" empire. In Daniel 2, the last pagan empire, the Roman Empire, was succeeded by the empire of Christ. What was more obvious than to suppose that the Christian empire manifesting itself in the fourth century was the promised Messianic kingdom of peace and righteousness, which destroyed all previous pagan empires? The territory of the Christianized Roman Empire was the realm in which the kingdom of Christ would develop, and the establishment of the earthly church through human activity would be the means to realize that kingdom of Christ, and thus to fulfill the prophecies. In reality, of course, exactly the opposite happened: not the church Christianized the empire, but the empire secularized and paganized the church. Not Christ triumphed over the pagan gods, but these gods triumphed over the Christian church.

The theology from after the "great turn" was, first, "supersessionism," that is, the theology that leaves to the Jews the announced curses, and claims for the church the blessings promised to Israel.[42] Secondly, it is "anti-millennialism," that

42. Often it is formulated differently: no "replacement" but the (few) believers in Israel have been extended with the believers from the nations, and together

is, it locates the kingdom of Christ no longer after his second coming but in its own time, that is, in the time that has begun with the "great turn." In his eulogy on Constantine, Eusebius called him a new Moses. Indeed, a new Mosaic theocracy arose, an imitation of ancient Israel, which itself allegedly had been discarded.[43] For the first time, genuine church buildings arose, splendid constructions, to a certain extent imitating Israel's temple, with an outer court for the uninitiated, the actual temple for the lay people, and the shielded sanctuary with the altar, only accessible to the priests.

Before the "great turn," Eusebius taught that Isaiah 35 and Psalm 46 referred to the future Messianic kingdom. After the "turn," he applied these chapters to the new church buildings of his time, such as the church of Tyre, which he circumscribed as a "new and much better Jerusalem." He now also claimed that the magnificent church which Constantine wanted to build in old Jerusalem, might be the fulfillment of the prophecy of the New Jerusalem (Rev. 21). The fact that in Revelation 12 the dragon is cast out from heaven was explained by Eusebius as Constantine's victory over the pagan empire. When Constantine let his sons and a nephew share in his imperial dominion, Eusebius saw this as the fulfillment of Daniel 7:18, "the saints of the Most High will receive the kingdom [or, kingly rule]."

Thus, the great revolution in prophetical views was neatly illustrated in Eusebius's new thinking. The same was true for many other teachers of the church. As a consequence of all the successes and new possessions of the church, its rising

---

they form the "Israel of God," that is, the church. *Materially*, the two circumscriptions involve exactly the same, for this church factually takes the place of 99% of ancient Israel, that is, "the" Israel still existing today. *Theologically*, the difference is also enormous: the Gentile believers did not join Israel, thus taking on Jewish characteristics, but Jewish believers had to join the essentially Gentile church, thus losing their Jewish identity (see extensively Ouweneel, 2014).

43. See for the descriptions of the views of the various church fathers especially Froom (1950).

glory and power, the expectation of Christ's second coming was pushed entirely to the background. Why look forward to a future kingdom of Christ if this kingdom was already clearly manifesting itself here and now? For three centuries, the great men of the church such as Justin Martyr, Irenaeus, Tertullian, Hippolytus, and Lactantius, had unanimously expected a millennial kingdom *after* the second coming. However, after the "great turn," the situation soon changed. Already Eusebius, and also Ambrose, Prudentius, and Jerome (the great composer of the *Vulgate*, the Latin Bible translation), rejected millennialism. Further we must mention the Donatist Tichonius, who is little known but who formed the source for the views of Augustine. Tichonius replaced the idea of a future millennial kingdom by the idea of a "millennial" kingdom *now* (started at the resurrection of Christ), whereas the second coming of Christ was pushed away to the last ("youngest") day of world history, literally at the end of time.

Augustine was the most important church father who, within a century after the "great turn," further developed the totally new view of the Messianic kingdom. The rule of the Messiah is not in the future but now, and receives shape within the Roman Empire under the guidance of the emperor, namely, through the universal church guided by the bishop of Rome. Revelation 20:1-6 was viewed as entirely fulfilled except for the "second resurrection," that is, the bodily resurrection of the dead at the second coming of Christ. The "first resurrection" was spiritualized and applied to rebirth. The "bottomless pit" in which Satan was bound was explained as the whole of the nations that had not yet been converted; at the end of world history, the devil was to be released for three and a half years. The "thrones" in v. 4 were the present-day ecclesial seats (or "sees"). The "camp of the saints" in v. 9 was the worldwide ("catholic") church. The Jews had to be converted to this church, and in this way fully abjure their Jewish background and identity. The Roman Catholic Church was the stone in Daniel 2, which destroyed the image, and was to grow into a world power. It is this church that is the "New Jerusalem" (Rev. 21).

History has shown to what dramatic consequences this doctrine has led. Less than a century later, around 500, Rome's bishop had developed into the absolute ruler within the Catholic Church, as we will see: the emperor's seat—the city of Rome—had necessarily to be the seat of the prelate as well: the pope. It is particularly supersessionism and anti-millennialism that have made of the "catholic" (or, universal) church a *Roman* catholic church. In the Western world, it would retain this universal character until the time of the Reformation (early sixteenth century).

5.4.3 Militarism

During the battle at the Milvian Bridge, the central question with which Constantine saw himself confronted was who was stronger: the God of the Christians or the ancient Roman gods. When Constantine gained the victory, this did not only demonstrate that Christ was stronger but also that he, by nature, was necessarily a god of war and triumph, that is, a kind of Ares, or Mars. The Christian draft dodger, who before that time had been a "soldier" of peace, now became a war soldier in Constantine's armies, which spread the Christian faith over Europe by means of the sword. Already two years after Constantine's victory, in 314, the Council of Arles decided that draft dodgers had to be banned from the church. Again, the situation had turned one hundred and eighty degrees. Of course, many Christians kept resisting the wars and, surely, great church fathers from after 312 condemned war crimes. But church fathers such as Athanasius, Ambrose and Augustine all approved of military service as a means to defend and strengthen the empire, and thus Christendom.

What happened in Christian thinking that, for instance, Tertullian and Origen had so sharply been *against* military service, and, for instance, Athanasius and Augustine *for* it? The cause of this change was that the church had cast itself hook, line and sinker into the arms of the "Christian" emperor Constantine and his successors. Before the year 312, the worst sins Christians could commit were veneration of the emperor and participation in the pagan cult. After 312, the Christians venerated no person on earth more strongly than the essentially still fully pagan emperor Constantine. Even though it lasted until 380 before Christianity, or actually, Roman Catholicism, was turned into the state religion, already from 324 the separation between church and state was in principle abrogated. After Constantine in 324 had given full right to Christianity within the empire, entire masses of people accepted Christianity because of the social and economic benefits. To put it a bit harshly: they were baptized in water but not in the Holy Spirit. They were ignited by the emperor's enthusiasm, and enlisted in his armies. Militarism had entered the church.[44]

In this context, the pagan cult too was adapted to Christianity, in that famous Christian soldiers were turned into saints, and were thus placed before the masses as examples to be followed. A striking example is, first, Saint George (Geourgios), mentioned above. He was a soldier that allegedly had been decapitated in 303. Afterwards, he was surrounded with legends (St. George and the dragon!), and, as I said, made the patron saint of England, and other places (§ 5.3.3-4). A second peculiar example is Saint Theodore of Amasea, a Roman Christian general, who died in 306 for his faith. Afterwards, a later Byzantine emperor made him the patron saint of Venice. "San Teodoro" still stands in Venice on a high pillar near the palace of the Doge. However, after the Venetians had taken the relics of Mark, the gospel writer, to their city, they preferred him as their patron saint. But the point remains: George and Theodore were examples to be followed: every young man was called upon to follow his emperor. Thus, they were to defend the Roman Catholic empire as well as spread the Roman Catholic faith, not only among the pagans, but also among the non-Catholic Christians.

44. It is to this militarism that Heering's book (1928) refers.

Chapter 6
The Roman Successors' Empires

6.1. The Frankish Empire
6.1.1. "Peter"

IN ISAIAH 14, WE SAW looming up behind the king of Babylon his angelic prince, Lucifer, in whom several church fathers believed to recognize Satan (§ 3.3.3). As said before, that is correct insofar as a direct line runs from the angelic prince of Babylon, the first of the four world-empires, to the "dragon," the angelic prince of the Roman, the last world-empire. In the book of Revelation, the Roman-Catholic power as a *system* is the "great Babylon" of the end time (that is, apart from the many faithful in that church). The deeper spiritual link between the "first" and the "last" Babylon has been extensively shown and described in Alexander Hislop's work, *The Two Babylons*. The American theologian Donald Grey Barnhouse (1895-1960) called this book "one of the great books in the Christian literature of apologetics." Therefore, this work, which in its original form was first published in 1853, has appeared in many editions, and even after one and a half centuries is still reprinted.

Hislop argues that almost all practices of the Roman-Catholic church go back upon Babylonian paganism (apart from, e.g., baptism and the Lord's Supper, which in their primordial form come from the New Testament). A number of the most ancient "saints" of this church seem to be angelic powers stemming from the pagan pantheon. The veneration of the Virgin Mary goes back upon the pagan worship of Ishtar (Astarte, Venus). In fact, behind this name a great number of spiritual powers are hidden. If people doubt this, they only have to find out why the Virgin of La Salette is thought to be more or less favorable than the Virgin of Lourdes; why the Virgin in the cathedral of Algiers is a negress; why pope John Paul II had such a preference for the Black Madonna in Poland, etcetera.

Another spiritual power hiding behind a very familiar name seems to be "Peter."[1] To understand the true nature of the Roman Catholic Church, the biblical figure of Peter is of tremendous significance, because he is considered to be the "founder" of the church in Rome, and because the bishop of Rome, later called the "pope" (= father), is regarded to be his successor. The "keys" of the kingdom of heaven, entrusted to Peter (Matt. 16:19), form a "key power" (the power based on these "keys") that is transferred from pope to pope. It is remarkable, however, that in the first centuries of Christendom we hear nothing about this "key." The special position of the bishop of Rome was based on nothing but the fact that Rome was the capital of the Roman Empire, and because the tombs of the apostles Peter and Paul were there. Only in the last quarter of the fourth century, the pope's "key power" began to play a role. This might be due to the fact that the "second" Rome, Constantinople, threatened to rival the "first" Rome. Therefore, a new argument for the superiority of Rome's bishop was necessary.

If we may believe Hislop, this new argument was found in the fact that around 378 the pope became the heir of the "keys" that were the symbols of two well-known deities in Rome. The one key was that of the god Janus[2] (after whom

1. Hislop (1959:206-209, 212).
2. Ovid, *Fasti* i.95,99.

the month "January" is called), the other one that of the goddess Cybele. This goddess, originally from Asia Minor, was called the Great Mother, or the Mother of the gods. Only around 200 BC, she had been introduced under that name in Rome; but the same goddess, with the "key power," had been worshipped in Rome centuries before, under the name Cardea, together with Janus.[3]

Apparently, these are the two keys that the pope bears on the sleeves of his garment. When, in the course of the fourth century, the "Christianized" Romans came to the conclusion that the bishop of Rome had taken the place of the representatives of Janus and Cybele, it seemed self-evident that he also deserved the keys. These keys were "Christianized" by associating them with the "keys" of Peter, in spite of the fact that *nothing in Matt. 16 suggests these "keys" to be transferable*; they only belonged to Peter in person. In 431, the pope for the first time officially claimed the keys of Peter. In an analogous way, the statue of Jupiter in Rome began to be venerated as an image of Peter. The "Peter" who is honored here was therefore in essence a pagan idol, although associated with the apostle Peter.

There is no historical evidence that Peter was the first *bishop* of Rome. But, writes Hislop,[4]

> while this is the case with Peter the *Christian*, it can be shown to be by no means doubtful that before the Christian era, and downwards, there was a "Peter" at Rome, who occupied the highest place in the *Pagan* priesthood. The priest who explained the Mysteries to the initiated was sometimes called by a Greek term, the Hierophant; but in primitive Chaldee, the real language of the Mysteries, his title, as pronounced without the points, was "Peter"—i.e., "the interpreter."[5] As the revealer of

3. Ovid, *Fasti* iii.101. See extensively about the mother goddess of antiquity, Ouweneel (1998).
4. Hislop (1959:208).
5. The Hebrew verb *phatar* (Accadian, *pataru*) means "to interpret" and occurs in Gen. 40:8, 16, 22; 41:8, 12-13, 15. The Biblical name Peter is Greek,

> that which is hidden, nothing was more natural than that, while opening up the esoteric doctrine of the Mysteries, he should be decorated with the keys of the two divinities whose mysteries he unfolded.[6] Thus we may see how the keys of Janus and Cybele would come to be known as the keys of Peter, the "interpreter" of the Mysteries.

Next, Hislop gives a great number of indications that in widely spread countries these keys were known as the "keys of Peter," namely, a "Peter" associated with Rome. Thus, in Athens there was an initiation book known as the *Book Petroma*, that is, "Pet-Roma," the "Book of the Great Interpreter," Hermes.[7] We saw that Hermes was considered to be the messenger and interpreter of the gods. In Egypt, Hermes was worshipped as the Great Interpreter, or "Peter-Roma"; in the language of the hieroglyphs, *ptr* means "to show." The fact that such a handy title as "the Peter [interpreter] of Rome" together with his keys already existed was, according to Hislop, a great help to the bishop of Rome. In his intertwinement of Christianity and Rome's idolatry, he was just too pleased to be able to take over this title and to associate it with the biblical Peter. Thus, so still Hislop, he became the representative of the god Janus with his two faces: one face for the blind Christians, who saw him as the successor of Peter, and one face for the initiated pagans, who saw in him the representative of "Peter," the interpreter of the Mysteries.

Janus is not just anyone. He was worshipped in Asia Minor, and from time immemorial, in Rome too. He is the "god of gods" (thus called in the most ancient hymns of the *Salii*,

---

derived from *petra*, "rock" (Matt. 16:18), and is in Aramaic sometimes rendered as Cephas (from *kéfa*, "rock": see, e.g., Gal. 2:9). However, if "Peter" is taken as a Grecianized Semitic word, it means "interpreter."

6. "The Turkish Muftis, or 'interpreters' of the Koran, derive that name ['Mufti'] from the very same verb as that from which comes *Miftah*, a key." (Note by Hislop, 1959:208).
7. In Acts 14:12, Barnabas is called "Zeus" by the pagans, and Paul is called "Hermes," "because he was the chief speaker," that is, he acted as the spokesman (interpreter) of the chief god.

the "leaping priests" of Mars), from whom all other gods originated, and who at every important occasion in Rome has to be called upon first. His original name was "Chaos";[8] he thus was the "god of confusion" – a remarkable name if it is remembered that *diabolos*, "devil," literally means "confuser."[9] We saw that Janus/Chaos is associated with Bel ("confuser") and Nebo ("oracler"), with Kronos/Saturn (both are the "hidden god," as Amon/Osiris), and with Osiris/Horus (both have two faces).

Janus had in his hands the rule over the world; to him belonged "all power in heaven and on earth and on the sea."[10] In this respect, this angelic prince of Rome is the imitator of Christ (Matt. 28:18), the *pseudochristos*, as he particularly will take shape in the Antichrist, who looks like the Lamb, but speaks as the dragon (Rev. 13:11). When we consider that, since the fourth century, the pope more and more became the earthly representative of Janus (= "Peter"), we can imagine that many theologians associated him with the Antichrist. The title *pontifex maximus*, which was transferred to the pope, had been carried before by the pagan chief priest of Rome, who had been the representative of the god Janus. Also, titles such as *vicarius Dei* ("substitute of God") and *sua Sanctitas* ("his Holiness") were transferred from the pagan representative of Janus to the pope.

In summary, Hislop believed to have identified in the Roman pantheon a deity who may be pre-eminently associated with the angelic prince of Rome: Janus, the *principium deorum*, "chief of the gods," Janus with the key (connected with the mother-lady Cybele with the key), and as such the same as "Peter" with the keys, the divine interpreter, introducer into the mysteries of paganism, that is, demon worship. Even if Hislop had exaggerated, and some of his arguments would

8. Ovid, *Fasti* i.104.
9. It is the more striking that Bel himself is "confused" by the God of gods, and Marduk "broken" (Jer. 50:2).
10. Ovid, *Fasti* i.117,120,125.

turn out not to hold water, enough would seem to remain to see in the Peter figure, coming ever more to the fore in the young Roman church, a mixture of the New Testament apostle and features of the god Janus, or more generally, of the Roman angelic prince. The astonishing way in which this "Peter" seems to push aside even Christ, as we will see, supports this metahistorical interpretation.

6.1.2. The Franks[11]

In the same century in which the bishop of Rome began assuming the features of Janus/Peter, the Germanic hordes began invading the Roman Empire for the first time. Already before the pope officially took over the keys of "Peter"—perhaps, Boniface I (418-422) was the first who did so—the West-Goths led by Alaric stood before Rome (410). When in 455 the Vandals sacked Rome, the pope, at that moment Leo I the Great, was already firmly associated with Janus/Peter. And when Odoacer in 476 overthrew the West-Roman Empire, the Roman ideal as well as the unity and continuity of the (West-) European world remained firmly rooted in the connection of the pope with Janus/Peter. None has contributed more to this than pope Leo the Great (440-461), who indefatigably defended the view that Peter was the first bishop of Rome and the chief of all bishops. Leo even claimed that, as it were, Peter on his see at Rome was continually "present," and that his power and authority continued to work in his successors, the bishops of Rome. When, at the Council of Chalcedon (451), the Eutychian Dioscurus was condemned, the sentence began as follows:

> Leo, archbishop of the great and ancient Rome (...) on the authority of the holy Peter, on which the Catholic church and the orthodox faith are built.

And when, during the Council, a letter by Leo regarding the

11. See for this section, Nitschke (1975); of course, for the interpretation of the Peter veneration I am responsible alone.

heresy was read, the participants unanimously exclaimed:

> That is the faith of the fathers; through the mouth of Leo, Peter has spoken!

Please note, it is not said that Christ or the Holy Spirit has spoken, but "Peter." In that same century, pope Gelasius I (492-496) further extended the central authority of Rome's bishop on the basis of the notion of the supreme power of "Peter's" see. It is not the pope who rules, but "Peter," as it were from his grave; the pope is only an instrument in his hand. Nothing was more holy and important at Rome, even on earth, than this place: "Peter's" tomb. It is very difficult to say what connotations this name "Peter" had in those times: was there more of the New Testament Peter, *or* of the ancient Roman gods that reverberated in this name? Why were the popes so keen on the title *pontifex maximus*, given the fact that this had been for centuries the title of the pagan high priest in ancient Rome?

The undeniable association of Rome and Peter—whatever Peter this is—would turn out to be of great religious as well as political significance. Most Germanic tribes had, insofar as they had been Christianized, adopted the doctrine of Arius—except the Franks, who in imitation of king Clovis (c. 500) accepted the "orthodox" doctrine of Athanasius. This in itself was positive of course; but much more was involved here than the conflict between Arius and Athanasius: it was a matter of non-Rome-bound confessions over against "Catholicism," the confession strictly bound to "Peter's" see. Thus, the peculiar situation arose that the *lie* of Arius held the Germanic nations at a safe distance from Rome, whereas those who accepted the *truth* of Athanasius, in so doing fell into the arms of Janus/Peter, which had incorporated this pure truth into its corrupt idolatry. It was therefore the Franks, and not one of the other Germanic nations, to whom the Roman Empire, the empire of Janus/Peter, was transferred in the eighth century, as we will extensively see.

Already in the seventh century, it was especially the Anglo-Saxon Christians who elevated "Peter" and his "successors" in Rome to their peculiar lord. The German historian, Johannes Haller (1865-1947), linked this with a typically Germanic feature: choosing at their discretion a deity, who subsequently is venerated and served in order to obtain his help and protection in return. In this way, the previously so independent and spiritual Anglo-Saxons chose Janus/Peter to be their lord, and preached this deity under the Franks. This was so successful that it led to the Franks' readiness to protect the "see of Peter" at Rome against the threatening Longobards and to give to the representative of Janus/Peter his own territory, which became the basis for the Papal State.

Long before that time, around 500, Clovis (or Chlodwig, or Chlodowech, in French corrupted into Louis), king of the Franks (or, as the French say, the first king of France), had adopted Catholicism, because he came to the conclusion that the "god" of the Catholics was more powerful than the gods of paganism or of Arianism. For the see of "Peter," he formed a very important bridgehead under the largely Arian Germanic nations. Considering the horrible acts of Clovis and his Merovingian successors it is not difficult to see that the "Jesus" whom he had accepted was "another Jesus" than the one of the Scriptures (cf. 2 Cor. 11:4). As once Constantine had been the emperor who, associated with his "Jesus," as the one sun benevolently shone upon all people (so Eusebius), thus Clovis too, with his "Jesus," had to stretch out for that one world-empire, upon which he as the one sun could shine—thus bishop Avitus of Vienne impressed upon him. Clovis himself made a beginning with the extension of his empire, his Merovingian descendants continued that work, but the work was finished by their Carolingian majordomos. After a great victory in 687, the majordomo Pepin II of Herstal was the mightiest man in the Frankish empire.

Meanwhile the star of Janus/Peter was rising. As I said, Anglo-Saxon priests and monks venerated the "Peter of

Rome" in a special way. Some years before Pepin's victory, in 663, a synod took place at Whitby (England), where the Northumbrian monk Wilfried, a great admirer of the Roman "Peter," managed to persuade king Oswiu to become Roman-Catholic, since the Catholic traditions stemmed from Peter. Oswiu replied that he did not want to contradict "Peter," since the latter guarded the gate of heaven and might not be willing to open this gate to him, Oswiu, when once he would arrive there. Thus, Northumbria became "Roman(-Catholic)," and through many Anglo-Saxon missionaries the same gradually occurred with the Frankish empire, which was already "Christian" but certainly not yet "Petrinian." In Gallia, particularly St. Martin of Tours was venerated, who had performed so many more miracles than Peter; but here too Peter's key power turned the scale. The best known of the Anglo-Saxon preachers of "Peter of Rome" became Willibrord, Boniface, and later Alcuin, a relative of Willibrord and the counselor and confident of Charlemagne.[12]

All along the Peter figure was central in this missionary work. Boniface had a chapel built from the wood of the Donar oak at Geismar to the honor of Peter. The greatest monasteries that he founded were consecrated to Peter and Paul, like the first church that Willibrord at Echternach (Luxemburg) received from the abbess Irmina. In England, Boniface ordered a copy of Peter's epistles written in gold, so that at his preaching his hearers could see with their own eyes the tremendous significance of Peter. And everywhere the rule was: the more attached people were to "Peter," the more ardently they linked themselves with Rome. Through "Peter," the gatekeeper, people counted upon entering heaven one day. In this respect, too, "Peter" is identical with Janus, the key-god. Janus is the god of doors and hinges, the god who has the *ius vertendi cardinis*, "the right to open the door" (literally, to turn the hinge), whether these are the doors to heaven, or the

12. Weiler (1989:55-79).

doors to peace and war on earth.[13] If Janus/Peter was the god of Rome, Boniface was his prophet, indefatigable as he was in fettering the Germanic nations to the see of "Peter."

Pepin's bastard son Charles Martel took a more reserved stand with regard to Peter and his Roman successor. Yet, he let himself be introduced into a prayer brotherhood consecrated to Peter, and had his sons, Carloman and Pepin, be educated in the Anglo-Saxon, that is, Petrinian spirit. Both were ardent "Petrinians," and ever more Frankish priests went in the same trail. Shortly after the death of Charles Martel, a great general Frankish synod came together led by Boniface, "who is an ambassador of the holy Peter" (747). At this meeting, all Frankish bishops signed a declaration that they would always obey Peter and his successors. They put this down in a charter, which was deposited at the tomb of Peter:[14]

> We have taken the decision, in mutual agreement and submission to the church of Rome, to hold until the end of the days or our lives to the Catholic faith, to own the authority of the holy Peter and his substitute, as archbishops to pray the see of Peter for the pallium,[15] and in all matters to follow the prescriptions of the holy Peter, in order thus to belong to the sheep entrusted to him.

After Carloman had retired to a monastery and Pepin had become the sole ruler, he, with the permission of pope Zacharias (741-752), dismissed the last Merovingian king and proclaimed himself king of the Franks (751). Probably it was Boniface, the "ambassador of Peter," who anointed him king. This Petrinian anointment had to make up for the lacking right of descent, which meant nothing else than that Pepin had been

---

13. Over against the pretensions of Janus/Peter, Christ presents himself to the faithful Christians ("Philadelphia") as "He who is holy, He who is true, He who has the key of David, He who opens and no one shuts, and who shuts and no one opens." In this way, He claims his own *ius vertendi cardinis*: "See, I have given before you an opened door, which no one can shut" (Rev. 3:7-8).
14. Nitschke (1975:303-304).
15. Shoulder-cape of archbishops, which is given to them by the pope.

put on the throne by Peter himself. When a new pope, Stephen II (752-757), was threatened by his enemies, Pepin swore an oath of friendship to Peter and his successor. Thereupon, the pope anointed him again, and bestowed upon him the title *patricius Romanorum*, "ruler of the Romans" (754). Pepin drove the enemies out, and laid the keys of the conquered cities as a gift upon the tomb of Peter (756). When subsequently the emperor of Byzantium (the East-Roman Empire) claimed Rome, Pepin explicitly declared that he could not give the land to him because he had not fought for men but for Peter. In his turn, the pope did not scruple to send in that year (756) a letter to Pepin in which Peter addressed the king personally—"I, Peter, the apostle"—with the words:[16]

> I assisted you and granted you by divine [!] strength the victory over your enemies. When you will obey me [!], your reward will be great. Through my [!] help you will prevail over your enemies in the present life, and long enjoy the earthly blessings, in order to rejoice afterwards in the everlasting life.

The German historian August Nitschke (b. 1926) accuses Pepin of "unadulterated naivety" because he took such letters seriously—but, in my opinion, Nitschke errs. Indeed, Pepin may have had a childlike faith, but it was not just based on deceit. The pope *was* the medium through whom Janus/Peter himself, the angelic prince of Rome, addressed the king. Even if the pope would have consciously deceived Pepin, which in itself is quite possible although I doubt it, he deceived himself too, for he *was* the representative of the "key-god."

One other event of great metahistorical importance has to be mentioned here. Shortly after the middle of the eighth century, from the contacts of pope Stephen II and Pepin the Short the "Papal State" originated. This was called the *patrimonium Petri*, the "heritage of Peter," which made the pope besides a spiritual also a secular ruler. In order to corroborate the papal claims no means were shunned. The most striking one was

16. Nitschke (1975:305).

the false *Donatio Constantini*, a charter that was concocted at that time in Rome. In this document, it was suggested that the first Christian emperor, Constantine the Great, had transferred to his contemporary, pope Silvester I, the city of Rome and the Western part of the empire. In the so-called Pepinian Donation, Pepin himself made territorial promises in Italy to the pope. On the one hand, Pepin's anointment ushered in the origin of a Roman-Frankish empire, on the other hand the Pepinian Donation turned the pope into a secular prince, with all kinds of consequences, as we will see.

6.1.3. Charlemagne

According to the medieval view, the empire of the Antichrist, and therewith the end of the present world, could not arrive as long as the Roman Empire continued.[17] Therefore, when the West-Roman Empire fell (476), people comforted themselves with the thought that the East-Roman emperors, who also in the West exerted a certain influence, still stood firm. When the power of the emperors in the West began to wane, this was compensated by the rise of popery in Rome. Thus, especially in Italy, the idea of the Roman Empire lived on unabated, also after the fall of Rome. One reason was that the Roman state institutions largely remained intact. The Germanic rulers "germanized" the empire—already before 476—not by replacing the Roman state institutions by their own, but by henceforth holding the Roman state offices themselves.

Yet, also after 476, the Romans always kept considering the invaded Teutons as strangers and intruders. Therefore, the ancient Roman Empire never passed to one of the Germanic tribes that had ensconced themselves on Italic soil. Only as in Gallia a totally new power developed, that of the Franks, the Roman Empire could be "transferred." Moreover, as I said, the Germanic tribes were Arians, except these very Franks. In the eighth century, the latter were "Roman(-Catholic)" like the West-Romans, and in Gallia they respected both the

17. See for the first paragraphs, Adamek (1938:4-9).

Roman culture and the Roman population in their midst. It was the Franks who also maintained close links with East-Roman emperors as well as with the popes at Rome. We saw that, on the one hand, Merovingians and popes, through their agents, had managed to bring the Irish-Scottish Christianity under the banner of Rome, and they romanized the Gallic church ever further. On the other hand, the West- and East-Romans grew more and more apart, both in the form and in the language (Latin vs. Greek) of the empires, as well as in their religious views (Catholicism vs. Orthodoxy). Moreover, the pope urgently needed help against the Longobards. Already in 739 therefore, the Senate and the people of Rome as well as the pope decided to turn away from the East-Roman emperor and to entrust themselves to the patronage of Charles Martel.[18] Eventually, in 800, this new relationship was sealed with the imperial coronation of Charlemagne.

In 768, Pepin the Short died. Already three years later, his son Carloman died, so that his other son, Charles, became the sole ruler. As Pepin had already risen to the rank of *patricius Romanorum*, over Charles even more Roman splendor was spread. At Easter, 774, Charles paid his first visit to pope Hadrian I at Rome. They met in the St. Peter, where they swore oaths to each other at the tomb of Peter. On this tomb, Charles placed a letter in which he confirmed the Pepinian

---

18. Notice the words with which this happened: *bis a Roma sede s. Petri apostoli beatus papa Gregorius claves venerandi sepulchri cum vincula s. Petri et muneribus magnis et infinitis legationem, quod antea nullis auditis aut visis temporibus fuit, memorato principi (Carolo) destinavit, eo pacto patrato, ut a partibus imperatoris recederet et Romano consulto praefato principi Carlo sanciret* (this weak Latin means more or less: "twice the blessed pope Gregory from Rome, the see of the holy apostle Peter, destined the keys of the venerable tomb [of Peter] together with the seal of the holy Peter and great and infinite gifts [or, tasks, responsibilities] the office of envoy [or, deputy commander]—which did not happened before in times heard or seen—for the mentioned prince (Charles), under this condition that [this office] resided with the tasks of the emperor and that he [the pope] would enforce it for the prince, Charles, according to the Roman decree mentioned before") (quoted by Adamek 1938:9).

Donation. The pope bestowed on him more and more rights that before had belonged to the emperor of Byzantium. From that time, Charles also began carrying the title *patricius Romanorum* ("ruler of the Romans"), which before had been granted to him together with his father.

In 795, Hadrian I was succeeded by pope Leo III, who immediately after his election sent the key of "Peter's" tomb and the standard of Rome to Charlemagne. In this way, he recognized Charles's suzerainty with regard to the Papal State. This is beautifully depicted in a mosaic in the dining hall of the ancient Lateran palace at Rome, dating from the same period, in which Leo III and Charlemagne are pictured as faithful followers of "Peter." The latter gives with his right hand the pallium to the kneeling pope, with his left hand he gives the standard to the kneeling Charles.

By the end of the eighth century, Charlemagne's power had grown so strongly in Western Europe that the Frankish court itself had already considered granting him the title of emperor. They liked to tie in with Roman tradition; some even considered the – Petrinian! – empire of Charles to be superior to the ancient Roman Empire. The matter was brought to a decision by the pope himself. Leo III fled before his enemies to Charles, who personally took him back to Rome. There, on Christmas day of the year 800, the pope unexpectedly crowned him emperor, while the people, according to the ancient custom and Roman rule, exclaimed, "To Charles, the most pious Augustus crowned by God, the great, peace-bringing emperor, life and hail!"

Tradition tells us that Charlemagne was crowned without himself being prepared for it. Moreover, at that moment he could not be entirely content with it either, first, because he received the imperial dignity out of the hands of the pope who after all was subordinate to him – and the same would happen to his successors. It was a very cunning move of the "Petrinian," which for centuries would have great consequences in Europe. Secondly, Charlemagne was concerned because he maintained good connections with Byzantium, the Byzantinian emperor still carrying the title *imperator Romanorum*, "emperor of the Romans." In order not to rebuff him, Charlemagne after careful consultation chose the less pretentious title, *Romanum gubernans imperium*, "governor of the Roman Empire."

However, the most essential point clearly came to expression in this title: Charlemagne ruled over the ancient *(West-) Roman Empire*. The pope therefore argued for the *translatio imperii*, the "transfer of the empire." Such a *translatio* had taken place before, when Constantine transferred the empire to the Greeks (that is, at Constantinople). Now the pope, on the basis of an authority founded on the see of "Peter," transferred the empire from the Greeks (that is, the still extant East-Roman Empire) to the Franks. This was what was called a *renovatio imperii Romani*, "renewal of the Roman Empire" (as Charlemagne wrote in his imperial bull) under Frankish authority.

Now, in the sense of Augustine's great work, *De civitate Dei* ("On the City of God"), the Roman Empire after all had primarily been the *civitas terrena*, the empire of the devil. What interest, then, did the pope, as the head of the *civitas Dei*, have in restoring this empire? The answer is that this restored empire was above all a Christian empire, the *imperium christianum*, as it was called even in the church liturgy. It is quite telling that *De civitate Dei* was Charlemagne's favorite book! His empire did not stand over against the *civitas Dei*, but represented the earthly part of the church, the "kingdom of everlasting peace in this world," as his court scholar, Alcuin of York, put it.[19]

It is to be constantly kept in mind that a "Christian" empire does mean here, a *Petrinian* empire, the empire of Janus, the angelic prince of Rome. That does not take anything away from the many good, positive-Christian things that existed in

19. Yates (1975:2-3).

this empire, and the many faithful Christians that belonged to it. But this was not only due to, but often also in spite of, Charlemagne. Notorious is the horrible way in which he forced the Saxons to be Christianized; that is, not winning them for Christ, but submitting them to the Janus of Rome. As Clovis before him, Charlemagne made it very clear to which god his life belonged. With the craftiest means, he extended his "Christian" empire. Every instrument to reach this end was permitted; presumably, he even had the king of Denmark poisoned, only because the latter wanted to revenge the poor Saxons.

Even the Anglo-Saxon Petrinian, Alcuin, abhorred of the atrocities against the Saxons, who had been driven with violence into the baptismal water. On the other hand, it was none other than Alcuin, Charles's most loyal friend and counselor, who, in a famous letter, strikingly characterized Charlemagne's significance. He compared him with the pope and with the emperor of Byzantium, and concluded that Charlemagne surpassed both men in wisdom as well as in power. It did offend Charlemagne, though, that the emperor of Byzantium could not accept him as a Roman emperor, and not even owned him as a Roman. Charlemagne would have liked to overcome this problem by marrying the East-Roman empress, Irene, the widow of emperor Leo IV. She was a bigot, a religious fanatic, and luxuriating in her power. In 790, she even had the nerve of having her own son's eyes gouged out; this was Constantine VI, then 27 years of age, who in name was the emperor. Charles's plan to marry this woman—she had already consented!—was frustrated by her early death in 802.

6.1.4. Franks and Jews

From a metahistorical viewpoint, the history of the Ancient World is the history of the conflict between Jacob and Esau, or, between the God of Israel and the angelic prince of Rome. This is a conflict quite varying in character. At times, the angelic prince fiercely turns himself against Jacob, as under Constantine the Great, at other times he closes him in the arms, as Esau once did with Jacob. But Esau cannot be trusted. The Jews experienced this again in the new, Germanic empires. At the outset, the new rulers in Italy, after the fall of the West-Roman Empire, assumed a benevolent attitude to the Jews. The East-Gothic king, Theoderic the Great, successor to Odoacer, as an Arian (!) ardently defended the Jews several times over against the population, which, because it was Catholic, did not sympathize too strongly with him.

In Northern and Western Europe, too, the Jews experienced a time free of care under the early Germanic rulers. As merchants, slaves, fugitives, ex-prisoners, soldiers, or homeless people, they spread over this part of the world on the traces of the Roman legions. There they arrived at esteem and prosperity. But during the very time when Clovis became a Petrinian the attitude towards the Jews changes. Just as the Arians were forced to become "Catholic"—that is, Petrinian—thus it happened with the Jews. Here too, therefore, the peculiar situation arises that the *lie* of Arius protected the Jews, whereas those who accepted the *truth* of Athanasius, but in this way unfortunately fell into the arms of Janus/Peter, began to persecute the Jews.

In 465, the council at Vannes (Bretagne) forbade the clergy to eat together with Jews. In 517, the council of Epaon (Burgundy) took the same decision. In 533, the council of Orléans forbade marriages between Christians and Jews. In 538, the council in the same city forbade a fugitive Christian slave to be handed back to his Jewish owner, and forbade the Jews to appear among the Christians from Maundy Thursday to Easter Monday. At the outset, this kind of decree produced only little effect. But especially under pope Gregory I the Great, who mounted the "see of Peter" in 590, the number of anti-Jewish decrees increased enormously. In no way anymore, Janus/Peter permitted any son of Abraham to exert any form of power over "Petrinians." Gregory did turn against the *persecution* of the Jews; more strongly so, he hoped with gentle means to turn the Jews into "Petrinians." This failed, however; in church history, neither means of coercion, nor peaceful attempts have ever led to a both *voluntary* and *massive* Christianization of the Jews. Better than many a willing Christian, they realized, because of an authentic and meta-historical consciousness, the true nature of the "Petrinians" and the Roman representatives of "Peter." When, therefore, at the time of Gregory the Great, one European territory after the other moved from Arianism to "Catholicism"—"Petrinism"—this was a catastrophe for the Jews. The German historian Edmund Schopen (1881-1961) says of this,[20]

> It was the heaviest blow of fate which could strike the Jews of Europe, for from this moment they are defenseless and unprotected over against the hostile attitude of Catholic Christendom, which has brought about the rupture with the severeness of Jewish monotheism.

As soon as the West is unified under the headship of Janus/Peter, the persecutions of the Jews break out. In all West-European countries, the ancient decrees of the councils are now legally enforced, while the Jewish congregations lose their rights. Already in 576, the Jews in Clermont are, for the first time, placed before the choice: to be baptized or to be banished. Elsewhere, similar measures are taken. At many places, the synagogues are destroyed. In 614, the bishops gathered at Paris decree that Jews are not to be allowed in governmental or military posts anymore. It is true that, at that time, the persecutions of the Jews in Spain or Byzantium, for instance, are at least as bad, or far worse, but I now limit myself to the Merovingian Empire.

The face of Janus/Peter is two-sided, however, and this comes out time and again. Under the Carolingians, Janus suddenly turns his other face to the Jews. Pepin the Short allows

20. E. Schopen, *Geschichte des Judentums im Morgenland*, quoted by Keller (n.y.:132).

the Jews their rights again. Charlemagne breaks even more forcefully with the persecutions of the Jewish people, in spite of the fierce protests of the pope. The rights and liberties that Charlemagne allows the Jews, and the way in which he protects them, are really astonishing. From a purely historical viewpoint, this fact can only be explained by Charlemagne's political and diplomatic geniality. For instance, he appoints a Jew called Isaac as an interpreter and guide for an embassy he wants to found at Baghdad. When in 802 Isaac returns to Charlemagne's court, he causes great consternation by the khalif's gift to the emperor: an elephant.

Also, Charlemagne's son, Louis the Pious, is—though the nickname "pious" here means Petrinian[21]—benevolent to the Jews. For instance, he replaces the market at Lyons from the Saturday to a common weekday to meet the Jewish merchants' wishes (though this deed was not free of some economic self-interest). Globally speaking, under the Carolingians the Jews have known a time of peace and prosperity that in European history is not equalled by any other period. In their turn, the Jews brought prosperity to Europe. For a considerable part, it was the Jews who brought the superior medical knowledge of the Arabs to the West. Their international contacts furthered world-trade and created the great, multinational bankers' houses of the Middle Ages. There where the Gentile, Christianized or not, blessed the Jew, he always received great blessing through the Jew.

---

21. Louis the Pious was an admirer of Claudius, a famous Spanish Bible commentator of that time. As soon as Louis became emperor, he appointed Claudius to be bishop of Turin. The latter supported the council of Frankfurt (794), which had been presided by Charlemagne and had condemned all venerations of images. Claudius immediately carried out these decrees, and removed all images, and even all crucifixes, from the churches of Turin. He also openly taught that the apostolic office of Peter had ended with his life, that the "key power" had been transferred to the *entire* episcopal order, and that the pope possessed apostolic power only insofar as he also led an apostolic life.

6.2. The Holy Roman Empire under the Emperor
6.2.1. The Ottonians

Of course, Charlemagne was Petrinian too—but how whole-hearted was that? The pope had crowned him, but in fact, Leo entirely depended on the emperor. Charlemagne, not the pope, was the *custos fidei*, "guardian of the faith," and the *defensor ecclesiae*, "defender of the church." When in 806 he divided his enormous empire among his three sons, he did oblige them, according to the firm custom of his family, to assist Peter and his representative. Therefore, the charter regarding the division of the empire was sent to the pope for his signature. But in 813—by then, two of the three sons had already died—Charlemagne induced his only remaining son, Louis the Pious, to have himself crowned co-emperor at Aix-la-Chapelle (Aachen), without pope Stephen IV and the Romans knowing of this. The Petrinian did not take it lying down. After Charlemagne's death, January 814, he crowned Louis again at Reims. In his turn, Louis induced his son Lothaire in 817 to have himself crowned co-emperor and successor—but here again, the pope repeated it in 823, now at Rome. Already here, a battle of competence revealed itself that would last for many centuries.

Only among Louis's three sons, the Carolingian empire was definitively divided, and that after a long conflict (843: treaty of Verdun). It is remarkable, however, that the first division of the empire had already taken place in 806: exactly one thousand years before the fall of the Eastern part of the ancient Carolingian empire. This is the empire that, since the thirteenth century, is called the Holy Roman Empire, *Sacrum Imperium Romanum*. In 1806, another "Roman" emperor, Napoleon I, put a formal end to this empire (or to what was left of it at that moment). Since the end of the fifteenth century, the title is limited to "Holy Roman Empire of the German nation." It remains to be called *Romanum*, however, even if it never had the size of the ancient Roman Empire. In the word "holy," the "Christian" character of the empire was expressed: it is the *imperium christianum.* In reality, *sacer* has here the original meaning: "holy" in the sense of "consecrated to the gods," or "God," who may be the God of the Bible but also the gods, the angelic princes of the empire, Janus/Peter in the first place.

One and a half century after the imperial coronation of Charlemagne, the resurrected *imperium Romanum* was so divided and weak that again it seemed to be nearing its end. But again, the pope as well as Italy were in distress, and again a mighty protector appeared: the German king Otto I from the Saxon house. This king in his turn had to function as emperor and peacemaker, and as *defensor ecclesiae.* Intentionally in the line of the Carolingian tradition, the *imperium Romanum* was founded again, namely in 962, when Otto I was crowned emperor. To be sure, the name "Holy Roman Empire of the German nation" presumably only dates from the end of the fifteenth century, as I said. In the tenth century, people spoke at best of a *regnum teutonicum,* a "German empire," or a "people's empire," the Germanic word "Teutonic" meaning both things. Yet, the coronation of Otto I the Great, with which again a great, West-European empire emerged, was certainly a "Roman" matter.

In fact, the Ottonian empire was even more "Roman" than that of Charlemagne and Louis in that people for the first time, because of the weakening of Byzantium, found the courage to call the German emperor the "august emperor of the Romans" (*imperator Romanorum augustus*). To this end, Otto gathered enough power in Italy, while the imperial coronation intentionally took place at Rome. Later, the title was even carried by the claimant to the throne, who was called *rex Romanorum,* "Roman king." It is characteristic that the Roman laws of the emperor Justinian, rediscovered around 1075, were simply added to the German-imperial laws, because the German emperors were viewed as direct successors to the Roman ones. In a continually renewed form, the idea of the Roman Empire remained fully intact throughout the Middle Ages. And although, or rather because, the city of Rome was the center of Petrinian Christendom, ancient tradition, the old-Roman customs and views, even the pagan habits at Rome were always held in esteem, not only in the Middle Ages, but in a newer way also later, during the Renaissance.

However, we have to repeat here that this "Holy *Roman* Empire" never encompassed the entire antique Roman Empire. First, there was still the Byzantine emperor, who considered himself to be equal to the "Roman"-German emperor. Neither the Carolingians, nor the Ottonians, nor the popes, ever viewed the German emperor as the emperor of the entire empire, or, as the only emperor. Moreover, the "Holy Roman Empire" never encompassed the ancient West-Frankish kingdom. Only emperor Henry VI (1165-1197) managed to force the English king Richard the Lionheart to honor him as the feudal lord of England, took the feudal oath from the kings of Armenia and Cyprus, wanted, together with Richard, to induce France to do the same thing, and even stretched his hand out to North-Africa as well as to the East-Roman Empire. When Henry died at 32, however, his card-house collapsed.

Neither France nor Byzantium ever belonged to the "Holy Roman Empire." On the contrary, the French-German antithesis would dominate the history of Europe for many centuries. In 954, the year in which the French king Louis IV (great-grandson of Charlemagne's grandson, Charles the Bald) died, the French abbot Adso, in his *De ortu et tempore Antichristi* ("On the Rise and Time of the Antichrist"), claimed that France was Francia, that the French kings were Frankish kings, successors to Charlemagne, and that their empire was the true continuation of the Frankish *imperium Romanum.*[22] This view did not change when in 987 Hugo Capet mounted the French throne. This rivalry even continued until far into the twentieth century, and only stopped after the Second

22. See Adamek (1938:79-80).

World War.

6.2.2. *Universitas Christiana*

In its later phase, already the ancient Roman Empire had a universal character. When, namely, under the influence of Greek thinking, it had laid down its strictly national character, it could grow into an all-encompassing "empire of mankind." It represented a certain world-order and world-culture that was no longer bound to a certain nation. He who had enjoyed the Roman education and had adopted the Roman customs was no "barbarian" anymore, but belonged to "the empire," to the *oikoumenè*, that is, civilized mankind.[23] When, moreover, Petrinian Christendom made Rome its religious capital and the *imperium Romanum* became the *imperium christianum*, henceforth every "Christian" automatically belonged to "the empire." The Petrinian theologians taught that, after God's counsel and providence, the Roman Empire was a preparation for the kingdom of God. This was because people were united and pacified by the Roman Empire, so that they could adopt the gospel more easily. Had not Christ made himself to be inscribed as a Roman citizen at his birth? And had God not taken care that in due time the Roman emperor had become a Christian one? Thus, according God's salvational plan, the whole world had become Christian, and this world was Roman; to be Christian is to be Roman, to be Roman is to be Catholic. Again, in anticipation we can see what rupture with the past the Reformation has brought about.

Even when, in the political sense, the medieval empire was no longer linked to Rome but, for instance, to Aix-la-Chapelle (Aachen) or Byzantium, the tomb and the see of Peter guaranteed the lasting central position of Rome. The place of Greek-Roman pagan culture had been taken up by Roman-Christian culture, which the church preached to the "barbarians." Christianity and barbarity could not go together. The bishops, often stemming from ancient Roman families,

23. Adamek (1938:12).

were the bearers of the Roman culture under the "barbarian" nations, such as the Germanic kingdoms. Where Roman-Catholic Christendom was established, in fact also "the empire" was established, be it not always in the political, then at least in the ideal sense. It was quite common to refer to the Petrinian Christians as *Romani*, "Romans."[24] The church of Rome took over the buildings of the empire—thus the ancient and famous temple of Vesta became a Marian church—as well as the governmental structure of the ancient empire: it called its regions "provinces," "dioceses," "praefectures," etcetera. The church also imitated the ancient *curia* of the Romans, took over its legislation and jurisprudence, and their main offices such as that of *pontifex maximus*. The church absorbed the empire as it were in its deepest inward parts, namely, in its liturgical prayers. Until the twentieth century, the significance of the medieval imperial idea could be found in these prayers, for instance, in the prayers for Good Friday.[25]

To return to the Ottonian period: the "Roman" character of the German empire at that time did not imply the supremacy of the pope. On the contrary, church and state were not yet divided; the emperor was the undisputed head of the undivided "empire of God," the *universitas christiana*. He was the one who gave every new bishop his staff, the one who remained the suzerain of Rome, and who kept a decisive voice at the papal election. Under Otto III this went even further: he led the synods where the pope was present; he could command the pope and appeal against the latter's decrees. Only on papal decisions in strict matters of faith he had no influence.

For the German empire, the Ottonian emperors have been of invaluable significance. It was in their time that this

24. Thus Orosius, Victor Vitensis, Gregory of Tours (see Adamek 1938:16).

25. *...respice ad Francorum benignus imperium, ut et Rex juste imperando, et populus fideliter obediendo, ad gloriam tui nominis et regni tranquillitatem, unanimi pietate conspirent* ("benevolently give heed to the empire of the Franks, in order that the king [= the emperor] by ruling righteously, and the people by obeying faithfully, in unanimous piety may cooperate to the honor of your name, and for the rest of the empire").

empire, which so far had still been rather barbarous, developed into a "Christian"—read, Petrinian—empire, and Roman civilization got a grip upon the population. That with which Charlemagne had made a beginning was now competed: the empire was bestrewn with churches and schools. Of this Roman Empire, emperor Otto III was the absolute Supreme Monarch. Therefore, for our purpose, this period in *political* respect is more important than the later history of the Holy Roman Empire, that is, after 1100, when the spiritual and the secular power were separated. The angelic prince of Rome was here still indisputably associated with the emperor: first, the Carolingians, then the Ottonians. Only from the eleventh century, the angelic prince of papacy manifested itself more and more. Charlemagne and Louis, and afterwards the Ottonians, not only ruled as "deputies" of the deity, but *gratia dei*, "by the grace of the god," that is, in them the deity ruled himself.[26] Indisputably they stood above the clergy, and even determined the election of every new pope.

Particularly in the case of Constantine the Great, we considered the fact that the angelic prince of Rome can assume all kinds of forms. A striking example is an illustration in an evangeliary of Otto III made in Reichenau, depicting the foot washing of Peter (John 13). Art historian Martin Gosebuch[27] believes that it is Christ "who dominates the situation and at the same time stimulates it." All figures visible to the right of Jesus are "carried out as energy in the commanding arm of Christ." At the right side sits Peter, whose attitude expresses

> curved submission and stormily bowing forward in one movement, desirous to receive the salvation going out from Christ.

For a moment, it seems as if the figure of Peter gives way to that of Christ—or perhaps I should say, "Christ," that is, "another Jesus," in the sense of 2 Cor. 11:4. In any case, in this

26. Cf. De Graaff (n.y.:14-15); my interpretation, for that matter, is quite a different one.
27. Quoted by Nitschke (1975:343).

new time we get to know the emperor as *typus Christi*, "image of Christ," that is, expression of the godhead. In the actions of the emperor, the "godhead" is personally "present" as it were. He is almost an embodiment of the godhead, as the ancient kings of the world-empires had been. This we also see in the coronation of Otto I to become king of the Franks and Saxons (936). His election was not "democratic," but a symbolic procedure in which the godhead himself pointed out the new emperor. At this election in the cathedral at Aix-la-Chapelle (Aachen), Otto lay on the floor with his arms stretched out in the form of a cross. In this way, he symbolically took the place of the "crucified god," while the bishops and priests, lying down beside him on the floor, took the place of the twelve apostles, the martyrs, and the confessors. Not the pope, but the king was the *typus Christi*. We will see several times, however, that the figure of Peter certainly does not disappear from the picture.

One of the most important features of the rule of Otto I was his Italian politics. By acquiring more and more power in that region, he obtained authority over the pope and his Papal State. When he protected pope John XII against his enemies, in passing he acquired at Rome the imperial crown (962). The pope was almost startled himself by this event, and sought protection at the emperor of Byzantium against the Saxon emperor, who acquired more and more power. Again, Otto came to Rome, now to teach the pope a lesson. The Romans had to swear that they would not elect a pope without the consent of Otto or his son! They did not obey, and the revenge of Otto that then descended upon them was terrible. At the zenith of his power, he was not satisfied anymore with the title *augustus imperator*, "august emperor," but began to call himself "emperor of the Romans and Franks."

6.2.3. Otto III

The highlights of the career of emperor Otto I were that he was recognized by the Byzantine emperor, that his son Otto

II of 12 was crowned co-emperor in 967 at Rome, and that pope John XIII in 972 at Rome celebrated in the St. Peter the marriage between Otto II and Theophano, a niece of the Byzantine emperor John I Tsimiskes.[28] In this way, in a certain sense a spiritual connection was made between the ancient West-Roman and East-Roman Empire. July 980, a child was born of this marriage, incidentally in the middle of the *Reichswald* (Imperial Forest) between Goch (Germany) and Nijmegen (Netherlands). This was the later emperor Otto III, in whom the unity of "Christian" civilization came to light in such a perfect way as afterwards never occurred again.[29]

The argumentation for this marriage between "East" and "West" was quite curious. At the solemnization of the marriage, a charter on purple parchment with golden letters was drafted, in which the marriage of Otto and Theophano was justified with "God's" desire that mankind would multiply in order to replace the angels who had left him by following Lucifer in his pride! What should we think of this? Lucifer ("light-bearer") is the "morning star" of Isaiah 14, the ancient angelic prince of Babylon, who in fact is identical with the angelic prince of the Roman Empire. What is the deeper, metahistorical link that is suggested here between Lucifer, the angelic prince of Rome, the "old dragon," on the one hand, and these two "Roman" princes on the other? A new, "Roman" generation, which can act as a *substitute* for Lucifer and his angels? Substitution or representation? The questions are not answered; one can only surmise.

28. She was a daughter of prince Constantine Skleros and Sophia Phokas. De Graaf (n.y.:457) rejects this with the argument that, according to Gerbert of Reims, Theophano stemmed *summo Grecorum sanguine* ("from the highest blood of the Greeks"), and that this can only be the imperial blood, namely, that of the famous Romanus II. However, after the death of this emperor, when his son Basilius was still a minor, two of his generals ruled *de facto* as emperors (963-976). One of them was a Phokas; the other, John I, an uncle of Theophano, is called "emperor" by none other than De Graaff (n.y.:63) himself! If Theophano stemmed from a Skleros-Phokas marriage, she still came from the "highest Greek blood."

29. De Graaff (n.y.:16).

In 973, Otto I died and was succeeded by his son. The emperor Otto II in his turn already died in 983, at Rome of all places, so that he, as the only German emperor, was buried in the atrium of the old St. Peter. His successor as king over Germany and Italy was his little son Otto, who was only three. At Christmas, Otto was crowned in Aix-la-Chapelle (Aachen). His grandmother and mother, the empresses Adelheid and Theophano, acted as regents. Shortly after, Otto was kidnapped by the duke of Bavaria, who claimed the throne for himself. When, however, the diet of the Empire spoke in favor of Otto, the duke gave the child back to his mother. That took place on June 29, 984, the feast of Peter and Paul. At the moment of transfer, heaven directly interfered in the affair: in broad daylight, a bright star or comet allegedly appeared at the sky!

From 985, the beautiful, highly civilized Byzantine, Theophano, was the only regent; she liked to sign as *Theophanou divina gratia imperatrix augusta*, "Theophano, august empress by divine grace." When in 991 she died at Nijmegen, the pious grandmother Adelheid again took the regency upon herself. She signed as follows: "Adelheid, empress by God's gift, by herself a sinner, the servant of the servants of God." In 994, at 14, king Otto at his own request was declared to be of age, after which he pushed aside his grandmother. The young German-Byzantine "Roman king," who was to become one of the greatest German emperors, wished to rule himself. The following spring, he, like so many German candidate emperors before and after him, marched over the Alps to Rome. On the way, he got the message that the pope had died, whereupon he appointed his cousin and domestic chaplain, Bruno, aged 24, to be the pope's successor. It demonstrates the power and determination of Otto that he, as a German, had the courage to appoint another German, and such a young one at that, as the next pope. It had not occurred in two hundred and fifty years that a "Roman" outside the city of Rome was appointed pope. Through this new pope, who called himself Gregory V,

Otto had himself crowned emperor on Ascension Day, May 21, 996, at Rome. Where could this take place better than at the tomb of Peter? At the time, the city was a muddle of many ruins with between them ramshackled palaces and temples; but the tomb of Peter was indestructible.

Thus it happened that a 24 year old German pope placed the imperial crown on the head of a 16 year old German cousin. Interestingly enough, at this solemn occasion the emperor wore priestly garments, to manifest very clearly that he, not the pope, was Christ's substitute on earth, the *ecclesiae protector ac defensor* ("protector and defender of the church"). In fact, Otto was a kind of secular priest, as the kings David and Solomon had been in old Israel. At his entry in the St. Peter, not only the imperial sword was carried along, but also the relics of the "true" cross of Christ, as well as the lance with which the soldier Longinus allegedly had pierced the dead Christ (John 19:34).

The "gods" had chosen as supreme monarch a "Roman" emperor who was so gifted that his contemporaries called him *Mirabilia mundi*, the "wonder of the world." Byzantine and German teachers taught Otto to speak Greek and Latin fluently, and made him conversant with philosophy, mathematics, music, and poetry. But he was also trained in horse-riding and military affairs. The friend and counselor of the young emperor was the theologian and philosopher, Gerbert of Aurillac (or, of Reims). In a writing of 997,[30] the latter praised Otto III as the

> emperor of the Romans, always increaser of the empire (...) stemming out of the noblest Greek blood, surpassing the Greeks in power, who by hereditary right makes the Romans obey, and who surpasses the Greeks in understanding and eloquence.

The conclusion which he drew was, "Ours, ours is the Roman Empire!" And thus it was in fact: after the fall of the West-Roman Empire, no emperor embodied the idea of the *imperium*

30. *Lettres de Gerbert*, ed. J. Havet, nr. 187, p. 173.

Romanum more outspokenly than this emperor of Greek and Germanic blood. Otto's political main idea was the *renovatio imperii Romanorum*, the "renovation of the Romans' Empire," which concretely implied that Rome again had to stand at the head of the empire. Germany and Italy were to be ruled from Rome. Therefore, Otto established his authority in the ancient imperial capital, and as the emperor constructed a citadel there, probably upon the Palatine. Again, an emperor resided at Rome! In 999, he appointed his friend Gerbert to be the new pope. The fact that the latter assumed the name Silvester II had a deep sense: he suggested in this way the same unity between emperor and pope as, according to the legend, it had once also existed between the emperor Constantine the Great and pope Silvester I.

In the year 1000, Otto marched to Aix-la-Chapelle (Aachen). Many people expected in that year the second coming of Christ; some sold their possessions, others lived merrily in the sense of, "Let us eat and drink, for tomorrow we die" (cf. Isa. 22:13). Out of a deep metahistorical consciousness, Otto, in that very year, opened at Aix-la-Chapelle the sepulchral vault of Charlemagne who, two hundred years before, had been crowned Roman emperor. He did it by night, in deepest secrecy, accompanied by a count and two bishops. The body of Charlemagne sat upon a throne, had a golden crown on its head, and a scepter in its hand. Otto bowed down deeply before the illustrious emperor, and vested him with white garments. The body had still not lost any limbs, except the nose tip, which Otto replaced by a golden prosthesis. He drew a tooth from Charles's mouth, also took the breast-cross, plus a little piece of the clothing, and had the tomb closed again. When his deed came to light, many blamed him for it. In the so-called Hildesheim Annals of the time, it was even asserted that Charlemagne's spirit appeared to him after this desecration of the tomb, and predicted him a bad future. Indeed, Otto had no two years to live anymore.

In the same year 1000, Otto III, then 20 years of age,

assumed a new title: *Servus Jesu Christi*, "servant of Jesus Christ." This title too does not mean that, in Ottonian times, the figure of Peter had to give way to the "other Jesus," the *pseudochristos*, whose representatives the Ottonians have been. On the contrary, Peter was not forgotten. In that same year, at Rome, Otto called himself *Servus apostolorum*, "servant of the apostles," that is, of Peter and Paul. In particular, this implied that he, together with the pope, wanted to act as "Peter's" substitute on earth. As such, he claimed the highest right of disposal over all the Roman-Catholic possessions, and thus he definitively regulated the territory of Peter and his successors. He did so as a "servant," but at the same time as a patron, who held the factual power over this *patrimonium Petri* in his hands. He called Rome *caput mundi*, the "head of the world," the Roman-Catholic church he called "the mother of all churches"—and he himself was the head of Rome, and factually the head of the church. He called the inhabitants of Rome "my Romans."

However, it must be added here that the Romans did not care very much for this "Germanic barbarian." When, in 1001, Otto arrived at Rome one other time, an uproar arose against him, while his troops unfortunately were encamped outside the city. With a small group of loyal people, Otto broke out of his palace, and fought himself through the narrow lanes to the Angel's Citadel. He reached the Citadel by the pure magic of the holy lance of Longinus, which was carried along by a bishop. The uproar stayed unabated, however. Otto was so disillusioned that perhaps, as has been presumed, he sought death. In any case, he left the citadel and exposed himself to the rebels. An eye witness reports:[31]

> With a pale face and a voice trembling of passion he said, encompassing all with one glance, "so that's you, those whom I called my Romans... I led you into the farthest regions of my empire, there where even your fathers, when they still

31. Quoted in Schoonwater (1986:39-40).

> dominated the world, had never set a foot. I regarded you as my sons, as children whom I preferred above all, so that I incurred the hatred and envy of others. And now, out of gratitude you attacked me in the back, me, your father, and killed my friends, and expelled me from your community..."

The miraculous power coming out of this emperor, only 20 years of age, was incredible. Standing between his enemies unprotected, he managed to bewitch them all with his word. The mood turned completely, and the instigators of the uproar were cast at his feet half-dead. Yet, Otto understood that Rome was untenable for him. While the spectators wept, he silently mounted his horse, and left the city. He was restless and depressed; he felt abandoned by his god, who did not need him anymore. He began to fast severely, visited several sanctuaries, and even considered to settle in a monastery. But no, he became active again. Once more, he attempted to take Rome—in vain. Rome was, and remained, a wish-dream, which estranged him from the German princes. One archbishop wrote that this was Otto's sin that he did not want to see his beloved German birth ground anymore:[32]

> like an ancient pagan king, he meddled in a purposeless way with the Rome that was rotten of old age...

What would have become of this man if a long life had been granted to him? We do not know; already the next year, he died, only 21 years of age. Before that, his pious grandmother Adelheid had received the message from the "gods." As the chronicler of Merseburg reports, one day she received a vision in the middle of a prayer. She fell on the ground at full length, and called in trance,[33]

> Lord in heaven... help, help... my son the king... I see him... many will find death in Italy... and then he will also languish there... he, Otto, of the imperial race...

32. Ibid. (1986:39-40).
33. Ibid. (1986:39-40).

It was the malaria that, after a short sickbed, felled Otto. When he sensed that his death-hour was near, he had the relic of Christ's cross and the holy lance placed by his bed. To bishop Heribert of Cologne he handed the regalia, and ordered him to bury him in Aix-la-Chapelle. January 23, 1002, he died at Paterno. The embalmed body was carried over the snow-covered Alps, while several times fanatical enemies trying to rob the body had to be repulsed. Finally, at Easter Saturday, the procession arrived at Aix-la-Chapelle, where at Easter Sunday the body was entombed in the cathedral.

Meanwhile, in South-Italy the Byzantine bride Zoe, intended for Otto, had arrived in vain. A new marriage between the two ancient parts of the Roman Empire was not granted to the pair because of the early decease of the bridegroom. The shock of Otto's death was tremendous. Already within a few years, the first legends began to be woven around his person. No "Roman" emperor had stirred the imagination more than he did. Even that other remarkable, European emperor, Napoleon I, could not withdraw himself from it. His strawman, bishop Marc-Antoine Berdolet, had Otto's great sarcophagus broken down, while the French prefect, Alexandre Méchin, opened the tomb. According to one tradition, the bones of Otto III were transferred to Paris, after some remains had been distributed among the bystanders. According to another tradition, the bones would have been interred again at the cemetery, since long dissolved, at the Monsheimallée in Aix-la-Chapelle (Aachen).

6.2.4. The Second and Third Rome

Perhaps this is a good point to say something more about that "other Rome," Constantinople or Byzantium, which for a moment, in Otto III, was so closely attached to the first Rome (be it not by his own marriage). In 326, Constantine the Great had chosen Byzantium at the Bosporus as the new capital of the empire, and gave it the name Constantinople ("city of Constantine"). One of the fascinating aspects of this city is that, as a *Christian* city, it explicitly took its stand over against the still essentially *pagan* Rome. For this reason, too, it received the nickname "Second Rome." This antithesis was sharpened by the division of the empire in 395 under the two sons of the emperor Theodosius. When in 476 Rome fell, and thus the Roman Empire factually ceased to exist, the East-Roman emperor Zeno at Constantinople was of a different opinion. He did not regard the imperial unity as further broken down, but rather as restored: where one emperor had fallen out, now the *whole* empire belonged to the one Byzantine emperor again. Zeno simply declared the new rulers in the West, Odoacer in particular, to be his subjects.

If the West-Roman Empire came to its end in 476, with the East-Roman Empire this factually happened in the beginning of the seventh century—not by conquest, but by the introduction of the "Greek emperorship" under the emperor Heraclius I. Henceforth, the emperor is the *basileus*, "king," of a Greek-Christian national state, even if he, in a purely formal way, is still the emperor of the Byzantine empire of the *Rhomaioi*, Greek for "Romans." The essence of this empire is formed by the *Roman* idea of the state, the *Greek* language and culture, and the *Christian* faith. That which the Franks were for the West-Roman Empire, was what the Persians and the Arabs were for the Byzantine empire, who in several wars were repulsed. In this way, room for great cultural bloom and political power was created.

After the year 1000, the Byzantine power gradually crumbled away. As in the Holy Roman Empire, the power of the feudal rulers grew, and the central authority was more and more diminishing. In 1204, Byzantium was even conquered by the collective crusaders—a sad conflict, in which the Western Christians did not fight against Islam, which had been the intention of the crusades (§ 6.3.4), but against their brothers in the East. The country was divided up, and a "Latin" empire was established. In the Hagia Sophia, the ancient church of Constantinople, Baldwin VI count of Hainault (that is, Baldwin IX count of Flanders) was crowned emperor (Baldwin I); he died a year later in Bulgarian captivity. After this episode, the empire was perceptibly falling off. Its territory was swallowed ever further, until the ancient imperial city in 1453 was taken by the Turks and turned into the capital of their Islamic empire. To some extent, this catastrophe was a blessing for the West because Greek scholars from Byzantium took the heritage of Greek antiquity to Italy—a tremendous injection for the Renaissance.

It is true that the Greek orthodoxy remained upon the Balkan, but the leading role within orthodoxy was no longer to be found there. It was taken over by Russia. After the slavification of the tribes at the Dnieper, these were called "Rus." Around the year 1000, grand-duke Wladimir "the Saint" at Kiev with an iron fist introduced Christianity in Russia. The new Russian church stood under the patriarchate of Byzantium, but the church language was Slavic. After centuries of war, confusion, and decay, we see the principality of Moscow rising in the fourteenth century, over which Iwan Kalita became grand-duke. Moscow became the see of the orthodox metropolitan (ecclesiastical ruler), and after long wars, the city became the undisputed center of a new, Great-Russian empire.

When in 1453 the Byzantine empire was conquered by the Turks, and thus the "Second Rome" collapsed, its role was taken over by Moscow, which after 1510, at the instigation of the monnik Filofei (Philotheos), was called the "Third Rome": the new bulwark of Eastern orthodoxy. From Byzantium it adopted its hatred against Rome and the church of Rome, and it despised the "Second Rome" because this city allegedly had been lost as a consequence of concessions to the Roman-Catholics. Henceforth, the "Third Rome" carried the pretension of gaining the world for true orthodoxy. Then, Iwan III the Great also assumed the title of *czar*, a corruption of *caesar*, that is, "emperor" in the Roman sense. The czar of Russia regarded himself as the spiritual successor to the emperor of

Byzantium, and took over all the latter's attributes. By also marrying Zoe, the niece of the last Byzantine emperor, Iwan made his charisma entirely unassailable.

In 1589, the church of Moscow, which in practice had since long severed itself from Byzantium, also formally became independent of it by being elevated to a patriarchate. The czar became officially the head of the church, as had been the case in Byzantium. Metahistorically, this was of great importance, because henceforth the czar was not only a "holy person," but was also "deified" to a certain extent. Such a thing always means that people are religiously conscious of the god, or gods (angelic princes), that are embodied in the ruler. The veneration of the czar was even included in the Russian-orthodox liturgy. In Byzantium, the god of the East-Roman Empire had made place for those of Islam. But in "Christian" Europe, apart from the gods of ancient Rome, henceforth those of the "Third Rome" were not to be underestimated.

In 1613, the Romanov dynasty came to the throne. Its name reminds us of ancient Rome and they were to remain in power until the Russian Revolution (1917). Around 1700, czar Peter I the Great, who lived for a while at Zaandam (Netherlands) to practice ship-building, led his empire into Western civilization. Little less than a century later, empress Catharine II the Great was even a representative of the French Enlightenment. After the Napoleonic wars, czar Alexander II introduced further reformations, but these could not prevent the Russian Revolution. After 1917, Lenin, and after him Joseph Stalin in particular, as the absolute sole ruler, became in fact a new czar.

From a spiritual and metahistorical viewpoint, it is an interesting question whether Russia belongs to Europe.[34] In the present European unification, this question becomes especially relevant. If one looks at the influence of the French Enlightenment in Russia, at the arts, music, and literature, oriented

34. Cf. Pomian (1993:131).

toward the West, and at the Russian role in Europe, especially during the Napoleonic and the national-socialistic period, Russia certainly belongs to the historical European cultural domain. However, there are other factors, which until today make of Russia a non-, or even anti-European power. That is, first, such a simple thing as its Cyrillic writing, by which it always stood at a distance of Western Europe, whereas other Slavic countries chose Latin writing.

Secondly, also after the fall of communism and of the Soviet-Union (1990), its autocratic governmental form was essentially maintained in the person of Boris Yeltsin, and subsequently Wladimir Putin, and still always places itself above all traditions and all commandments of religion.

Thirdly, there is the still mighty influence of Russian orthodoxy, which, apart from a few Balkan countries (Romania, Serbia, Bulgaria, which each have their own Orthodox Church), is shared by no European country, and which continues to be sharply opposed to everything that has to do with the "first Rome" (not to speak of Protestantism). It is striking that after the fall of communism, the bonds between orthodoxy and the new regime have been strongly renewed. Even today, a sharp line runs from North to South through Europe, separating Catholicism and Protestantism in the West from Orthodoxy and Islam in the East.

The contradictory answer to the question as to whether Russia belongs to Europe—yes and no—is connected with a serious discord within Russian culture itself, going back to the time that czar Peter the Great introduced the Western achievements in Russia. It is the discord between slavophiles and Western-minded people, which today is still alive (and today keenly sensible in a country like Ukraine). The frightening nationalism of the Russian Wladimir Zhirinowski, but also the still mighty communist party belong to the first, the Western orientation of Putin, and more clearly the democrats and the reformation-minded belong to the second wing.

6.3. The Holy Roman Empire under the Pope

6.3.1. The Beginning Conflict around the Investiture

Metahistorically speaking, the importance of the further history of the German-Roman emperorship consists in the conflict around the so-called "investiture." This is the (right of) establishing a bishop in his office. The emperor argued that, because many bishops were also secular rulers of their dioceses (like those of Utrecht, Münster and Cologne, for instance), they were his vassals, and therefore only *he* had the right to install them in their offices ("invest" them with the robe). The pope contested that, because the bishops were clergymen, serving the church, only the head of the church had the right to install them in their offices. Since the Christianization of the Roman Empire (fourth century), there had always been two captains on the ship: the head of the Roman Empire and the head of the Roman Church.

Undisputed, the emperor had always been the greater of the two. In the eleventh century, this began to change. During this conflict, the power gradually moved to the pope at Rome. Much more emphatically than before, the angelic prince of Rome chose his seat at Rome, which now was papal Rome. Otto III was succeeded by his second cousin, emperor Henry II, who still held great power over the church, and was called the "substitute of God [read, the god] on earth." At his death, with which the Ottonian house died out, he was lamented as "the lord of Rome, the lord of the church." He was the only emperor who was ever canonized (declared a saint) by Rome, and thus at least still gave some substance to the sacral character of the "holy" Roman Empire.

After Henry II, the Salian house came to power, which did descend from Otto I, for that matter. The first emperor of this house was Conrad II, who was crowned emperor in 1027 at Rome. At that occasion, the archbishop of Mainz spoke the telling words, "You climbed to the highest dignity, you are the *vicarius Christi*," that is, the substitute (or deputy) of Christ. Conrad's successor was his son, emperor Henry III, who, entirely in line with Otto III and his own father, felt closely related with Rome. The circumscription of the empire as *Romanum imperium*, the "Roman Empire," became more and more popular. Already by his father Conrad, in the latter's first imperial charter, Henry was depicted as *Heinricus spes imperii*, "Henry the hope of the empire." In the second charter we find *aurea Roma*, "the golden Rome," depicted with the subscription: *Roma caput mundi tenet orbis frena rotundi*, "Rome, the head of the world, holds the reins of the earth globe." Since then, this device was written in the seals of the German-Roman emperors.

However, it was at the time of Henry III that the first overt protests arose against the emperor's supremacy over the pope. In a work, *De ordinando pontifice* ("On Appointing the Pope"), it was openly contested that the emperor had the right to steer the papal election. Henry was not bothered much by this and kept influencing the papal elections. However, he was confronted with an extraordinary opponent: the theologian, lawyer, and diplomat Humbert, consecrated by pope Leo IX to be the cardinal-bishop of Silva Candida. Humbert had very outspoken viewpoints, and exerted great influence. One of the points that he fought for was precisely a new respect for Peter, of whom he even asserted,[35]

> Peter carries in the first place the whole weight of the Christian building (...) on his inflexible neck he lifts all members of Christ heavenward.

In line with this, also the deputy of Peter at Rome had to be respected, to such an extent that the emperors of the East- and West-Roman Empire clearly ranked second. He called them only the "arms" of Peter's deputy, that is, they were just the executives of the pope's will. He despisingly called the Ottonians "new converts." In his view, the church was the "soul," the empire was only the "body." As a consequence of this, the

35. Quoted by Nitschke (1975:382).

bishops were to be invested with the tokens of their dignity (the "investiture") no longer by the king, but by the higher clergy, ultimately by the pope. It was still the "deity" who was to appoint the candidates for the office—also the Carolingians and Ottonians had viewed it this way—but it was no longer to be done by a layman, but by a clergyman.

In 1050, the pope appointed Humbert archbishop of Sicily. That was quite presumptuous because Sicily, though at that moment occupied by the Saracens, nominally still belonged to the East-Roman Empire. This challenging of Byzantium led from one thing to the other. The deep cleft between the Eastern and the Western empire turned out to be a cleft between the Eastern and the Western church as well. It was none less than Humbert who at Constantinople, in the Hagia Sophia, put all Eastern church leaders under the ban, and thus caused the notorious schism of 1054. Of course, the actual causes were much older and deeper; but the immediate occasion was the "Roman" and Petrinian Humbert.

The schism was only the beginning. The reformational movement started by Humbert and continued by Hildebrand not only insulted the Eastern Empire and the Eastern church, but also the German emperor's house. Against the latter's will, Alexander II was recognized as pope, a man who was wholeheartedly attached to Hildebrand and the reformers. Through him, knight Erembald received the "vane of Peter," in order to combat under that standard the non-reformation-minded priests. With a similar "vane of Peter," that is, with the support and blessing of the reformation-minded pope, the duke of Normandy, William "the Conqueror," conquered England in 1066, and laid it at the feet of Peter. With a similar "vane of Peter," Roger I combated the Saracens in Italy. Humbert "supported" all this with his interpretation of Daniel 2: the "stone" coming down from the mountain is not Christ coming again, as the large majority of the ancient church fathers had taught, but the Petrinian papacy, which had become an enormous, strong and impressive mountain.

Peter seemed to have definitively chosen the side of the reformation-minded, that is, the side of the pope over against the emperor. In a dramatic way, this finally came to light for all people to see. In 1065, the son of Henry III, who had succeeded him as king Henry IV in 1056, came of age. Henry first collided with pope Alexander II, but the latter died in 1073 and was succeeded by none less than the ardent reformer, Hildebrand, henceforth called Gregory VII. He was a Petrinian to the bone, who regarded himself almost as the embodiment of Peter. In him it became sharply visible that Peter henceforth was not to be identified with the emperor anymore, but with the pope. The pope "was" Peter: when the pope read letters, it was Peter who read those letters; when the pope answered them, it was Peter who through the pope dictated the words. Because of this identification, Gregory proclaimed that all popes by definition were "saints." Christ prayed for the faith of Peter (Luke 22:32), and thus also for the representative of Peter on earth, and therefore the pope was in his decisions holy and infallible.

6.3.2. Separation of Church and State

The things Humbert had preached as ideals could be realized by Gregory in his papal office. Everlasting life was only destined for those who were in contact with Peter, that is, with his representative at Rome. If at all possible, the believers ought to make a pilgrimage to Peter's tomb at Rome. Opposing the pope was opposing the "rights of Peter," and had to be suppressed with violence. Indeed, the pope did so with the help of the so-called "faithful of Peter," that is, the papal troops. Through Gregory's far-fetched Petrinian mysticism, not only Peter got to the first rank, but in this way papacy too; just read Gregory's famous *Dictatus papae*, in which the position of the pope was established. The roles had been turned upside down: not the emperor appoints the pope or the bishops, but the pope appoints bishops and also dismisses them, and can even dismiss emperors.

It turned out that a conflict with king Henry IV about this matter could not be avoided. Because the king continued appointing bishops, he incurred a sentence involving that he no longer belonged to the "sons of Peter." Gregory earnestly threatened Henry, whereupon the latter convened the diet at Worms. The German bishops chose the side of the king. In Worms, cardinal Hugo Candidus even accused the pope of illegitimately occupying the "see of Peter." Thereupon the diet decided to dismiss the "false monk Hildebrand," and to inform him of this in a letter. When Gregory received the letter, he banished king Henry and his men from the church *in a prayer to Peter*:

> ... with the fetters of the ecclesiastical bull I bind them in your stead [cf. Matt. 16:19], so that all nations know and recognize that you are Peter, and that on this *petra* the son of the eternal God has built his church, and the gates of hell will not prevail over her [v. 18].

When some contested the pope's right of the bull he appealed to Christ, who had said to Peter, "Tend my sheep" (John 21:16), and explained,[36]

> When with those words the Lord entrusts his church to the apostle Peter, does not everyone then see that, if God thus particularly on him confers the power to bind and to loose in heaven and on earth, he did not exempt anyone from this and withdrew no one from that power? (...) If, in virtue of the power transferred to it by God, the holy apostolic see judges the spiritual things on the highest level, why will it not do the same with the secular affairs? When spiritual persons belong to its jurisdiction, why will secular persons not do the same, when they do something wrong?

The whole conflict in fact turned around the question: on whose side stood Peter, or, the angelic prince of Rome? For a long time, Janus had shown his two faces: one to the emperor

36. Gregory's letters 4,2; quoted by De Visser (1926:141).

of Rome, the other to the pope of Rome. Now he was forced to choose, or, he was the one who steered the whole process—and he did. Henry demanded of Gregory that he would abandon the "see of Peter," but this put pressure on the German princes and bishops. At the summit of the conflict, the pope and the king traveled in each other's direction, and met in Northern Italy, at Canossa. On January 26, 1077, Henry, in spite of the fierce cold, appeared barefoot and in a penitential garment before the gate of the castle where the pope stayed. For three days, the pope refused to receive to him. Finally, under the pressure of his friends, he gave in, gave the king absolution, and together with him celebrated the Eucharist. Henry submitted to the pope, and thus acknowledged that henceforth Peter was on the side of the Roman(-Catholic) empire's spiritual leader. The king was no more a *typus Christi* as the Ottonians had still been. Gregory clearly formulated this:[37]

> The Lord Jesus Christ, the king of honor, appointed the blessed apostle Peter to be *principem super regna mundi* [prince over the empires of the world].

Of course, the Bible says nothing of the kind—yet there is truth in this statement: it is the angelic prince who is in charge. His earthly deputy, the Petrinian pope, is the sun. The emperor and all earthly princes are the moon, who receive their light from the papal sun. In this sharp form, this idea is new and unheard of. Gregory even ventures to compare an earthly prince forcing the "priests of the Lord" to bow down before him with the devil at the temptation in the wilderness, who demanded the same thing of Christ[38]—and that while his own angelic prince, Janus/Peter, was only an angel of the devil. More forcefully than anyone before him, Gregory VII established the church as the *secular* Roman Empire of Peter.

---

37. Gregory's letters 1,63.
38. Gregory's letters 8,21; cf. 1,63; 4,23.24. See on the whole conflict extensively the discussion by Holland (2012).

In other words, as from his rule, the Roman-Catholic church itself is, for some centuries, the factual metahistorical continuation of the ancient Roman Empire.

The conflict between emperor and pope was certainly not definitively decided for that matter. Over against Henry, a counter-king was appointed, Rudolf of Rheinfelden, who in 1080 received the support of the pope. Shortly after, however, the German and Italian bishops elected a counter-pope, Clemens III. A battle between Henry and Rudolf led to the death of the latter. On the same day, Gregory's army was defeated by that of Clemens. Now Henry marched to Rome, and the tables seemed to be turned. In 1083, he conquered the St. Peter. The next year, Rome opened the gates for Henry, and Gregory was deposed. Clemens was officially established as pope, and shortly after crowned Henry emperor. Heavy fights sprang up at Rome, which even led to the destruction of whole quarters of the city.

Only under the successors, king Henry V and pope Pascal, the situation became clearer. In 1110, Henry came to Rome, and demanded the acknowledgement of the royal right of investiture. Pope Pascal considered a compromise that so far would have been inconceivable, namely a separation of the *spiritualia* and the *temporalia*, the spiritual and the secular rights. That was new. Neither the Carolingians and Ottonians, nor Humbert and Hildebrand (Gregory VII), had ever thought in terms of "church and state," let alone a separation between them. They knew and accepted only the one Christian community in Europe. Therefore, the conflict between Henry IV and Gregory VII was not a conflict between the "state" and the "church," but a battle for the supremacy in the "Kingdom of God," the *civitas Dei*. The spiritual and the secular dominion were the two "swords" of which Jesus had spoken (Luke 22:38), and which both belonged in Peter's hand.[39] Priesthood and kingship were the two "eyes" in the

39. In 1232, the later pope Gregory IX gave a further explanation of this: "Please notice what the Lord in the Gospel of Matthew tells Peter: 'Put your sword

one face of the *civitas Dei*.

Now the two separated. Later, we will examine the metahistorical backgrounds of this separation within theology, philosophy and the arts of that time, and in the centuries afterwards. We now limit ourselves to stating that Henry V accepted the proposal of pope Pascal: the "servants of the altar" did no longer have to be "servants of the court" as well. At Rome, Henry was received by Pascal in the St. Peter. The emperor renounced his claim of investiture, while the pope proclaimed that the priests who had received possessions and public rights (*regalia*) from the king had to give these back to him. A storm of protests broke out in the church, and also in the city fights sprang up. Henry had to leave Rome, but took the pope and his cardinals with him as hostages. After weeks of negotiation, finally an agreement was reached: the king would only invest the priests with the possession of the ecclesial territories, whereas only the pope would invest them with the spiritual office.

Now Henry could return to Rome, where on April 13, 1111, he was crowned emperor in the St. Peter. The conflict around the investiture was not yet over, though. Only on September 23, 1122, a definitive Concordat was worked out at Worms. The emperor returned the possessions and *regalia* of Peter, renounced his right of the investiture, but the elections of the highest churchmen would take place in his presence. In case of a difference of opinion, he had to gain the counsel of the

---

into its sheath.' By this 'your sword' he means the material sword with which Peter had beaten the servant of the high priest. Concerning the spiritual sword there is no doubt, since he gave him, that is, Peter, the power of binding and loosing by means of the hight of his spiritual status. Both swords were therefore handed to the church. However, the one is carried by the church, the other is drawn for the church by the hand of the secular prince; the one is used by the priest, the other at the sign of the priest by the warrior" (quoted by De Visser 1926:169; also cf. 191-193, where we hear the same, now in the bull *Unam Sanctam* by pope Bonifatius VIII, of 1302: the pope is *episcopus universalis*, and it is necessary for every man's salvation to be submitted to him!). Here lies the basis for the Inquisition: the church pronounces the sentence, the secular authorities carry it out.

archbishop. This did fall in with the wishes of the reformation party, but at the great, ecumenical Lateran Council (1123) it turned out that many had great difficulty with the separation between *spiritualia* and *regalia*. However, what had been done could not be undone. Henceforth, there is a Christian—read, Petrinian—church, which will forever be separated from that which will be called the "state": the temporal, natural side of society.

6.3.3. Pope Innocent III

It took a long time before the separation between the spiritual and the natural was fully achieved. On the one hand this was because of the emperors Frederic I Barbarossa (1152-1190) and his son, Henry VI (1190-1197), on the other hand because of pope Innocent III (1198-1216). In 1158, Barbarossa undertook a campaign to Italy, where he subdued the Lombardian cities. At a diet on the Roncalian fields near Piacenza he again established the sovereign rights of the emperor. This was done according to the principles of the ancient Roman emperorship, which since the end of the eleventh century were propagated again by Bolognese lawyers. Contrary to the Concordat of Worms, the emperor again placed the church possessions under himself, and within the city of Rome, and the Papal State in the wider sense, he again claimed the suzerainty as the Carolingians and the Ottonians had possessed it.

Under his son, Henry VI, German emperorship even reached a summit: as said before, the emperor obtained a universal European position, and strived for the feudal supremacy over all European countries. He died young and suddenly, however. And when a year later (1198), the brilliant and dominant pope Innocent III came to power, the European power center moved from the German emperor to the pope in such a drastic way as has never occurred in history before or after. As the great German historian, Leopold von Ranke (1795-1886), expressed it, the actual successor to emperor Henry VI was... pope Innocent III.

Count Lothaire of Segni was only 37 years old when he, as the successor to a weak old man and as the youngest of the cardinals, came to papal power under the name Innocent III. He seemed such a brat that the German troubadour Walter von der Vogelweide complained: *hilf herre diner kristenheit.*[40] He could never have been more wrong, for pope Innocent was going to rule over Europe with an iron fist, including kings and emperors. He was what emperor Henry VI had wanted to be: head of the *populus christianus,* the "Christian people." He claimed the patronage over the Roman Empire for himself, so that under him even the emperorship became a loan of the pope. France listened to his commands, king John received England from him as a loan, Portugal had to pay feudal taxes, Pedro II received from him the crown over Aragon and had to own him as feudal lord, and even Eastern powers as Byzantium, Armenia, Serbia, and Bulgaria owned for a time the suzerainty of Rome. The lord of the world was Innocent, who did not hesitate to apply Isaiah 42:8 to himself: "... my glory I give to no other." That is said there of YHWH, who was thus challenged by the "god" of Innocent.

It is interesting to see how the pope founded this right of invention in the affairs of the "Holy Roman Empire." He based it upon the *apostolica sede (...) quae Romanum imperium in persona magnifici Caroli a Graecis transtulit in Germanos,* "the apostolic see [...] which the Roman Empire in the person of Charlemagne transferred from the Greeks to the Germans."[41] The reasoning was that the same papacy that had entrusted the Roman Empire to the Germans (the *translatio imperii*) also had the right to decide at its own discretion the affairs of the Holy Roman Empire. Charlemagne had not acquired or conquered the emperorship but it had been given to him by the pope. In this way, pope Innocent claimed, it had been shown once and for all that the pope, or actually Peter, possessed the supremacy. The "Roman" emperor was only a vassal (feudal

40. "Lord, help your Christendom"; quoted by Seppelt & Löffler (1939:248).
41. Letter of March 1202 to the duke of Zähringen; quoted by Kocken (1935:XI).

tenant) of Peter.

It is fascinating to see how Innocent III found new "evidence" in the history of the biblical Peter to strengthen his own position. Well known of course are the references to Matthew 16:19 (where Christ gives to Peter the keys of the kingdom of heaven) and John 21:17 (where Christ entrusts his flock to Peter). From Matthew 14:29, where Peter walks on the sea, the pope concluded that Peter has dominion over the "sea of the nations" (cf. Isa. 17:12; Rev. 17:15). From Matthew 18:15-18, he concluded that *ratione peccati* ("because of sin") he had the right to judge over and between princes, since in every dispute the possibility of sin can be supposed, and to judge over sin is the domain of the priest. From Matthew 28:18 ("all power in heaven and on earth has been given to me"), the pope concluded that Christ had transferred to Peter the dominion over both the "heavenly" and the "earthly" things, the *spiritualia* as well as the *temporalia*. And from Acts 10:13 ("Rise, Peter, kill and eat") he concluded that Christ renews here Peter's dominion over all *spiritualia* and *temporalia*. He summarized:[42]

> the distinct princes have been placed over the distinct kingdoms; the holy Peter and his successors over all.

And when he called the successor of Peter "less than God, more than a man," in fact he, who himself was perhaps the highest embodiment of Janus/Peter of all times, pronounced a pure truth, be it in another sense than he himself probably intended. He was a *daimonion*, a lower godhead between the supreme God and mankind.

Innocent was notorious for his "crusades" against the Jews and the Albigenses, which clearly show on whose side he was. He abused his power in the service of foreign gods, both in the secular and in the spiritual domain. However, although both domains were united under him, the *antithesis* between the temporal, natural empire, which in particular took shape

42. Quoted by De Visser (1926:166).

in the state, and the eternal, supernatural empire, which in particular took shape in the church, could not be abolished anymore. Theoretically, this antithesis found its brilliant formulation in the doctrine of nature and grace of high scholasticism, which was shortly after Innocent III (§ 6.4.2).

During the same time, German emperorship became weaker and weaker. The factors that enhanced this were (a) the great power of Innocent III, under whom papacy became a world power, (b) the double imperial election in 1198, which led to a disastrous civil war, (c) the rise of national states around Germany, and (d) the increasing independence of the German princes. Once more the idea of the Roman Empire seemed to revive under the highly gifted emperor, Frederic II.[43] But after his death in 1250, the emperorship rapidly declined. Germany lost the supremacy over Italy and its leading role in Europe. Toward 1300, Italian historiographers repeatedly expressed the conviction that with Frederic II the German-Roman Empire had ceased for good. New solicitors came up, however, who, over against the Italians as well as the French, defended the Germans' title to the Roman Empire.

After the Reformation, and particularly after the Peace of Westphalia (or Münster, 1648), at which all the German princes were proclaimed sovereign, the German emperorship became an empty notion, while papacy too was finished as a world power. Those who triumphed were the larger as well as the smaller neighboring countries—such as the Netherlands—and the German princes within the ancient empire. If the *imperium christianum* in political respect was already gone, spiritually speaking it still appeared to exhibit a measure of unity in the fifteenth century. But the Reformation put an end to this.

France in particular became Germany's equal, and at times Germany's superior. France had never belonged to the "Holy Roman Empire." On the contrary, already from the twelfth

43. Yates (1975:8) calls the empire of Frederic II "the fullest and most consistent attempt to restore the Roman Empire" (see p. 5-8).

century, France continually vied with the German empire. As before the French abbot Adso (ninth century) had proclaimed, the illustrious French abbot, statesman, master-builder and biographer, Suger of St. Denis, in the twelfth century openly proclaimed that not Germany but France was the true heir of Rome. According to him, not the German emperor but the French king was the actual successor to the "Roman" Charlemagne. The great French poet, Chrétien de Troyes, pronounced that, according to God's will, the world-empire had been transferred from Greece to Rome, and from Rome to France. The poet Ruteboeuf even connected this with the *presence* of God: "If God dwells anywhere in the world, then no doubt in France." In metahistorical respect, this raises the fascinating question as to what (Roman) god is intended here. What angelic prince dwells like God in France?

6.3.4. The Roman Empire and the Jews

In order to understand the deeper, metahistorical significance of the Holy Roman Empire, we will again have to pay attention to the fate of the Jews. That does not mean that this fate metahistorically can always be easily explained, on the contrary. For instance, the persecution of the Jews under the Merovingians does not astonish us, but the protection of the Jews under the Carolingians and Ottonians does. Although all these imperial houses were Petrinian, Janus in their times subsequently shows his two very different faces. Thus, it was striking, but for that time still very common, that Charles the Bald (823-877), grandson of Charlemagne and ruler in the West-Frankish Empire, had the Jew Juda as counselor, and the Jew Zedekias as physician at his court.

However, as the power of the Carolingians crumbled away, Janus again began showing his other face now and then. The Petrinian bishop Amulo published in 846 his writing, *Contra Judaeos*, "Against the Jews," in which he enlarged on the dangers of the Jews for Christianity, and pleaded for a sharp separation from Jewry. Amulo got support from high

French churchmen, but for the time being their decrees still produced little effect. Only here and there, riots sprang up which aimed at the Jews. Yet, it took until the last of the Ottonians before the tide for the Jews turned. The emperors Otto I and Otto II entrusted the protection of the Jews to the local bishops, under whose regime the Jewish communities flourished.[44] Only in 1012, under the last Ottonian emperor, Henry II, suddenly the order was decreed in Mainz that the Jews had to be baptized, or had to leave. The order was of a temporary nature, however.

One can only make a guess at the backgrounds of this turn. But one thing is certain: it was at that same time that the first reports arrived about violations of many churches and persecutions of the Christians in the Holy Land by the Egyptian khalif, Hakim. Rumors went around saying that the Muslims had been poked up by Jews. Just because of this news, at many places in France persecutions broke out.

The crusades, planned to free the sacred places in the Holy Land, were manifestations of the unity of the *imperium christianum* and of the veneration for the Petrinian pope. For the European Jews, the era of these crusades became a time of great horror. For the first time in November 1095, the call of pope Urban II and many knights reverberated through Europe: *Deus vult*, "God wants it!" God wanted a crusade against the "unbelievers" in the Holy Land. One wonders: what god wanted this? The call by itself was enough to murder the Jews in Cologne as "arch-enemies and murderers of Christ." The crusade against the Muslims in the Near East was accompanied by a crusade against the Jews at home. In 1096, many "warriors of Christ" marched from place to place to ransack all Jews whom they met, and to kill all those who refused to be baptized. Within a few months, many thousands of Jews in France and Germany met their death.

44. Well-known is the story—told again by De Graaff (n.y.:64)—about the Jew Kalonymus, who in 982 saved the life of emperor Otto II over against a band of Muslims.

Not all leaders agreed with this massacre. Several bishops resisted, and emperor Henry IV protested equally vehemently. He allowed the baptized Jews to return unpunished to Judaism. However, this led to heated objections by pope Clemens III, who called it "sin" if the baptized Jews were allowed to apostatize from the church and to violate the sacrament of baptism. The emperor was not intimidated, however. The conflict between emperor and pope around the investiture found a striking counterpart in this conflict about the Jews. The battle around the investiture eventually led to the sharp cleft between church and state; the conflict about the Jews led to the definitive cleft between Judaism and Christianity—a cleft as had actually never existed before in Europe in such a smarting way. Also the subsequent crusades (1146-47 and 1189-93) led to terrible persecutions of the Jews.

A lowest point was reached during the third Lateran Council (1179) and under pope Innocent III (1198-1216), who humiliated the Jews most of all, and pushed them away as pariahs to the lowest level of society. New life was breathed into church laws from the time of the Merovingians, both in 1179 and during the fourth Lateran Council in 1215. Again, Jews and Christians were sharply separated. Again, in public life Jews had to distinguish themselves from Christians by certain signs. Ideas such as that of the Jewish star did not primarily come up in national-socialist, but in Petrinian heads: henceforth, for many centuries, the Jews were to be dishonored by this kind of decree. Time and again, the popes ensured the observance of these humiliating decrees, in all countries of Europe. True, some emperors like Frederic II, and popes like Innocent IV and Gregory X, were cast in a better mould. But the diabolical flood that was poured out over European Jewry could not be dammed anymore.

The horrible persecutions of the Jews in those centuries cannot be severed from the supremacy of the papacy at that time. For instance, these persecutions received a wholly new impulse by three disgusting Petrinian accusations: the Jews allegedly were "murderers of God" (for they had killed Jesus), committed ritual murders (particularly during the Passover feast), and were host desecrators. The Petrinians themselves worshipped a Roman "god," and had thus denied the God of Scripture. Therefore, the fact that they accused the Jews of having "murdered God" sounds quite cynical from their mouths. Through Humbert, the Petrinians had also alleged that

> bread and wine are not only sacraments, but the true body and the true blood of the Lord (...) the body of the Lord is broken in reality, and ground by the teeth of the believers.[45]

Against the background of such a vulgar doctrine, eventually leading to the official doctrine of transubstantiation—"chew your own god"—it is cynical to hear the Petrinians accusing the Jews of ritual killings and of having "murdered God."

Was it a "coincidence" that the Jews had their greatest peace and prosperity in Europe at the time of the Carolingians and Ottonians, that is, *when the supremacy was in the hands of the emperor*, and their most horrible period since the reformational movement of Humbert and Hildebrand (Gregory VII), that is, *when the supremacy moved to the hands of the papacy*? It is difficult to believe that. The Carolingians and the Ottonians were full-blooded Petrinians, that cannot be denied. But did they still form a counter-weight against the power of the angelic prince Janus/Peter? A counter-weight which falls away when the actual power in Europe moves to the hands of the pope, that is, of Janus/Peter? It is difficult, if not impossible, to give a final judgment on this matter. But if we are prepared to accept the fate of the Jews as an indicator for the metahistorical developments in Europe, we will have to ask such questions time and again. It is not for nothing that the thirteenth, fourteenth, and fifteenth centuries are the centuries in which papacy experienced its moral decline. Only during the Reformation, when the spiritual power of Janus/Peter was

45. Quoted by Nitschke (1975:382).

broken, new light began to shine in Europe, also—be it faintly—for the Jews.

For those who can interpret it metahistorically I have kept the greatest surprise until the end. If it is true that at the time of Hildebrand (pope Gregory VII) the worst persecution of the Jews began, what to think of the fact that *Hildebrand, as well as his predecessor and teacher, Gregory VI, had himself Jewish blood in their veins?* Both originated from the wealthy Jewish family Pierleone at Rome.[46] The patriarch of the family, Baruch, was a rich Jewish businessman in the Jewish quarter of Rome, who in his time had been a counselor and financier of pope Benedict IX. The latter told him that, if he wanted to maintain his business relationship with the pope, he had to become a Christian. Eventually Baruch consented, was baptized, and assumed the name of his connection (Benedict), which happened to be the Latin translation of his name, Baruch ("blessed"), but remained associated with the Jewry. His son was steward of another pope, Leo IX, had himself baptized too, and also assumed the name of his master, Leo. Our Hildebrand, the later pope Gregory VII, was born of a daughter of this Leo. Because of his character as well as his piety, the theologian Peter Damian († 1072/3) once called him a "holy devil."

When speaking at all of Jewish popes: a son of the same Leo was Peter Leonis (Peter, son of Leo), or, in Italian: Pierleone. By the end of the eleventh century, the family Pierleone was a significant factor in the Roman financial world. It was in the interest of the family to maintain close connections with the church, and therefore one of Pierleone's sons, Pietro, followed a church career and rose to the rank of cardinal. When pope Honorius II died in 1130, in the same night two popes were elected: sixteen cardinals chose Gregory Papareschi, who assumed the name Innocent II, and twenty of them chose the Jew Pietro Pierleone, who called himself Anacletus II. A

46. See extensively Prinz (1966).

conflict of years broke out between the two popes, in which both men collected many followers and excommunicated the other. Several historians have expressed their conviction that particularly the Jewish descent of Anacletus procured the counterparty so many adherents. The most important supporter of Innocent was the illustrious abbot Bernard of Clairvaux, who stated that it

> was a shame for Christ that a Jewish descendant had occupied the see of St. Peter.[47]

For convenience he overlooked the fact that Peter himself had also been a Jew. Another "objection" against Anacletus was that he looked so "Jewish," and that he was an unreliable and ambitious man. Nonetheless, Anacletus quietly remained pope at Rome. Only after his death (1138), Innocent II came to Rome and, after having resisted another rival, finally occupied the Petrinian see. Intriguing and telling is the fact that, in the official Roman-Catholic historiography of the popes, Innocent II is viewed as the successor of Honorius II, and that Anacletus II only figures as "antipope."

6.4. Philosophical Developments

6.4.1. The *Filioque* Question

We have seen that, after the year 1000, an antithesis originated between the realm of the temporal, natural things and the realm of the eternal, supernatural things. In practical respect, the first realm took shape particularly in the state, and the second particularly in the church. The background of this was not just a changed theoretical understanding, but I hope to make it likely that this can only have been a reflection of *metahistorical* changes. I believe this change to become visible already in the well-known schism between the East-Roman and the West-Roman church. Theologically speaking, the most important issue was the question whether the Holy Spirit "proceeds" from the Father alone (*processio ex patre*), as

47. Quoted by Goldberg (1976:118).

the East taught, or "proceeds" from both the Father and the Son (*processio ex patre filioque*), as the West believed. Note, this is thought of as a "proceeding" *from eternity*; the Spirit is the "eternal Spirit" (Heb. 9:14).

This issue is so remarkable because not even the slightest biblical argument could be adduced, neither for the one, nor for the other viewpoint. In John 15:26, we do hear of the "spirit of truth," who "proceeds from the Father," but that evidently refers to the pouring out of the Holy Spirit on earth, which is recorded in Acts 2. Therefore, theories about the Spirit's "eternal proceeding" from the Father (and, if so desired, from the Son) are nothing but theological speculation. It is an interesting theory, but no "divine truth," not something to be enforced upon the Christians with an *anathema*, as occurs in the Athanasian Creed. However, it got even worse when this purely theological-speculative issue was also extended to the question as to whether the *processio* is only *ex patre* ("from the Father"), or *ex patre filioque* ("from the Father and the Son"). It has been cynically said that in 1054 the whole Christian world was torn apart because of that single non-biblical word *filioque*. How could such a thing happen?

The Nicene Creed only spoke of the Spirit's "proceeding from the Father." It was not before the third synod of Toledo (589) that the *filioque*, as found in the creed of the West-Gothic king Reccared, was inserted into the text of the Nicene-Constantinopolitan creed. Such an insertion was formally incorrect, as pope Leo III admitted, who advised Charlemagne to leave it out of the creed. Only in 1014 (!), pope Benedict VIII, at the instigation of the German emperor, Henry II, gave to the *filioque* the character of an official dogma of the Western church. The consequences of this illegitimate act have been disastrous, since the Eastern church could not and wished not to accept this insertion.

Of course, there were other (especially political) causes for the schism; but still: how could the *filioque* question lead to such a catastrophic division? What was behind it? For the Eastern church was certainly prepared to accept that the procession of the Spirit, though "from" the Father, was also "through" the Son. The Western church did not object to this, but felt it did not go far enough. It wanted to see emphasized that the Father and the Son are "one beginning (or, principle)" (*unum principium*) with regard to the Spirit's "proceeding." The Eastern church, on the contrary, accused the Western church of starting from two principles (*principia*, or Gr. *aitiai*, "causes"). The layman will wonder what the importance of such a theological dispute may be. He will be astonished to learn that both Western (Catholic as well as Protestant!) and Eastern theologians connect this question with nothing less than the whole Eastern and Western Christian mentality and culture.

Strangely enough, both the Western and the Eastern complaint involved accusing the other party of a deeply rooted *dualism*. Because the Eastern thinkers "severed" the Son from the Holy Spirit—as the Western theologians argued—a dualism arose between the orthodoxy and the mysticism of the Eastern church. Their view implied that there are two ways to the Father: one through the Son, leading to *knowledge*, and one through the Spirit, leading to *exaltation*.[48] I leave aside the question in how far this accusation is justified. I am more interested in the accusation of the Eastern church, because this might touch upon the metahistorical nature of Western culture. As I said, this accusation implied that the Western church assumed two "causes" ('sources," "principles," "starting points") for the activity of the Holy Spirit.

Several Eastern theologians, like Leo Karsawin (1882-1952), have tried to derive the inner dualisms of Western culture, to this day, from this dualism. One may think particularly of rationalistic science (including theology), which led to

48. Dogmaticians such as Herman Bavinck, Karl Barth, Gerrit C. van Niftrik, Ben Wentsel, and Jan van Genderen, have all leveled this reproach toward the Eastern church.

the de-Christianization of the West, versus practical faith.[49] Essentially this was the reproach of scholastic thinking. While the Western world accused the Eastern world of an orthodoxy-mysticism dualism, one might wonder whether it is not far more appropriate to accuse the Western world of this, or a comparable, dualism of "doctrine" and "practice." Karl Barth[50] blamed the Russian theologians and philosophers of religion for blotting out without any restraint all boundaries between philosophy and theology, between reason and revelation, between Scripture, tradition, and immediate enlightenment, between mind and nature, between *pistis* (faith) and *gnosis* (knowledge). But precisely that makes me suspicious. If Barth presumed that this blotting out was caused by the Russian rejection of the *filioque*, I begin to wonder whether Barth's own (and the usual Catholic and Protestant) scholastic separations between philosophy and theology, between reason and revelation, between mind and nature, between faith and knowledge,[51] were not caused by, or are related with, the *acceptation* of the *filioque*.

Please note that my point is absolutely not whether omission or insertion of the *filioque* is the most biblical. I said before that this is a highly speculative question, about which Scripture is simply silent. No, my point is not the *theological* aspects, but much more to discover the *metahistorical* backgrounds of the *filioque* question. In that case, it seems to be quite telling that Eastern theologians equal the acceptation of the *filioque* with the acceptation of two divine "principles" or "starting points." They even connect it with the distinction of, or even separation between, two "spiritual" realms, the sacred and the secular realm. It is not so strange, as Barth believed, that Karsawin (see note 2) even linked Kantianism with the *filioque*, because Kant too was still interested in the distinction of, or separation between, the sacred and the secular. That is, the

49. See particularly Karsawin (1925:356-365).
50. Barth (1932:505).
51. See extensively Ouweneel (2013).

distinction of, or separation between, the higher and the lower realm of the spirit. The first is the domain of the church, but also that of theology, of faith, of the soul, of Scriptural revelation, of the Holy Spirit; the second is the domain of the state, but also that of philosophy, of reason, of the body, of natural revelation, of the secular.

Now, who can deny that this distinction has anything to do with the new spiritual developments in the West after the year 1000? Under the Carolingians and the Ottonians, the *oikoumenè* was still the one, undivided Christian community. To be sure, it was governed by both the emperor and the pope, but some distinction between "church" and "state" was entirely foreign to it. However, in the eleventh and twelfth century this distinction developed: church and state became manifest as two distinct realms of the Spirit. *Therefore, the* filioque *question in 1054 was definitely of eminent importance.* It was a matter of the greatest metahistorical significance. Whereas the East held to the one undivided (Eastern) Christendom under the two-headed guidance of emperor and patriarch, the West arrived at a division of church and state, or—the bare truth must be told—two realms, not of the Spirit but, *of the spirits.* The one realm was the supernatural realm of "grace" under the guidance of Janus/Petrus, the other realm was the natural one. The latter was the realm that in the late Middle Ages would, in *political* respect, disintegrate into the first national states of Europe, all with their own angelic princes, and in *ideological* respect would get into the grip of the rising natural sciences' humanistic ideal of the control of nature.

6.4.2. Development of the Nature–Grace Scheme[52]

At the time of the great church father Augustine (c. 400), a division of church and state, therefore also of theology and philosophy, was still inconceivable. He called theology *philosophia christiana*, "Christian philosophy," and asserted that the *verus christianus* ("true Christian") is *verus philosophus* ("true

52. See for the following sections extensively Ouweneel (2014b and d).

philosopher").[53] Over against the Greeks (to begin with Xenophanes), who had alleged that only philosophy, and nothing else, is the "true theology," Augustine and other church fathers claimed that theology, and nothing else, is the "true philosophy." In this way, they tried to separate Greek philosophy from Christian theology. But apparently, they did not see how much Greek thinking had already factually intruded into their own thought systems.

Augustine rightly rejected the false idea of the autonomy of philosophical thought, and rightly stated that reason cannot discover any truth apart from the illumination by God's revelation. That was a tremendous gain in comparison with the later reason—faith dualism of high scholasticism. However, Augustine failed to develop his own *Christian* philosophy, that is, an encompassing worldview founded in God's revelation. Instead of submitting pagan thought to *Scripture*, with the help of a *Bible-oriented* philosophy equal to this task, he tried to submit it to dogmatic theology, which was not up to it. As a consequence, exactly that happened which he wanted to avoid, namely the intrusion of pagan thought into Christian theology. The church fathers did not subject philosophical problems to a rigorous immanent criticism, with the help of a Christian-philosophical apparatus, but only dealt with them in a theological context. In this way, the unavoidable *had to* occur: the adoption of all kinds of particularly neo-Platonic and Aristotelian thought-contents within theology, which have remained there to this day.

Augustine and his contemporaries emphatically tried to keep theology and philosophy "together," but in my opinion they did it the wrong way. As a consequence, medieval Christian thought was not equal to the entirely *new* approach which in the eleventh century penetrated Western thinking and which was brilliantly formulated particularly by Thomas Aquinas (1225-1274). Augustine had identified dogmatic

53. *De Civitate Dei* 8.1.

theology with Christian philosophy, as well as with Christian religion. That was incorrect and harmful, but after all it was better than what Thomas did. Thomas emphatically rejected the mentioned identification. In itself this seemed to be positive, for theology *is* not "Christian philosophy," and *cannot* be that at all. But Thomas did not recognize any *other Christian* philosophy as such. He accepted philosophy as an *autonomous* science, that is, a science essentially severed from the authority of God's Word. In his opinion, this philosophy did include so-called "natural theology," which claims to prove the existence of God, but it does so exclusively by the light of natural reason. This philosophy in the Thomistic sense is essentially nothing but the philosophy of Aristotle, mingled with some other philosophical ideas, and here and there adapted to Catholic theological views.

Apart from and beyond this Aristotelian philosophy, Thomas elevated Christian theology to the status of "supernatural" knowledge. This surpasses the "natural" knowledge of philosophy (which at that time still included the present-day special sciences) as a consequence of its infallible, supernatural principles, derived from God's revelation. The significance of this scheme is that "sacred" theology is distinguished here from the other, "profane" sciences. Whereas Augustine viewed philosophy as Christian, because it was identified with theology, Thomas emphatically viewed philosophy as non-Christian, "neutral." Only theology is "Christian," because it works with the *ratio fide illustrata*, "reason illuminated by faith." The other sciences, however, are allotted to the domain of "neutral" knowledge, which only works by the *lumen rationis naturalis*, "the light of natural reason," that is, reason as not illuminated by Scripture.

In this way, a tremendous switch was made, which was of the greatest metahistorical significance.[54] In their doctrine, Thomas and his predecessors only expressed the general

54. De Graaff (n.y.:125ff.) also gave some attention to this point.

feeling of their time, as does, by the way, every genial philosopher (and artist, for that matter). Even John Scotus Eriugena (ninth century) had still viewed true religion as the true philosophy, and for instance concluded from this that every doubt with regard to religion or theology can and should be refuted "philosophically," that is, by reason. But Gerbert of Reims, the later pope Silvester II, the friend and counselor of emperor Otto III, around the year 1000 for the first time abolished the subordination of the seven "free arts" to theology. Those "free arts" were the special sciences of those days. Gerbert submitted them to philosophy, and also called theology "just" one of the special sciences. If rightly understood, this was perfectly correct. But Gerbert claimed, moreover, that Man in the domain of the "profane" sciences does not need any supernatural illumination of reason, but that the light of natural reason suffices him. Thus, the sciences were "liberated" from the grip of theology without submitting them to Scripture, or to a Scriptural worldview (or philosophy). Gerbert immediately showed the practical results of this "liberation" by some revolutionary renovations in the field of the natural sciences.

Anselm of Canterbury (1033-1109), after Eriugena called the "second father of scholasticism," followed him in his coupling of philosophy and theology, but without Eriugena's overestimation of reason. In imitation of Augustine, he put faith first: *credo ut intellegam*, "I believe, in order that I may understand." Peter Abaelard (1079-1142), however, shifted the primacy back to reason. This enlightened philosopher even asserted that the church in disputes not merely was to appeal to its doctrinal authority, but to reason. Neither Scriptures, nor miracles, but only reason has demonstrative force. To be a Christian means to be a logician, for Christ is the Logos. This question of the supremacy of either reason or faith was solved by Albert of Bollstädt, called Albertus Magnus (1193?-1280), by no longer choosing between a primacy of either reason or faith, but by allotting to both of them their own domain. Very practically, Albert arrived at this solution by following Augustine in faith matters, and by following the recently rediscovered Aristotle in scientific matters. Thus, he arrived at the distinction that afterwards became so important: the distinction between natural (i.e., philosophical and special-scientific) and theological knowledge, which he, by the way, tried to merge into a harmonic unity.

6.4.3. "Nature" and "Grace" Grow Apart

Albert's great pupil—whom he survived—was Thomas Aquinas. He followed Albert both in his distinction between "nature" and "grace," and in his attempt to keep the two together in a harmonic unity. The historic significance of his doctrine is that, since 1870, Thomism is the official philosophy and foundation of the theology of the Roman-Catholic Church. Thomas's "nature" comprised matters such as philosophy, reason, body, state, earth, general revelation. His "grace" comprised theology, faith, soul, heaven, special revelation. Both distinguishing these two domains and keeping them together was of great importance to Thomas. His "nature" was distinguished from "grace," but it was still oriented upon the latter. First, the "natural truths" investigated by reason were also part of God's revelation. Secondly, "nature" was not severed from theology, for natural reason investigates also that part which is called "natural theology." Thirdly, natural reason "leads on" to "grace"; natural theology is a *praeambula fidei*, "entrance-hall of faith."

Conversely, "grace" remains oriented upon "nature." The supernatural domain of "grace" is supra-rational, but not contra-rational; reason is not abolished. True, the sacred truths can only be investigated in the light of special revelation and on the basis of grace, but illuminated reason is of assistance here by refuting, for instance, arguments against the supernatural truths. Grace does not cancel nature, but *perfects* it (*perficit naturam*). In the political philosophy of Thomas, this means that the Christian empire is still viewed as a unity, in which the world monarch rules over the realm of "nature," but is appointed to this end by the pope from the realm of "grace."

In this way, Thomism at least tried to combine "nature" and "grace" in a synthesis. But in later scholasticism, this well-intended synthesis collapsed. Precisely because it was a *synthesis* of unequal and unfitting elements it *had to* collapse. The first late scholastic to be mentioned in this context is John Duns Scotus (c. 1268-1308). He loosened the bond between "nature" and "grace" by taking away natural theology from the domain of "nature." That is to say, according to Duns, such natural-theological matters as the creation of the world in time and the immortality of the soul cannot be demonstrated by natural reason either (*contra* Thomas). Here too one could only speak of faith. Time and again, Duns placed the *philosophi* over against the *catholici*, and thus loosened science out of the grip of Rome. The unity was even dissolved to such an extent that, for instance, things that might be true to the philosopher might be wrong to the theologian (as after him particularly Occam would argue). Faith and reason had to cooperate, but the cleft between theology and (Aristotelian) philosophy was so deep that the two had to be separated. Thus, Duns inadvertently helped to prepare the de-Christianization of science.

William of Ockham (Latin, Occam) (c. 1290-1349) was the most important late scholastic. He emphatically alleged that over against reason the Christian dogmas could only be preserved by radically and definitively severing the bond between theology (which to him actually was no science at all) and philosophy. For instance, the existence of God could not be demonstrated by reason (*contra* "natural theology"), but at most be made plausible to the sympathetic listener. Even of dogmas like, for instance, the Trinity and the incarnation of God it should not be said that they surpass reason, but that they contradict reason, and as such they are to be accepted. The ancient *credo quia absurdum* ("I believe because it is absurd," after Tertullian) was in vogue again.

Interestingly enough, in this way Scripture became more important again. Whereas Abaelard believed to be able to derive all truths of faith by means of reason, and thus hardly seemed to need Scripture, Occam's view implied with regard to the absurdity of the truths of faith that we can only know them through Scripture. However, at the same time this truth of faith was sharply separated from the "natural" truth of philosophy, it being totally uninteresting whether they seemed to contradict each other in certain respects. This was the "double truth" of faith and (secularized) science—a fiction that to this day dominates Western thinking. Henceforth, faith and reason, theology and philosophy, would go their own ways. It would take long before people would again be concerned with the relationship between faith and knowledge.

As the first thinker in this domain, Occam also clearly proclaimed that the separation between theology and philosophy also implied separation between church and state. This fact led this Franciscan mendicant friar into a sharp conflict with the secularized, highly ambitious pope Boniface VIII, so that he had to seek refuge with Louis the Bavarian. To him he said, "Defend me with your sword, then I will defend you with my pen." In 1326, his doctrine was condemned by the inquisition at Avignon, and in 1340 rejected by the university of Paris. But after his death (1349), Occam soon got an enormous following. His nickname was *doctor invincibilis*, "invincible doctor"; this was correct in so far as in this late scholastic the signs of a new time became visible. That was the time of expanding humanism and Renaissance. But also the Reformer, Martin Luther (c. 1500), would still say, *Ich bin von Occams Schule* ("I belong to Occam's school"), as indeed was clearly shown by his separation between theology and philosophy (*sapientia humana*), and between church and state.

I finally mention here the view of the great writer Dante Alighieri (1265-1321) in his three volumes, *De Monarchia*.

In volume 1, he presented his ideal of one indivisible world monarchy with an emperor at its head. In volume 2, he defended the Roman people's God given title to that world monarchy. The emperor therefore was to reside at Rome, and from there was to bring about the good for mankind. There was a direct continuity between the antique and the medieval Rome. In volume 3, he claimed that this Roman emperorship did not depend on the pope, but exclusively on God. On the one hand, we see here in Dante's case how vibrant the "Roman" ideal still was. On the other hand, we hear sounds here that already pointed forward to the Reformational view: not the church, but the emperor was to possess the world monarchy—but both church and emperor stood under the highest supremacy of God.[55]

6.4.4. Two Realms of the Spirit/Spirits

As said before, the deeper significance of the scholastic nature–grace dualism really opens up to us only if we try to penetrate into its metahistorical backgrounds. True philosophers have an antenna that is oriented to the epoch in which they live. They voice the experiential world of (thinking) people, as artists do in their own way. Thus, the scholastics did not just invent interesting solutions to purely theoretical questions, as if they had no tie with their time. No, as good philosophers they *interpreted* their time; that means essentially, they reflected that which occurred in the invisible realm.

We saw that, in the eleventh century, the antithesis between church and state arose. That was the antithesis between the Petrinian "empire" (church) of Rome's angelic prince and the rising national states in Europe, each with its own angelic prince. For us, the Janus/Petrus figure is the most important prince, for in him we have to do with the actual angelic prince of the Roman Empire, who for the time being was particularly a "Roman-Catholic" prince. That which happened with the secular empire and the national states was not so threatening

55. Cf. Yates (1975:8-12).

for the Roman(-Catholic) angelic prince. On the contrary, he only welcomed their continually progressing secularization as a consequence of humanism and Renaissance. The fact that the Roman angelic prince furthered the Renaissance can be easily shown. Some of the popes, like Sixtus IV (1471-1484) (after whom the Sistine chapel was called), Julius II (1503-1513) (nephew of the latter), and Leo X (1513-1521), originally Giovanni de Medici—we will meet him again —were themselves pronounced Renaissance popes. And Nicolaus Cusanus (or, von Kues) (1401-1464) was indeed a cardinal in the Roman-Catholic church, but at the same time one of the most characteristic interpreters of the transition to an entirely new time. This was shown by his rejection of the church's sovereignty.

Some of the most important pioneers of humanism and Renaissance were and remained faithful sons of the church. One of them was the "father of humanism," Francesco Petrarca (1304-1374), who entirely stood in the Roman as well as in the Christian tradition, and as an Italian was deeply convinced of the "Latin mission" in this world. What else is that than a plea for the Roman(-Catholic) angelic prince? And yet he was at the same time the first "humanist," pleading for the true self-knowledge and individual control of his own life by the *pia philosophia*, "pious philosophy." And what to think of the faithful Christian-humanist, Erasmus of Rotterdam (1466-1536), who had tremendous expectations of the newly developing natural science, preached the "freedom" of the individual conscience, but at the same time remained a faithful son of Rome? Also pronounced Renaissance-rulers as king Francis I in France, emperor Charles V in Germany, and king Philip II in Spain, did not contemplate for a second abandoning the Roman(-Catholic) angelic prince.[56]

56. Henry VIII, Renaissance king of England, seems to be an exception because he does sever himself from Rome. However, his deed was not Reformational in nature at all, but Machiavellian: the deed of an absolutistic Renaissance prince (see § 7.3.5).

No, the greatest threat for Janus/Petrus was not in the first place a political, or an artistic, or a Roman-philosophical one, but one that struck him in the heart, that is to say, affected the position of the pope and the church. Many individuals as well as whole movements (Waldenses, Albigenses, Lollards, Hussites, Moravian Brethren) had already openly cast doubt upon the sovereignty and the authority of the pope and the church, and had been condemned as heretics. But as long as they remained coming to the church in order to receive, through her sacraments, the "divine" grace for time and eternity, and to enter heaven through her angelic prince—Peter at the alleged gate of heaven—things did not alarm Rome too much. But these were the very things that were heavily attacked by the German monk Martin Luther. In short, humanism and Renaissance played into the angelic prince's hand; the great threat came from the Reformation.

That which occurred in the domain of nature, for that matter—its being severed from Scripture, its continuing secularization—was for believing thinkers an outright disaster. The natural and the supernatural were about to part for good, so it seemed. The divine realm withdrew from the natural realm. Janus/Petrus retired from nature, without nature being brought back under the dominion of the true Christ and his Word. Even the Reformation failed almost completely in this respect, for that matter, as we will see. Nature was given up to new, yet unknown spiritual powers: the powers particularly behind secular science and technology. These new powers brought much outward blessing; how else could they have been so successful? But the *ideology* hiding behind these powers, or rather, the *idols*, the "spiritual powers" dominating them, meant a disaster to the Western world.

The "liberation" of nature from the grip of the ancient gods of Rome seemed at first sight a great blessing. In the sixteenth century this came to expression not so much in natural science—its time was still to come—but particularly in the arts. While, before the eleventh century, the natural and the supernatural still formed a harmonic unity, the "natural" realm had only been an imperfect place of sin and curse, which had to be saved and ruled by the "supernatural" church. As the natural and the supernatural parted, however, the man of "nature" was no longer a weak and sinful man, dependent on the "supernatural" (Petrinian!) grace infusions of the church, but a free artist with unlimited possibilities and creative urge. Man, divested of his Creator, himself became a creator—creative person —who rubbed his eyes and suddenly recognized the world as a beautiful, harmonious work of art, animated by entirely new "gods."

The outburst of artisticity to which this development led was in fact unequalled in history. Think in Italy of the universal genius, Leonardo da Vinci, of painters like Sandro Botticelli, Raffael, and Titian, of a painter-sculptor like Michelangelo, of a composer like Giovanni Pierluigi da Palestrina, of belletrists like François Rabelais in France, Miguel de Cervantes in Spain, and Christopher Marlowe and William Shakespeare in England, of German painters like Albrecht Dürer and Hans Holbein, and in the Netherlands of Roemer Visser, Pieter C. Hooft, and Joost van den Vondel.

On the one hand, their artistic expressions differed from the earlier arts, which had never been secularized, on the contrary, which always retained a sacred splendor. Painting, literature, music, were emphatically subservient to religion, and that could be seen and heard in every respect. But the art of the (Southern) Renaissance also emphatically differed from the later Northern art, such as the Dutch masters of the seventeenth century: Rembrandt and his contemporaries. They too did not only paint religious objects but also nature for its own sake, as a beautiful creation of God, and not just as a symbol which had only significance insofar as it referred to the supernatural. No, nature had a value of its own, was allowed to be itself. And yet, their work usually contained a deeper meaning, derived from the God of the Bible. Their work did not follow the first, traditional way, that is, it did not refer to the gods of Rome. It did not follow the new, *second* way either, that is, it was not secularized and bereft of all divine splendor. It followed a *third* way, that is, this art was only possible and understandable because of the God who, after many centuries, had been rediscovered in the sixteenth century. Their work breathes the spirit of Reformation.

Chapter 7
Reformation and Renaissance

7.1. The Resistance to Rome

7.1.1. Previous History

Do we really have to assume that, after all these centuries, only at the time of the Reformation the light in Europe began to shine? Do we indeed have to assume that *all* Christians from the fourth to the fifteenth century had put themselves unconditionally under the authority of Janus/Peter? Certainly not. Already at the time of Constantine the Great, there had been Christians who strongly resisted the union of the spiritual and the secular power, through which the gods of ancient Rome penetrated the Christian church. The power of Rome, which during the persecutions of the Christians had turned against the church for such a long time, now got into the hands of the church. It did not take long before this power turned against the dissidents; the persecuted became themselves persecutors. The hand of Constantine and his successors, which lasted so heavily upon the Jews, turned equally strongly against the Christians who resisted the entering of Janus/Peter.

The congregations that were stamped as heretics by the church of Rome were the spiritual descendants of those congregations that, from apostolic time, to a greater or lesser extent had remained loyal to the God of Israel, that is the God of Jesus Christ. Examples of such groups were from the second century the Montanists who—though there were excesses among them—rightly emphasized personal spiritual life. The Catholic bishops were interested in as many souls as possible, groups like the Montanists were interested in the converted and pious souls. This antithesis has continued until today in the contrast between the Protestant national churches and the smaller faith communities.

Another group was that of the Donatists in Northern Africa, called after bishop Donatus. This movement originated in 311, that is just when Constantine's star was rising. They too laid great emphasis upon sanctification, such as the personal holiness of the priests; sacraments administered by unholy priests had no value for them. They appealed to the new emperor to pronounce a sentence in their case. Constantine heard a great number of bishops from both parties, but a synod at Rome (313) finally decided against the Donatists. The formal standpoint prevailed over the spiritual standpoint. The Donatists did not submit to this decision. Constantine persecuted them for a time, but from 321 the Donatists could spread undisturbed. Under emperor Valentinian they were persecuted again, however.

Their greatest opponent they found in the great church father, Augustine. When he was bishop at Hippo Regius, the Donatists still formed a majority there as compared with the Catholics. From 411, the church father allowed the authorities to proceed violently against the Donatists. Augustine, who in many regards was such a Scriptural thinker, had the weakness of defending the Petrinian church, and of asserting that the "communion of the saints" was to be found in this church alone, that there was no salvation apart from her, and that only in her the true sacraments were administered. Over against the Donatists, he claimed that the force of the sacrament was independent of the priests' attitude—a view that was not free of the danger of magic. It is also shocking that

Augustine openly preached the doctrine that the erring sons and daughters of the Catholic church ought to be violently driven back to the mother-church.

One could mention many other examples of Christian movements that tried to hold to principles of congregation building and personal piety as unfolded in the New Testament, and which were fiercely persecuted for it by the Petrinians. For centuries, they were found in Ireland and Scotland, in Northern Africa, in Spain (the Priscillianists), in Armenia (the Paulicians), in Byzantium (the Nestorians), in France and Italy (the Waldenses and Albigenses), in England (the Lollards), in Czechia (the Hussites, the Bohemian and Moravian Brethren). Of course, this summary does not mean that I agree with all doctrines and practices of these very diverse movements. Far from that. But there was much authentic Christianity among them, much longing for New Testament church building and lifestyle, much hunger for the pure Word, and much resistance against what we have called Petrinian Christendom.

Several of these movements were true forerunners of the Reformation. Among themselves, they were not entirely without contacts; thus, the French and Italian Waldenses, various German congregations, and the Bohemian Brethren used the same catechism, a booklet that from 1498 to 1530 was regularly reprinted in the four languages involved. They also exhibited a clear congeniality with the "Brothers of the Common Life," a community founded by Gerard Groot at Deventer (1340-1384), a pupil of the great mystic, John Ruusbroeck (1293-1381). This school formed such great men as Thomas à Kempis, the writer of the devotional book, *De Imitatione Christi* ("On the Imitation of Christ"), which till today has known a tremendous circulation; further such diverse figures as Nicolaus Cusanus, Rudolf Agricola, and Desiderius Erasmus, spiritual men with one leg in the biblical tradition, and with the other in the Petrinian camp.

7.1.2. "Thyatira"

Even though, throughout the centuries, many faithfully believing and pious Christians belonged to the Petrinian church, we should not despise them for it. Prophetically this is shown in the epistle to the church at Thyatira (Rev. 2:18-29). We already briefly looked at the epistle to Pergamus in coherence with the general prophetic character of the seven epistles in Revelation 2 and 3. The "Thyatira" phase of church history was that of medieval Petrinian papacy. The fame of this tremendous spiritual power actually began with pope Gregory I (c. 600), who as the first pope had authority over the whole Catholic church. But, as said before, this authority reached its summit when the pope had finally won the battle over the investiture in a definitive way. Nowhere the "Thyatira" character of papacy came to light more clearly than in a pope such as Innocent III, without whose permission no king or emperor in Europe could lift his little finger. That is the spirit of Jezebel that reigned in European Christendom.

At the town of Thyatira, the god Tyrimnos was worshipped as its guardian angel; this god was identified with the Greek sun god Apollo. In the Orphic Hymns, Apollo is addressed as the "two-horned god," so that he resembles the beast which had two horns like the Lamb, but spoke like the dragon (Rev. 13:11). We already met Apollo as the son of the chief god, Zeus, just as the Roman emperor too was regarded as the son of Zeus/Jupiter. Over against the radiant sun god Apollo, son of the chief god, Christ presents himself to the church of Thyatira as the "Son of God," with his "eyes like a flame of fire, and his feet like fine brass," the "bright morning star" (vs.18, 28) (see more extensively Appendix 9). In the Roman church, Peter was factually introduced as a replacement for the Son of God. For, in Matthew 16:18, either it is the Son of the living God himself who is the *petra* of God's true Church, or Jesus refers to the believers *like* Peter who form the foundation of the Church.[1] Rome alleges that not only Peter in person, as the first "bishop" of Rome, was this *petra*, but also all his alleged "successors."

"Thyatira" as a medieval *system*—not to speak of the many faithful individuals in it—worshiped a false son of god. With the true Son of God Thyatira/Rome did not know very well how to deal; either it substituted Peter for him, or it turned his house, over which the Son of God has been set (Heb. 3:2,6), into its own house—the Catholic church—or it made of him the Son of the holy virgin, so that the attention was moved from him to the Madonna. If we take all this into account, it is the more striking that the epistle starts in such a positive way! No church receives such exuberant praise as this very Thyatira:

> I know your works, your love, your faith, your service, and your patience, and that your last works are more than your first.

This means that the Lord has not forgotten all those Waldenses, Albigenses, Lollards, Hussites, Bohemian and Moravian Brethren. They were faithful to the Lord; yet, many of these believers still stood with at least one leg in the medieval church in which "the woman Jezebel" was active. She does not belong in the church, she is a foreign, pagan element (cf. 1 Kings 16:31), just as Janus/Peter, and all the other angelic powers of Rome, the innumerable gods whom Rome annexed among the many nations, until it became a "habitation of demons" and a "prison of every foul spirit" (Rev. 18:2). Yet, "Jezebel" claims to be a prophetess, which means that the Petrinian church pretends to be the mouthpiece of God. As Jezebel, however, was only the mouthpiece of the false gods, so the Roman system. As a consequence, throughout the centuries papacy fell time and again into "pornocracy," that is, the rulers threw themselves away on fornication (cf. Rev. 2:20-21), particularly during the time immediately preceding the Reformation, with pope Alexander VI as the absolute nadir.

1. See extensively Ouweneel (2010:§2.1.3).

In Revelation 2:24, the faithful in the Petrinian church are distinguished from the others. They are those who did not know the "depths of Satan," that is, who do not belong to those who pretend that they did experience the deep things of Satan. Probably, this means that the unfaithful in Thyatira pretended to have experienced the depths of *God* (cf. 1 Cor. 2:10), whereas the Lord shows here that these were in reality the depths of Satan. This is significant! The medieval Petrinian church alleged to know *God,* but—apart from the many faithful individuals in her—she only knew *a god,* Janus, the *diabolos* or "devil," the ancient Bel/Nebo of the Babylonians, the "morning star" of Isaiah 14, the great imitator of Christ (cf. Rev. 2:28!), the treacherous angelic prince of Babylon and Rome, the "dragon" in the book of Revelation. The deep things that Rome pretended to know were the deep things of Satan.

Let me underscore here that in this and the previous chapter we constantly speak of the *medieval* Roman church. This is not "some other" church than many of my readers may belong to, but the church of virtually *all* Western Christians since, say, the sixth or seventh century. Even the staunchest Protestants always have to remember that during the Middle Ages the Roman Catholic Church was the church of their ancestors, and therefore "their" church. Moreover, during the sixteenth century also the Roman Catholic Church itself experienced a great inner reformation. This is why nowadays some church historians no longer speak of "the" Reformation, but of Luther's reformation, Zwingli's reformation, Calvin's reformation, the Anabaptist reformation, the Mennonite reformation, as well as the inner Roman Catholic reformation. For the sake of convention, we will still refer to "the" Reformation, although we will notice the differences between, say, Martin Luther, John Calvin and Menno Simons.

7.1.3. The Battle against Petrinism

The Protestant Reformation that Martin Luther (1483-1546)

started found its primary source of inspiration in the Bible. However, the outer events that gave rise to the Reformation can reveal much regarding its metahistorical backgrounds. These backgrounds may become clear if we begin with paying attention to the construction of the new St. Peter's church at Rome. It was the Renaissance pope, Julius II, who in 1506 began the construction of this church, that is, in the year that Luther took his vow as a monk. Julius was attached to Peter, so much so that he even conceived the plan of erecting for himself a magnificent tomb in the new St. Peter. This did not succeed, however; his indeed splendid tomb (including Michelangelo's wonderful Moses) remained in his earlier titular church, St. Peter in Vincoli. But he retained the "honor" of having been the instigator of the new St. Peter, to which end he employed such great artists as Bramante, Michelangelo, and Raffael. It was Bramante who designed the gigantic plan of replacing the decaying St. Peter by a new, colossal church in the form of a Greek cross with equal arms and a dome in the middle.

Julius II died in 1513, that is, in the year that Luther at Wittenberg began his significant courses on the books of the Bible: first the Psalms (1513-15), then the epistle to the Romans, which was so important for his spiritual development (1515-16). In that year, Julius II's successor was Leo X, the pope who in 1521 would put Luther under the ban, and would die in that same year. Leo's own name was Giovanni, third son of Lorenzo de' Medici; he brought to the papal court the true Renaissance atmosphere of his family. In order to finance the new St. Peter, Julius had offered a plenary indulgence, which was renewed by pope Leo X. This was necessary, for Michelangelo submitted to pope Leo the definitive design of this gigantic church, which demanded enormous sums.

No wonder, for the church was to become the greatest of Christendom, a mighty monument for the "god" of Rome, Janus/Peter, a shrine for the relics of Peter, a temple like the one for Osiris in Egypt and the one for Zoroaster in Babylon, which preserve the bones of their god-men. This is where that striking metahistorical connection is to be found: humanly speaking, there would never have been a Reformation if Luther with his 95 theses had not stood up against Johann Tetzel's disgusting trade in indulgences. These monstrous practices would not have occurred to such a tremendous extent if Rome had not emphatically wanted its new, pompous temple for Janus/Peter.

It is no coincidence that the first St. Peter, which had stood on the same spot, had already been built by emperor Constantine the Great (326-333) above the place where, according to tradition, the apostle Peter had been buried. It was in this basilica that the Petrinian Charlemagne had been crowned emperor at Christmas 800. In the middle of the fifteenth century, the church had become so ramshackle that already pope Nicholas V had commanded the construction of a new basilica. In total, this construction took about one hundred and seventy-five years!

It is striking that the shape of the church was a matter of such long discussions. Was it to be a Greek cross (with four equal arms), or a Latin cross (with one long arm)? Only when the building was almost ready, pope Paul V, in the early part of the seventeenth century, decided to make it a Latin cross after all. However this may have been, the "sign of the cross" played a dominating role in the Roman-Catholic liturgy. The outright magic meaning which was attached to the sign of the cross can only be explained from the fact that this sign, with exactly the same magic meaning, had been used before in the Babylonian Mysteries and had enjoyed there exactly the same veneration.[2] Janus/Peter, the "interpreter" of the Mysteries, deserved a building in the form of the cross. "Mystery" is Rome's essence, "Mystery" is also its name (Rev. 17:5).

When Luther fought against the system of Rome, he fought against Janus/Peter, the "god" (angelic prince) of

2. Cf. Hislop (1959:197-205).

Rome, in fact even against Samael himself. Luther is reported to have once said that Satan is much more powerful than the believers, but that, if we have Christ on our side, we are more powerful than he is. In the titles of some of his works, this clearly comes to light. Already in 1520, he wrote *De captivitate Babylonica ecclesiae* ("On the Babylonian Exile of the Church"; cf. Israel in the grip of Bel; cf. Rev. 17 and 18, and see § 3.3), and in 1545 his *Wider das Papsttum zu Rom, vom Teufel gestiftet* ("Against Popery, Founded by the Devil"). Luther's fight against Rome, which was so incredibly successful, can only be genuinely understood on the meta-historical level.

Of course, many purely historical factors can be pointed out; it is not my intention to deny them, on the contrary. One might just think of the Renaissance's emphasis upon the individual, upon man's own, free choice, which in the Reformation meant among other things: the emphasis upon the "universal priesthood" of the believers, upon the necessity of a personal conversion and rebirth, upon the personal relationship with God, upon the personal study of the Bible. One could also think of the terrible abuses within the Catholic church of the time, particularly within the papacy itself—I mentioned pornocracy—which made many Catholics long for reformation, renewal. This is all true. But it does not explain enough. Here too, we are to learn by viewing things in a metahistorical light.

7.2. Reformation and the Gods

7.2.1. Two Opponents

Luther saw himself placed over against two "spiritual realms," or put more accurately, two "realms or *spirits*." On the one hand, there were the ancient "gods" of Rome, who kept claiming the absolute supremacy in the *spiritualia*. *Nulla salus extra ecclesiam* ("outside the church no salvation"), that is, only through Janus/Peter's "key power," lying in the hands of the papacy, Rome promised access to heaven. On the other hand, there were the *temporalia* ("temporal [mundane] matters"), which had been entirely loosened from the grip of Rome, and, since late scholasticism, were being fully secularized. But "secularizing" meant being governed by the *saeculum*, that is, this world, and this meant being governed by the *Deus huius saeculi*, as the Vulgate puts it: the "god of this age (or, world)" (2 Cor. 4:4). Secularization means: pushing aside the God of the Bible to the edge of society;[3] but that means irrevocably: filling the gap thus originating with the "god" of this *saeculum*. This is exactly what happened during the Renaissance: the "natural" world (science, state, society) was withdrawn from the power of papacy *without submitting it to the God of Scripture*, so that it was filled with entirely new spirits. It is irrelevant that many Renaissance men were Christians (at least nominally); what matters is that consciously or unconsciously the Renaissance secularized both nature and culture.

Therefore, the choice for the Reformers was: Rome or the Renaissance—or was there a third way? Let us consider the two questions that occupied Luther and Calvin, respectively. Luther's central question can be formulated as follows: "How can a man be righteous before God?"[4] One could emphasize here the word "righteous": how can a man become *right* before God? One could also emphasize "God": how do the righteous escape from the gods of both Rome and the Renaissance, to be righteous before *God*, the God of the Bible?

The central question of John Calvin (1509-1564) can be formulated as follows: "How does God come to the honor he deserves?" Here, the emphasis can be explained even more easily: how, in a world that has fallen apart into two domains—church and state, theology and philosophy/science, dominated respectively by the gods of Rome and the gods of the Renaissance—can the *God of the Bible* receive his place? Is

3. See extensively Ouweneel (1994), especially ch. 2.
4. Cf. Job 9:2; see De Graaff (n.y.:172ff.), but with great reservation, because his views do contain many points of light, but are spoilt by his unacceptable view of "the death of the god."

there in this bipartition of the world still place for this God, not only in the one but also in the other domain? Ought perhaps a kind of third little domain be created for him where he can get some room?

Let us remember that Luther as well as Calvin knew both Rome and the Renaissance from the inside. Luther got to know the Renaissance thoroughly at the university of Erfurt, and Roman-Catholicism particularly as an Augustinian monk and theologian. His great colleague, Philip Melanchthon (1497-1560), as well as the Reformer Ulrich Zwingli (1484-1531), were outright humanists. Calvin too is sometimes simply reckoned to "French humanism." They all thoroughly knew the new manner of life that had originated since late scholasticism. And yet they did not stay in Rome, nor were they absorbed by humanism or the Renaissance. Nor did they seek and find that third domain to which I just referred. No, in the deep spiritual crisis of the New Era, the Reformation came to its breathtaking discovery: it *rejected* the very bipartition, and submitted the *one, undivided world* in its entirety *to the feet of the God and the Christ of Scripture*. And, for the sake of clarity, this Christ had nothing to do with the pseudochrist worshipped in Rome, nor with the pseudochrists worshipped by all kinds of enlightened Renaissancists and humanists.

This was not only unheard of and revolutionary, it was moreover daring and challenging. For this was not just a new "theology," a doctrine that had to compete with the doctrine of Rome and the doctrine of the Renaissance, but this was a proclamation for the true God *of gods*. Here a standard was raised for the God of Scripture in a way that could not but kindle the terrible wrath of both the gods of Rome and those of the Renaissance. The Reformation was a *spiritual* conflict in the sense of a conflict between the spirits. Luther and Calvin were only little human, earthly instruments. Their factual opponents were not the pope, or (the forerunners of) René Descartes, were no people of flesh and blood, but the spiritual "principalities and powers," the "rulers of the world of darkness," the "spiritual [hosts] of wickedness" in the heavenly realms (Eph. 6:12). The fact that we should not underestimate this battle is shown by the fact that, humanly speaking, Luther and Calvin to some extent lost it.

7.2.2. The Lost Battle of Protestantism

There are at least three points on which Protestantism lost the battle against Rome and the Renaissance. First, against Rome it lost the battle because Counter-Reformation managed to restrict the "success" of the Reformation to a limited part of Europe. Secondly, Protestantism largely failed in its attitude towards the Jews. Thirdly, against Renaissance Protestantism lost the battle because it reintroduced the scholastic bipartition of the world, and thus conceded "natural" life to the gods of the Renaissance. Let us examine these three important points a little more closely.

First, the Reformers only managed to reform a limited part of the Roman church in a lasting way. In France, the Southern Netherlands (now Belgium), and several parts of the German empire, the rising Reformation was almost entirely suppressed by the Counter-Reformation. This was in particular the work of the Jesuites, the *Societas Jesu*, the society of the "other Jesus." Its founder was Ignace of Loyola (1491-1556), who was a true lover of Christ but whose love was mixed with his affection for Janus/Peter and for the Madonna (the ancient "queen of heaven" of the Babylonians, not to be confused with the biblical Mary). In the monastery Mansera, he even received through meditation a visionary encounter with the Madonna. In his rigidly mystic-ascetic work, *Excercitia spiritualia* ("spiritual matters"), he described his ideal of a training to become a soldier and knight in the army of Rome's angelic prince, of submitting all means to that one goal, of unconditional obedience to Petrinism.

It is striking that the Counter-Reformation was associated with unvarnished hatred toward the Jews—metahistorically of the greatest significance, because hating the Jews is always a sign that a certain movement has become a prey of Samael. Pope Leo X was benevolent to the Jews; but the later *Societas Jesu* demanded from each of its members evidence that he had not had Jewish ancestors since five (later three) generations. The Inquisition aimed equally fiercely at the Jews, as well as at the Protestants. Not only over against the Reformation, but also over against the Jews, the Counter-Reformation loaded upon itself a blood-guilt which cannot be obliterated. When John describes the New Testament "Babylon" (Rome) as "drunk with the blood of the saints and with the blood of the witnesses (or, martyrs) of Jesus" (Rev. 17:6), the latter have been especially the Protestants. But the "saints" include the "people of the saints of the Most High," Israel, persecuted by the Roman beast (Dan. 7:21-27).

Secondly, particularly Luther failed in his attitude toward the Jews. At the outset, Luther ardently protested against the persecution of the Jews, especially because he was convinced that he would be able to win the Jews for his new doctrine. Although the Jews showed him their gratitude for his brave support, they remained in the faith of their fathers. Luther was so deeply disappointed about this that he turned from a warm admirer and defender of the Jews into a bitter opponent. When in 1537 the elector Frederic of Saxony, Luther's great friend and adherent, banished all Jews from his country, he received Luther's full support for this. The Jews sought Luther's support, but he did not even want to receive them. Shortly after this he wrote his first work against the Jews (1538): *Brief wider die Sabbather* ("Letter Against the Sabbath Keepers"), in which he called them "possessed by all devils" and "damned" by God. After this letter, his tone, both in the pulpit and in his famous table conversations (*Tischreden*), became fiercer and fiercer. The absolute nadir was his two works of 1543, three years before his death: *Von den Juden und ihren Lügen* ("On the Jews and Their Lies") and *Vom Schem Hamphoras und vom Geschlecht Christi* ("On the Unknowable Name and on the Generations of Christ"; see Matt. 1:1-17).

The reformer of the Alsace, Martin Bucer (1491-1551), was an equally bitter hater of the Jews. Did Calvinism perhaps fare better in this regard? Calvin too was bitter against the Jews because they did not wish to accept Jesus as the Messiah. Thus, he too arrives at a not very lofty conclusion; he had spoken much with Jews, but[5]

> I never found a trace of piety or a grain of truth or uprightness; yes, I never encountered in any Jew common sense.

For such a statement, one could today be charged with anti-Semitism in a court of law! It should be added, however, that from the latter part of the sixteenth century the Calvinistic Netherlands became a safe haven for the European Jews. It was just about the only country where they could live free of persecutions, and enjoy perfect liberty to practice their religion. Yet, it should be remembered that this freedom was granted to the Jews by the liberal regents, who certainly were not very Calvinistic. Historian Hajo Brugmans (1868-1939) wrote:[6]

> With regard to the attitude of the authorities toward the Jews in the days of the Republic, we can say: that of the authorities was benevolent and tolerant, that of the church disapproving and intolerant, and that of the population moderate and indifferent.

Here, the simple truth is expressed that the very sons of the Reformation in the Netherlands were not at all very benevolent toward the Jews; on the contrary, they were quite hostile. In correspondence with the Augustinian theory of spiritualization, according to which the church regarded itself as the "spiritual Israel," claimed for itself the blessing of Abraham, and left the curse to the Jews, Israel was treated as rejected by God. The Reformed synods, and also local consistories, at times demanded more severe measures from the authorities against the Jews. Reverend Abraham Coster even wrote a

5. Corpus Reformatorum 40,605.
6. Brugmans & Frank (1940:642).

Historie der Joden ("History of the Jews"), which clearly brought to light his anti-Jewish attitude. Usually, such appeals against the Jews fortunately had no effect for that matter.

7.2.3. Reformation against Renaissance

We now come to the third point in which Protestantism badly failed, namely, in its battle against the Renaissance. The Reformation clearly preached the *Sola Scriptura* in this sense: Scripture alone has absolute divine authority, and that over the entire, undivided life of man, of society, of church and state. That was a tremendous gain, especially if we compare this with the three alternatives available:

(a) The medieval dialectic thinkers, but also the new rationalism coming up in the Renaissance, finding in René Descartes (1596-1650) its first great representative, sought the authority for each view in human *autonomous reason*. In the New Era this factually meant that they sought this authority in the new gods of the Renaissance. In the latter part of the fifteenth century, Pico della Mirandola (1463-1494), in his *De hominis dignitate* ("On the Dignity of Man"), had called man "a god clothed with human flesh"; that means in reality, man under the influence of the new gods.

(b) The Roman-Catholic church knew as its source of authority only the *ecclesial doctrinal authority*, that is, the power of the ancient Roman gods and goddesses: Janus/Peter, the Madonna, and especially, behind them, Samael.

(c) The mystics of the later Middle Ages (Meister Eckhart [1260-1328] in particular) and the New Era accepted as their source of authority only individual *inner experience*, flowing from the union with the godhead. Here one should mention especially the German, bigoted, theosophically, and even pantheistically colored mysticism of Andreas Osiander, Kaspar Schwenckfeld, Sebastian Franck, Valentin Weigel, and in particular Jakob Böhme. They discovered their own, occultly tainted gods, and thus paved the way for the intrusion of Eastern mysticism in the nineteenth and twentieth century.

Over against these alternatives, how refreshing was the fourth "alternative": the direct biblical testimony of Luther and Calvin. Luther turned against both Rome's doctrinal authority, and the notion of autonomous reason, as well as against occult mysticism, and thus against all the false gods of his time. It is no wonder that his whole ministry, oral and written, was pervaded so strongly by his battle against the devil himself! He was the preacher of the Word concerning the sin of man, the cross of Christ, and justification by faith alone. He sharply criticized all thinking glorifying autonomous reason and free will, and consequently the self-rebirth ("renaissance"!) and self-justification of man. However, neither Luther nor the other Reformers designed a thorough Christian-philosophical view of reality.[7] Therefore, within the domain of the sciences they had little impact. But it was this very domain where the strength of the Renaissance manifested itself most clearly! Consequently, the co-workers and successors of the Reformers (Philip Melanchthon, Theodore Beza) introduced the same bipartition of reality as the medieval scholastic thinkers had done: the Word was mainly effectuated in the "supernatural" (church, personal devotion, theology), whereas in the "natural" the gods of the Renaissance were given free play.

In Lutheranism, this treason to "nature"—and to Christ as the Head of "natural" life as well—had in fact been committed already by Luther himself, particularly in his view of the state.[8] In his opinion, church and state, that is, the spiritual and the temporal realm respectively, have no inner point of contact whatsoever. The state, or the prince, receives authority from God, and is responsible to him. But it principally did not matter to Luther whether the ruler was a Christian or a pagan. For the earthly matters with which the state is concerned, there are not only no ecclesiastical, but even no biblical rules. Luther therefore expressly exhorted the princes not

7. See extensively Ouweneel (2014b).
8. See extensively Ouweneel (2014c).

to consult the Bible and the pastors in the execution of their task, but the laws of the country. That may have been well intended in order to prevent biblicism and ecclesiocracy, but it furthered neutralism, and never arrived at the pivotal question whether at least these laws ought not to be based upon a radically Christian view of justice and the state.

Philip Melanchthon even went much further. He sought a harmony between the Spirit of the Reformation and the spirits of humanism and Renaissance, and introduced at the Lutheran universities a softened Aristotelianism plus Cicero's doctrine of the "light of natural reason." He also taught the "free will," that is, man's will as governed by the gods of the Renaissance, and defended natural theology, which can only derive something about the "gods," not of the God of gods. His study books dominated German education for a long time, and paved the way for the absolute, humanistic secularization of Protestantism at the time of the Enlightenment. This is the general line in Lutheran thinking to this day. No wonder that, for instance, the well-known Lutheran theologian, Gerhard Ebeling (1912-2001), fully accepted the scholastic bipartition of our culture, and tried to live with it and to reason on the basis of it. As I said, already Luther himself claimed to be of Occam's school, and this clearly came to light in his dualism of law and gospel, which goes back upon his dualism of philosophy (*sapientia humana*, "human wisdom") and theology.

Calvin rejected the scholastic dualism of the natural and the supernatural, and, much more clearly than Luther, pleaded for a Reformation of the entire life, an active submission of personal and societal life to the God of gods. Thus, he founded in 1559 a reformational university at Geneva, and even arrived at the notion of a *philosophia christiana*, a "Christian philosophy," that is, a biblically based and scientifically warranted view of creation, of church and state, of art and science, etcetera. But unfortunately, Calvin did not arrive at an elaboration of this view either. Thus it could happen that, in

Calvinism too, the bipartition of culture was reintroduced by Theodore Beza (1519-1605). He again lauded Aristotelianism, now adapted to Reformed theology, as the true philosophy. In the Calvinistic Netherlands, during the seventeenth century, Descartes was fought by the illustrious Reformed theologian, Gisbert Voetius (1589-1676)—however not with the help of a Christian-philosophical view, but with the help of Aristotle, whom he called "our philosopher."

In this way, Protestant scholasticism came up, which again divided reality into a domain of faith where Scripture has its say—and even there only partly, since Aristotle also strongly dominated theology—whereas "natural" life was in fact delivered to the new gods of the Renaissance. The practical application of the Reformation to the life of the church and society was, at least in the Protestant countries, enormous. But this application was by far not so extensive in the domain where the gods of the Renaissance had exerted their greatest influence: the domain of thinking. For the time being, the power of these gods remained limited to an elite: to the private studies of the continental rationalist and the British empiricist philosophers. But in these parts of Europe, they did indeed form a powerful bridgehead within European culture. And when their time had arrived, that is, in the time of the so-called Enlightenment (eighteenth century), they came forward, and within a short time, without much resistance, adopted the lead of the entire Western culture. This will be dealt with more extensively later.

7.2.4. "Sardis"

Again, the developments described are prophetically indicated in the very significant seven epistles of Revelation 2 and 3.[9] "Thyatira," the idolatrous papacy of the Middle Ages, is followed by "Sardis." It represents prophetically an entirely new start, comparable with nothing less than the apostolic time. For it was the truth of the apostles that emerged again

9. See more extensively Ouweneel (2011:ch.2).

at the time of the Reformation. We see this in the parallels between "Ephesus" (the post-apostolic time) and "Sardis" (the time of Protestantism): in both epistles, Christ presents himself as the One holding the "seven stars" in his hand (2:1; 3:1). In both epistles the complaint is heard, "but you have..." (2:6; 3:4), as well as the exhortation, "Remember therefore ... and repent" (2:5; 3:3), as well as the threat, "if not, I come" (2:5; 3:5). As in the post-apostolic time the apostolic heritage is darkened; globally speaking, Protestantism has darkened the reformational heritage.

The Reformation was a work of God; Protestantism was a work of men—more accurately, of the gods of the Renaissance. This does not take way anything of the many precious things that have been preserved in Protestantism—but that was equally true of Rome (cf. Rev. 2:19) and the Renaissance. *Grosso modo*, Protestantism failed in at least the three points mentioned. Christ tells Sardis (v. 1), "I know your works, that you have the name that you live, and you are dead." In spite of the numerous truly living souls, Protestantism *as a system* is dead. Only relatively few people came to the "new doctrine" of the Reformers out of a personal conviction. The others had only followed the political authorities and the spiritual leaders. Luther and Calvin very consciously chose a Protestant national or regional church instead of congregations of believers. It caught the masses that fled out of Rome without asking too much about their inner convictions. However, just as the Donatists and others blamed the Catholic church of their days that it did not demand inner sanctification, thus it was with the faithful believers at the time of the Reformation. They also turned their backs to Rome, but they did not want to join a national church either. The (moderate) Mennonites—precursors of the later Evangelical movements—were the most conspicuous, but they were not alone.

Protestantism factually withdrew the entire "natural" life from the authority of Scripture by reintroducing scholastic thinking. Even Protestant dogmatics involved no complete return to the writings of the apostles. Therefore, Christ says in v. 2, "I have not found your works perfect before God." Of what works could we think here? "Sardis" endeavored to develop a "pure doctrine," but demanded too little the elaboration of it in a pious life (which, by the way, was a little made up for by the Dutch Second Reformation [*Nadere Reformatie*] in the Netherlands, pietism in Germany, and puritanism in Anglo-Saxon countries). Just as little as Rome did Protestantism develop a lively expectation of the soon coming again of Christ (cf. v. 3b). As Rome did, Protestantism in general sought the ordering of church life in a rigid ecclesial structure and organization. To this day, the Evangelical communities that do not go along with this are, even for this simple reason, often called "sects," or today, a little more mildly, "free" (non-institutional) churches. But it was "Sardis" itself that failed: it sought the ordering of its church life not in him who has "the seven Spirits of God," that is, in him who wishes to lead his church primarily by his Spirit, not human institutions. On the whole, Protestantism also adopted from Rome the disastrous theology of supersessionism, and therefore could never find the right attitude toward the Jews.

"Sardis" must become "watchful," and strengthen the little life that is still there; thus it is called upon. It must remember how it had received and heard God's Word during the Reformation, and keep it, lest it would also lose the little that is "left" (v. 2-3). However, the latter is exactly what happened, unfortunately. The naturalistic and positivistic "higher biblical criticism" did not primarily come up in Rome, but in "Enlightened" Protestantism. In this way, by far the largest part of Protestantism lost precisely the greatest treasure that the Reformation had recaptured: the Word of God. But fortunately, there are also "a few names [of persons] in Sardis that have not defiled their garments" (v. 4), and they have remained within State Protestantism until this very day. Within Protestantism as a whole, however, their voice is hardly heard. Their time is over. Therefore, in the nineteenth century a "Philadelphia" had to come, a revival movement, in which Scripture would again really open up and would be lived out.

When comparing the "fall of Protestantism" with the "fall of Christendom" (§ 5.4), we are struck by the following points:

(1) *Caesaropapism* (the church subservient to the state, the church leaders subservient to the emperor) returns with Luther in such a way that the "Evangelical" (Lutheran) church in Germany everywhere placed itself under the protection of the Lutheran princes. In the classical Reformed view too, the state must support the church to further the Kingdom of God. To this belongs also the battle against false religions and churches (see the unabridged article 36 of the Belgic Confession: "... upholding the sacred ministry, with a view to removing and destroying all idolatry and false worship of the Antichrist"). However, the prince or the state, respectively, does *not* receive authority over the church. On the contrary, under the influence of scholastic dualism the state secularized entirely. In the (post-)Constantinian empire this was still inconceivable. Because of this same dualism, the secularization of society, science and culture is strongly furthered by Protestantism (§ 7.3.2).

(2) The horrendous *persecution of the Jews* arising after the Constantinian upheaval receives its counterpart in the unrestrained anti-Semitism of the late Luther (§ 7.2.2).

(3) The *healing miracles*, decreased by the inner spiritual weakening of the church, are hardly restored in the Reformation. On the contrary, Calvinism in particular had strongly suppressed the healing ministry.[10]

(4) Unfortunately, the especially Augustinian *antimillennialism* is fully maintained by Luther and Calvin, be it that in the later Dutch Second Reformation (*Nadere Reformatie*) (Netherlands), pietism (Germany) and Puritanism (Anglo-Saxon countries), here and there the theological picture of Israel and

10. See Ouweneel (2003b:§2.2.1-2).

the future Messianic kingdom is restored.[11]

(5) Also *militarism*, arising after the Constantinian upheaval, receives its counterpart in Protestantism, namely, in the political and military protection that Luther sought with the "Evangelical" German princes and in the way in which he, for instance, defended the suppression of the German peasant revolts.

7.3. The New Powers

7.3.1. Charles V

In 1520, pope Leo X finally entered into an open fight with Luther. On June 15 a papal threatening bull (*Bannandrohungsbulle*) appeared, in which the Lutheran "heresies" were rejected. All those who had openly pronounced themselves for them and did not revoke within sixty days, were threatened with all kinds of ecclesial punishments. Luther immediately wrote a pamphlet against what he called "the cursed bull of the Antichrist." On December 10, 1520, Luther convened a meeting at the famous "Luther oak," just outside Wittenberg, together with colleagues and students. Solemnly they burned a number of books about church law, which had been so cruelly violated by the church, and finally Luther cast a copy of the bull into the fire. In this way, the bond between Luther and the Roman-Catholic Church was formally cut through, although Luther never officially left that church. On January 3, 1521, the final banishing bull was promulgated against Luther; in this way, Rome on its behalf cut the bonds with him.

In the same time, Luther received a remarkably gentle invitation to come and give an account before a young man, who now deserves our special attention: the Holy Roman emperor Charles V. This account was to be given at the Diet at Worms. On April 17 and 18, 1521, Luther actually stood before the emperor. After a first hearing and a night of deliberation, Luther came with a statement that, for that time, was revolutionary and in fact incredible. He stated that he was not

11. See extensively Van Campen (2006).

prepared to simply believe what the pope and the councils taught, but that he wanted to lean on Scripture alone. His conscience was entirely caught in God's Word, therefore he could not and wished not to revoke anything. This was unheard of! Here, one single monk ventured to contradict the whole holy Roman-Catholic Church as well as the whole Holy Roman Empire. Here, one man ventured to openly pronounce, for the first time, that, if all popes and councils spoke this way, but the Bible spoke that way, he would choose the Bible. *Here, one man ventured to choose the side of Christ over against all the ancient – imperial and ecclesial – gods of Rome.* The consequence was that now the emperor too pronounced the imperial ban on Luther. This Edict of Worms appeared on May 26, 1521.

Who was this emperor? If we want so see where the ancient Roman ideal of the one (Roman) Empire and the one (Roman-Catholic) Church was left, if, in the New Era, we again want to find a figure in whom this ideal received once more a magnificent form, we should consider Charles V. All the factors that were to lead him to his great position were present already before his birth, in 1500 at Ghent (now Belgium). Only look at his four grandparents: the parents of his father, Philip the Fair, were the Habsburgian Maximilian I, emperor of Germany, and Mary the Rich, hereditary daughter of Burgundy. From his grandfather he inherited the Austrian, from his mother the Burgundian hereditary goods. The parents of his mother, Joanna the Insane, were Ferdinand of Aragon and Isabella of Castile, the Spanish royal pair. From them, he inherited the title to Spain's royal throne.

Already in 1515, Charles was declared of age and became lord over the Burgundian hereditary lands, which encompassed more or less the present-day Benelux (Belgium, Netherlands, Luxemburg) as well as the duchy of Burgundy. In 1516, after the death of his grandfather, king Ferdinand, he received the sole dominion over the Spanish kingdoms. And in 1519, after the death of his other grandfather, emperor Maximilian, Charles became candidate for the German emperorship. The fact that he indeed became the German emperor, and not his strongest counter-candidate, king Francis I of France, was particularly due to the Italian statesman, Mercurino Gattinara, who had a prophetic eye. He saw Charles called to world dominion, in order to "unite the world under one shepherd." To this end, Charles had to become emperor of Germany, and to pronounce claims on Italy. Thus it happened: in Frankfurt, June 1519, Charles was unanimously chosen by the electors.

In October 1520, Charles V, twenty years old, arrived for the first time in the Holy Roman Empire. On October 23, he was crowned "Roman king" in the cathedral of his illustrious predecessor and namesake, Charlemagne, at Aix-la-Chapelle (Aachen). This traditional title is significant; it means pretender of the Roman (!) crown and throne. Charles swore loyalty to the empire as well as to the Catholic Church. With papal warrant, he was now allowed to call himself "elected Roman emperor." His first important governmental act was the opening of the Diet at Worms (April 1521), where, without him being aware of it, Luther's steadfastness was the beginning of the deepest split within the empire that this dreamer of the *Monarchia universalis*, the universal monarchy concentrated in one single person, could imagine.

It still took ten years before Charles was effectively crowned emperor by the pope. In 1527, Charles's mutinying Spanish and German soldiers sacked and ruined the city of Rome, which by many, Catholics included, was regarded as a divine judgment on the secularized papacy. Because of this *sacco di Roma*, the humiliated city was not fit for the imperial coronation, which therefore took place at Bologna. When Charles V arrived there on December 6, 1529, he was welcomed by triumphal arcs, which not only showed the Habsburgian coat of arms, but also pictures of Roman emperors. At Charles's thirtieth birthday, February 24, 1530, pope Clemens VII splendidly crowned Charles *Imperator Romanorum*, "emperor of the Romans." That meant that, after the discovery of America,

Charles became *dominus mundi*, "lord of the world," in a more literal sense than ever before.

The melancholic aspect of the event was that this would turn out to be the last time that in this way a Roman emperor was crowned. A new era had started; an era not only of church dissension, but also of the rise of national states, which would make the ancient Roman Empire fall apart. As English historian Frances Yates (1899-1981) expressed it:[12]

> It is as a very phantom that Charles's empire was of importance, because it revived the imperial idea and spread it through Europe in the symbolism of its propaganda, and that in a time that more advanced political thinking rejected it. (...) Each revival of the empire in the person of some great emperor, brought with it as a phantom the revival of a universal imperialistic hope. These revivals, that of Charlemagne not excepted, were never politically real or politically lasting; it was their phantoms that lasted, and exerted an almost ineradicable influence. The empire of Charles V, which was a late revival of the "espérance impériale" in connection with the bearer of the imperial title, transferred the influence of the phantom to the modern world.

7.3.2. Church and State[13]

In a certain sense, Charles V was the last medieval emperor, and at the same time he was the first Renaissance emperor. In him, once more the universal imperial idea was concentrated. This idea connected the self-consciousness of his dynasty with the religious notion of the universal responsibility for the one Christendom. The one empire with the one church—that was an ideal that precisely under Charles V experienced both its highlight and its collapse. Because of the conquered territories in the new world, an empire had arisen that was so large and so powerful that it was truly an empire "in which the sun never sets," as Charles put it himself. Under him

12. Yates (1975:1-2; cf. 20-28).
13. See extensively Ouweneel (2014c).

revived once more the splendor of the Carolingian kingship. His name sufficed to connect him with Charlemagne, who with regard to Charles V was Charles I. Never after Charlemagne, had so much power, so much territory, and so much wealth been united under one head as under Charles V. He was also an emperor of truly international grandeur: emperor of Germany, and king of Spain, but as to education, mentality, and culture, a Netherlander and Burgundian.

The German historian, Dietrich Schäfer (1845-1929), was right in stating that the Christian Roman Empire had never been closer to its realization than under Charles V. But at the same time, it became clear under Charles V that a supranational empire had become outdated. The first really national states came to light: Spain, France, England. The Northern Netherlands (which we call today "the Netherlands") would fight themselves free in a long rebellion. By long religious wars, Germany was going to be divided into a patchwork of little Protestant and Catholic states. Outwardly the Holy Roman Empire continued its existence but it was almost an empty shell. In 1555, the actually not yet very old emperor (55) had seen enough of these processes to abdicate as a tired and disillusioned man. Because of the division of the "world-empire" by his son, Philip II, and his brother, Ferdinand I, the dream of the *Monarchia universalis* came to an end. Unity and universalism had given way to disunity and pluralism. Would there ever be new chances for one, undivided European empire?

As I said, Charles V was not only the last medieval, but also the first Renaissance emperor. The cunning political and ecclesial diplomacy, the calculated conduct of wars, the astute propaganda, these were elements of the New Era. The same combination of medieval and Renaissance elements can be encountered with his contemporaries, king Francis I of France and king Henry VIII of England. None of them still viewed himself as a "feudal tenant" of the pope; even Philip II saw himself rather as a tutor than as a son of the mother-church. The medieval ideal of the one empire, the one church, and the one prince was gone. Out of the ashes, three entirely different powers arose: Protestantism, the new natural sciences, and state absolutism. If Protestantism had fulfilled its historical calling, both the new sciences and the new political system would have been based upon a radically Christian view of science and the state, respectively. Unfortunately, as I said, it was (part of) the fall of Protestantism that it, apart from its sad attitude towards the Jews, largely delivered both the domain of science and that of the political system, as far as their underlying views are concerned, to the gods of the Renaissance, and later to those of the Enlightenment.

In Christian thinking, since the Christianization of the Roman Empire (fourth century), time and again the question had come up as to whether the government of God was to be associated primarily with the pope, or with the emperor. And if with both: who of the two had the primacy? It is understandable that now the one, now the other answer was given. If one emphasizes the spiritual character of the Kingdom of God, one will give the primacy to the church, for the church is sacred, and the state is secular. If, however, one emphasizes the government of God over the entire mankind, one will give the primacy to the state. And if people would avoid such a choice, they will construe a *duplex ordo* ("double order") as high scholasticism had done, that is, a scheme in which the two, church and state, as two "empires" or "regiments" (that is, regimes) stand next to each other: two facets of the one government of God.

"Empire" and "regiment" by the way are not the same. Those speaking of two "empires" could mean by this the empire of God and the empire of the devil. But Luther's term "regiment" implies that in both the church and the state we have to do with a *divine* regime. With the one rule (of the "gospel") God leads people to faith, with the other rule (of the "law") he keeps the unrighteous under control. The first "regiment" (i.e., "rule") has to do with the *iustitia fidei*, the "righteousness of faith," the second one has to do with the *iustitia civilis* or *politica*, the "civil" or "political righteousness," the outward righteousness of societal life. This is related to the Lutheran dualism, already mentioned, of *law* and *gospel*: The law is the norm of the first, the gospel the norm of the second empire. In Lutheran terminology, they are the empire at God's left, and the empire at God's right hand, respectively. The first empire is not independent of God, for the authority of the secular authorities is also God-given. In this respect, this domain too is a divine "empire" or "regiment," in which God realizes certain aims, namely of maintaining order and rest in temporal, earthly life and to keep a check on the unrighteous. But this empire is yet far removed from the actual Kingdom of God, the spiritual kingdom of his Christ, which realizes itself within the church.

The most striking characteristic of any type of "two-empires" doctrine is the *secularization of the state*. The sacred (spiritual, devotional) life is confined to the church, or even to personal, inner, devotional life, but for the rest the whole life of the believer is secularized. According to this thinking, the life of the Christian, apart from the ecclesial and the inner devotional life, is just as secularized as that of the non-Christians. Professional life, science, politics, the arts, etcetera are "neutral." A "Christian" state is regarded as a fundamental impossibility, and, for instance, "Christian" schools are tolerated insofar as they are entirely financed by the parents. Only the church represents the Kingdom of God on earth; at best, the state can serve the Kingdom of God by supporting the church, and by defending it against outsiders.

With regard to the relationship of church and state, of course, many varieties can be, and have been, proposed. For instance, it makes quite a difference whether the state is especially viewed as the domain of the devil, or whether the state is also seen as an "empire" ("regiment") of God, be it sharply distinguished from the Kingdom of God. According to the *Lutheran* view of the state, church and state as the spiritual and the temporal empire have no inner point of contact.

However, the state is not "neutral" but "sacred," because the prince receives his authority from God and is responsible to him, not to the church. At best, there is a relationship with the church insofar as the latter, apart from being a spiritual empire, is also an earthly institute, which as such falls under the jurisdiction of the state. The state does not meddle in ecclesial matters, however, just as the church does not occupy itself with state affairs.

A closer relationship between church and state—be it still under the viewpoint of the nature-grace dualism—is assumed by the following two Protestant standpoints. Here, the state has the divine commission to help, to support, and to defend the church. In the *Anglican* view, the state does so from a *higher* position than the church, for the church is here a part of the state. Therefore, the British king is also the head of the Church of England and "defender of the faith." In the case of conflicting or overlapping interests, the church therefore stands under the state. The state rules over secular as well as sacred matters, therefore also over the internal functioning of the church, but it does not meddle in the actual spiritual tasks of the church: the ministry of the Word, and the sacraments.

In the *classical-Reformed* view too, as formulated particularly by Calvin, the state is to support the church in order to further the Kingdom of God. To this also belongs combating false religions and churches.[14] As the spiritual kingdom of Christ, the church is higher than the state, but that does not mean that she has authority over the state. In this regard, the state therefore does not have a lower position than the church, as in the Roman-Catholic view, nor a higher position, as in the Anglican view, but an *equal* position, in that both church and state are under the authority of Scripture, and both give account to God alone.

14. Cf. article 36 of the Belgic Confession; in the twentieth century, the words quoted in the text have been rightly omitted by several Reformed denominations.

7.3.3. The Republic of Letters

As to the three Protestant views mentioned, the classical-Reformed view of the state is closest to Scripture, because both church and state are seen here as equally standing under God's Word. Yet, this view too still presupposes the scholastic nature-grace scheme. Consequently, with regard to "natural" life, in this view the Renaissancistic approach still has too much free play. It is no wonder that in the very confusion of the sixteenth century, in which so many signs of the New Era became visible, a totally new philosophy of law and state came up within secularized thinking. This new reflection was necessary because of the rise of cities and citizens, of capitalism, and the traffic economy, of nationalism and the first sovereign national states, of the continuing separation between church and state, the German peasants' revolts around 1525, and the regal absolutism caused partly by the failure of these revolts.

I noted already that, apart from Protestantism, the New Era was going to be governed especially by two new categories of gods: those of the new natural sciences, and those of the new regal absolutism. By way of introduction, let me make one remark about the connection of this absolutism with the earlier German-Roman emperorship. Already since the Treaty of Verdun (843), the territories outside the East-Frankish empire were in fact independent of any German emperor whatsoever. But the German-"Roman" emperors might still play with the thought that the princes of the neighboring countries were "in fact" their feudal tenants. As I said, emperor Henry VI cherished this thought in the most conspicuous way, be it without success. Shortly after him, it was the Englishman Alanus who, already in the early part of the thirteenth century, placed the rights of the various kings in their *regna* ("kingdoms") on one level with those of the emperor in his *imperium* ("empire"). His doctrine gained increasingly more influence, and in the second half of the same century it took shape in the famous formula, *Rex est imperator in regno suo*, "the king is emperor in his kingdom." This meant, the one "Roman" emperorship of old had now been broken up into a whole variety of "little Roman emperors," who each received more power than the German emperor had factually ever possessed.

Yet, the notion of a European unified empire was, even at that time, not entirely forgotten. Petrarca (1304-1374), the great Roman-Italian patriot, spoke a little scornfully about the Holy Roman Empire of the *German* nation, and wonders, "If the Roman Empire is not at Rome, where then is it?"[15] He therefore supported the republican ideals of Cola di Rienzi in 1347, who wished to unite divided Italy under an emperor at Rome (cf. § 8.4.2). Finally, he aimed at a restoration of the Roman Empire with Rome as its capital. Rienzo even wrote about this to the German emperor of his time, Charles IV; his message implied that the emperor actually ought to reside in Rome, and that the Roman Senate ought to appoint him.

Some centuries later, the French king Henry IV (1553-1610) with his minister Maurice de Sully designed a new unification plan. It was a proposal of cooperation for the "Christian" states of Europe with the aim of banishing war between these states, to preserve the religious peace, and to keep the Turks at a distance. Even the possibility of a real confederation with a general council was discussed, in which the member states were to be represented according to their sizes. But this plan was not taken seriously, particularly by those who saw in it a secretive attempt of France to gain the supremacy in Europe. How would history have looked if one had indeed strived for such a confederation precisely to keep France's possible supremacy within restraints—exactly like, since World War II, the European Union is considered to fulfill such a task with respect to Germany?

At a different level, we hear in this very time of political dissension of a new, quite different European unification of a "Roman" nature. The French philosopher and historian of

15. *Liber sine nomine* IV; quoted by Yates (1975:14). Also see Petrarca's *Epistolae the iuribus Imperii Romani et iniuriis Papae Romani eiusque asseclarum.*

Polish descent, Krzysztof Pomian (b. 1934),[16] calls the Carolingian empire the "first attempt to European unification," and calls the Renaissance the real "first European unification," in a cultural sense, that is. He calls the new culture of the elite in this period "the return to ancient Rome." By the "second European unification" he understands the *Respublica Litteraria*, the "Republic of Letters," which arose after the Reformation in Europe. It was an elite of both Catholic and Protestant (!) men of letters in all countries of Europe, writing to each other, and during their travels conversing with each other, in Latin, the language of ancient Rome.

It may seem far-fetched to associate this Empire of Letters with the ancient Roman Empire, but the literary men of that time did not view it as exaggerated at all. Humanist scholars such as Poggio Bracciolini (1380-1459) and Pico della Mirandola (see before) understood by the Western empire not primarily a political, but a cultural empire in the best traditions of ancient Rome. The Italian humanist Lorenzo Valla (c. 1407-1457) expressed it even more acutely: *Ibi namque Romanum imperium est ubicumque Romana lingua dominatur,* "Everywhere, namely, where the Roman language dominates, there is the Roman Empire." Even poor Gerrit Witse, who, according to Hildebrand's famous Dutch novel, *Camera Obscura,* in the nineteenth century in the Netherlands still had to do his medical exam in Latin, "demonstrated" in this way that the Netherlands still lay within the sphere of influence of the Roman Empire.

In spite of the nationalist crumbling of Europe, the continent as a whole still upheld the same ideals shaped by antiquity and Christianity. Even where Catholics and Protestants had gone apart, some common culture remained intact, as it continued especially at the courts, the salons, and the lodges. If the "Roman Empire" of the newer time was indeed a cultural empire, then it was the culture of these courts, salons,

16. Pomian (1993:ch. 4, 8-9, 12-13).

and lodges. At the outset, it was the language of Rome that kept this intellectual elite together. The same Latin that in the Middle Ages had warranted the ecclesial unity of Europe now guaranteed a lasting cultural unity. Gradually, Latin passed into the Romanic language that far into the nineteenth century would remain Europe's language of unity: French. What else is French but a special continuation of Latin?

Does this Latin character of French also underline the supremacy of France over Germany? The great composer and little writer, Richard Wagner (1813-1883), defended the thesis that the French were inferior to the Germans since the latter had kept to their mother's language, whereas the West-Frankish tribes had exchanged it for the language of the Roman invaders.[17] But why could we not reverse this thesis? Why should the French not be superior, since they adopted the Latin *language of culture*, whereas the Germans had kept to their "barbarous" Germanic? With such arguments anything can be proven. But the subject does illustrate again how strongly, since the Middle Ages, the French-German relationship determined European history. If we may make somewhat large jumps, the pendulum swings from Charles V to Louis XIV, back to Frederic the Great, back to Napoleon I and III, back to Wilhelm I and II, back to France triumphing in 1918, back to Adolf Hitler. And then? Konrad Adenauer as well as Charles de Gaulle; Helmut Kohl as well as François Mitterrand, Angela Merkel as well as Nicolas Sarkozy and François Hollande. How will history go on? But we get ahead of our story.

Only this: if the language would be determinative for the nature of the European "empire," it has since long become an Anglo-Saxon empire. If an Englishman coming in the nineteenth century to the Netherlands still spoke French with the *haute société*, today the Dutch and the French, and even Dutch and Germans speak more and more English together. This does not yet necessarily imply an Anglo-Saxon "empire"

17. Wagner (n.y.).

(see chapters 8 and 9); or is English, that striking mixture of French (Latin) iron and Germanic clay, not pre-eminently the language for a modern Western "empire"?

7.3.4. The Republic of Scholars

The Republic of Letters also comprised the Republic of Scholars. This was the "empire" of the new natural sciences. Evidently, the publications of these Scholars were primarily written in the language of Rome. Their results supported the new mentality. Since Aristotle, people had believed in the distinction between the perfect superlunary and the imperfect sublunary world. Nicholas Copernicus (1473-1543), however, developed the heliocentric worldview, which removed the earth from the centre of the universe. Galileo Galilei (1564-1642) tied in with this, and, among other things, formulated the laws of movement for falling and thrown bodies. Isaac Newton (1642-1727) reduced these laws as well as those for the celestial bodies to one system of gravitation laws.

Often, this whole complex of scientific results has been interpreted in such a way that the earth, and thus man, would have been tarnished and pushed from the throne. In my opinion, the reverse could be argued for as well. Because the laws of movement on earth turn out to be the same as those that hold for the universe, the earth has been *promoted* to be one of those *celestial* bodies which before had been viewed as perfect. Man, before viewed as "just" an earth-dweller, thus became, so to speak, a "celestial" being. This re-evaluation fitted entirely into the mentality of the Renaissance: man had penetrated the empire of the gods. We have seen before (§ 2.1.2) how deeply rooted was the notion of the celestial bodies being associated with gods. If Pico della Mirandolo calls man "a god clothed with human flesh," natural science has corroborated this by placing man in the celestial empire of the gods.

The fact that between this new science and regal absolutism a much closer connection exists than may seem at first sight, has been made evident by the great pioneer of the new philosophy of law and state, the Italian Niccolò Machiavelli (1469-1527). This Italian nationalist ardently longed for the unity of his land and therefore hated papacy, which in his opinion hampered this unity. In fact, he longed for the Roman Empire from before the Christianization, and greatly regretted the fall of that ancient empire. Machiavelli developed a philosophy of law and state that was thoroughly secular-scientific. The new natural science, based on the principle, *Knowledge is Power* (see § 7.3.5), supplied him with the mechanistic view showing how this power could be politically translated. In his main work, *Il Principe* ("The Prince"), of 1513—the time of the young, rising Charles V!—he taught that the people and the prince are especially mechanic "power quanta." I say, especially, not exclusively: Machiavelli too recognized that goodness is higher than ability. But still, at the prize of all moral as well as immoral means the prince must attempt to keep his quantum largest. The great historian Machiavelli supplied abundant "evidence" for this thesis from history. Only by strong government, he taught, the state can maintain itself and extend its power. Very realistically, Machiavelli based this on the corruption of man, for which the educational mission of the state is the divine emergency solution. For the rest, he too recognized that not the state, but ethics and religion were the highest value.

A similar view was presented by the Englishman Thomas Hobbes (1588-1679), who had been influenced by Machiavelli. In fact, he used the expression *Scientia potentia est* ("Knowledge is power"). According to Hobbes, too, the people are power quanta, governed by blind "natural forces." At first, in his opinion, there was the "state of nature," in which "nature" means the jungle, governed by the law of taking and raking, that is, by brutal power. This state entails continuous war, in which *homo homini lupus*, "man is toward man a wolf," until the second phase sets in: the making of a *state-treaty*, in which people renounce the "right of nature." The state is therefore not founded in the social urge of man, as Aristotle and the Dutch scholar Hugo Grotius (1583-1645) too had claimed, but in the "natural" (biological) urge to self-preservation. Hobbes assigned to the state, personified in the prince, absolute power, but this absolutism was to be based upon reason, and thus upon justice and loyalty. Only that which is recognized as such by the state is justice, morals, and religion. The whole political system is only a state of organized greed. Hobbes therefore called the absolute prince the Leviathan devouring everything—and knowing the angelological background of the notion of "Leviathan"[18] we view this as hitting the mark more than Hobbes himself probably realized.

In this "natural-scientific" approach of Machiavelli and Hobbes, based on the "nature" of man, on "natural laws" governing political systems, on the "cycle" of history, etcetera, the deeper, metahistorical connection between the new philosophy of the state and the new natural science became visible. Both systems of thinking were based on a *physical* notion of *power*. Modern natural science no longer accepted that

18. Leviathan presumably means in Hebrew "twisting, tortuous," and refers to a dragon-like sea monster. Possibly, in Ps. 104:26 and particularly in Job 40:20 a literal water animal is intended—according to many, the crocodile—but even then with metahistorical implications (cf. Hartley 1988:521-522, 524 [nt 10], 529 [nt 23-24], 530 [nt 35], especially about the mythical meaning of the crocodile in Egypt). In Isa. 27:1, the word is twice a reference to world powers—or rather, their angelic princes—which have been hostile toward Israel, presumably Assyria and Babylonia. Ps. 74:14 seems to refers to Egypt (cf. the "dragon" in v. 13), in connection with the exodus of Israel from Egypt. But it cannot be excluded that the psalmist thinks of the chaos angels of God's creation, who are subdued by him through his creational power (cf. v. 16) (cf. § 3.1.2). Perhaps, the psalmist thinks of both: the chaos powers of Gen. 1:2, once subdued by him, raise as it were their monstrous head again at the redemption of God's own people, and are defeated anew by him. Ancient Ugarit knew Lotan, the sea monster, described as a twisting serpent, or a seven-headed dragon (cf. Rev. 12:3), defeated by Baal. In general, Leviathan is the personification of all powers resisting God's power and attempting to turn order into chaos, and harmony into disorder. In Job 3:8, "those who are ready [or, have the skill] to rouse up Leviathan" are people who, as diabolic instruments, are able to work mischief.

meaning and destination of man might lie outside this life and this world, namely in God (or, in the gods), but aimed *on its own authority* at the enrichment and ennoblement of human life—or at that which was viewed as such. This was to take place by setting free the slumbering potentialities of human nature and unfolding them, apart from of any conceivable "force," that is, subjection to norms and rules, particularly those of religion, of God.

In the new nature-freedom motif of humanism and Renaissance, on the one hand the scholastic motif of grace had been humanized and secularized into the motif of freedom. This motif was based on the new personality ideal of the absolutely free, autonomous man, who is governed by reason. The grace *of* God has been replaced here by the freedom *without* God (be it *with* the new gods). This new personality is nothing but a "god created after the (idealized) image of man." On the other hand, the motif of nature was developed into the science-ideal of the free subject, that objectifies nature and lays it at his feet in order to exert absolute, sovereign power over it. For nature offers infinite possibilities for satisfying the creative urge of subjection and dominion of self-begotten "modern" man. Thus, nature too is "re-created" after the will of man.

7.3.5. The Natural-Scientific Notion of Power

Just like the new philosophy of the state furthered regal absolutism, the new natural science furthered the notion of absolute human power over nature. The gods of the New Era were "creators" just like the God of gods: they created a new (free) man, a new nature, a new society, new scientific power, and new power of the state.

Francis Bacon (1561-1626), great statesman under queen Elisabeth I of England, pleaded for a true scientific *method*. Only if there is a method, true knowledge of nature can be obtained, and only if there is knowledge of nature, domination of nature is possible. Bacon too wrote *Scientia potestas est*, "knowledge is power." Although Bacon viewed this ideal in the light of the kingdom of God, we have to do here primarily with a typically Renaissancistic domination ideal. Thus, René Descartes (1596-1650) too asserted that, if we would obtain knowledge according to his methods, we would become "masters and possessors of nature." He said, and Immanuel Kant repeated it, "Give us materials, and we will build a world for you." And Thomas Hobbes said that theoretical thinking can create just like God. That is significant enough.

With regard to Descartes one more remark. If so far, God, or rather, the pantheon of Rome, had been the reference point of all Western thinking, Descartes once and for all placed this reference point in man's own self. In this way he became the father of modern philosophy. Man as it were has himself become "god." But a fact that is not so often told is that Descartes on November 10, 1619, shortly after he had laid the foundations of his philosophy—he was then 23 years old —three times in succession dreamed that he was to seek the truth by means of reason. He made the vow of making a pilgrimage to Our Lady of Loreto (Italy). Because of his military service and travels, only in 1623 he managed to fulfill his vow and to thank the Virgin for his philosophical discovery. This is quite peculiar! Descartes was called to his task from the realm of the gods, and he knew exactly to which address he had to send his thanks for his mission and discovery. He was not ashamed of the fact that he was in the service of the higher powers.

The gods of the new scientific thinking were acutely depicted by Johann Wolfgang von Goethe (c. 1800), following Christopher Marlowe (c. 1590), namely in the figure of Dr. Johann Georg Faustus (c. 1480-c. 1540). (Goethe's play was inspired by an earlier play called *Cenodoxus* written by the German Jesuit, Jacob Biderman [1578-1639].) Goethe supplied this figure with contours fitting into the time of Enlightenment. Faust wrestles restlessly in order to obtain true understanding, and even to learn to passionately taste life itself.

The dark spirit, Mephistopheles,[19] becomes his *genius,* so that Faust can subdue everything around him to himself, including the innocent soul of a woman. In this way, he has at his disposal power, riches, and pleasure, as the serpent already in the garden of Eden had promised this to Man (Gen. 3:5). But in this very way, he destroys the most beautiful, namely, love and innocence. In paradise too Adam had lost his innocence, and because of him, mankind entered upon a road of hatred and destruction. German historian Oswald Spengler (1880-1936) saw this. In his famous work, *Der Untergang des Abendlandes* ("The Decline of the West"), he compared civilizations to living organisms having a soul and a body. Thus he called the "soul" of antique culture the *Apollinian,* but that of modern Western civilization the *Faustian* "soul." The "body" of this Faustian "soul" is that civilization which,

> with the birth of the Romanic style in the tenth century, began to flourish in the northern plains between Elbe and Tagus.[20]

In describing the Faustian "soul," Spengler placed other accents than I do. But the fascinating thing is that he not only called our culture Faustian but moreover viewed this as the soul of a living being. In my opinion, Spengler in fact pronounced the same as what I have tried to express with the notion of the "god" (*genius*) of a certain culture or a certain empire. The Faustian angelic power(s) of modern Western culture are the soul of that culture; the princes, scholars, and artists are only the body.

Characteristic of the "Faustian" pretension of modern science and technology is the longing for knowledge inspired by the new gods, so that the new Man can dominate, manipulate, and reform that reality scientific-technologically, according to

19. The name occurs in Shakespeare as Mephistophilus (*The Merry Wives or Windsor*, r. 135), which is perhaps a corruption of the Greek *Mè-photo-philos*, "he who does not love light" (which forms a contrast with Lucifer, "light-bearer"). Also other explanations have been given.
20. Spengler (1923:234).

his own views and aims. But in reality, the ideology of technology leads to his fall. His unfettered lust of power evokes—to quote also Goethe's poem *Der Zauberlehrling* ("The Sorcerer's Apprentice")—"spirits" (!) of which he cannot get rid anymore (*Die ich rief, die Geister, werd ich nun nicht los*). In this poem, the only one who can control the "spirits" that have been released is the old *Hexenmeister* ("master-wizard"). This is the highest angelic prince in the spiritual world.

Concretely this means that Man is in danger of destroying himself by nuclear armament, by genetic manipulation, by environmental pollution, by the problem of the ever richer nations over against the ever poorer countries, etcetera. Man thinks he can continue on this way without giving account to God. He really believes he can allow himself to be no longer *theonomous*, that is, "subject to God," but *autonomous*, that is, only "subject to himself." He does not see that he who does not wish to be *theonomous* can only be *diabolonomous*: subject to the Confuser, the Disturber. The "bottomless pit" has been opened, and a cloud of "locusts" has escaped (Rev. 9:1-11). The spirits have been set free and cannot be collected anymore. Their tails are like scorpions to hurt men. Their king is the angel of the bottomless pit; his name is in Hebrew, Abaddon ("destruction"), in Greek, Apollyon ("destroyer"; notice the relation with Apollo).

Renaissance and Reformation both contributed to the scientific de-deification (*Entzauberung*, disenchantment, demythologizing) of nature. The Reformation, however, kept to the *God* of nature, whereas the Renaissance eventually placed God outside its thinking, thus falling into the hands of the gods. Exactly the same happened in regal absolutism, which was metahistorically related to it. In the sixteenth century it rose, and in the seventeenth century it reached its summit. We see this most clearly in Louis XIV, King of France, who did not own any suzerain above him, not the Roman pope, and even less the Roman emperor. The court priest, Jacques-Bénigne Bossuet, even supported him in his striving to obtain the say over the Roman-Catholic Church within his kingdom. Louis only ruled "by the grace of the god"—a pretended *droit divin* ("divine right"), which implied nothing but the "grace" of the new "gods" of the Renaissance. Deposition of the prince could not take place through the pope, nor through the high nobility, and even less through the subjects. The king's state philosophers, submissive courtiers, but also his own degenerated court noblemen, and even his confessor, père François de Lachaise, assured him, as well as us, that his power was derived directly from "god," and was indivisible, that he did not have to give account to any person on earth, and that all his whims were inspired by "god." They were right; the question is only, what "god"?

How strongly the absolutistic princes were identified with their "god" or "gods" is strikingly shown by the miraculous healing power that was ascribed to them. The French king also possessed a kind of "priestly" office by the grace of (the) god, which abundance of "grace" came to expression in his healing power. By the laying on of hands, he could heal people of glandular diseases. Whether it was the re-Catholicized Henry IV, or Louis XIII, or Louis XIV, they all have laid hands on many thousands of ill people. And it "worked"! The gods of the prince supplied him with such magic power as the medieval priests had possessed, who with their conjurations healed cattle and people. On whose sides the gods were standing, through them they brought about their occult healings.

In this way, the people "benefitted." But was it a "benefit"? Actually, the greatest benefit of the people was the return of hundreds of thousands to the Word of God. They were the Huguenots (French Protestants). But their reformation was suppressed by Louis XIV with all possible violence. The king healed the glandular diseases of his people—but by exterminating or repelling the Huguenots he struck the people an economic as well as spiritual blow of which they have recovered only with great effort.

7.3.6. King-Stadtholder William of Orange

Regal absolutism was of the greatest importance for the development of Europe. That was true in a positive sense, because it put forever an end to the secular power of the pope—but also in a negative sense. Regal absolutism formed the most important foreboding of the French Revolution and the rise of emperor Napoleon. In the latter, as a fruit of the Enlightenment, the ancient Roman ideal once more got shape in an entirely new way—and that again particularly in a negative sense. There runs a direct absolutist line from Louis XIV through Napoleon Bonaparte to Adolf Hitler. And there is one colossal opponent of this absolutism to be pointed out at the time of Louis XIV, whose influence was even felt still in Napoleon, even until the British battle against national-socialism. This opponent was William III (1650-1702), stadtholder of most of the Dutch provinces, from 1689 William of Orange, king of England, Scotland and Ireland.[21]

The metahistorical task of this prince has been gigantic—but he was up to it. As a deeply believing Christian, notwithstanding all his faults, he was the fierce opponent of absolutism. The fact that he wanted to reign "by the grace of God" meant something, for he knew both the God of the Bible and the grace of that God. If anywhere, Reformation was allowed to behold in him the personification of the great reformational ideal, which in practice usually failed so badly. This ideal involved the submission of the whole (personal as well as societal) life to God and his Word. In the Netherlands, William's opponents were the absolutistically minded regents, conspiring with Louis XIV, under the guidance of Johan de Witt, key Dutch politician, and on the British Isles, the Roman-Catholic henchmen of Louis XIV and the short-sighted parliament.

---

21. De Graaff (n.y.:195, 261, 270-281, 316-317, 340, 346) has said magnificent things about this matter, which, unfortunately, as always are spoilt by his theory about the "sacrificial death" of the incarnated "god," Otto III. Thus, the authority of a Louis XIV does not come from this "dead god" (p. 261-262), but from very lively gods.

Already in his descent, William of Orange exhibited the greatness of his calling. He was a descendant of prince William the Silent and of the great French Huguenot leader, Gaspard de Coligny, as well as of the pious Huguenot Jeanne d'Albret (mother of Henri IV), but also of the Danish-Norwegian king, Frederic II, James I of England, and Francis I of France, even of the house of Habsburg. Growing up in solitude, William was conscious of his high calling from his early youth. Particularly the education by the reverend Cornelis Triglandt prepared him for his great task. Drawing on the power of prayer, William of Orange did not primarily serve the interests of his house, or even those of "the people," but first aimed at the honor of God. In that strength, he managed to turn the catastrophic year 1672 in the Netherlands for the better by standing up to Louis XIV. Even the pope, very afraid of the "Roman-Catholic" Louis, preferred William of Orange to gain the victory instead of Louis XIV. In God's strength, William of Orange also ventured his Glorious Revolution in England (1688), where he substituted the kingship "by the grace of God" for the absolutism of James II. In fact, in European history, this kingship has become unique. The Peace of Utrecht (1713), brought about after William's death but fruit of his unmatched statesmanship, brought peace to Europe for a long time.

William of Orange knew the hidden spiritual strength that was able to stand up to absolutism. Even Napoleon seems to have realized his importance: he asked the Dutch prince of Orange, the later King William I, for a portrait of King William of Orange. Even the British resistance against national-socialism was an after-effect of the anti-absolutism which William of Orange had so strongly propagated in England. In this connection, his relationship with the Jews is quite remarkable. De Graaff says of this:[22]

> not only the Calvinists, also the Jews recognized William III as

22. De Graaff (n.y.:281).

> redeemer of God's people. The Portuguese Jew [F. Lopez] Suasso lent William III two million guilders without a debenture for the invasion in England. The relation with the Jews was such that William as king even lodged at Amsterdam with the Jew [Hieronymus] Nunes da Costa. William gave the synagogue of Amsterdam, which he visited regularly, marble pillars. [Antonio A.] Machado provisioned William's armies. He was often charged by him with diplomatic missions.

A similar relationship we find with William's successors. Isaac the Pinto was "court Jew" (money-lender, tradesman) of Prince William IV, and Tobias Boas functioned as such for Prince William V. When in 1785 the latter had to flee before the France-oriented "patriots," the wealthy tobacco manufacturer, Benjamin Cohen at Amersfoort, offered shelter to the prince (his "House with the blue window-glasses" still exists).

At the same time, it must be said that the reformational splendor of William of Orange was far less under his Dutch successors. In the Netherlands too, the century of the Enlightenment had begun. That was the century of deism, the doctrine owning a Creator-God but rejecting any intervention of this God in the history of the world. This implies that the possibility of miracles and of a divine revelation is rejected too. Deism is not so much, like in scholasticism, concerned with the relationship between, and the distinction of, faith and reason, but rather with the demand that each religious belief is founded upon reason. The Enlightenment was prepared in Great Britain (John Locke, David Hume, John Toland, Anthony Collins, Matthew Tindal), then blew over to France (Voltaire [François-Marie Arouet], Jean-Jacques Rousseau, the Encyclopedists), Germany (Gotthold E. Lessing, Frederic the Great), and to all Europe.

The Enlightenment was the spiritual movement that sealed the separation between the domain of "grace" (of God, the church, theology) and the domain of "nature" (of reason, society, philosophy, and science). On the one hand, the "Nearer

Reformation" (the Netherlands) and pietism (Germany) withdrew themselves into the former domain, and left the latter one to the new pagans, so that they lost all effectiveness in culture. On the other hand, liberal, ethical, humanist Christianity and the new agnosticism only accepted a religion that was entirely covered by reason.

Into this religious consciousness, an image of God did still fit. The Enlightenment philosophers in general even spoke with respect about God/god. But this notion only involved the "god of the philosophers and scholars," of whom French thinker Blaise Pascal (1623-1662) had already warned that this god had little to do with the God of Abraham, Isaac, and Jacob. Enlightenment was nothing but the great "liberation" of the people from the latter God. Thus, Immanuel Kant (1724-1804) did try to save religion by means of the distinction between theoretical and practical reason, and therewith between the secular and the sacred domain. But with him, the sacred was nothing but some decent moralism. He too, the former pietist, had effectively placed the God of the Bible outside the horizon of man. Modern man has been delivered to the "divine" powers dominating the Enlightenment in Europe.

Chapter 8
The Seventh Empire

8.1. Post-Roman Empires
8.1.1. An Exegetical Question

When in the nineteenth century, during the European Réveil, thousands of Christians received an entirely new insight into the prophetic Word, this had great consequences. They again got an eye for the glorious future of the converted ethnic Israel in the Messianic kingdom of peace; for the future restoration of the ancient Roman Empire in an entirely new form (see chapter 9); for the literal interpretation of the Old Testament's prophecies; and therefore, also for the eschatological interpretation of the book of Revelation. Certainly, the spiritual descendants of the Réveil exhibited great differences in their exegesis of this Bible book. But the main points were clear: the futurist-eschatological, premillennialist explanation was to be preferred.[1]

Also, with respect to the difficult prophecy in Revelation 17:7-14, more clarity was achieved. I already pointed to the various interpretations of the "seven kings" mentioned there (see § 1.2). The futurist-eschatological exegesis has thought here of seven historical phases, or of seven political forms of the Roman Empire, or of seven subsequent world-empires.

1. See Ouweneel (1988b:38-40); see also Ouweneel (2012).

The latter is the exegesis that I present here. At any rate, in both the two latter interpretations, the "sixth king" is the (head of the) Roman Empire, and the "eighth king" is the future (head of the) restored Roman Empire. But then, in both exegeses the problem presents itself, *Who is the "seventh king"?*

I pass here the view of Bible scholar William Kelly (1821-1906), who identifies the seventh and the eighth head.[2] In my opinion, the text clearly distinguishes between them. I also discard the view of those who equate the seventh head with the ten kingdoms in v. 8. This is not impossible,[3] but the objection against this is that the ten kings do not have a head which might function as the "seventh king." In my opinion, a "king" is not just a political system here, as a confederation of ten states, but an empire with a mighty head of state, and an angelic prince identifying himself with that empire and embodied in that head of state. It is precisely the "eighth king" who becomes that mighty head of the ten states (v. 12f.), so that it seems hardly possible to view the confederation of the ten states itself as the "seventh king."

Who then is the "seventh king"? It is interesting to listen to the most influential premillennialist expositor of the nineteenth century, the Anglo-Irish John Nelson Darby (1800-1882). His second given name he owed to his godfather, Lord Nelson, the great British opponent of Napoleon. I mention this because of Darby's interpretation of the "seventh king": he liked to think here of Napoleon. In this context, he also mentioned the historicist exegesis of the book of Revelation, which sees in this book a prophetic sketch of the whole of Western history, and in the "seventh king" sees Charlemagne. The idea is, then, that the "sixth king" is the Roman Empire, which in the West was overthrown in 476; Charlemagne would then have been the "seventh king" following upon this. In Darby's own futurist-eschatological exegesis, he

2. Kelly (1904:203).
3. I myself defended this view before (1990:166). It is, among others, the view of Grant (1902:464) and Scott (1920:352).

rather thought of a figure in the "end time," that is the time just before the second coming of Christ and the Messianic kingdom of peace. Already in his rather early commentary upon Revelation (1839) he therefore wrote,[4]

> One brief-lived [seventh] head of the beast was to arise before the last [the eighth], after the apostle's days,

and then said in a footnote on the seventh head:

> I feel that probably this has passed, if we take the protracted [= historicist] course, in Charlemagne; if [applied to] the closing scene, in Buonaparte, because the Roman Empire had been destroyed in its full character before Charlemagne; and this [the latter's empire] was a renewal of what [for a time] was not [cf. vs. 8]. Nominally it continued until Buonaparte, who, as the agent of the French republic, broke it to pieces and renewed the imperial power for a little season.

The idea is that the Carolingian empire actually represented a new empire, which in the form of successively the Carolingian and the Holy Roman Empire continued until Napoleon. The latter abolished in 1806 the Holy Roman Empire, and called a whole new empire into existence, be it "for a short time" (cf. v. 10). Precisely because of this "short time" it is difficult to think of the Carolingian and the Holy Roman Empire,[5] but one could possibly think of Napoleon, who placed an empire over against the Holy Roman Empire, and that "for a short time." In a much later, undated commentary, Darby expressed himself a little more carefully, and said of the

---

4. Darby (n.y.,2:242).
5. *Contra*, for instance, William Hendriksen (1988:170), who asks, "Is this seventh head the collective title for all antichristian governments between the fall of Rome and the last empire of the Antichrist...?" In a footnote (p. 226) he says, "some make of this seventh head papacy; others the nominally Christian Roman Empire, beginning with Constantine the Great, still others, the Germanic nations, prevailing over Rome." The great objection against all these interpretations is that it cannot be maintained in any way that the intended empires "remained a short while."

"seventh king":[6]

> perhaps Napoleon I; in the protracted [= historicist] system, Charlemagne.

Also, expositor Edward Dennett (1831-1914) carefully wrote in his commentary (last part of the nineteenth century?),[7]

> If Napoleon I is, as has often been suggested, the one who was to make the seventh, there remains now only the appearance of the "beast" to fulfil the angelic prophecy.

And contemporary Edward H. Chater wrote with regard to the seventh head,[8]

> The writer shares the thought of many that this is a reference to the first Napoleon, who rose into power and conquered most of the territory comprised in the old Roman earth. "When he cometh, he must continue a short space." From the Isle of Corsica, in the midst of the sea, he rose from obscurity to imperial power, continued a short space, and disappeared from the stage of this world, to spend the short remainder of his life in another island of the sea.

The exegesis became more doubtful when Darby did not express himself in a careful way anymore but with great confidence. Thus he wrote during the empire of Napoleon III,[9]

> As much excitement has been caused by the question, as to whether Louis Napoleon is the Antichrist or not, I add that I have not the smallest doubt [!!] that he is the great agent of the formation of the Latin or ten-horned beast at present, and that his operations distinctly mark the rapid approach of the final scenes.

He added wisely, though:

---

6. Darby (n.y.,30:389).
7. Dennett (n.y.:224).
8. Chater (1914:196-197).
9. Darby (n.y.,11:386-387; also cf. 15:258).

> (...) the computation of dates is all unfounded. There are general analogies, I have no doubt, as there have been many Antichrists who were not the Antichrist. (...) It is to be feared England will be dragged into the vortex of the ten kingdoms [cf. vs. 12]: God knows. (...) I think Louis Napoleon a sign of prophetical progress towards the close (...) though events have made progress, the view of the position of Louis Napoleon falls in entirely with Faber's view of the first Napoleon, that he was the seventh head of the beast who was to continue for a short time; indeed, it was that of others too.

These are typical examples of an interpretation of the prophecies with the help of the newspaper: reading contemporary events into the prophetic Word. This is not forbidden; we will also "trespass" in this respect ourselves. But it always remains risky, because later events often seem to yield a far more striking and accurate interpretation of the prophetic Word. In this respect, it is worthwhile to compare Darby's conjecture with that of another expositor, namely, Alfred H. Burton, also physician, and remarkably enough the man in whose arms Darby deceased in 1882. In 1932 (!), Burton wrote the following:[10]

> Along with others we used often to suggest that Napoleon Bonaparte might have been this seventh [head]. The brief description here given seemed to have had its fulfilment in his extraordinary rise to power, and his equally sudden fall. But the present remarkable developments in Italy make it much more likely that Mussolini may be this seventh, for after all, Napoleon's seat of government so long as it lasted was Paris, whereas Mussolini's is Rome. Time will shew. (...) that what we are now witnessing in Italy may be, and most likely is, the immediate preparation for the actual Beast of prophecy.

Here again we find a striking example of interpreting a portion of Scripture in the light of contemporary events. One is inclined to think: if Burton had waited a few more years, he

10. Burton (1932:232).

might have seen arising a figure in Berlin that would eclipse Mussolini in every respect. The bond with Rome remains preserved for that matter, for in 1936 Hitler concluded a treaty with Mussolini, and the "Berlin-Rome axis" would dominate the war in Europe.

Reverend Leonard Sale-Harrison (1875-1956) wrote a remarkable little book concerning the revival of the ancient Roman Empire in the same period, that is, shortly before World War II. As far as I can verify, the first edition of this book appeared in 1928, while the version which is at my disposal apparently stems from 1939 (at least, that is the youngest year mentioned in it).[11] Although Sale-Harrison in this last edition knows of course about the rise of Hitler, to him too the "Roman" Mussolini is the fulfillment of prophecy. He mentions some striking facts with regard to him, which will be dealt with below, facts that at least make of Mussolini too, a forerunner of the beast. Yet, we now know that he was not the beast—if only because Hitler was a far greater "beast" than he.

As an illustration, let us look at a still later commentary, now written in the 1950s, by August Van Ryn (1890-1982). We quote his remark concerning the confederation of the ten states:[12]

> No doubt [!!] the main reason for this coalition of Western European nations is for the purpose of resisting the aggression of Communistic powers, with Russia seen as the chief aggressor. We see the foreshadow of such an alliance already very clearly in our day.

Again, prophecy is read through the glasses of the media! Thirty years later, there were no "communist powers" anymore in Europe, and former communist countries are pushing to join the European Union (ten of them already did). In short, the scene changes continually, and we will have to exercise

11. Sale-Harrison ([1939]).
12. Van Ryn ([1960]:195-196).

the greatest care not to let the newspaper govern the exegesis. We propose therefore not to tie ourselves down to the identity of the "seventh king." In this chapter, we will simply pay attention to the two chief persons mentioned so far: Napoleon Bonaparte and Adolf Hitler. Perhaps, the "seventh king" is still going to appear; but then we will be allowed to view Napoleon and Hitler at least as forerunners of this figure.

We will see below how much more Hitler resembled the "beast" of Revelation than Napoleon, for that matter. The latter was (more or less) a Jews' friend, Hitler a Jews' hater like biblical Haman. In this respect, it is striking that national-socialism so emphatically harked back to Germanic paganism. If all seven world-empires had and have their own, though closely related, angelic princes, then the sixth empire was dominated by Zeus/Apollo, and the seventh empire by Wodan. These angelic princes are different, and yet so akin. It is one and the same diabolic power hiding behind the world-empires, manifesting itself in them, and through them assaulting God's people.

8.1.2. England and America

In the present study, two empires are hardly dealt with. They are "cleared off" in this section, although both of them did enjoy the honor of being named "world-empires." They certainly deserve our attention if we adhere to the theory mentioned before that the succession of the world-empires moves from East to West. After the Roman Empire in its diverse varieties, the *translatio imperii* moved further to the West, to arrive first in Great Britain for the time being. Already in the fourteenth century, this thought was pronounced by Richard the Bury, bishop of Durham:[13]

> *ad Britanniam, insularum insignissimam quin potius microcosmum, accedit feliciter:* happily has she [Minerva, in this case as the goddess of wise government] now approached Britain, the most

13. R. de Bury (1960), see the whole section: p. 98-115.

> remarkable of the islands, even a world in little.

The English speaking authors referred to in the previous section were very moderate compared with the English nationalists who, in earlier centuries, shortly after the Reformation, even managed to apply the Bible books of Daniel and Revelation entirely to themselves. The theologian Thomas Brightman (1562-1607) saw a glorious future for the English nation in the approaching kingdom of God. Some Protestants united in a group calling itself the *Fifth Monarchy Men,* the men of the "fifth empire," that is, the kingdom of God, which replaces all previous, godless empires (Dan. 2 and 7). One of the leaders was rev. William Sedgwick (c. 1610-c. 1669), who described England as the "bosom of the earth, where the divine glory chooses to preserve its richest jewels," and as "a happy Canaan." And Timothy Dwight (1752-1817), president of Yale University, made a link with the world-empires again:[14]

> The Assyrian empire was surpassed by the Persian, that again by the Greek empire, and all were wrapped up in the splendor of the Roman greatness. That one in its turn, however, has been surpassed by the science, the power, and the grandeur of England. (...) The world-empire of North America will be the last on earth (...) It will also be the most glorious one. Here the progression of all the earthly will be completed on the way to perfection.

Does not even the one-dollar bill speak of a *novus ordo seclorum,* "new world-order"? In the nineteenth century, there really was a British *imperium* that "ruled the waves," and thus spread over oceans. Yea, there was the triumphant *pax Britannica,* which put the *pax Romana* in the shadow. This was a "Christian" empire, as many underlined, a blessing for the whole world—not the least for the colonies, as some taught in a patronizing way. This triumphant attitude was connected with a racist nationalism, which certainly did not yield to

14. From an address to students in 1776; quoted by Schulte Nordholt (1992:136).

German racism. English politician Sir Charles W. Dilke (1843-1911) wrote in his *Greater Britain* (1868, only 25 years old) about

> the grandeur of our [Anglo-Saxon!] race, which already like a belt encompasses the earth and which perhaps is destined to eventually spread over that whole earth.

The first fulfillment of this was seen particularly in the "Anglo-Saxon" United States of America. In 1883, historian Sir John R. Seeley (1834-1895) in his *The Expansion of England* (1883) proclaimed that civilization was clearly moving westward, away from Italy (Rome) and Germany. Westward meant, England and America. Interestingly, here again history itself relativizes all bravado. Since the decolonization, nothing is left of the British Empire. In the European Union, England is a nation that clearly stays behind Germany and France in power and significance. And the United States? Of course, for those who adhered to the theory of the East-West movement of the *translatio imperii* America was the glorious final goal. Dutch historian and America expert Jan Willem Schulte Nordholt (1920-1995) devoted a whole book to this "myth of the West" (1992), according to which America would be "the last world-empire." This myth primarily flowed forth from British nationalism, since America was originally seen as "a new Britaine in another world" (J.E. Gillespie). American diplomat Alexander Hill Everett (1792-1847) wrote in 1827 that the United States, as the mightiest and most populous nation of English origin, of itself would take the place of the British Isles. Already the English poet George Herbert (1593-1633) drew a line from Egypt through Babylon, the Jews, Greeks, and Romans, to Western Europe, and from there the gospel would travel to the New World.

The well-known bishop and philosopher, George Berkeley (1685-1753), even wrote a poem about this apotheosis in the West. California, which itself forms the West of the United States, was so grateful to him for this that it called a whole city and university after him (near San Francisco). In the last stanza, Berkeley wrote some words that have become famous:

Westward the course of empire takes its way;
The four first Acts already past,
A fifth shall close the Drama with the day;
Time's noblest offspring is the last.

What Berkeley says is this: the world-empires follow a westward course; four empires have already been, the fifth and most Western one forms the glorious conclusion. There has been enormous speculation concerning this poetic statement. What are these words from a Christian mouth supposed to mean? According to Christian expectation, is the fifth empire not the empire of the Messiah? Is the Messianic empire to be localized in North America? The thousands of poor and straying, who found their dreams of bliss realized in America, might like to believe this just all too greedily. Many American preachers have supported this thought. Increase Mather and his son, Cotton Mather, Samuel Sewall, William Smith, Jonathan Edwards, Samuel Langdon, they all hailed America as "God's own country," the new Canaan, or as president Abraham Lincoln put it, God's "almost chosen people." The young American poet Philip Freneau (1752-1832) described in *On the Rising Glory or America* (!) the millennial kingdom of peace as described in Revelation, and pronounced the presumption that the New Jerusalem would descend in America:

And when a train of rolling years are past,
(So sung the exiled seer in Patmos isle)
A new Jerusalem, sent down from heaven,
Shall grace our happy earth, – –perhaps this land [America],
Whose ample bosom shall receive, though late,
Myriads of saints, with their immortal king,
To live and reign on earth a thousand years,
Thence called Millennium.

Even in the nineteenth-century, such dreams struck a responsive chord with Dutch Reformed dissenters (*Afgescheidenen*) and the men of the Réveil. Rev. Hendrik P. Scholte (1805-1868) and rev. Albertus C. van Raalte (1811-1876), who both transplanted a group of dissenters to America, believed that the Lord opened a new future in the New World. We find the same, again based on the notion of the East-West course of civilization, with Dutch Jewish convert Isaac da Costa (1798-1860), especially in his great poem, *Wachter, wat is er van de nacht?* ("Watchman, what of the night?"). Dutch scholar and prime minister Abraham Kuyper (1837-1920) proclaimed the same East-West theory in his famous Stone Lectures, held in America about Calvinism, and viewed the "stream of life" moving from Middle-Asia and the Levant through Europe to America,

> at the beach of the Pacific reverently waiting for what further course God has ordered for it.[15]

Perhaps the economic power Japan, the "Asian tigers" (Hong Kong, Singapore, South Korea, Taiwan) and especially the rising economic world powers India and China...? Kuyper's daughter, Henriette S.S. Kuyper (1870-1932), who spent some time in the New World, painted an even more fantastic picture. She expected that once the East–West circle would be closed, when the center of civilization again would be localized in Asia, she wondered if Christ would then return.[16] Triumphant Americans, so far away from Rome, even claimed the ancient Roman ideal for themselves. The illustrious lawyer, Oliver Wendell Holmes (1809-1894), exclaimed, "We are the Romans of the Western world!" Many others made similar statements. Peter Chardon Brooks Adams (1848-1927), grandson of president John Quincy Adams, foresaw that the United States would become a greater seat of wealth than England, Rome or Constantinople had ever been.[17] And perhaps

15. Kuyper (n.y.:25-27).
16. H.S.S. Kuyper (1907:442).
17. Adams (1900:12).

America never behaved more "Roman" than in the twentieth century, when it proclaimed itself the keeper of world peace, as it demonstrated from Korea to Kuwait, Iraq and Afghanistan. Gerhard F. Mehrtens devoted an interesting study to this subject; he calls the Americans the "new Romans."[18] After the *pax Romana* and the *pax Britannica* people now speak of the *pax Americana*, which the conservative powers would like to establish in the whole world.

For many non-Anglo-Saxons, it was not so easy to be congenial with these pretentions, certainly not for the Germans. The great German philosopher Georg W.F. Hegel (1770-1831) said it quite clearly in his *Philosophie der Weltgeschichte* ("Philosophy of World History"):

> *Europe is schlechthin das Ende der Weltgeschichte, Asien der Anfang.*

("Europe is simply the end of world history, Asia the beginning.") World history reaches its summit, "its perfect maturity," in "the Germanic world," and that's it. The essential component of the United States, however, is just as "Germanic" (viz., Anglo-Saxon) as Western Europe. None could say with certainty which of these two "Germanic" worlds will form the end point of the history of world culture. Today, the European Union comprises more territory and more people than the United States do. In 2012, according the International Monetary Fund, the World Bank and the CIA World Factbook, the GDP (Gross Domestic Product) of the European Union was larger than that of the United States. Yet, the European Union is less powerful than the United States. That which Europe lacks is a *central* economic, political and military power, to push it up to the first place on the world scene. But here we again got ahead of our story. First, we will have to take up the thread at the French Revolution.

18. Mehrtens (1987).

8.2. Napoleon

8.2.1. The Rising Star-God

Secularization, de-Christianization, "Enlightenment," and then finally, revolution in France, and the rise of Napoleon Bonaparte. For the French revolutionaries, ancient Rome was again the great ideal. Many a decree therefore started with this phrase, *Ainsi faisaient les Romains...* ("Thus did the Romans..."). The Swiss historian, Jean de Müller (1752-1809), called the day that the Bastille fell the most beautiful day of world history since the fall of the Roman Empire. In the little general Bonaparte, after a long time the Roman ideal was revived in a still much more striking way. The metahistorical conditions were all present, if at least we may believe the stories. For instance, it is told that a comet with a gigantic tail appeared two weeks before his birth on August 15, 1769. We are also told that a comet announced his death—as is also said of his illustrious "Roman" predecessors: Julius Caesar, Charlemagne, Charles V. In the evening of May 3, 1821, a servant came to Napoleon and told him that a comet had been discovered at the Western sky. "A comet?" exclaimed the exile of St. Helena, "once that was the harbinger of Caesar's death too!" The next day, a violent storm raged; sky-high the waves struck the steep rock shores of the island, and the rain gushed down. It was as if the "elementary spirits" wished to announce the decline of this star-god. At sunset on Saturday, May 5, 1821, the last Roman emperor died.

There, at St. Helena (saint Helena had been the mother of the first Christian Roman emperor!), Napoleon unfolded how he had imagined the empire founded by him. It looks very much like the European Union which is being developed at present: a European confederation of sovereign states, each with their representatives in Paris, one generally valid code of law, one international court of law, one common currency. He also desired, if at all possible, the one ecumenical deistic, rationalist world religion of the Revolution. Napoleon certainly was not the only one who had such dreams caused by the

Revolution. In 1804, czar Alexander (1777-1825), influenced by the revolutionist, playwright and critic Jean-François de La Harpe (1739-1803), had submitted to the English government a daring plan for European unification. Thus, the restored Roman Empire could have originated as a voluntary union of the European states. But for this, it was still far too early.

Napoleon had almost been a real "Roman": only two years before his birth, the isle of Corsica, where he was born, had passed from Genoese into French hands. In any case, he always remained a Corsican, as was evident from his bad pronunciation of the French and his limited French vernacular. The pre-eminent historian of Napoleon's time and empire, Louis Madelin (1871-1956), tried to furnish extensive evidence for Napoleon's "Roman" descent. Napoleon himself, too, liked to boast of his "Roman," or even his "Etruscan" descent. The fact that he got himself the title of "consul" points to this orientation to the Roman Empire. At the very least, Napoleon's *empire* was "Roman"—more "Roman" than that of Charles V, whose empire did not comprise France, of all countries. It was a long time ago that a "Roman" emperor could reckon such a large part of Europe to his territory, or to his allies, as Napoleon could in 1812: from Spain to Denmark and East-Prussia, from the Netherlands to the kingdoms of Hungary and Naples. Napoleon's famous codes of law stood in the best of Roman traditions.

Already in 1793, Napoleon Bonaparte's military talent came to light. When in that year several rebellious cities were subdued by the new regime, he distinguished himself as captain of the artillery at the siege of Toulon. Shortly after, he was promoted general. At the same time, in the Notre Dame at Paris, the Cult of Reason was instituted; the universal anti-Christian feelings led to the closure of many churches. In 1796, Napoleon undertook his great campaign in Italy, where he defeated many times the Austrians—nominally, that still implied: the Holy Roman Empire, or what was left of it—and coerced the pope to peace. In 1797, Austria, at the Peace of

Campoformio, ceded the Southern Netherlands to France in exchange for Venice, and accepted the ceding of the territory West of the Rhine to France.

In 1798, the French occupied Rome and led pope Pius VI as a prisoner to France. In that year, Napoleon's expedition to Egypt started, where his fleet was defeated by the British admiral, Lord Nelson, though. After his return from Egypt, Napoleon, late 1799, overthrew the French regime (the *Directoire*) and became first Consul, with Charles-Maurice de Talleyrand as his minister of foreign affairs. In 1800, Napoleon again defeated the Austrians; at the Peace of Lunéville (1801), the Peace of Campoformio was reinforced. In 1802, Napoleon made the Peace of Amiens with England. In that year, he became Consul for life by means of a plebiscite. He "reconciled" himself with the Roman-Catholic Church in a concordat, and carried through many political reformations. On December 2, 1804, on the basis of a new plebiscite he became "emperor of the French," and a year later, king of Italy.

The subsequent years were dominated by war against England, Russia, Austria, and Sweden. In the "Three Emperors' Battle" at Austerlitz (1805), the last "Holy Roman" emperor, Francis I, and the emperor of the "Third Rome," czar Alexander I, fought against the new, self-made "Roman" emperor, Napoleon Bonaparte. Three "Roman" emperors, fighting each other! In 1811, Napoleon, after many victories, was at the summit of his power; but the next year, he got stuck in Russia. In 1813, at Leipzig in the *Völkerschlacht* ("Battle of the Nations"), he was severely defeated by the allied Russians, Prussians, Austrians, English, and Swedes. Napoleon refused peace. In 1814, he had to abdicate and was banished to Elba. The following year, however, he landed again in France, acquired a large army, but was permanently defeated at Waterloo by the English and the Prussians. He was banished to St. Helena, where, as said before, he died in 1821.

8.2.2. Napoleon the "Roman"

Now what are the aspects of Napoleon's career that might help us further to get some insight into the metahistorical background of this "Roman" emperor? For instance, his second marriage with none less than a Habsburger, Marie-Louise of Austria, of whom he hoped that she, after his childless marriage with Joséphine the Beauharnais, would give him a successor on the imperial throne. Indeed, finally the long expected son was born: Napoleon II, *Roi de Rome*, "king of Rome" (!), who, by the way, would never mount the throne. Speaking further of the Habsburgers: Napoleon's inane brother, Joseph, became king of Spain as Joseph Napoleon I, and as such occupied nothing less than the throne of Charles V.

Napoleon's relationship with the pope of Rome has been peculiar. He made the power of the Gallic church—the Roman-Catholic Church in France—strongly dependent on the state's power in a way that deeply grieved Rome, without the pope having the power or the courage to undertake anything against it. We will see later how Napoleon coerced pope Pius VII to cooperate in his coronation at Paris, how he himself placed the crown on his own head, and how the pope had to bless him from the foot of the throne. Seldom a pope has been so deeply humiliated as Pius VII at Paris, from the moment he arrived until he left. In everything, Napoleon made it clear that he regarded himself as the lord of Rome. And when, in his opinion, Pius VII did not sufficiently support his politics, Napoleon first took the papal citadel, Ancona, and then took the city of Rome, revoked the so-called Donation of Constantine, and incorporated the estates of the pope into the French empire. When the pope excommunicated him in powerless anger, Napoleon laconically put him into prison for almost five years.

In numerous ways, Napoleon managed to affront the Roman-Catholic Church. His birthday, August 15, that is, the day of the Assumption of Mary, was henceforth to be the "feast of the holy Napoleon." Yet he was not a-religious, but then in the way a son of the Enlightenment is "religious." He venerated the "god of the philosophers," the natural idea of god, the god of natural theology, the god of modern natural science—his *own* god, which had led him to this imperial summit. He even managed to have a "St. Napoleon" introduced into the sacred calendar.

As the French Revolution, according to De Graaff, was a "Luciferic revelation," he therefore calls Napoleon "the great Luciferic genius,"[19] and says of him,[20]

> As the positive genius seeks an instrument that is excellent, that is, which has great talents, so Lucifer sought in Napoleon a man with the greatest talents. (...) Napoleon disposed of the greatest talents. He was not only the greatest general of all times, but also a great statesman, economist, lawgiver, manager, and a great judge of people. The question is whether Napoleon was overpowered by Lucifer. I believe that God gave Man a power that for the kingdom of darkness is unassailable. Only voluntary permission by Napoleon must have preceded the submission to Lucifer. For the crowd, the lack of divine splendor is replaced by Napoleon's spectacular deeds. (...) The crowd is content with a surrogate of a divine justification. When the people lose their god, they turn into the mob, which serves an idol. With Napoleon, the mob did not feel lost anymore without a god and without a master [*ni dieu ni maître*] in the world. With Napoleon, the mob did not feel alone anymore over against the absurd nothingness.

When Napoleon at St. Helena tried to justify himself with the words, "I am no man like others; the laws of ethics and conventions cannot be applied to me," in a metahistorical sense he was right. He was no common man, but the immediate instrument of the god or the gods of the New Time. Napoleon himself once said that in all things he felt impelled by a

19. De Graaff (n.y.:335).
20. Ibid. (n.y.:336-337).

hidden force. That force pushed him to a certain goal, which he himself could not have more accurately described. But he did know that, if that force would once forsake him, it would be over with him. Without that force he would "become weak, and be as another man," as Samson once said to Delilah (Judg. 16:7, 11, 17). He also realized that that force was a "divine" force; therefore, at his command an imperial catechism could be used in the schools in which it was taught that serving the emperor implied serving "god."

When Napoleon himself pronounced that above all he wanted to establish the ideal of the Enlightenment, the kingdom of reason, he very clearly presented himself as the instrument of this "god." He defended himself before the forum of history by appealing to his, indeed enormous, administrative, technical, and economical achievements. The fact that he sacrificed hundreds of thousands of human lives he deemed of secondary importance. In this connection, we should not overlook, by the way, the person of Talleyrand, Napoleon's most important statesman and counselor. In fact, it was this failed priest, a genial and brilliant man, who led Napoleon to power, and also overthrew him. It is quite fascinating that De Graaff compares this man to Goethe's Faust, while he compares Napoleon to Mephistopheles (not the other way around).[21]

8.2.3. The Coronation of Napoleon

The imperial coronation (*le Sacre*) of Napoleon[22] was entirely directed at imparting to Napoleon's rule the splendor of the gods who governed him. The whole territory of Roman Christendom had to be collected under one emperor again; the political unity that had been lost since Charlemagne was to be restored. Paris, that chief Roman cultural center, was to become the new "Rome," and the Romanic French, for the elite since long the language of unity, was to become the

21. Ibid. (n.y.:348-349).
22. See Presser (1978:206-214).

lingua franca. It was to become an empire with one scepter, one center, one political structure, one culture, one language, one army, one police. Napoleon strived for a lofty goal, so lofty, that a failure *a priori* seemed unavoidable.

In itself the institution of the Napoleonic emperorship was already a miracle, since through it the "free citizens" of the Revolution were again degraded to silenced "subjects." This institution was "legalized" by a plebiscite that was manipulated from the beginning to the end. Dutch historian Jacques Presser (1899-1970) called the *Sacre* itself

> the most beautiful piece of stage-management of Napoleon's entire reign, perhaps of the whole of French history.

The aim of the imperial consecration was inspired by Charlemagne, who had fascinated the new emperor since quite some time. At Aix-la-Chapelle (Aachen), he even had a statue erected for the great Charles. An entire Charlemagne cult was set going, with extensive glorifications in the press. On December 2, 1804, three marshals solemnly paraded with the crown, the scepter, and the imperial gown of precisely ten centuries ago. Napoleon's coronation gown was an imitation of a rediscovered Merovingian gown. Charlemagne's scepter was uncovered in the Louvre—although wicked tongues alleged that it was nothing but an imitation concocted by the museum's director.

It was a pity that Napoleon's coronation had not taken place already in 1800, exactly one thousand years after that of Charlemagne! Nevertheless, the coronation was to be an imitation of Charles's—and thus the pope had to be involved. Pius VII did not particularly like the idea, yet he was persuaded to come to Paris. There, as I said, Napoleon managed to offend and affront the poor pope in numerous ways. On one point, however, the pope could not be talked round: the marriage with Joséphine had only been concluded before the civil authorities, and therefore first had to be concluded ecclesially too. In spite of Napoleon's great anger, this occurred in the night before the coronation through his own uncle, Joseph Fesch (a scoundrel who had managed to become a cardinal), with Louis-Alexandre Berthier and Talleyrand as witnesses.

The coronation took place in the Notre Dame. It was a mad masquerade, a foolish imitation of the coronations of the Holy Roman Empire—and moreover an affront for the last emperor of that empire, Francis II, who at that moment was still in power! The celebration involved a scepter, a sword, and an orb, all blessed by the pope, and moreover, in between all the "religious" hotch-potch, a civic oath upon the constitution. The show was so ridiculous that, as one spectator told, if someone had begun laughing, all would have burst out in roaring laughter. While the emperor yawned continually, the pope performed the infinite "religious" activities, such as the sacred anointments on the forehead and the hands. When the pope finally exclaimed, *Vivat Imperator in aeternum,* "Long live the emperor in eternity," the public, that was supposed to jubilate, remained conspicuously silent.

The historian and French statesman, Louis A. Thiers (1797-1877), has come up with the fine story that Napoleon at the supreme moment unexpectedly grabbed the crown out of the hands of the pope and placed it on his own head. Presser calls the story incorrect; but other present-day authors keep repeating it. However it may be, it was a pope after all who crowned a "Roman" emperor. But then a deeply dishonored pope, who did not elevate some descendant from an illustrious dynasty, but a son of low Corsican nobility to be *imperator.* A sad performance—yet not merely show business. Napoleon was allegedly touched by it to some extent; something great had been reached.

But what then was that something great? Had Napoleon not become in this way a new absolute prince after all, a new "Louis," who legitimated his reign with a new *droit divin,* but who in this very manner got estranged from "the people"? An interesting feature: when the "revolutionist," the composer Ludwig van Beethoven, who had just completed his symphony *Buonaparte*, heard the news of the imperial coronation, he became infuriated and exclaimed, "he too is nothing but a common man after all! Now he will ride roughshod over all human rights, only give rein to his ambition; he now will put himself higher than all others, become a tyrant!" He took the manuscript of his third symphony, tore the title page apart, and gave it a new name, *Sinfonia Eroica* ("Heroic Symphony").

With regard to Napoleon, I have still to refer to one correspondence with Charlemagne. On the whole, both took a positive attitude toward the Jews, even if this was never free of self-interest. In 1799, during his campaign through the Middle-East, Napoleon brought out a statement in which he demanded the restoration of a Jewish homeland in Palestine. Later he did come back upon this; like under emperor Julian the Apostate it was still too early for such an idea. More positive was, or seemed to be, the fact that in 1807 he as emperor called together the Great Sanhedrin in France, which met from February 9 to March 9. It was the first great meeting of the international Jewish spiritual leaders since antiquity! But when we look deeper, we are shocked by the fact that Napoleon affronted the Jews just as he had done with the pope. Thus, he deliberately opened this Jewish congress on a Sabbath. Moreover, not all participants were religious, and only a few rabbis of name had been invited.

Napoleon was also responsible for several limiting measures against the Jews. Yet it was he who in 1808 instituted a central administration of the Jewish congregations. Moreover, he granted the Jews the same civil rights as his other subjects, not only in France, but also in the other countries that were under his dominion. This attitude of Napoleon tremendously advanced the full emancipation of the European Jews in the nineteenth century. By the way, this emancipation so strongly stirred the jealously of the demons that it became unintentionally one of the greatest causes of the most barbarous Jewish persecutions of all times: the holocaust. Or was the emancipation nothing but a *dirty trick* of the demons in order to destroy in this way the Jewish identity, and was this prevented by this very holocaust? That is a very deep meta-historical puzzle!

8.3. The New Great Powers

8.3.1. The Holy Alliance

After the Napoleonic Empire had fallen apart, Europe was again "divided up" by the Congress of Vienna (1814-15). That illustrious and notorious Congress was one big show of pomp and circumstance, of feasts and banquets, of balls and concerts, but also, of well-attended church services and "brotherly" consultation between Roman-Catholic, Lutheran, and Calvinist Europeans. Above all, it was a Congress of diplomatic intrigue and far-reaching political decisions. Talleyrand, the loser but ever cunning diplomat, and his Austrian opponent, Prince Klemens von Metternich (1773-1859), set the tone, the first behind the screens, the second officially. The smaller states with their leaders, including the pope, were only allowed to come and hear what the Great Powers had decided over them. For that became the new situation: the one Napoleonic Empire had been defeated and was now replaced by four new powers, Austria, Prussia, England, and Russia.

The period between the two "beasts" (to anticipate the Book of Revelation), Napoleon and Hitler, was characterized particularly by three peculiar political developments that are of interest for our subject: the French empire of Napoleon III, the second German empire, and the Holy Alliance. The developments in Europe were confusing and complicated; in a letter to Metternich, German statesman Friedrich von Gentz (1764-1832) compared them with the outbursts in Europe after the fall of the Roman Empire.

Further below we will speak of the new French and German emperors; now first something about that remarkable phenomenon of the Holy Alliance. Surely remarkable, because it came up in the mind of a man influenced by a remarkable woman. The man was czar Alexander I, the woman was Madame de Krüdener (born Barbara Juliane von Vietinghoff, 1764-1824), a baroness of high Russian nobility. She was a mystic, influenced by the Moravian brethren and the German pietist, Johann Heinrich Jung Stilling. The Dutch neo-Calvinist politician, Albertus Zijlstra (1874-1968), who by the way published a fascinating book about "world politics in the light of Scripture," cast her, as a good follower of Abraham Kuyper, in one heap with the whole millennialism of the time of the Réveil.[23] How unfair this is, is shown by the fact that by far the most important millennialist of the Réveil, John N. Darby (mentioned before), swept the floor with the mysticism of the baroness.[24] About millennialism we will have to say more; but with the kind of mysticism of Mrs. de Krüdener not many millennialists would have anything to do.

It was this lady who exerted so much influence upon the czar that she managed to inspire into him the notion of a Holy Alliance: the idea of a Christian empire in Europe. We might almost say that the czar aimed at a new shape of the Holy Roman Empire, now in the form of a confederation of the four great European powers at the time. In the last part of 1814, at a meeting of the great powers at Paris, the czar suddenly launched the assertion that God had made it clear to him that the princes in Europe were again to rule according to the principles of the Gospel. His plan upset the Viennese Congress, as the czar's plan itself was again upset by the escape of Napoleon. After the latter's defeat at Waterloo and his banishment (1815), the thread of the Viennese Congress was picked up again, but also the czar returned with his idea. He offered a *Manifest of the Princes to the Nations*, of which text baroness de Krüdener afterwards alleged to be the author, to the displeasure of the czar.

With drastic alterations by Metternich, a text was

23. Zijlstra (1950:194-195).
24. Darby (n.y.,32:218-226).

produced that was eventually signed by the Roman-Catholic emperor of Austria, the Lutheran king of Prussia, and the Orthodox czar of Russia. In it, they declared "in the name of the most-holy and indivisible Trinity" that they had arrived at the conviction that they were to "found" their mutual relationships "on the great truths that the imperishable religion of the divine Savior teaches." On the basis of these truths, they wished to reign and determine international relations. They declared that they regarded each other as "brothers" and "compatriots," even as "members of one and the same Christian [European] nation," and only viewed themselves as "instruments of Providence," yes, "in truth had no other Lord than the divine Savior Jesus Christ, the Word of the Most High, the Word of Life."

The three sovereigns also invited other Christian states to join their holy covenant. Indeed, it did not take long before all European powers joined, except Turkey (which was not Christian), "insular" England (that shrugged its shoulders), and the Papal State. The latter was no wonder, of course. How could pope Pius, who only owned a Roman-Catholic Christendom, of which he was the head, join as a "common" member to an ecumenical alliance? Since Constantine the Great there is only one holy Christian empire, and that is either imperial-Roman or papal-Roman. In this respect, it is a piquant detail that within the Alliance the czar had the supremacy, not only because he was a mighty man and the Alliance's instigator, but also because as head of the Orthodox church he was the spiritual leader within his own empire.

What became of this Holy Alliance eventually? Nothing. It was not yet the time for a real European confederation. And if such a thing would ever originate, it would be far from holy or Christian. Even at that time, there were already enough "enlightened" liberals in Europe who saluted the Holy Alliance with scoffing. That scorn further increased when Metternich abused the "religious" alliance for his own political goals, and therefore even managed to call upon the Holy Alliance to support the Islamic Turks against the Christian Greeks! And how "holy" was czar Alexander himself who, craving for power, managed to pick up the greatest part of Poland (the duchy of Warsaw)? Thus, nothing became of this new "Christian" European empire. Two empires, sharply opposing each other, took its place: France and Germany. In the Franco-German War of 1870-71, France ceased being an empire (Napoleon III being its last emperor), and the second began becoming one: the "German Empire" (William I being its first emperor).

Emperors, greater and smaller, were there enough in nineteenth-century Europe—"and so few world-empires," says Schulte Nordholt.[25] Apart from the French, the Russian, and the Austrian emperor, there was the new German emperor since 1871, while British queen Victoria since 1876 was "empress of India." Empty phrases these were. Europe would have to wait a little longer before it would see another truly European "world-empire": the *Third Reich*.

8.3.2. The Second German Empire

After Charlemagne, the Frankish-Roman Empire had fallen apart into three sections, the middle one of which, that of Lothaire, eventually for the greater part landed either in the Western or in the Eastern section, that is, in France and Germany. Since then, the French-German antithesis dominated the political history of Europe. From an early stage, over against the Holy Roman Empire of the German nation stood the much more coherent French kingdom. Over against Charles V, who was one of the main German emperors, stood king Francis I. Whereas the German empire became ever less coherent, France became more and more a political unity, finding its summit in the Sun king (*Roi soleil*), Louis XIV. But the mightiest product of mighty France was emperor Napoleon I. Once more his empire seemed to revive under his nephew, Louis Napoleon, who in 1852 mounted the throne as Napoleon III, "emperor of the French." It was the very Germans

25. Schulte Nordholt (1992:200).

who in 1870, through their great victory over the French, put an end to that empire.

Already in the eighteenth century, the German empire had become very weak. Actually, this had begun in 1648 at the Peace of Westphalia, because at that moment all German princes were declared sovereigns. Legitimately the empire continued, in practice it fell apart into about 300 states and cities. At that time, the political position of the ancient empire was taken up by the two German states which were by far the largest, Austria and Prussia, where Maria Theresia and Francis I as well as Frederic William I and Frederic II the Great, respectively, established regal absolutism. The German-Roman imperial dignity remained in the hands of the Austrian princes, who, however, had nothing to say over the other German lands anymore. In fact, the most magnificent German prince in the second half of the eighteenth century was rather Frederic the Great, the most important, intelligent and culturally outstanding prince of enlightened absolutism.

Austria and Prussia each fought their own battle against Napoleon. At the outset, both countries suffered losses against him, and in 1806, emperor Francis II, who since 1804 as Francis I was emperor of Austria, after an ultimatum by Napoleon, laid down his dignity as Roman emperor. That also implied the legitimate end of the Holy Roman Empire, which in practice had not been extant anymore since a long time. Therefore, after the fall of Napoleon, this Roman Empire was not restored. Other relations showed up in Germany, which however again would lead to a German empire.

During the Viennese Congress of 1815, the German *Bund* (League) of thirty-five sovereign princes and four free cities was established. This empty shell without a head of state served as a surrogate for the lost Holy Roman Empire. The highest body in this league was the diet in Frankfurt, consisting of princes and burgomasters and presided by the Austrian delegate. It is striking that the king of England was also a member of the league, namely in his quality of king of Hannover, and the king of the Netherlands as well in his quality of grand duke of Luxemburg. It is equally striking that already in the revolution year 1848 people spoke of a Pan-German unitary state, even with the involvement of Austria.[26] The latter did not like such an idea, and moreover, the Prussian king, Frederic William IV, refused to become emperor of the remaining Little-German empire.

After 1848, the call for German union became increasingly strong, particularly because the Napoleonic supremacy had supplied abundant evidence of the inner weakness of divided Germany. In this striving for unity, the Prussian prime minister, Otto von Bismarck (1815-1898), played a central role. In their fight for the German hegemony, Prussia and Austria collided with each other in 1866, after which Prussia formed the North-German Bund, of which Bismarck became the chancellor. In 1871, when the battle against France was almost settled, the South and the North joined to form the new German empire. The treaty was effectuated in the just conquered Versailles, of all places. The fact that William I, the king of Prussia, was proclaimed hereditary German emperor, underscored the desire to emphatically regard this empire as the successor to the Holy Roman Empire. At his coronation, William even spoke of "the *restoration* of the German empire," and of a taking up again of "the German imperial dignity now suspended since sixty years," that is, from 1806 to 1871. This "Little-German" empire, without Austria, was a federation, of which Bismarck became the imperial chancellor, until he was dismissed in 1890 by the young emperor, William II.

---

26. During a congress in 1849, where the great belletrist, Victor Hugo (1802-1885), gave a speech, he even proclaimed that one day war in Europe would be over and that all European nations would unite "in a superior unity" and would form a "European brotherhood," with a European parliament and a European legislation. These "United States of Europe" would be brought about by Providence, that is: Progress! Three West-European wars and more than a century had to pass before the words of Victor Hugo received a beginning of fulfillment.

In the meantime, the antithesis with France became sharper as a consequence of the French defeat and the loss of Alsace-Lorraine as well as the rise of this mighty German empire. Besides many other factors, the First World War (1914-1918) was particularly a conflict between the two ancient European hereditary enemies (*Erbfeinde*), which together had formed the ancient Roman Empire, France and Germany. This time, France with its allies became the great victor; in the Armistice of Versailles, Germany was deeply humiliated. The year 1918 also became the end of the "second" German empire. Germany became a republic, and former emperor William II took off to the Netherlands (Doorn). In fact, already in Versailles the germs were laid for a new world war. In 1918, the plan for a League of Nations originated, which began its work in 1920. In 1926, Germany was accepted into the League of Nations, and even became a permanent member of the League's Council.

Already shortly after the First World War, the peace-loving French statesman, Aristide Briand (1862-1932), had started a campaign for French-German friendship as a "pilgrim of peace." In this matter, he found the German statesman, Gustav Stresemann (1878-1929), on his side, and together they received the Nobel prize for peace in 1926. On September 4, 1929, in the assembly of the League of Nations, Briand made the proposal to arrive at the *United States of Europe*, primarily in the sense of a customs and economical union. This proposal was part of a much wider movement striving for European unity: the "Pan-Europe" movement of the Austrian-Japanese count Richard Nikolaus von Coudenhove-Kalergi (1894-1972). But it was still too early for such a European unity. First, Europe was to be ravaged by another war, which neither Briand nor Stresemann lived to see. Once more, Europe was to be forged together with brutal violence, on the anvil of Hitler's national-socialism and in the furnace of the Second World War.

In 1933, Austrian born politician Adolf Hitler (1889-1945)

was appointed chancellor by German president Paul von Hindenburg. In that same year he established his national-socialist dictatorship, and Germany left the League of Nations. This definitely did not please Hindenburg. This old war-horse actually dreamed of a restoration of the German empire of the Hohenzollern house, and the corporal/painter Hitler "on the seat of Bismarck" was a thorn in his side. But Hindenburg died in 1934; the way was free for a wholly new German empire, in which the sole ruler, no matter how short, would possess more power than factually any German prince before him had ever had.

8.4. The "Third Reich"[27]

8.4.1. The Magic Corporal

Before they gained their fame, many great ones in history had an important prognostic dream, which pointed to their connection with the world of the gods. Adolf Hitler had such a dream during the First World War. As a corporal he was part of the Bavarian troops lying in 1917 at the Somme front over against the French troops. One day, Hitler had a nightmare there, in which he saw himself buried under an avalanche of earth and melted iron, and felt blood running over his breast. He woke up with a start, and noticed that he was still safely lying in his trench. However, he could not keep lying quietly. A mysterious force drove him out of the trench and toward the dangerous no man's land between the two armies. Reason told him he was a fool in thus exposing himself to the danger of bullets or grenades, but yet the inner force drove him on. Suddenly there was heavy gunfire and a thundering explosion, which smote him to the ground. Hitler hastened back to his trench, but it turned out to have disappeared. At that spot, a deep crater had originated, and everyone at that spot in the trench had been buried alive. Only Hitler had miraculously survived. From that moment he was convinced that "god"

27. Apart from the primary literature, I was much helped by Mellen (1988) in my analysis of Hitler.

had entrusted him with a special mission, and that he was heading for a great future.[28]

At another occasion, he was eating in a trench with a few comrades, when he suddenly heard a voice saying to him, "Rise, and go thence!" The voice was so clear and commanding that he automatically obeyed, got up, and went twenty more meters through the trench, with his feeder still in his hand. He had hardly sat down to continue eating when an enormous explosion was heard. A stray bomb had come down upon the group that he had just left, and each man had been killed on the spot.[29]

The well-known German astrologer, Elsbeth Ebertin (1880-1944), regularly published an almanac. In the July 1923 issue she did one of her most famous predictions. One of Hitler's many female fans in Munich had sent his birth date and hour to Mrs. Ebertin with the request to cast his horoscope. Ebertin wrote,[30]

> a man who knows how to manage things, born on April 20, 1889 (...) can expose himself to personal danger through precipitate actions. He surely might cause a great crisis. His horoscope shows that this man yet has to be taken very seriously. He is predestined to fulfill a leader's role in future battles (...) the man whom I have in mind and who is strongly influenced by the sign of Ram will sacrifice himself for the German people. Audaciously and courageously, he will know to face all circumstances, even when it is a matter of life or death. He will suddenly and unexpectedly give the impulse that will lead to... but I do not want to anticipate things. Time will tell...

28. *Grote Mysteries* (1978a:187,189).
29. Told by Hitler himself in an interview to Ward Price; quoted by Toland (1976:68).
30. *Grote Mysteries* (1978b:154). Speaking of prophecies: Nostradamus wrote in 1555 (*Prophéties the Maistre Michel Nostradamus*), "In Germany, several sects will arise / which will come very near to happy heathenism / the constraint of the heart and the small outturns / will open the way for paying the true toll."

Indeed, four months after Ebertin's prediction, Hitler committed his "precipitate" *Putsch* (coup) in Munich, which failed and brought him into prison. He "sacrificed himself for the German people" by committing suicide in his Berlin bunker in May 1945.[31] Hitler himself continuously demanded astrological predictions (just like Napoleon, for that matter). SS commander Heinrich Himmler (1900-1945) in particular was a fanatical occultist. It is a fact that Hitler's "gods" preserved him many times in a miraculous way, until the day that they dropped him. Not only during World War I, but also at the murder attempts of 1939 and 1944, Hitler escaped miraculously.[32] In October 1914, he went through the first battle at Ieper (Flanders), where a shot knocked off his right sleeve, but left him unhurt; of the three thousand five hundred men in his regiment only six hundred survived.

In my opinion, this occult aspect is of great metahistorical significance. Numerous theories have been launched to explain the miraculous phenomenon that national-socialism could emerge in such a short time out of nothing, and managed to acquire the absolute and undivided power in Germany. American journalist and Germany expert George Bailey (1904-1985) said,[33]

> [the German people] had of course been betrayed: that which had happened with the Germans no people would wish for themselves. They had been deceived, enchanted: Hitler was a sorcerer, whom they had erroneously taken for an oracle.

In a similar sense, Hermann Rauschning (1987-1982), who knew Hitler so closely, called him a "Shaman," a sorcerer and witchdoctor as found among primitive nations, a mediator

31. Indeed, Hitler himself regarded this as a sacrifice: "In the hour of utmost danger I must sacrifice myself for the people" (Rauschning, 1940:252). His sacrifice as a "lamb" (a young ram; see the quotation of Ebertin!) is a grotesque imitation of Christ (cf. Rev. 13:11).
32. See Hesemann (2007:433-435).
33. Bailey (1972:121f.).

between the world of the spirits (gods) and that of men.[34] American historian Rudolph Binion (b. 1927) compared Hitler with Dionysus as described in the *Bacchae* of Euripides, the son of Zeus, who managed to bring the whole city of Thebe under his corrupting mass enchantment.[35] This "divine" power explains the nature of Hitler's sorcery. It explains how, for instance, the German horde could shout unceasingly, "We want our *Führer*," and, when he appeared for a moment on the balcony, totally got out of control: women fainted, the crowd pushed forward to better see their messiah. It explains why even outspoken Nazi opponents, in Hitler's presence, in the midst of the crowd could hardly (or not!) refrain from shouting *Sieg Heil* or *Heil Hitler*.

The magic hypnosis emanating from Hitler has been unique, and cannot be explained in common terms of demagogy, hysteria, and mass psychosis. I think I know why: it can only be explained from the demonic prince, the Super-Intelligence, whose embodiment he was. Albert Speer (1905-1981), for such a long time Hitler's collaborator and entirely under his enchantment, afterwards sharply summarized it in one sentence: "He really came from another world."[36] It seems to me that this was perfectly true.

8.4.2. Hitler's Genius

Hitler himself said several times that the people needed an "idol," that is, a false god; it was he himself who was

> voluntarily and incessantly presented to the masses as a godhead—the only savior of the nation. The messiah figure of the leader is the indispensable center of their propaganda.[37]

That is what he was to 95% of the Germans, a messiah, that is, someone with an anointing from the higher world.[38] In

34. Rauschning (1940:259).
35. Binion (1984:91).
36. Speer (1976:19).
37. Rauschning (1939:35).
38. Shirer (1984:119). Hermann Göring overtly called him a *Heiland* ("savior")

relation to Christ, this means an anti-messiah, an anti-Christ, a *pseudochristos*, an embodiment of an extraordinarily powerful angelic adversary of Christ. As several persons attending the passion games of 1934 at Oberammergau expressed it more or less at the moment that "Jesus" was hung on the cross, "There is he, that is our Führer, our Hitler."[39] Hitler himself once told Nazi-official Martin Bormann (1900-1945),[40]

> I am about to become a religious figure. In a while I will be the great Chief of the Tartars. Arabs and Moroccans already mingle my name with their prayers. Among the Tartars I will become Khan.

This represents to some extent the fact that he saw himself more or less as a deity. German-American historian George L. Mosse (1918-1999) wrote that the children of Cologne began and finished each lunch with a prayer to Hitler, containing phrases such as:

> Führer, my Führer, protect and keep me as long as I live, stay with me, leave me not, my faith and my light, be assured, my Führer, that you are great.[41]

Hitler permitted to be written on tombstones that the departed was "deceased in Hitler." Each candidate for the SS, Hitler's paramilitary organization, had to learn his "catechism," which included the question, "Why do we believe in Germany and the *Führer*?" And the answer was:[42]

> Because we believe in God, we believe in Germany that he created in his world, and in the *Führer*, Adolf Hitler, whom he sent to us.

Hitler himself, by the way, saw all "Aryans" (the Germanic

(Quinn, 1978:XIV).

39. Toland (1976:376f.).
40. Cameron & Stevens (1976:167).
41. Mosse (1981:241).
42. Hohne (1983:168). Cf. the Muslim slogan, "There is no god but God, and Mohammed is his messenger."

race) as god-men. Therefore, he viewed himself as absolutely one with the people. Perhaps there never was an angelic prince who identified himself not only with an earthly prince, but also very strongly with a whole nation. The Nazi propaganda expressed this in quite a striking way:[43]

> Nowhere in the world is there such a fanatical love among millions of people for one man (...) this alone justifies the phrase, "Hitler is Germany—Germany is Hitler." (...) Adolf Hitler never uttered anything else than what the people thought in their deepest soul; he never did anything else than what all the people wanted to do. He (...) is not, and never will be, a dictator who enforces his own personal tendencies or his craving for dominion upon the people. He truly is only the *Führer*, and that is the highest that can ever be said of a person. (...) Never before was there such a person as the *Führer*. This happens only once in the world.

Hitler was the *genius* of the German people, and his angelic prince was the *genius* of Hitler. In his notorious work, *Mein Kampf* ("My Struggle"), written in prison, he himself often referred to his genius as *das Schicksal*, "Destiny," even from the very first sentence:

> I now regard it as a fortunate steering of Destiny, that it assigned to me precisely Braunau on the Inn as place of birth.

And at the beginning of his second chapter:

> When my mother died, Destiny had in one respect already decided concerning my fate,

etcetera. To Speer he said about his difficulties in younger years,[44]

> Everyone else would have given up. But Destiny wanted it so.

43. Quoted by Quinn (1978:17-22). The same idea was expressed by the national-socialist, Ernst Rudolf Huber, quoted in Murphy et al. (n.y.:74f.).
44. Speer (1976:236). Others spoke likewise, for instance Joseph Goebbels (1948:8), "I thank Destiny which gave us this man."

Providence helped me.

Destiny, or Fate, is the *fatum*, the divine oracle, the decision of the gods; or, in Germanic mythology, the steering of the "fates," the three Norns (or "weird sisters"), who at the beginning of Richard Wagner's *Götterdämmerung* ("Twilight of the Gods") weave the threads of fate. Hitler madly venerated the fierce anti-Semite Wagner (1813-1883), was intensively inspired by him, and referred many times to him.[45] Viewed metahistorically, the *Götterdämmerung*, as a prophetic painting of the Germanic *Ragnarök* (the perdition of the "world" with its ancient gods), described the decline of the "Germanic" empire, whether this regards the First, the Second, or the Third Reich. It is significant that, sometime before the fall of Berlin in 1945, national-socialist leaders once more attended a performance of the *Götterdämmerung* by the Berlin Philharmonic Orchestra. It was as if they watched their own fall. At the end of the opera, the world of Wodan breaks down; that was the world of Hitler's and Nazi-Germany's own "Germanic" angelic prince. But in the opera, Siegfried falls too. Hitler felt himself to be so powerful that he even challenged the gods. He had been the god-man Siegfried, who had challenged the world of Wodan; but eventually the hero himself is slain.[46]

Hitler also felt strongly attached to another Wagner figure: the Roman hero Cola di Rienzi, who persuaded the Roman people to cast out the corrupt Senate by reminding them of the glorious past of the Roman Empire (cf. § 7.3.3). After a

45. See extensively Hesemann (2007).
46. In 1936, Jung (1984:45-58) wrote a fascinating article about "Wodan" in relation to the German spirit and national-socialism: "Wodan disappeared when his oaks were felled, and returned when Christianity turned out to be too weak to keep Christendom from a terrible fratricide at a large scale [the First World War. WJO]. When the Holy Father at Rome, divested of all power, only to God could complain about the grex segregatus (divided herd), the one-eyed old hunter laughed at the border of the Germanic forest, and saddled Sleipnir" (49). Jung speaks of the "parallel between the revived Wodan and the social-political and psychological situation sweeping present-day Germany [1936]" (50).

performance of the *Rienzi* overture, Hitler said to Speer,[47]

> When as a young man I listened to this blissful music in the theatre of Linz, I had the vision that one day I too had to succeed in uniting the German Empire and making it great again.

As a consequence of the *Reichskonkordat* ("Imperial Concordat") that national-socialism concluded in 1933 with the Roman-Catholic Church, in which all "quarrels" between the two powers were settled, the Vatican got the reputation of collaborating with the Nazis. Janus/Peter watched in a perplexed—or amused?—way how gods out of the underworld launched a new religion, and how the Jewish people were massacred. Or was it one and the same power: Janus with the two faces? After 1945, Janus/Peter was all too eager to let many Nazis escape, through the Vatican travel-office, to South-America and elsewhere. The two faces of Janus always keep confusing us, always remain inscrutable.

8.4.3. Hitler and Rome

Hitler was a Teutonic god, in the tradition of the Holy Roman Empire of the German nation. Already nearly at the beginning of *Mein Kampf,* Hitler gave expression to the Roman-German ideal. In his description of the collapse of Habsburg Austria, which he hated, he referred back to the earlier Holy Roman Empire as follows:[48]

> The destiny of this state [Austria] is connected so much with the life and growth of the whole German nation that an attempt to split history into a German and an Austrian half simply has to end in a miserable failure. Yes, when Germany eventually fell apart into two powers, this very division became an event in German history. The Imperial Ornaments kept at Vienna, *symbols of the earlier greatness and glory of the Empire,* seem in their wonderful splendor to be a *pledge for the everlasting unity of the*

47. Speer (1976:96); to his friend August Kubizek, Hitler said something similar (Hesemann 2007:52-55).
48. Hitler (n.y.:11f.).

> *German lands*. That cry of the German-Austrian people, welled up deep from the heart, "One again with the German motherland!" in the days that the Habsburg state collapsed [1918], was only the effect of that feeling of nostalgia for the never forgotten father's house, which lived in all the hearts. [italics added]

Hitler did not dream in the first place of restoring the "second" empire, because that had only been a "Little-German" empire. No, the "third" German Empire (*Reich*) was to be a revival of the "first" one, the ancient German unitary empire. Moreover, Bismarck's empire had "only" been a federation, at least nominally; in reality, it gradually became more and more a unitary state. The new empire was to be a Great-German, centrally governed state. Berlin was to be the capital of this new empire, only comparable with ancient Egypt, Babylon or Rome. In 1936, the Nazis solemnly celebrated in Quedlinburg the millennial memorial of the death of Henry I (876-936), nicknamed the Fowler, founder of the Ottonian dynasty of the Holy Roman Empire, one of the great examples for Hitler.

The expression "Third Reich" was not Hitler's, by the way. In fact, it goes back upon medieval notions. The monk, Joachim of Fiore (1130/35-1202), alleged that in the Easter night he had received a vision in which God had unfolded to him his plan for history.[49] After the empire of the Father (that of the Law) and that of the Son (the empire of the Gospel), he saw a "third empire" coming up, the millennial kingdom of the Holy Spirit, the kingdom of Love and Freedom, in which the corrupt church was to be restored in its original purity. Joachim of Fiore's followers expected this kingdom in 1260 in connection with emperor Frederic II (1212-1250). They regarded this "emperor of peace"—*fred* in "Frederic" (cf. German *Friede*) means "peace"—who was exceptionally gifted both in political and in scientific respect, as the Antichrist. This

49. Cf. Hartvelt (1977, ch. 4: "the triplet of time: Joachim of Fiore") and Tuveson (1949:19f.), whose study also describes many other ancient "millennial" views.

astonishing person, nicknamed *stupor mundi* ("the amazement of the world"), indeed exhibited a kind of alleged "end time" character. This comes to light, among other things, in his ardent conflict with pope Gregory IX, in which each of them depicted the other as the Antichrist.

In fact, Joachim was the forerunner of the post-millennialists. These are Christians – among others several Reformed theologians of the "Nearer Reformation" – who believed and believe in a future millennial kingdom preceding the second coming of Christ (*post* means "after": the second coming takes place *after* the millennium). Later German philosophers such as the Enlightenment thinker, Gotthold E. Lessing, and the German idealist, Friedrich Schelling, each in their own way have played with the notion of a Third Empire. Lessing found the idea of a triple empire not unattractive, but blamed Joachim and his associates for having proclaimed the Third Empire as being so near. Schelling saw, after a "Petrinian" (Roman-Catholic) and a "Paulinian" (Germanic-protestant) empire, a third, "Johanneic" empire coming up, which would know only one world religion. The German idealist, Georg W.F. Hegel, inspired, with his dialectic notion of thesis, antithesis, and synthesis, quite a few philosophers of history. Thus, the Norwegian Henrik Ibsen spoke of a Third Empire which would be a synthesis of antique culture (thesis) and Christianity (antithesis), and Russian novelist Dmitry S. Merezhkovsky (1866-1941) saw a Third Empire as a synthesis of religion and science.[50] With Russian novelist Fyodor M. Dostoyevsky (1821-1881) and German historian Oswald Spengler (mentioned before) we encounter similar notions.

The person that inadvertently most influenced the national-socialist idea of the Third Empire was the German political writer Arthur Moeller van den Bruck (1876-1925) who in 1923, two years before his suicide, published his book, *Das dritte Reich* ("The Third Empire").[51] He too interpreted the notion

50. See especially his novel *The Death of the Gods* (1901; Russian edition: 1895).
51. See Hesemann (2007:158-159).

of a Third Empire in a Hegelian-dialectic sense, namely, as an eschatological-millennialist synthesis of the Holy Roman Empire (thesis) and the "second" German empire (antithesis). In this sense, the term was adopted by national-socialism, be it that the latter gave it a form very different from what the writer had intended. The Nazis meant by the Third Reich the "millennial empire" (compare Joachim!), which after the "first" and the "second empire" was founded by national-socialism in 1933.

The German people regarded the Weimar republic as a historic disgrace. Therefore, in the nazistic propaganda the term "Third Reich" was very useful to rouse the people's longing for a state in which the ancient German imperial idea would receive some form again. Already in *Mein Kampf*, Hitler gave his own view of the history of the first Reich (concentrated in Charlemagne) and the second Reich (in fact founded already by Prussian king Frederic the Great). These were the two empires which the "Aryans" had founded since the fall of Rome, and which in his opinion had been miserably overthrown by the Jews. Hitler regarded himself as the new "Jesus," the new Charlemagne, the new Frederic the Great, in short, a new embodiment of the Teutonic deity. This time, this deity would succeed, namely, by destroying the greatest threat to the Third Reich, the Jews. In his opinion, total eradication was the *Endlösung* ("final solution") for the greatest problem menacing any "Aryan" empire. When this problem would have been definitively solved, it would be possible for the Third Reich, the millennial kingdom, to finally break through.

Again, Hitler was "right" in a tragically distorted sense: the God of Israel is the greatest "threat" to any world-empire or any opposing angelic prince whatsoever. To put it even more strongly, the true millennial kingdom can only arrive when the God of Israel in the *Jew* Jesus Christ, the Messiah of Israel, will prevail over all pseudochrists and their embodiments, from the Pharaoh till the Beast and the Antichrist.

The "thousand years" of Hitler ultimately became only twelve (1933-1945), that is four times as short as the second empire (1871-1918). Only the first German Empire did, if we begin to count from the division of the empire in 806, last exactly one thousand years, until 1806.

In the above quotation from *Mein Kampf*, Hitler speaks of the *regalia* of the ancient Holy Roman Empire, which were kept at Vienna, as the pledge for the "everlasting unity" of all German lands. These *regalia* spoke much to his imagination, because they warranted the continuity of the Third Reich with the "first" one. In 1934, at the annual Nuremberg party congress, in the town hall a replica of the imperial symbol of Charlemagne, and in 1935 of the imperial sword, was offered to him.[52] According to Hamilton T. Burden, these medieval symbols of imperial authority served to give expression to "the historic connection between the First Reich of the ninth century and the Third Reich."[53]

Already as a young man, Hitler was highly fascinated by the history of the Holy Roman Empire of the German Nation. After the so-called *Anschluss* ("junction") of Austria, he immediately liked to see the insignia of the Holy Roman Empire. For an hour, he was left alone with these precious treasures, which deeply touched him. They were the crown, the scepter and the sword of the empire, and the *Reichskreuz* ("Imperial Cross") with two precious relics (parts of the cross of Jesus and the holy spear [John 19:34]). Hitler knew that, according to an ancient legend, he who would claim the spear and would reveal its secrets, would receive the power to determine the destiny of the world, either for good or for evil. Think of the role of this spear in *Parsifal* of Hitler's great idol, Wagner! In 1938, Hitler had the insignia brought over to Nuremberg as an expression of his conviction that his Great-German Empire was the legitimate heir of the Holy Roman Empire. (In 1945, the Americans brought the treasures back to Vienna.)

52. Burden (1967:102).
53. Burden (1967:79).

Even as late as 1942, Hitler said:[54] "If we want to claim the world at all, we must appeal to the history of the German emperor... [this is] the most overwhelming epos... the world has ever experienced." It is an unanswerable question what would have happened if the Third Reich had existed much longer. Would Hitler, as an imitation of the Holy Roman ("First *Reich*") and Hohenzollern emperors ("Second *Reich*"), as well as of Napoleon of course, have stretched out to the imperial crown? As a support for this, the *regalia* of the Holy Roman Empire would have been indispensable.

It is not too far-fetched to claim that Hitler regarded himself as the new Charlemagne. Hitler's mountain-citadel in Obersalzberg lay over against the Unterberg, where, according to the legend, Charlemagne (in other versions: Frederick Barbarossa, 1122-1190) still "sleeps" until the hour of distress, when he will rise again. To Speer, Hitler once said in his citadel,[55]

> There you see the Unterberg. It is no coincidence that I have my residence over against it.

Barbarossa, one of the greatest emperors of the Holy Roman Empire, was one of Hitler's greatest examples. He called his campaign against Russia *Unternehmen Barbarossa* ("Operation Barbarossa") because, according to legend, one day Barbarossa would lead the Holy Roman Empire back to its former grandeur. This would lead to a millennial empire of peace. Hitler saw himself as the man in whom Barbarossa had revived and in whom the legend would be fulfilled.[56]

Hitler's association with another Frederick, Prussian king Frederic the Great, was perhaps even more important. Hitler's installation in the Garrison's Church at Potsdam (March 21, 1933) only served to make symbolically clear that Hitler had taken the place of Frederic the Great. The same held for

54. Picker (2003:140); cf. Hesemann (2007:125-129).
55. Speer (1971:131).
56. Hesemann (2007:415).

the opening of the *Reichstag* (the diet), the church service, and the laying of the wreath on the tombs of the Prussian kings. Hitler's own address underlined the connection between these kings and himself. In this way, they each became a John the Baptist pointing to him, the new messiah.

This also makes clear that Hitler was not primarily interested in the Holy Roman Empire; in fact, he was only concerned with the empire of the German nation. The Third Reich was a *Great-German* empire. Therefore, Hitler first of all aimed at getting all "German" territories back into that empire again, and only secondarily at restoring the Roman Empire in Europe. To achieve this goal, he enacted in 1934 the law concerning the "restoration" of the empire, in 1935 hauled in the Saar territory, in 1936 occupied the demilitarized zone of the Rhineland, in 1938 enforced the *Anschluss* of Austria, and occupied the Sudeten territory, and in 1939 Bohemia and Moravia as well because of their large German populations. The invasion of Poland in the same year, which rang in the Second World War, had a similar goal: Danzig had to be incorporated into the empire, and a traffic road through the Corridor had to be mastered. The fact that subsequently Hitler also occupied other countries around Germany was caused by the requirements of the disastrous war he had unchained: Denmark and Norway, then the Netherlands and Belgium, and particularly the ancient hereditary enemy, France.

The beginning of the Second World War laid the whole of Europe at the feet of Hitler, with the exception of his allies as well as of Great Britain and of Russia, where Hitler got stuck in the same way as had previously happened to Napoleon. Once more a Roman-German unitary empire existed in Western Europe, centrally and dictatorially governed, and based on bloodshed and terror. The ultimate termination of the war implied a catastrophe for the entire world, and the decline of fascist Germany and Italy. Thus, the last revival of the West-European unitary empire collapsed, while immediately afterwards a totally new objective came up: the amalgamation of Europe into a union, this time not based on violence and oppression, but on the voluntary junction of sovereign European states.

8.4.4. Hitler and the Jews

We have seen that the notion of Destiny (*Schicksal*) played an important role in Hitler's life and thought. This word becomes peculiarly striking when he speaks of the Jews:[57]

> ... when I thus examined the influence which the Jewish people had exerted upon human history for many centuries, suddenly the anxious question came up in my mind whether perhaps, after all, unfathomable Destiny, for reasons unknown to us miserable people, had decided the final victory of this little nation in its eternal, unchangeable counsel? Would it be to these people, who always live exclusively for the earthly things, that the earth has been allotted as a reward? Do we have an objective title to the struggle for our self-preservation, or is this, too, only a subjective conviction? While I investigated the doctrine of Marxism, and thus soberly and objectively examined the influences that went out from the Jewish people [Marx was a Jew! WJO], Destiny itself gave me the answer. (...) Therefore it is my conviction that I work in the spirit of the almighty Creator: *For in resisting the Jew I fight for the work of the Lord.*

For a moment Hitler doubted! Might his genius after all stand on the side of the God of Israel? Will the future millennial kingdom be for Israel after all? But no, his *genius* reassures him: the "Jewish" doctrine of Marxism, that is in fact, the Old Testament promise of the restoration of paradise on earth, would involve a destruction of the cosmic order. That implies, an abolishment of the consequences of Man's fall into sin! Therefore, Hitler's *genius* resists with all strength the notion of a millennial kingdom of which Israel would be the center. Hitler said many times that he, in his battle against the Jew, carried out the "work of the Lord," and again he was

57. Hitler (n.y.:71f.).

"right" in a tragically distorted sense: his work was the work of his lord.[58]

Hitler's *genius*, who made him "genial," is a demon of the blackest kind. Indeed, his *literally* demonic character comes to light in the most acute way in his anti-Semitism. It did not start with him; the *Endlösung* ("final solution") had been propagated already in 1899 by the Anti-Semitic German-Social Party, and even emperor William II was open to it because of his court-chaplain, Adolf Stoecker. By the way, for instance the Dreyfus case shows that the situation in France was not much better. Hitler's anti-Semitism, however, is of the dirtiest, grossest kind ever shown. Already *Mein Kampf* is full of his revolting insanity with regard to the Jews. In his own way, he saw the "realms" of Aryans and Jews in a metahistorical light by describing them as

> the people of God and the people of satan. The Jew is the anti-man, the creature of a different god.[59]

In my opinion, this must be read as follows: the "Aryans" (as the embodiment of Hitler's angelic prince) were people of Hitler's god, the Jews were the people of the adversary (Heb. *satan*!) of this god, that is, the God of Scripture. The Jew who serves God belongs to him, and stands over against all those who are children of the adversary (Satan) (cf. 1 John 3:10). It is significant that Hitler ascribed all the good that had existed in other civilizations to the "Aryans." In his opinion, all empires that we have dealt with, Egypt, Assyria, Babylonia, Medo-Persia, Greece, Rome, had been essentially "Aryan" empires. In these empires, according to Hitler, it had always been the Jew who attempted to destroy this Aryan element. Metahistorically this means, the driving "Aryan" force in all world-empires is the force of the angelic princes who governed these empires

58. As said before, "lord" is a reference to a "god," a national angelic prince (see Isa. 26:13; 1 Cor. 8:5).

59. Quoted by Rauschning (1940:241), who also speaks of two "gods": "the one god excludes the other" (235).

and who were always against Israel. Indeed, Israel, or rather, the God of Israel, was the greatest threat to the demonic powers governing the world-empires. Hitler pronounces here a profound truth that he, with a perverse exchange of good and evil, converts into a satanic lie.

Of course, such a spirit is also fundamentally anti-Christian. To be sure, Hitler uttered some praises about Jesus Christ, but he denied him his Jewish descent, and ascribed to him an anti-Jewish attitude. According to Hitler, the apostle Paul was the Jew who, against the mind of Jesus, proclaimed Christianity as a kind of forerunner of the hateful Bolshevism. The true "Aryan" religion is "heroic faith in God in nature, God in our people, in our destiny, in our blood."[60] The "god" in nature comprises the gods whom we have called "elementary spirits." The "god" "*in* our people" is the angelic prince who was embodied by Hitler and his followers. This "god" stands filled with hatred over against the God of Israel and of the Christians; as Hitler put it,[61]

> we will be able to destroy Christianity because there is in [the masses] a true religion rooted in nature and blood.

Of course, numerous things have been written about Hitler's anti-Semitism and the holocaust, but less about the highly peculiar *personal* relations that Hitler had with the Jews. Here we find some remarkable metahistorical connections. In the first place, Hitler anxiously wondered whether he himself possibly had some Jewish blood in his veins. His father had been an illegitimate child, begotten by a man whose identity has never been established beyond all doubt. However, there may have been some hints, pointed out by the Nazi, Hans Frank, who spoke about it in the Nuremberg trials, that Hitler's grandfather was Jewish. The mother of Hitler's father, Maria Anna Schicklgruber, worked as a maid in the house of a Jewish family in Gratz, named Frankenburger, where she,

60. Quinn (1978:49).
61. Rauschning (1939:56).

according to Hans Frank on the basis of letters of the family, had been made pregnant by the son of the house. In another version of the story, stated by Walter C. Langer in a secret psychological report about Hitler to the American government,[62] Langer wrote that Maria Anna at that time worked in Vienna with the Jewish family Rothschild. Of course, that does not necessarily mean that Hitler's grandmother had been seduced by a member of that family. There is no convincing evidence that Hitler's grandfather was a Jew. But the most fascinating part of the story is that *he himself* unmistakably believed that he was one fourth Jewish! Of course, according to Jewish law, Hitler would only have been a Jew if his mother had been a Jewess; but according to his own "biological" theories it was a horrible thing that he (as he believed) was a quarter Jew.

There are more peculiar points to be mentioned concerning Hitler's relations to the Jews. If it was not for his weird theories, he would have had every reason to count the Jews among his best friends. It was Jewish art-dealers who took pity on the young, poor Hitler in Vienna, and "paid generously for his mediocre water colors."[63] Most of the paintings that Hitler ever made have been bought by Jewish dealers. Also, his landlady was a Jewish woman, who had mercy on him and therefore asked but a small rent. At one time she even moved out of her apartment to offer more space to Hitler and a friend. Another Jew who at that time became interested in Hitler was a Hungarian ragman, who gave him a long black coat. Hitler entirely wore out the coat, which resembled a Jewish caftan. Reinhold Hanisch, a friend of his youth, wrote that "Hitler at that time looked very Jewish."[64]

For his merits in World War I, Hitler received the Iron Cross of the first and the second class. He was very proud of it, exploited this high military honor politically, and wore the medal everywhere he went. It was quite remarkable that this

62. Published later (Langer 1972).
63. R.G.L. Waite in an Epilogue in Langer (1972).
64. Quoted by Goldberg (1976:27).

medal was awarded to an officer of such a low rank and without distinct military achievements. The only reason for this award to be thought of was the sympathy that the lieutenant of the regiment, the Jew Hugo Gutmann (1880-1962), had for him. It was this Jew who made indefatigable efforts that Hitler was honored with the Iron Cross.

Once he was the Führer, Hitler employed a Jewish woman, Miss Kunde, to cook for him. She had been sent to him by the Nazi boss of Romania, who like Hitler had stomach troubles. When Himmler carefully asked whether it was appropriate that the Führer had a Jewish cook, Hitler became furious. Even more striking was his relation to Eduard Bloch (1872-1945), the Jewish physician of the Hitler family during his youth. Doctor Bloch had accompanied Hitler's mother on her deathbed, and after the funeral Hitler told him, according to Bloch, that "I shall be grateful to you forever."[65] From Vienna, he sent Bloch two picture postcards, of which he had painted one with his own hand. On both cards he expressed his warm appreciation. In the mentioned report by Langer, the latter wrote that these postcards to a Jew form

> one of the very few cases of which we have any record where Hitler showed any lasting gratitude.[66]

Is a more painful example conceivable in which Jacob blessed Esau so much—and in which Esau nevertheless became the bitterest enemy of Jacob? Israel was not only a blessing to Hitler personally, but also to Germany. Just before the holocaust, the Jews formed not even one percent of the German population, but they comprised 16% of the German practicing lawyers, 10% of the doctors and dentists, 17% of the bankers, 11% of the real estate agents, 25% of the retail business, 30% of the clothing business, 70% of the warehouses. On the other hand, however, for instance 25% of the 170,000 Berlin Jews lived on social welfare. The Jews have contributed

65. Goldberg (1976:28).
66. Goldberg (1976:29).

tremendously to Germany's greatness. From the first existence of the Berlin stock exchange this was particularly a Jewish institution; two of the four presidents and ten of the 23 members were Jews. Germany's war navy in World War I had been mainly the work of the Jewish captain of industry, Albert Ballin (1857-1918), counselor of emperor William II. In that war, almost one fifth of the German Jews served in the German forces; 13% of them fell for their fatherland. An almost equally large number received the Iron Cross. After the war, it was the Jewish lawyer, Hugo Preuss (1860-1925), who wrote the concept of the new Weimar constitution. From 1905 to 1931, ten German Jews gained Nobel prizes in the natural sciences.

In spite of this tremendous blessing of Jacob to Esau, the Nazis exclaimed that the Jews formed the greatest conceivable threat to Germany and the world. One of the mightiest means for the Nazis to extirpate these Jews consisted of the European railway network, for the most important concentration camps were situated near railway stations. That railway network had been designed mainly by the Jews, especially by the Rothschilds. Through this tremendous intellectual and financial contribution to the modern European infrastructure, the Jews inadvertently helped to dig their own graves. Trains have transported them by the tens of thousands to the gas chambers. Esau refused to bless Jacob, but cursed him.

Hitler's name probably comes from *heidler*, which means as much as "heathen." He was the heathen *par excellence*, with all connotations of primitive demon power, occultism, and polytheism involved in the term. The word "heathen" (as *heidler*) comes from "heather," that is, the uncultivated countryside, where the primitive live who do not yet know the Christian civilization of the city.[67] That is Esau: a hunter, a "man of the field" (Gen. 25:27). Jacob, on the contrary, "dwells in tents," and it is only in the tents of Sem/Jacob that Japheth/Esau

67. Cf. Latin *paganus* (Eng. pagan), which literally means "rural," and hence "rustic, illiterate."

can be blessed (Gen. 9:27). Jacob is a blessing to Esau; what is Esau's reply to this? The most hideous answer to this question ever given came from Adolf Hitler. Therefore, no man in history approximates the apocalyptic "beast" more than this "heathen." To which European country have the Jews, throughout the centuries, been a greater blessing than to Germany? And what country has reacted to this with a greater curse than (Nazi) Germany?

8.4.5. Benito Mussolini

If Hitler was primarily interested in a *German* Empire, yet, viewed metahistorically, it is striking that within Europe he found his ally in the Italy of the fascist Benito Mussolini (1883-1945), who was in power there already since 1922. In June 1934, the two leaders met for the first time. On October 25, 1936, a German-Italian treaty was put into effect, in which Germany owned the Italian annexation of Abyssinia (Ethiopia), and together they owned the fascist government of generalissimo Francisco Franco (1892-1975) in Spain. In an address a week later, Mussolini launched for the first time the name "Berlin-Rome axis," meaning that the two new, fascist-totalitarian power centers in Central Europe had to act as an "axis" between the "decadent democracies" in the West and the "bolshevist danger" in the East. Thus, the intended German Empire was linked after all with ancient Rome: around the "Berlin-Rome axis," the history of Europe henceforth was to turn. In May 1939, Hitler paid a visit to Rome, and in September of that year, Mussolini was gloriously received in Berlin.

The person of Hitler has obviously been of much greater significance than Mussolini, yet I want to devote a few words to the latter because of his connection with Rome. For if anyone in the last decades before the war had both the dream and the power to work for a restoration of the ancient Roman Empire, it was Mussolini. In the years before World War II he allegedly said,[68]

> There can be no turning back. We shall ever march onward towards that Imperial Rome which is our dream and our faith.
>
> Within five years Rome must become the most wonderful city in the world in the eyes of all people of the globe (..) Vast, well-ordered, powerful as in the days of the first empire of Augustus.
>
> We are repeating history in these days, the history of the Roman Caesar (Julius), my great inspirer, whose bust I have before me all the time.
>
> Rome, capital of the new Roman Empire...

Or, as Desmond wrote in April 1926 in the magazine *Forum*:[69]

> I believe from conversation of two of his lieutenants that what the Italian superman is aiming at is a sort of Holy Roman Empire—at the head of it God and His superman. In the Dictator's own words, "Powerful as in the days of the first Empire of Augustus, Rome must again become the wonder of the whole world. I am the State. I, because of God, I am called. I, because I am the superman incarnate, even as that Napoleon of whom I secretly believe I am the incarnation, was the heaven-sent. I, because like Napoleon, I am a law-giver as well as war lord."

Mussolini's Rome was conscious of its divine *genius*. In February 1926, the magazine *Dawn* quoted from Italian reports the new "ten commandments" of fascism, which begin as follows:[70]

> 1. I am Italy, thy mother, thy sovereign, thy goddess.
> 2. Thou shalt have no other mother, sovereign, or goddess above me.
> 3. Thou shalt honour her god and keep her festivals.

68. Sale-Harrison ([1939]:60,62,64f.).
69. Sale-Harrison ([1939]:61).
70. Sale-Harrison ([1939]:63).

At the summit of his fame, Mussolini built for himself a statue, ten times as big as himself, with the laurel-wreath of the Roman emperor on its head, as on the image of Julius Caesar, Mussolini's great example. Italian newspapers published headlines such as, "Revival of the spirit of the Romans of antiquity."

From a metahistorical viewpoint, Mussolini's relations to the Jews are of importance too. At the time, Leonard Sale-Harrison reported the alleged view that Mussolini had Jewish blood in his veins,[71] but I do not know whether there exists any confirmation of this. It is known, however, that among his many mistresses Mussolini had no less than two Jewish ones. This fact was afterwards quoted by his wife, in her biography, as evidence that Mussolini was not an anti-Semite! The one mistress was Margherita Sarfatti (1880-1961), who wrote a biography about him and of whom it is told that she inspired into Mussolini most of his original social reformations, and who broke up with him when he "picked up with Hitler." The other mistress was the socialist Angelica Balabanoff (c. 1878-1965), who was five years older than he, also exerted great influence upon his thinking, and, when he became the editor of the newspaper *Avanti!* at his insistence was appointed co-editor.

When he came to power, Mussolini several times appointed Jews as ministers such as Aldo Finzi and Guido Jung, the latter as minister of finance, because the duce felt that "a Jew should be at the head of finance."[72] Under the *Fascisti*, the four most influential leaders were Jews. On the whole, the Italian Jews seem to have welcomed Mussolini, and he himself spoke several times in a very positive way of them as well as of the Jewish case in Palestine. Therefore, many were the more perplexed when in 1938 Mussolini adopted the anti-Semitic ideology of German national-socialism, and enacted several anti-Semitic laws. Thus, all Jews who since January

71. Sale-Harrison ([1939]:107).
72. Goldberg (1976:25f.).

1, 1939, had entered Italy and the Italian possessions, had to leave within six months. However, the anti-Semitic laws in Italy were never as drastic and rigid as those in Germany.

In various respects, it is understandable that authors such as Alfred H. Burton and Leonard Sale-Harrison (also see § 8.1) saw in Mussolini's rise the first signs of the restoration of the Roman Empire. Yet, we now know that Mussolini was not the "beast," but at best a foreshadow of the "beast." At the end of World War II, both Hitler and Mussolini perished in the most shameful way, and their empires collapsed. A new era began, in which in a totally new way the unification of Europe loomed up.

Chapter 9
The Eighth Empire

9.1. The Beast

9.1.1. The Identity of the Beast

IN ITS FIRST YEAR OF PUBLICATION, the Dutch Réveil magazine *Nederlandsche Stemmen* ("Dutch Voices," 1834) contained an article which does not mention the author's name, but which was probably written by Isaac da Costa (1798-1860). This great Dutch Réveil man, poet and Bible teacher was a Christian of Portuguese-Jewish descent. It is worthwhile to quote a portion from the article:[1]

> However strange it may seem: the Fourth Monarchy [= the fourth empire of Dan. 2 and 7] is truly the last one! The Roman Empire was not transferred to Constantine the Great, nor to Charlemagne. For these did not stand over against Christendom, but were Christians themselves. Rome [= Roman-Catholicism] alone has, under the Christian dispensation, insofar as it opposes pure and true Christianity, and oppresses it, its own relation to it as Babylon once had to Jerusalem; therefore the city on the seven mountains in John's Revelation is explicitly called by that name; it [Rome] could bear that [name Babylon] with the greatest emphasis in the times of the Reformation; and it is predestined, according to the word of Prophecy, to reveal itself

1. *Nederlandsche Stemmen* 1834, nr. 17 (Aug. 30).

> once more in the fullest force of the word as the anti-Christian Babylon. But then it will see approaching its total destruction and perdition, at the appearance of the Son of man.

There are a few things that strike us here. Da Costa (if it is he) actually does not regard the Roman Empire as being continued in the empires of Constantine and Charlemagne, because these were Christians, whereas "Rome" represents the anti-Christian power. In his opinion, "Rome" relates to the Christian empires and states as Babylon to the ancient Jerusalem. In the Book of Revelation, Rome is indeed called "the great Babylon" (Rev. 17 and 18). Since this power offered resistance especially during the Reformation, da Costa apparently thinks here particularly of the Roman-Catholic Church. But apart from this, in the end time, the anti-Christian Babylon/ Rome will once again manifest itself in all its strength, but will then be promptly destroyed by the Son of man, coming with the clouds of heaven. The present chapter is concerned with this manifestation of anti-Christian Rome in the end time.

We will find a key to the understanding of large portions of the books of Daniel and Revelation, as well as of European history, if we start from the viewpoint that "the beast" in the Book of Revelation—the "first beast," rising from the sea (Rev. 13)—represents the Roman Empire restored in the end time.[2] Some expositors prefer, for instance because of the "speculations" of American evangelist Hal Lindsey or the fear to turn the Bible into a "puzzle-book," to speak as vaguely as possible of some "eschatological, anti-Christian world-power." But they cannot wipe out this exegetical datum *that this end-time world-power is the risen Roman Empire*. This is clear from a great number of indications, which each in itself may not be decisive, but I believe they are if taken together.

Thus there is, first, the clear parallel with the fourth, Roman, beast in Daniel 7, which also has ten horns. John obviously refers to this chapter because "his" beast also exhib-

2. See Ouweneel (1990 and 2012) on Rev. 13 and 17.

its features of the first three empires. For the church fathers, too, it was evident that the beast represents the emperor of Rome, or the Roman Empire. The Reformers saw the history of Rome continued in the Roman-Catholic Church, and therefore identified the first beast with "popery," an idea that is still maintained by some Reformed expositors. In my opinion, however, it is obvious from Revelation 17 that not the beast but the great whore is popery. The beast is not primarily a religious, but a political power, as was the Roman Empire.

We have emphasized how essential it is for the interpretation of the Book of Daniel that the four world-empires come to their end at, and as a consequence of, the second coming of Christ (Appendix 5). This too was for by far the most church fathers an established fact. It is the Son of man, *coming with the clouds of heaven,* who in Daniel puts an end to the power of the fourth (Roman) beast, and therewith to all four world-empires. If therefore the Roman Empire is destroyed by Christ only at his second coming, this implies that this empire has to reappear on the scene some time before that second coming. To be sure, if this were purely a logical consequence of the previous reasoning, I would suspect it. I mean, we need some further Biblical confirmation that indeed there will be such a thing like the re-erection of the Roman Empire in the end time. I believe that this further confirmation can indeed be found in Scripture.

To begin with, even the first revelation with regard to the four world-empires, in Daniel 2, already suggests a certain bipartition of the Roman Empire. The first form of the empire is represented by the two iron legs of the image, which clearly seem to refer to the bipartition into the East- and the West-Roman Empire. The second form of the empire is represented by the feet with the toes, which are partly of iron, partly of clay (v. 41-42). The distinct reference to the toes seems to point to the division of the empire into ten parts, as mentioned in Daniel 7:24 and Revelation 17:12-13 (the ten horns of the beast). In Daniel 2, the image of Nebuchadrezzar is struck at the feet, that is, in the last form of the fourth world-empire, and this fourth empire is then immediately replaced by the Messianic kingdom of peace and righteousness.

In Daniel 7, too, the Roman Empire is destroyed in the stage in which it consists of ten parts ("ten kings"), namely, at the coming of the Son of man with the clouds of heaven, and replaced by the latter's everlasting empire. Just before the second coming of Christ, the Roman Empire therefore exists in its last form of ten parts. Even if in Daniel 7 this may not yet be perfectly clear, it becomes so in Revelation 17, where the ten horns are ten "kings," who lay their power into the hands of the beast, which is subsequently destroyed by the Lamb. Notice that in Revelation 13 and 17, the beast represents both the Roman Empire and the *head* of that empire. Also notice that the Roman Empire in its past history never knew this form with ten parts to which Daniel 7 and Revelation 17 allude.

It is probably hardly necessary, yet I briefly point to an older interpretation which sees in the "ten kings" in Daniel and Revelation the more or less ten kingdoms that in the fifth and sixth century allegedly arose out of the perished Roman Empire. All sorts of lists of these ten kingdoms have been suggested by expositors, without much agreement between them. One correspondence there is, however, and that is the common basic mistake: the ten kingdoms do not at all exist *after* each other, over a period of several centuries, but (a) *alongside* each other, (b) during a *short* time ("one hour"), (c) they apparently form a kind of confederation, (d) they lay their power into the hands of a central dictator, and particularly, (e) the whole system *is destroyed by Christ at his second coming.*[3]

9.1.2. Decline and Revival

If the evidence given above might not yet be entirely convincing, we now have to pay attention to two passages in

3. Cf. Ironside (n.y.:37-38).

Revelation which, in my opinion, round up the argumentation.[4] The first is Revelation 13:4, 12, 14, where it is said that the beast is wounded to death, but comes to life again. It must be admitted that many different expositions of this Scripture have been given. Often, the beast's head wounded to death and healing again has been interpreted to refer to a literal historical person, who died and in the end time allegedly will be revived by Satan. Expositors think of various Roman leaders, from the murdered Julius Caesar to emperor Nero, or even of Judas Iscariot, but also of twentieth-century diabolic dictators, particularly Hitler, Stalin, or Mao Zedong. The main objection against this interpretation is that it is hardly acceptable to assume that Satan would be able to raise a man from death.

In fact, Revelation 13 does not have to refer to the death and resurrection of a certain person. The beast is primarily the empire, only secondarily the head of that empire. We therefore rather think of the "death" of the empire in the fifth century and its revival in the end time. The continuation of the Roman ideal in the empires of the Carolingians, the Ottonians, the Habsburgers, the Bonapartes, the "Third Reich," are as it were a vivid memory of the once deceased, but once reviving real Roman Empire. These memories always involved phantoms of the ancient empire evoked by war and violence, but the Roman Empire never really rose again. That which was never achieved with violence, however, will in the end time succeed in that, according to Revelation 17:12-13, the ancient Roman Empire revives in the form of a federation of "ten kings" (or, kingdoms, nation states), who subsequently lay all power into the hands of the sole ruler. This seems to imply that the empire revives through a "democratic" (?) process of voluntary junction of the ancient countries of Roman Europe, but that this "democratic" process comes to an end when the ever continuing centralization finally degenerates into a new totalitarian regime.

4. Cf. Ouweneel (1990, s.v.) and Medema (1992: ch. 11 & 13).

This dictator receives his power out of the hands of the "ten kings." But at the same time people will realize that he receives his power out of the hands of the dragon, the angelic prince of the Roman Empire, the evil *genius* behind the beast (Rev. 13:4). The goals of, for instance, the New Age movement—no matter if it will still exist by that time or not—will have been achieved: one world government, one world religion, one world teacher, who receives his mandate from the *archonts,* the cosmic world-rulers. The Age of Aquarius will seem to have arrived, a new era of justice, harmony, wholeness of creation, freedom, and peace. Christ said that if the "strong man" (Satan) keeps his domain, all that he has is "in peace" (Luke 11:21). Never will that word of Christ be borne out more than in that very era. Just shortly before sudden destruction comes upon the people they will shout, "Peace and safety" (1 Thess. 5:3).

The second passage that is of importance for our subject is Revelation 17:8, where it is said of the beast that it "was," that it "is not," and that it will "ascend out of the abyss." Here again it is important not to think of a person but of the empire. There was a long time that it "was" (first phase), since many centuries it has not been anymore (second phase), and in the end time it will come up out of the "abyss," the realm of death, of Satan and his demons (cf. 9:11; 11:7) (third phase). The origin of his revival is purely demonic, and this explains its heinous character. But it is destined to "go to perdition"; that will be the fourth and last phase of the empire. The way in which this will take place is explained in Revelation 19, although already in chapter 17:14 we find a hint: "the Lamb will overcome them."

Nation states, world-empires, civilizations rise, flourish, wither, and perish to rise no more; thus it has always been. But the miracle of the eschatological Roman Empire is that it will essentially be the same empire as in antiquity. Therefore, the whole of mankind will "marvel" about the beast, says both Revelation 13:3 and 17:8 (indicating that these two passages refer to the same event). It is new in history that a world-empire "revives," and this, as will be clearly recognizable, in a similar form as before, and that after so many centuries. Of course there will be differences; in a thousand respects our time can never be an imitation anymore of the first centuries of our era. Yet the rising empire will, recognizably for everyone, be a revival of the ancient Roman Empire.

In Revelation 17:11 it is said that "the beast that was, and is not," that is, the revived Roman Empire, "is himself also [the] eighth." This means: the seven heads of the beast refer to the seven earlier world-empires, that is, the Egyptian, Assyrian, Babylonian, Medo-Persian, Greek-Macedonian, Roman, and also the "seventh empire," which we associated with the last centuries particularly stamped by Napoleon and Hitler. But the beast is itself the eighth empire, which follows upon the seven previous empires. Here too, the beast is both the empire and the head of that empire. It is "of the seven," that is, it is a revival of one of the previous empires, namely, as said before, the Roman Empire of antiquity. The eighth empire starts as a "democratic" confederation, and finishes as a centralistic dictatorial empire. The "ten kings" lay their power into the hands of the beast, that is, the chief of the revived Roman Empire. This will not take place without difficulties. For it is true, during "one hour" (a short time) the "ten kings" receive "authority as kings with the beast," and therefore, even if they have given away their sovereignty, they will retain their power. But Daniel 7:7-8 mentions (not repeated in Rev. 17) that three of the ten "horns" are plucked out by the roots. This seems to imply that, although the "ten kings" will give their power to the beast, it will find the opportunity to overthrow three of those "kings."

All this will probably take only a short time, for already the next verse speaks of their perdition, namely, at the appearance of the Lamb. Elsewhere in Revelation, even a very precise time indication is given. The period in which the empire will manifest itself in its most diabolical form only lasts forty-two months (Rev. 13:5; cf. 11:2), that is one thousand two hundred and sixty days (11:3; 12:6), or "a time [= one year] and times [= two years] and half a time" (12:14), that is in each case three and a half years. Of course, there have been numerous speculations with regard to these time indications. People have tried to turn the 1260 "days" into years, or into an indefinite, though very long, period. However, there is in this case a very clear and simple reason to take the one thousand two hundred and sixty days literally. They correspond, namely, with the expression "a time and times and half a time" and the somewhat longer periods of one thousand two hundred and ninety and three thousand and thirty-five days in Daniel 12:7, 11-12 (cf. 7:25), which unmistakably tie in with the half of the "week" in Daniel 9:27, that is, the half of seven years (cf. 7:25; 8:11-12).

Indeed, it cannot be reasonably doubted that the one thousand two hundred and sixty days correspond with a half year-"week" in Daniel. The "week" (actually, "sevens") in Daniel 9 are literal sevens of years, for the first 69 "weeks" precisely form the 483 years from the command of the Persian king Artaxerxes to restore and rebuild Jerusalem until the appearance of Christ. But in that case, half a year-"week," that is, a period of three and a half years, has to be taken literally as well. This is the (brief) period of the "great tribulation," of the heaviest persecutions for the believers, of the extirpation of all true religion on earth, of the darkest days since creation, just before the "sun of righteousness" appears at the horizon.

9.1.3. The Dragon-Killing Son

Of course, in a study concerned with the "gods" behind the world-empires we are particularly fascinated by the diabolical world behind the beast. As earthly-human as the beast will be, as much will he be an embodiment of a spiritual power: the dragon, Satan. From the resemblance between the dragon and the beast (Rev. 12:3 and 13:1) we concluded that the dragon—"the old serpent, called Devil and Satan" (12:9)—is the *genius* of the ancient as well as of the restored Roman Empire. Behind the scenes of world history, the actual battle is fought, the one between the Lamb and the dragon. Just as the dragon Rahab (Isa. 51:9) threatened Israel in Egypt, and Israel was led out and redeemed on the basis of the blood of the Lamb, thus the dragon threatens the Son of Man as well as his people in Revelation 12. But his people will overcome the dragon "by the blood of the Lamb and by the word of their testimony" (v. 11).

In the light of this mythologically sounding language, it is no wonder that precisely in connection with Revelation 12 so many present-day expositors point to pagan mythologies. The theme of the woman with the divine child, threatened by a monster, seems to give them every reason to do so. In Greek mythology, Leto is made pregnant by Zeus, and therefore is persecuted by the great dragon, Python, who has heard through an oracle that a son of Leto will kill him. She is protected by Poseidon, however, so that the twins, Apollo and Artemis, are safely born. Four days later, Apollo, the sun god, has already arrived at masculine maturity, and kills the dragon.

Even older is the Babylonian myth concerning Damkina, the queen of heaven, ornamented with sun, moon and stars (cf. Rev. 12:1), sustained by an eagle in giving birth to the sun god Marduk (cf. v. 14). The dragon Tiamat (see § 3.1.2) knows the destination of the child, and threatens the mother, but a divine being puts the baby in safety in heaven. When Tiamat wants to pursue the child there, a heavenly army casts him on the earth. The dragon now turns against Damkina, she is saved by the earth and by the eagle, whereupon Tiamat turns against her other sons. When Marduk is grown up, he defeats the dragon and chains it in the abyss.

There are also parallels with the Persian myth around Ormuzd, the good spirit fighting with a three-headed dragon, and with the Egyptian myth around Isis, who is persecuted by the red (cf. 12:3) dragon, Typhon, yet gives birth to her child, Horus, who afterwards defeats the dragon.[5]

It is rather cheap to explain this kind of striking parallel such as if John had "adopted" his story from one or more pagan sources. If one believingly accepts the divine inspiration of Revelation 12, one cannot speak of an "adoption," whereas at the same time the parallels have to be taken seriously. British apologist Clive S. Lewis (1898-1963) has pointed out repeatedly that mythical themes such as that of the dragon threatening the woman with the divine child, and afterwards defeated by that child, go back upon a primordial revelation of God. In Scripture, however, the truth is handed down in its pure form because it is God who reveals it directly to us. But that truth has been corrupted in pagan mythologies, and mingled with polytheism and bombastic speculation. Not the prophets and apostles adopted the myths, and purified and historized them, but rather the reverse: the pagans only managed to preserve God's primordial revelation in the most corrupted form.

However, we have to add a thought element that is often overlooked by conservative expositors too. Do we really find in the pagan myths a vague and corrupted pre-knowledge of *Christ*? Or do these myths not rather speak of their own gods, that is, of the demonic powers? Was Hislop[6] possibly right, who adduced numerous arguments for the idea that, whether it concerns Zeus and Leto (Apollo's parents), or Osiris and Isis (Horus's parents), these are always references to the Nimrod (alias Ninus) and Semiramis of Babylonian mythology—a Nimrod also known from Gen. 10:9-10? In other words, we do not (only) have to do here with a version of some primordial revelation of God corrupted by the pagans, but (also) with a deification of the historical man Nimrod, and of his wife, and his son Tammuz. The Bible does not inform us any further about Nimrod's history; we depend here on pagan tradition

5. Cf. Van de Kamp (1990:219-236).
6. Hislop (1959: see about the dragon especially 225-242).

to find more data.

However this may be, such a view implies that the pagan myths concerning the mother and the dragon-killing child are no longer a foreshadowing of Christ, but an *imitation.* Do we possibly have to do here with demonic imitation, just as also the second beast in Revelation 13 is an imitation of the Lamb? This beast has two horns, as those of the Lamb, so that one might be confused for a moment; but when it opens its mouth, one hears the dragon speaking, so that it is impossible to be mistaken (v. 11). The "divine" world to which the mythologies of the pagans refer, and of which, in however corrupted a form, they have learned so much by occult means, is possibly full of such false divine imitations (see Appendix 3 about a depth-psychological approach to this problem).

To mention only one more example: in Micah 5:1-7 we find the pre-existent Messiah ("his goings forth are from of old, from the days of eternity") and his association with an age of paradise-like fertility. Rudolf Kittel (1853-1929) believed that this presentation points to the influence of pagan mythical elements regarding a returning king from the past or of the first man from paradise. In that case, we would in particular have to do here with the Egyptian myth of Osiris.[7] My interpretation is exactly the opposite: it is not so that in Micah 5 we find traces of the Osiris myth, but the Osiris myth itself is an occult imitation of the Messiah. If the wicked pagan Balaam, through the Spirit of God, could have knowledge of Israel's Messiah and his glorious and paradise-like future,[8] why not the antique pagans in general? They were not ignorant with regard to "the truth"; on the contrary, they knew it, but suppressed it "in unrighteousness" (Rom. 1:18).

9.2. The Revived Roman Empire and the World Situation

9.2.1. Old Predictions

We now come to the difficult question as to what connection

---

7. Kittel (1924:64ff.).
8. See Num. 23 & 24, particularly 23:24; 24:5-7, 17-19.

there is—if any—between the Biblical prophecies regarding the reviving Roman Empire on the one hand and our present-day world situation on the other. We already found several examples from the nineteenth century and the first half of the twentieth century that gave us every reason to be careful. With what aplomb have the prophecies been associated with Napoleon I or III, with Bismarck, with the League of Nations, with Hitler or Mussolini. And in the strict sense of the word, all these expositors were proven wrong. Much more recent "prophets" such as Hal Lindsey, too, will have to adjust their books, for how different does the world situation look—if alone since the fall of communism—compared with 1970 when Lindsey's *The Late Great Planet Earth* appeared.

Until 1989 Europe was divided into two, the democratic West and the communist East, and this bipartition was "explained" on the basis of the prophecies. Nowadays, on the contrary, we find ourselves in the situation in which the countries of Middle and Eastern Europe have joined the European Union, or are sitting in the waiting-room in order to be admitted (Montenegro, Serbia, the Republic of Macedonia) (although Russia remains an unstable and unpredictable factor). Whereas some expositors jubilated when the number of countries belonging to the EEC had increased to exactly ten (cf. Rev. 17:12), the EU now already comprises twenty-eight countries, and there is every appearance that this number will still increase.

On the other hand, a unique situation presents itself today, one that is totally new in the history of Europe. In previous situations, where people believed to recognize a revival of the Roman Empire, it was never a matter of a voluntary joining together of the countries of Western and Middle Europe. The United Nations Organization (UNO) does entail such a voluntary union, but that involves all countries of the world, and that is presumably something else than the revival of the ancient Roman Empire. Perhaps it seems "cheap" to associate the present-day voluntary joining together of the countries of

Western Europe with the revival of the Roman Empire. But let us at least establish the fact that already in the nineteenth century many expositors of prophecy have more or less exactly predicted the situation as we experience it today. Of course, that is not "proof" that we experience the revival of the Roman Empire today, but it is at least striking and totally new.

First, I refer to the most significant prophetic expositor of the nineteenth century, who became the teacher and inspirer for hundreds of other expositors: John N. Darby (1800-1882). In 1840 he gave eleven French lectures about prophecy at Geneva, which have been translated under the title, *The Hopes of the Church of God, in Connection with the Destiny of the Jews and the Nations As Revealed in Prophecy*. It is interesting to mention that the well-known Reformed pastor of the *Afscheiding* ("Secession") in the Netherlands (1834), rev. Hendrik P. Scholte (1805-1868), who later emigrated to the United States, was so impressed by these lectures that he published them in Dutch shortly after they had been held. I give here some passages from the English edition:[9]

> When the Roman Empire existed under its pagan form, it had not ten kings; but when this beast reappears (let us keep in mind that it is the Roman Empire), ten kings will give their power to it, instead of ten kings replacing it [as in 476 AD and afterwards. WJO]. More than this, it is after having been destroyed that it will come again into existence. In a word, it is not the pagan beast, nor the history of the middle ages, nor of ten barbarian kings (if indeed ten could be pronounced upon with any certainty) who have taken the place of the empire, but [it says in 17:8: it "was, and is not, and will ascend out of the abyss"]; that is, the mortal wound will be healed [13:3], and the imperial beast will re-appear.
>
> The ten kings "shall give their strength and power unto the beast" [17:13]; there will be an imperial head—an emperor, and

9. Darby (n.y., 2:329f.).

> ten kings, who will give him their power; the kingdoms will continue in existence, but it will be a confederation of them. As an illustration, we may refer to the kingdoms of Spain, Holland, Westphalia, etc., under Napoleon. There has been the beast; there have been, it may be, ten kings; but *never yet ten kings giving their power to the beast who was not, and who came anew into existence.*
>
> "The seven heads are seven mountains." (We are still occupied with the Roman Empire.) "And there are seven kings; five are fallen, and one is"—namely, the imperial one which existed in the time of John,— "and the other is not yet come; and when he cometh, he must continue a short space. And the beast that was, and is not, even he is the eighth (because the seven have passed), and is of the seven, and goeth into perdition." That is, there will be an eighth head, one of a peculiar character, who will re-unite all the power of the beast, who will be the beast himself, and who, whilst a head apart, is still one of the seven. It is the imperial head under a new form; for there are to be ten kings, who will give their power to this eighth head; and it is in this form that it will go down to destruction.

Here we have, already in 1840, the "program" as it since then has been repeated by Darby and by numerous other interpreters. To me, this early exposition seems to be still acceptable, even if by "kings" we would not necessarily think of literal monarchies anymore.[10] However, let us notice particularly the sentence which also in the original is printed in italics: never before has Europe known a situation in which there were ten "kings" (government leaders) who ruled at the same time, and collectively and simultaneously gave their power to a dictator—and that moreover to a dictator over an empire which had existed in an earlier age, had not been in

10. In the widest sense of the word each "regent" (or ruler, coming from the Latin, regula) is a "king." The words "regent" and regula are related to the Latin rex (genit. regis), "king." Ten "kings" are ten governments or heads of government.

existence for centuries, and reappears in the end time. Nobody can prove that the present-day European unification is the fulfillment of this prophecy; but we can state that Europe has never known a situation which comes so close to Darby's circumscription as the present situation.

Let me give one more example, this time from one of Darby's most gifted pupils, Bible expositor William Kelly (1821-1906). In 1860, he published in the magazine edited by himself, *The Bible Treasury*, a series of articles about the Book of Daniel, which in 1902 were published in unaltered form as a book. I quote from this the following:[11]

> The iron [of Nebuchadnezzar's image] was the original element [of the Roman Empire]: the clay was brought in subsequently, and properly did not belong to the great metal statue; it was a foreign ingredient. When and whence did it come? I believe that the Spirit of God in using the figure of clay refers not to the original Roman element, which had the strength of the iron, but to the barbaric hordes, which broke in at a later period, weakening the Roman power, and forming by degrees separate kingdoms. I can, however, only state this as my own judgment, founded upon the general use of Scripture language and ideas. We have [here] what was not properly and originally Roman, but was brought in from elsewhere; and it is the mixture of the two elements that is productive of the weakness, and that finally leads to divisions. These hordes of barbarians, that forced themselves in at first, professed not to be conquerors but guests of Rome, and finally settled themselves within its limits. This it was that subsequently led to the division of the empire into a number of separate independent kingdoms, when the power and pride of imperial Rome was broken. Charlemagne, later on, cherished the desire of universal empire, which he labored hard to realize: but it was a failure; and all that he acquired in his life was separated in his death. Another man attempted it in our days: I mean, of course, the exile of St. Helena [Napoleon]. He had at

11. Kelly (1860:25; 1952:49-50).

> heart the same universal monarchy. What was the issue? His success was still more short-lived. All was completely broken up into its original constituents before he had breathed his last. And so it will continue in the main, until the moment spoken of here [in Dan. 2], but more fully entered into in the Book of Revelation.
>
> This is, I believe, what Scripture lays down about the matter. There will be, before the age closes, the most remarkable union of two apparently contradictory conditions—a universal head of empire, and separate independent kingdoms besides, each of which will have its own king; but that one man will be the emperor over all these kings. Till that time comes, every effort to unite the different kingdoms under one head will be a total failure. Even then it will be not by fusing them together into one kingdom, but each independent kingdom will have its own king, though all subject to one head. God has said they shall be divided. This then is what is shown us here. "They shall not cleave one to another, even as iron is not mixed with clay." [Dan. 2:43b] And if there ever was a portion of the world that has represented this incoherent system of kingdoms, it is modern Europe [of 1860!]. As long as the iron predominated, there was one empire; but then came in the clay, or foreign material. In virtue of the iron there will be a universal monarchy, while in virtue of the clay there will be separate kingdoms.

More clearly one could not wish to read it in a publication of 1860. And the striking thing is here, of course, that these expositors wrote in a time that there was not the slightest indication of a union of Europe. Even some countries such as Germany and Italy were no national and political unities as yet, leave alone (Western and Middle) Europe as a whole. The great powers usually stood in sharp opposition to each other, and in fact all the way to 1945, three great wars have torn apart Western Europe (1870-71, 1914-18, 1939-45). Yet dozens of expositors in the nineteenth century wrote without any restraint about a coming unification of Europe. A unification not by conquest or intrigues, but because ten "kings" (states? blocks?) voluntarily join together, presumably into a kind of confederation, and subsequently, while maintaining their own position, transfer the power to a central ruler with totalitarian aspirations.

9.2.2. Link with the Present Situation

Let us briefly summarize what we have found.[12] The last world-empire, just before the second coming of Christ, is an astonishing revival of the ancient Roman Empire. This was itself the sixth empire. The seventh empire presumably comprises the most shocking revivals of the empire that could be seen in European history up till the eighth empire, with as a nadir (so far?) national-socialism with the holocaust. The eighth empire is the last, greatest, and ultimate revival. This empire starts off as a confederation of ten distinct "kings" (government leaders), who are joined together not by violence, but by mutual consent (Rev. 17:12-13), and subsequently bring their "kingdoms" together under the authority of the central dictator.

The metahistorical dimension of the empire implies that this empire, and particularly its head, is an embodiment of the dragon, that is the Devil, the Satan, the "god" of this world (*aiôn*, 2 Cor. 4:4), and especially of the ancient Roman *oikoumenè*. The most significant outer characteristic of the eighth empire will therefore be the burning hatred against Jesus Christ, against the true faithful among his people of Israel, and against all forms of the true religion of the God of Scriptures. All the power of the beast will therefore culminate in the "war" that he will undertake against the Lamb and the faithful belonging with him (Rev. 17:14; 19:19-21). In the battle of the eighth king against the ninth King, world history reaches its "apotheosis"[13], at least in a certain sense: in fact,

12. Cf. Pentecost (1964:323f., 332-334).
13. Here in the semi-literal sense of divine highlight and end point, ultimate highest manifestation of the truly divine.

the battle has already been fought at Calvary. In Harmagedon, only the final results of what was already accomplished at Calvary will become visible.

What can we say further about the identity of this eighth empire? We remember again the dangers of a strong coupling of the prophecies with the daily news. Yet we have seen that it is very difficult to sever the prophetic development of the Roman Empire from the present-day unification of Europe, precisely because *for the first time in its history* we have to do here with a *voluntary joining together* of the various European states. A joining together that started with the Treaty of Rome (!) of the two former "hereditary enemies," Germany and France, plus Italy (the central part of the Roman Empire) and the Benelux countries (the personal hereditary lands of emperor Charles V). The historic treaty was signed at Rome on March 25, 1957, and was effectuated on January 1, 1958. The United Kingdom, Ireland and Denmark joined in 1973, Greece in 1981, Spain and Portugal in 1986, Austria, Sweden and Finland in 1995, Cyprus, Czech Republic, Estonia, Hungary, Latvia, Lithuania, Malta, Poland, Slovakia and Slovenia in 2004, Bulgaria and Romania in 2007, and Croatia in 2013.

What had been attempted for centuries and never succeeded, the formation of a strictly voluntary political or economic unity, finally began taking shape.[14] In 1979, the European Parliament was formed, which is elected by the population of the European Union. The executive branch of the EU, the European Commission, has a president, who is the most powerful officeholder in the EU. Since the Italian Romano Prodi (in office: 1999-2004), this "president" has so much power that he can be called the prime minister of the EU. From 2004 to 2014 it was the Portuguese José Barroso who occupied this post. In 2009, the Belgian Herman A. van Rompuy (b. 1947) became the first president of the European Council, which is the institution of the European Union comprising the govern-

14. See more extensively Medema (1992, particularly ch. 3-6).

ment leaders of the EU member states. *De facto*, Brussels—the old seat of emperor Charles V—is the capital of a Union containing more than five hundred million people.

To be sure, a real federacy with a federal government still seems far away—the idea even reviled by many Europeans—and this holds even more for a government with totalitarian authority. But the process of centralization is continuing all the time; more and more bits of sovereignty are being perforce transferred by the distinct states to "Brussels." This process of federation formation and centralization is being speeded up by the economic crisis going on since 2008. Also military reasons, such as holding up a common fist against Islamic terrorism, could enhance this process. And only staunch idealists and optimists could really believe that a Napoleon, a Hitler or a Stalin has for ever become impossible in Europe, or also, that under peculiar circumstances the European Union could not choose a central dictator, just as ancient Rome did so once in a while for a period of six months.

9.2.3 The Western World

Yet I would suggest that the reviving Roman Empire might have a much larger extent than the ancient Roman Empire, or even than Europe. At times, older expositors have stressed the idea that the new empire ought to have exactly the same borders as the old empire, but I see no reason for this in Scripture. On the contrary, purely geographic borders mean nothing at all in metahistorical respect. If we do apprehend the spiritual character of the Roman Empire, as it possessed at the time of its fall in the fifth century, we will understand a very important element in Revelation 17. That is the close relationship between the beast and the great whore. In my commentary on Revelation I have argued that this whore is nominal Christendom, especially characterized by popery, though not popery alone (if the great whore is popery, then who are her daughters? Rev. 17:5). The two, empire and church, closely belong together. It was the Roman Empire with *papal* Rome that already in the fifth century was overthrown. The whore itself was not overthrown, but she did "ride" no longer on the beast. But when one day the empire will revive it will be ridden again by the whore (Rev. 17:3, 7, 9). It controls the beast, that is, the city with the seven hills, Rome.

This datum might supply an indication for establishing the borders of the Roman Empire. British-American Bible expositor Frederick C. Jennings (1847-1948), who became known for his commentary on Isaiah, wrote in an article of 1940 the following:[15]

> [In] the seventeenth chapter of the book of the Revelation, we see the whole stage filled with two personalities only: a "Beast" and a "Woman" (...) there can be no argument or discussion as to this speaking of both the Civil and Ecclesiastical conditions that will rule and characterize that part of the earth that is within the limits or boundaries of Prophecy. The whole of it will be filled with what shall answer to this "Beast" and this "Woman." The two are thus indissolubly co-related, and tell us to what end all (...) are trending; and that is that there will eventually be one World-Empire and one World-Church, and these will cover the whole of what is now called Christendom; the one Empire supporting the one Church, and the "Beast" in the Scripture supports the "Woman," and the "Woman" is supported by the "Beast." So that wherever one of those may be, there will inevitably the other be, too, and the boundaries of the one inevitably mark the boundaries of the other...
>
> (...) we are compelled to see that the boundaries of the Empire will be the boundaries of the professed, but utterly apostate Christianity; and vice-versa the boundaries of the apostate Church will be exactly co-terminous with those of the Empire. But that being assured and clear, it follows beyond all question, that the revived Roman Empire will include (...) every country everywhere in which there is any claim to apostate Christianity

15. Jennings (1940:387-389).

> at all, and so, will include North and South America.

Whether this conclusion is so "assured and clear" as Jennings claims is a matter of dispute. But he no doubt gives some striking arguments. Reasoning along the same lines I myself would put it this way. Where do we find today the cultural heirs of the ancient Roman Empire with its "Christian" church, that is, popery as well as its "daughters" (cf. Rev. 17:5), including Eastern "Orthodoxy" and the protestant national and state churches (apart from the many faithful believers in them)? Today these heirs live not in Western Europe alone anymore, but also in Eastern Europe, in North and South America, in parts of Africa, in Australia and New Zealand. It is therefore quite conceivable, though we cannot "prove" it, that the reviving Roman Empire will comprise the entire so-called "Western" world. It is to be seen to what extent institutions such as NATO and GATT, or even the UNO, will play a role in it.

In this context, I refer again to the study mentioned before by Gerhard F. Mehrtens,[16] who in his book, *De nieuwe Romeinen* ("The New Romans"), defends the thesis

> that the mechanisms which once, under Rome's guidance, managed to unify the scattered pre-Roman world usher in, today again, but now from the American cultural-technological high pressure area, a comparable development.

In other words, the Americans are the "new Romans." Mehrtens points to the numerous correspondences that exist between the two "super powers." According to him, all that Rome once brought about repeats itself today on a world scale in the United States. This implies that he, arguing from the development as well as decline of the Roman Empire, also believes he can make predictions about the future of the United States. Indeed, the parallels that Mehrtens points out are often quite surprising. If his view is correct, this would imply for

16. Mehrtens (1987:30).

our view that the reviving Roman Empire would comprise not only the whole Western world, but that the United States would belong to it, or even would form the kernel of it. Washington DC, after (the first) Rome, Constantinople and Moscow, the "fourth Rome"? In any case, there are nowhere so many Roman pillars, colonnades, and imitation temples as in America, especially in Washington DC. Statues of presidents as Jefferson and Lincoln have again been erected in antiquity type temples, the United States Congress meets in a genuine Capitol, the school youth again wear at official occasions the Roman toga, etcetera.[17] And these are but some of the outer parallels. The correspondences in mentality, life style, world language, megalomania, imperialism, technological superiority, etcetera, etcetera, go much deeper.

For the idea that the reviving Roman Empire will know a much wider extension than Western and Middle Europe, we find a forceful argument in Revelation 13:7-8:

> authority was given him [= the beast] over every tribe, and people, and language, and nation. And all who dwell on the earth will worship him.

This kind of language must probably be limited to that part of the earth that lies within the scope of biblical prophecy (also cf. Rev. 16:14 and 17:15). In other words, it is just as well possible that the revived Roman Empire will only comprise the united Europe after all. The United States struggle with problems which Europe knows too, but not at the same scale as in America: criminality, such as nocturnal unsafety, the drugs problem, the saddening level of public education, the abuse of freedoms, the crumbling down of the conventional family, and the effects of this for raising children, the advance of pornography, and the consequences of this for the general morality. The well-known American TV personality, Alistair Cooke (1908-2004),[18] believed that this moral decline of America will

17. Mehrtens (1987:171).

18. *The Financial Times*, Oct. 5, 1991.

necessarily lead to a significant historic turning-point, such as a second civil war (like between poor and rich), or the rise of a dangerous demagogue. In my terms: in the coming generation, America might very well either fall back to the level of a second-rate power, *or* it will overcome all its difficulties in a miraculous way, and give guidance to an all-powerful Western block, that can resist not only Russia but especially China and the Islamic world.

9.2.4 One or Two World-Powers

Things might, however, also take a very different direction. Everything is possible. It is no use to enter into further speculations regarding the question as to whether the reviving Roman Empire will, or will not, comprise America. An important question, which in a much more direct way touches the exegesis of the prophecies, is whether in the end time there will be one or two anti-divine world powers, which historically are opposed to each other, but metahistorically are both opposed to the Lamb. Compare the angelic princes of Greece and Persia, two countries that were at war with each other, whereas their angelic princes were both aiming at Israel and its God (Dan. 10). Apart from the eschatological Roman Empire, the prophecies speak of the "king of the North" in the end time (Dan. 11:40-45), of "Gog" (Ezek. 38 and 39), and of "Assyria" in the end time (e.g., Isa. 30 and 31; Mic. 5). Presumably these circumscriptions refer to one and the same power. Some believe that this power will remain until the end, and is destroyed by Christ himself at his second coming. Others believe that this power is destroyed already before, namely, at the beginning of the last half year-"week" of Daniel. In that case, subsequently the whole (Western?) world will really lie within the sphere of influence of the beast.

Please note, these are all considerations *not* inspired by the present world situation but by the problems in the exegesis of the prophecies themselves. One might neglect these problems and get rid of them—"the Bible is no puzzle book"—but then one offers no alternative exegesis. On the contrary, careful and detailed exegesis is simply declined. I speak of those who circumscribe the various eschatological powers opposing Israel ("Assyria," "the beast," "Gog," "king of the North") vaguely and indiscriminately as "anti-divine" or "anti-Christian" powers. I would call this non-exegesis, or the fear of exegesis. The reluctance of such expositors may be praiseworthy—speculations do not lead us anywhere—but we simply have the duty to *expound* Scripture. The Bible is not unclear about the fact that in the end time, that is, the time just before the second coming of Christ, there exists a Roman beast, an Assyrian king, a "king of the North," a Gog of the land of Magog. We cannot refer them back to the distant past, because their destiny is linked with the appearance of Messiah from heaven and the majestic establishment of his kingdom of peace and righteousness. Nor can we get away from them by very vague terms. We may not have a solution for all exegetical problems, but the least is that they are acknowledged.

9.3. The State of Israel

9.3.1. Old Predictions

Much more than our predecessors before World War II, and even more than those in the nineteenth century, we have every reason to believe that we live in prophetic times. First, this holds for the unification of Europe, and beyond that for the unification of the whole Western world. Secondly, this holds for the unification of—largely liberal—Christendom in the so-called World Council of Churches. It was founded in 1948, the year in which, as a phase in the European integration, also the Organization for Economic Cooperation and Development (OECD) was founded. The year 1948 was also the one in which the third significant prophetic development took place: the foundation of the state of Israel.

Here again, it is of interest to pay attention to nineteenth-century expositors who have clearly foreseen the foundation of this state, although nothing at their time pointed into that direction, and even Zionism (the longing for a Jewish state in the Holy Land) did not yet exist. Today, *after* the origin of the state Israel, thousands of Christians have come to the understanding that God still has a future for ethnic Israel, and that the "land promise" (God's promise that Israel one day would be restored in its own land) is not to be spiritualized and transferred to the Church. To put it more strongly, those who do not "see" it even now, have a grit in their spiritual eye. But it was a different matter at the beginning of the nineteenth century. When nothing of this could be seen in the Middle East, there were men who saw *from Scripture* that in the end time the state of Israel was to be restored.

Honesty commands us to say that also in seventeenth- and eighteenth-century Protestantism (Britain, Germany, the Netherlands) there have been expositors who saw the future spiritual restoration of ethnic Israel in its own land.[19] However, with them this insight was usually mingled with the confusing and unbiblical post-millennialism: the doctrine of an inner-temporal kingdom of peace *before* the second coming of Christ. The view of Israel could only be cleared up when people began to see that the restoration of Israel takes place before the Messianic kingdom of peace, that is, at the second coming of the Messiah.

I might quote here again from British expositors such as Darby and Kelly, particularly because their writings are of a still older date, but I now choose as a witness the most gifted Dutch expositor in this field, Herman C. Voorhoeve (1837-1901). Already in 1866, he wrote his book about eschatology, which since then has been reprinted many times unaltered. His son, Johannes N. Voorhoeve (1873-1948), wrote in 1922 in the preface of the eighth edition:[20]

> If one attentively reads this book one will be astonished about the fact that it is in no way contradicted by what happened

19. See extensively Van Campen (2006).
20. Voorhoeve (1922:6).

> afterwards, on the contrary, is corroborated by the events. The reason for this is that the author decidedly and exclusively held to Holy Scripture.

In 1866, Herman C. Voorhoeve indeed wrote:[21]

> There will be a time when Israel will return to the land of its fathers, will rebuild the city [Jerusalem] and the temple, under the renewed favor of Jehovah will again enjoy the light of his friendly face, and will safely dwell under the palm-trees and cedars of the promised land.
>
> Our exposition of "the second coming of Christ on earth" already made it clear that the Jews are to return to Palestine. For if the Lord will come from heaven with his heavenly saints to assume the dominion over his people, if his feet will stand on the Mount of Olives, and he again will enter into Jerusalem, and will be received and worshipped by Israel as the true Messiah, then of course this nation must have returned to its land before that time, and have rebuilt the city and the temple.

In order to corroborate this conclusion, Voorhoeve deals with Isaiah 14:1-2, Jeremiah 16:10-15, Ezekiel 34, 36 and 37, Daniel 9:24-27, Matthew 24, Isaiah 18, and Revelation 11 and 12. He then repeats the conclusion quoted above, now enriched with many prophetic details. The most significant error committed by Voorhoeve is that he believed the political restoration of Israel to take place only after the so-called "rapture" of the Church (cf. John 14:1-3; 1 Thess. 4:13-18), whereas this political restoration is now already more than sixty-five years old. There is nothing in Scripture that would force us to assume that the re-foundation of the state of Israel could only take place after some "rapture" of the Church. However, expositors like Voorhoeve and others lived so strongly in the daily expectation of the Lord coming to take away his Church that they placed *all* fulfillments of prophecies after this "rapture," also when Scripture did not explicitly demand this. In fact,

---

21. Voorhoeve (1922:108-109).

this error only underlines their true piety.

It is important that Voorhoeve wrote in a time (1866) for which the following was true:

> The tribes of Israel are still scattered over all the earth, the promised land is still waste, the city and the temple are still trampled by the Gentiles, the King of Israel is still hidden from their eyes.[22]

Today these same "tribes of Israel," insofar as they have survived the holocaust, have returned by the millions to Palestine, have founded there the state of Israel, have miraculously cultivated the land that had lied waste for centuries. Since the Six-Day War of 1967, "the city" is in Jewish hands, and in 1980 it was declared the "eternal capital" of Israel. Only the so-called "Third Temple" has not yet been rebuilt, although there are ultra-orthodox organizations that have the plans and materials for that rebuilding largely prepared (see the Temple Institute in Jerusalem). Above all, the King of Israel is indeed still hidden from the eyes of the mass of the Jews, but has been revealed to the eyes of the thousands (!) of "Messianic" Jews in Israel. These are the Jews who have learned to believingly accept and confess Jesus of Nazareth as their Messiah and Redeemer.

9.3.2. The Domain of Abaddon

The metahistorical vicissitudes of the apostate part of Israel in the end time are strikingly described in Revelation 9:1-6. There we hear in verse 1 of the "abyss" (Gr. abyssos) as the domain of a special angel, in Hebrew called Abaddon ("destruction") and in Greek, Apollyon ("destroyer") (v. 11). It is the diabolical domain from which ascends the beast (11:7; 17:8), and where Satan afterwards is bound a thousand years (20:1, 3). The "pit of the abyss" is figuratively described as a deep shaft, leading from the earth to the underworld. Perhaps that is the same as what is meant in Romans 10:7, the realm of

22. Voorhoeve (1922:55).

the spirits, *hades* (cf. Acts 2:27). If we consider that the beast is said to rise out of both the "sea" (13:1) and the "abyss" (17:8), we may presumably say that the abyss figuratively contains waters. Perhaps we must think here of the primordial ocean, the *tehôm*, which in Babylonian mythology lives on as the monster Tiamat. The Hebrew word *tehôm* is rendered either as "flood," or as "the deep" (abyss) (Gen. 1:2; cf. Gen. 49:25; Deut. 33:13; see § 3.1.2). According to the pseudepigraphic book 1 Enoch, the abyss is the dwelling-place of Satan, of fallen angels, and of fallen men.

The "star" in verse 1 is an evil power, probably an angelic power (cf. 12:4 or 12:7-9), or the false prophet (cf. 13:11-12). This person receives (from Christ?) the "key" to the abyss, that is, the command over the evil powers enclosed in it (cf. 1:18; 3:7). When the pit is opened, smoke comes out of it. If the abyss is also hades, this is presumably the smoke rising from the torture of the damned (cf. 14:11 and Luke 16:24). But it may also be that the "smoke" only looks like smoke, and is in fact a swarm of "locusts" set free from the abyss (cf. v. 3). These locusts are demonic powers released on the earth. Apparently, Palestine in particular is intended because verse 4 shows that the locusts are only allowed to harm those who do not have the seal of God on their foreheads. Since the 144,000 sealed ones in Revelation 7:4 are of Israel, chapter 9 apparently refers to the unbelieving mass of Israel, that is, those who do not care about the God of Jakob and his Anointed and who will bow before the image of the beast (see § 9.3.3).

Hostile powers are compared with locusts in other Scriptures too, as in Joel 1:4-7. If we consider that the plagues of Egypt were directed against the gods of Egypt, the locust plague (Exod. 10:12-20) must also refer to the evil powers that held Israel captive. They are insects that destroy everything that is in their way. That which is commanded to them in verse 4, namely, not to harm the trees or the green grass, is therefore in total conflict with the nature of ordinary locusts. This point underlines their symbolic character here. They are to "harm" the unsealed ones. In such a case, the intention of *diabolical powers* is to torture men; the intention of the *God of gods* is that men will repent after all (cf. v. 20-21; 16:9). These locusts receive a devilish power as the scorpions have it, namely, to inflict upon people their very painful sting in a secretive and crafty way (cf. v. 5 and 10; Luke 10:19).

The "false prophet" will be pre-eminently the embodiment of this devilish power. Through this power he will seduce both the nominal Christians and the unbelieving Jews to believe in the most perverse doctrines (cf. Matt. 12:45; 2 Thess. 2:11-12; Rev. 13:11-18). The heresies will be so vicious that people will try to escape from them by seeking death, but "they will not find it" (v. 6). In verses 20-21 we get an impression of these satanic influences: occultism, spiritism, magic, fortune-telling, sexual perversity, satanism. The spiritual torture by the locusts is like that of a scorpion when it stings a man: it cunningly injects its poison, without people noticing it. Similarly, people will unsuspectingly submit to the satanic power of the Antichrist, and be spiritually harassed and tormented.

Just like the dragon, the Rahab and the Leviathan, these locusts are a symbolic representation of real diabolical powers, which will probably torture people by means of human instruments, as the Antichrist and his companions. The symbolism of the description is underlined by the association with the aggression of war horses, with wreaths of victory, and with the brutality of lions. They have faces like men, but from behind they look like women because of their long hair. This long hair possibly speaks of submission (cf. 1 Cor. 11:15), and indicates that they depend on a higher power: Abaddon, the high angelic prince (v. 11). The latter point again corroborates their symbolic character, for common locusts have no king (Prov. 30:27). The locusts have as their king the angel of the abyss.[23] His Hebrew name suggests a relationship with

23. Cf. Job 18:14, which speaks of the "king of terrors," that is, the king of *Sheôl* (hades, realm of the dead). In Ugarit this was the god Mot (that is the Aramaic

the unbelieving mass of the Jewish people, his Greek name a relationship with nominal Christendom. Both the unbelieving Jews (John 5:43; 1 John 2:22; Rev. 13:11) and the unbelieving "Christians" (cf. 1 John 2:23; 2 Thess. 2:3-4; Rev. 13:12-17) will be the prey of the diabolical powers' cunningness, manifesting itself through the beast and the false prophet.

Many expositors have been struck by the fact that the name Apollyon much resembles the name Apollo. Indeed, this latter name is derived from the same root, "destroying," the locust being moreover one of the symbols of the god Apollo. It seems therefore that our verse alludes to this sun god, who, as we have seen, was so closely associated with the Roman emperors. Both the emperors of ancient Rome, even including Constantine the Great, and the future beast are embodiments of the sun god Apollo, or also of his father, Zeus (see § 9.3.4). In other words, the king of the diabolical powers in Revelation 9 is none less than the angelic prince of the Roman emperors. Therefore, Abaddon/Apollyon is presumably just another name for the dragon.

9.3.3. The Abomination of Desolation

Daniel 9:24-27, the prophecy concerning the seventy year-"weeks" briefly referred to before, still forms a key to the understanding of the Biblical prophecies in general, certainly when the future of Israel is at stake.[24] Without arguing extensively for this, I state that (a) the "weeks" here are periods of seven years, (b) the seventy "weeks" (four hundred and ninety years) continue until the Messianic kingdom of peace (cf. v. 24), (c) the Messiah is "cut off" after sixty-nine "weeks," that is, four hundred and eighty-three years since the command by the Persian king Artaxerxes to rebuild Jerusalem (v. 25-26; cf. Neh. 2), and (d) there is a gap between the sixty-ninth and

word for "death"). His firstborn was a demon who brought "terrors" over the people that they would land in *Sheôl* (Nahum M. Sarna, quoted by Hartley 1988:279; also cf. Heb. 2:14f.; Rev. 9:5-6, 10-11).

24. See for a present-day exposition, Fijnvandraat (1990:147-174), and the literature quoted there, as well as Ouweneel (2012:§6.5).

the seventieth "week." Recognizing this gap has always been the greatest stumbling block for the understanding of this prophecy because, if the gap is denied, the seventieth "week" has to be pressed into the final days of Christ and immediately afterwards, which is simply impossible.

The fact that a gap has to be assumed between verses 26 and 27 is obvious from at least three indications. First, verse 26 mentions an event that apparently takes place *after* the sixty-two (with the first seven, in total sixty-nine) "weeks," but before the seventieth "week," namely, the destruction of the city and the temple (70 AD). Secondly, the events of the seventieth "week" so far have never taken place. Thirdly, since the seventy "weeks" close the history of Israel's "exile," the seventieth "week" must take place immediately before the appearance of Christ. This is supported by verse 24: the seventy "weeks" end with the "transgression" being finished, "sin" being put to an end, "iniquity" being atoned for, "everlasting righteousness" being brought in, "vision and prophet" being sealed (viz. through their fulfillment), and the "Holy of Holies" (the Messianic temple) being anointed.

The events of that seventieth "week" (seven years) are very concisely described in verse 27. Because of this conciseness as well as biased views of prophecy, the verse often gave many problems to both translator and expositor. I believe I might translate the verse as literally as possible in the following way:

> And he will confirm a covenant with the many, one "seven."
> And [at the] half of the "seven" he will put an end to sacrifice and offering.
> And on the [or, a] wing of abominations [comes] a desolator
> or, on a wing [he places] an abomination [bringing] desolation
> or, because of the wing [= protection] of abomination [gods] [comes] a desolator
> until the consummation

> determination is poured out on the desolated [city]
> or, until the determined consummation is poured out on the desolate.

Without entering into all the details of the exposition, some points have to be emphasized. First, that the "he" in the beginning of the verse can be best understood as referring back to the person mentioned last, that is, "the coming prince" (v. 26), namely, the *future* prince of the very nation that in ancient days destroyed the city and temple of Israel (70 AD), that is, the Romans. Thus, the coming prince can only be the ruler of the Roman Empire reviving in the end time, that is, the beast.

Secondly, it is stated here that the beast concludes a firm covenant with "the many," that is here, the mass of the Jewish people restored in their own land. This mass stands over against the "remnant" of Israel, which serves YHWH, learns to trust in the coming Messiah, and does not want to have anything to do with the Roman Empire, the empire of the dragon, and therefore will be terribly persecuted.

Thirdly, there is a clear allusion here to the "abomination of desolation" mentioned also in Daniel 11:31 and 12:11. An "abomination" is an idol, here in the sense of an idol that, because it is worshipped, brings desolation over its worshippers. This desolation of the state of Israel in the second half of the seventieth "week" is followed immediately by the redemption of the believing "remnant" at the appearance of Christ. We are not concerned now with the question how this desolation will exactly take place. It is important that, on the one hand, in Israel the spectacular conversion of a "remnant" will take place (see, e.g., Isa. 10:20-23, where we also find again some terms from Dan. 9:27), and that, on the other hand, the mass of Israel will worship this "abomination."

What exactly this "abomination" that brings desolation will be, is also obvious from Daniel, but even more so from Revelation 13. We remember that in the last "week" there will be a firm covenant between the beast and the state of Israel. This is a covenant with "death" and with the "underworld" (*sheôl*), as Israel boasts in Isaiah 28:15, in a situation clearly exhibiting an eschatological dimension, thus forming a typology of the end time. Here again the metahistoric aspects clearly come to light. This covenant of the seventieth "week" is a covenant of the underworld, a diabolical league between the beast, with behind him the dragon, on the one hand, and the unbelieving mass of Israel on the other. This covenant is sealed by an "abomination," an idolatrous image representing the beast and erected by the "beast out of the earth," that is, the "false prophet" (Rev. 13:15; cf. Dan. 3:5-6):

> And he [the false prophet] was granted [power] to give breath to the image of the beast, that the image of the beast would also speak and cause all those not worshipping the image of the beast to be killed.

In my opinion, if we carefully compare Daniel 9, 11 and 12 with Revelation 13, and also adduce Matthew 24:15-21 and 2 Thessalonians 2:4, there can be no doubt that this very ingenious occult image will be erected in a restored temple in Jerusalem.

9.3.4. Zeus Sotèr

The erection of the image in Revelation 13 reminds us, even in its details, of the work of Antiochus IV Epiphanes. This Syrian king of the second century BC, who at the time was also king of Israel, desecrated the temple at Jerusalem, and erected in it an image of Zeus. Therefore, Daniel makes a clear connection between the time of Antiochus and the end time. Christ did the same. He announced in Matthew 24:15 that also in the end time, just before his second coming, there would be an "abomination of desolation" again "in the holy place." This casts light upon a quite striking passage in Daniel 11:36-39. The great exegetical difficulty lies here in the question as to where the description of Antiochus stops and where that of the "end time" (v. 40!) begins. The final part of the chapter can hardly be associated with the life of Antiochus. Possibly verses 36-39 still deal with him, but verses 40-45 are not applicable to him anymore.

Some expositors have pointed to the remarkable fact that, whereas the chapter everywhere speaks of "the king of the North" or "the king of the South," verse 36 briefly speaks of "the king." It has even been presumed that in verse 40 the word "him" refers back to this "king," and that "he" has to be distinguished from both the king of the North and that of the South. However this may be, already in verses 36-39 many expositors see a transition to the situation of the end time, when a wicked "king" will rule over the unbelieving mass of Israel. "The king" is therefore either Antiochus as a type of this future leader, or he is this leader himself. The terminology of verse 36, in comparison with 7:25, 2 Thessalonians 2:4 and Revelation 13:5, clearly suggests an eschatological meaning. Let us now pay attention to verses 37-39:

> And he shall not regard the gods of his father (...) nor regard any other god, for above [them] all he shall magnify himself. And he shall honor the god of fortresses in their place, and the god whom his fathers did not know he shall honor with gold, silver, jewels and precious things. And he shall assault the mighty fortresses with [the help of] the foreign god.

With regard to Antiochus Epiphanes, these words mean that he no longer honored the local Syrian gods, but as a Hellenist worshipped Zeus. The god whose image he placed in the temple at Jerusalem was the Syro-Phoenician god Baal-Shamen, the "lord of heaven," the equivalent of the Greek celestial god, Zeus Olympios, or the Roman celestial god, Jupiter Capitolinus. "Father Zeus," *Zeu pater*, corresponds etymologically with "Jupiter," *Diov pater*, "celestial father," and, by the way, also with the Aryan god, *Dyaus pitar*. Thus, the "god of fortresses" in verse 38 (*èloah maᶜuzzim*; LXX: "the god Maôzeim") is in the first place Jupiter Capitolinus, that is, the Jupiter worshipped in the Capitol, the citadel at Rome, where the great temple of Jupiter stood. The Capitol hill was very important because, according to Roman historian Aurelius Victor (c. 320-c. 390), already before the rise of Romulus' Rome a Babylonian "god" (angelic prince) was worshipped there. Thus, there exists at that place a very ancient connection between the gods of Babylon and the gods of Rome, so that we indeed can state that Baal-Shamen is identical with Zeus, or Jupiter Capitolinus.[25]

By erecting this image of Zeus/Jupiter in the temple at Jerusalem, Antiochus also honored himself on the standpoint that an earthly prince is one with, or is an embodiment of, his angelic prince. Therefore, Antiochus had himself depicted on coins as the god Zeus. Yet the meaning goes deeper, and that is understandable, for we saw that Zeus/Jupiter belongs to a whole complex of divine figures, all seeming to point to the same angelic power. That even holds for certain *goddesses*. The Hebrew does not use a separate word for them, so that the word *èloah* could point here just as well to a "goddess." Cybele, the Phrygian goddess, often represented as a mother goddess and (as we saw) as the "goddess of the key" associated with Janus, is usually depicted with a crown of walls and turrets, that is, with a "fortress" on her head. Also, the "Artemis of the Ephesians" (Acts 19:28, 34) is a mother goddess,

25. Tarn (1978:128-129) has described how the Seleucids restored the ancient Babylonian culture with its pantheon (cf. Martin 1993:133-134). Already Alexander the Great started the restoration of the temples of Bel and Nebo. The Seleucids adopted the gods and the rituals of the Babylonians, even if these ancient Babylonian gods received Greek names. Alexander was convinced that the Babylonian and the corresponding Greek gods were basically identical, for that matter. Thus Baal-Shamen, the "lord of heaven," was regarded as the equivalent of the Greek celestial god, Zeus Olympios. Through the Seleucid Empire many Chaldeans with their gods and customs eventually landed in ancient Rome. It was nothing but the Chaldean-Syrian sun god Bel who in the third century AD was proclaimed by emperor Aurelian to be the official god of the Romans, the *Sol Invictus* (see ch. 5!) (Cumont 1956:22, 120-125, 198-200; 1960:69-75, 89-90; cf. Martin 1993:127-147). Bel = Zeus/Jupiter/Apollo!

as is evidenced by her many breasts; she is the full sister of Apollo. She too is depicted with a "fortress" on her head.[26] As "mother goddesses" these goddesses also blend with Rhea, the wife of Kronos and the mother of Zeus. Since the attributes of Kronos and Zeus merge, we automatically arrive here at Zeus again. And from Zeus we land in the whole circle of chief gods: Osiris, Asshur, Bel/Nebo, Mithra, Wodan, who essentially each represent the same angelic power. The "fortress" is the fortified city, which in its negative meaning of a power hostile to God can be found throughout the Bible, from Cain (Gen. 4:17) to the great Babylon in Revelation 17 and 18.

In the end time, the same will happen as what Antiochus did, namely, that the "false prophet" will erect an image of the beast in the temple at Jerusalem. The connection here goes very far, for in a certain sense it is again an image of the "god of fortresses." The beast is the prince of the Roman Empire, the embodiment of the chief god of Rome. We know this angelic prince as "the dragon," but in Roman tradition this is Jupiter Capitolinus. Perhaps there is nothing that underscores the Roman character of this world-empire of the end time so strongly as the fact that the god – read, angelic prince – of that empire is the same as that of the ancient pagan Rome. In spite of all "Christianization" of that empire and all its "Christian" history, it is still nothing but the same gods that dominate the ancient, and also the restored empire. In the end time, other, associated Roman gods, whom we met in the "Christianized" Rome, particularly Apollo, Cybele and Janus, throw off their "Christian" masks as well. They manifest themselves in their true diabolical form as angels (or even embodiments!) of the dragon, that is, Zeus/Jupiter.

I already briefly indicated that "Zeus" and "Jupiter" are derived from an Indo-European word for "heaven." In Latin, *sub Jove* ("under Jupiter") can mean, "under the open sky." To this must be added that Osiris (Bel, Mithra, Apollo) is the sun

26. See the illustration in Hislop (1959:29).

god. When in Revelation 8:12 and 16:8 judgement is poured out over the "sun," it is the dragon that is struck in this manner: either the sun (god) becomes a plague for the people (16:8-9), or the sun itself is struck and its kingdom darkened (16:10-11). Zeus/Jupiter, or the dragon, is the usurper, the false, rebellious "celestial king," and also that name "celestial king" is a real name for the sun. In paganism of antiquity, the sun was often associated with the dragon (or serpent).

In the view of the Greeks, Zeus resides upon the Olympus, the mount of the gods, where the dragon too tries to find its domicile (cf. Isa. 14:13-14; Ezek. 28:14). But Revelation 12 shows how it is not the Lamb that takes action, but "only" the archangel, Michael, who with his heavenly powers is sufficient to cast Zeus from the Olympus, Jupiter from the Capitol, the dragon from the mount of the gods: "and their place was not found in heaven any longer" (v. 8). Christ already announced, "I saw Satan fall like lightning from heaven" (Luke 10:18). That is not Zeus who as the god of thunder casts lightning and thunder from the mount of the gods, but who himself as a lightning is cast from the "Olympus." In his stead steps the Ninth King, who as a Stone is cut out of the mountain and destroys the Roman colossus (Dan. 2:44-45). He shall appear just as the *lightning* comes from the east and flashes to the west (Matt. 24:27). It is the Lamb himself who deeply humiliates the "celestial king" cast out of heaven by throwing him first, at the beginning of the thousand years, into the "abyss," and after the thousand years into the "lake of fire and sulfur" (Rev. 20:1, 10). There the unholy pseudo-trinity of dragon, beast and false prophet are united in eternity.

Zeus is a "divine" being, that is an imitator of Christ and therein manifests his diabolical character. His grandmother Gaia, the earth goddess, gave birth to Typhon, a horrible monster with a hundred fire-breathing heads and larger than the highest mountain, and she set him against the gods. Zeus attacked the monster, was in danger of being beaten, but finally managed to kill the monster with his flashes of lightning (his hall-mark). In Revelation 12, however, it is "Zeus" himself who is the seven-headed monster that is fought against and like a lightning falls out of heaven. Zeus's well-known outbursts of anger remind us of the devil who is cast on the earth "with great wrath" and in rage turns against the "woman" (Israel) (v. 12, 17).

Remarkable for this great imitator is also his nickname, *Sotèr*, or *Aphesio*, or with the Romans, *Jupiter Liberator*. That is to say, this god presents himself as the great "liberator," whereas in fact he leads the people into slavery (Heb. 2:14-15). Zeus is the god of light, in the Bible he is the prince of darkness (cf. Luke 22:53; 2 Cor. 6:14-15; Eph. 6:12). Jupiter is called the *Optimus Maximus*, the "very good and very great one," but in the Bible he is the embodiment of evil. Even in the earliest Greek legends Zeus is described as a god who was always searching for love-adventures with goddesses, nymphs, and mortal women.[27] To reach his goal he sometimes even appeared in the form of an animal: a swan, as with Leto, or a bull, as with Europa, the daughter of the king of Tyrus. Zeus, in the form of a bull, abducted Europa and fathered with her Minos, the founder of the royal house of Crete. In the fact that a whole continent received the name of this seduced woman a deep thought lies concealed. Zeus is the dragon, the angelic prince of the (mainly European) Roman Empire, the great deceiver of Europe. The Antichrist is the last great embodiment of Zeus/Satan, the "deceiver" (2 John v. 7), the evil spirit that once more, for the last time, will corrupt Europe with its deceptions. We read of the "false prophet" (the beast from the earth; Rev. 13:14),

> It deceives those who dwell on the earth by the signs that he was given to do in the presence of the beast,

---

27. Compare with this the very ancient story, preserved in the Bible, of the "sons of God"—angelic powers—who begot with mortal women "mighty men" (Gen. 6:1-4), as Zeus begot with a mortal woman the hero Heracles (Hercules).

and the "earth" is here the Roman *oikoumenè*, with Europe as its heart.

Chapter 10
The Ninth King

10.1. The Last Battle
10.1.1. Armageddon

No one saved lady Europa from the power of the bull that overpowered and raped her. For centuries it seemed as if no power whatsoever could save the continent Europe from the claws of the dragon, "Zeus," the great angelic prince, the pseudo-deliverer and deceiver. Zeus is too great. The Stoics sang of him in the words of Greek philosopher Cleanthes (c. 330-c. 230) as "the supreme lord of the universe," apart from whom "nothing on earth, nothing in the lofty heaven, nothing in the sea is performed." Even Typhon, the hundred-headed giant monster, was no match for this mighty god. What kind of being does the God of gods have to send in order to overwhelm this angelic prince? A thousand-headed monster, not as large as the highest mountain but as the entire globe? Or a thousand of such monsters?

No. The greatest miracle of the whole Bible, and of all world history, is that the destiny of Europe, and of the whole world, which is in the power of the dragon, lies in the hands of a Lamb. As a symbol one could not imagine a more defenseless animal. A lamb has no claws to tear apart with. It has no teeth to devour with as the muzzle of the dragon

(Job 41:5; Jer. 51:34; Ezek. 29:4). And the summit of defenselessness is a lamb of which the neck is cut through (cf. Rev. 5:6, "standing as slain"). Yet the Lamb prevails over the dragon. By its utter frailty, as slain on Calvary, the Lamb destroys the dragon's supremacy, which threatens everything and seems invincible.

Already during the Babylonian exile there was the dragon by which Israel had been devoured (Jer. 51:34):

> Nebuchadrezzar, king of Babylon, has devoured me,
> he has frightened me,
> he has made me an empty vessel,
> he has swallowed me like a dragon,
> he has filled his belly with my delicacies,
> he has pushed me away.

And when Israel wishes to be delivered out of the Babylonian exile, it thinks back to the exodus out of Egypt, when it was also delivered from the dragon (Isa. 51:9-10):

> Awake! awake! put on strength,
> o arm of YHWH,
> awake as in ancient days,
> [in] the generations of old.
> [Were] you not he who has cut down Rahab,
> who pierced the dragon?
> [Were] you not he who has dried the sea,
> the waters of the great flood [*tehôm*],
> who has made the depths of the sea a way
> for the ransomed to pass through?

At the exodus out of Egypt, Israel's redemption was founded in the blood of the Passover lamb (Exod. 12), and at the exodus out of Babylon, the Redeemer is the suffering Servant of YHWH, who was led as a lamb to the slaughter (Isa. 53:7). In the same way, the great final victory over the dragon lies in the hands of the Lamb. It is against him that the dragon will one day mobilize all his forces and powers:

> And I saw three unclean spirits like frogs coming out of the mouth of the dragon, and out of the mouth of the beast, and out of the mouth of the false prophet; for they are spirits of demons, performing signs, which go out to the kings of the whole earth, to gather them to the battle of the great day of God the Almighty. (...) And he gathered them at the place called in Hebrew, Armageddon (Rev. 16:13-14, 16).

Armageddon presumably means "mountain of Megiddo," and the actual battlefield might thus be the great plains of Jezreel, stretching out at the foot of that mountain. But Armageddon is also translated as "mount of prey," or something similar; *magedon* would then be derived from the Hebrew *gadad*, "to attack, to plunder." In Jeremiah 51:25 we find a similar expression. There we hear of Babylon as a "destroying mountain," and this could be applied to the parallel Rome. Other translations are "fruitful mountain" (Zion?), "desired city" (Jerusalem?), "mountain of his gathering of troops." Of interest is also the interpretation which reads Armageddon as a corruption of *har mo^ced*, "mount of the congregation," which might refer to the mount of the gods in Isaiah 14:13 and Ezekiel 28:14. Is that the place where the great final battle is fought? Even then the word might still have an earthly-geographical meaning, because for Israel in fact Zion was the "mount of the gods," as we saw in Psalm 48:3.

10.1.2. War Against the Lamb

> And the ten horns that you saw are ten kings who [in John's days] have received no kingdom as yet, but they receive authority for one hour as kings with the beast. These are of one mind, and they will give their power and authority to the beast. These will make war with the Lamb, and the Lamb will overcome them—for he is Lord of lords and King of kings—and those [who are] with him, called and elected and faithful ones (Rev. 17:12-14).

In his unimaginable arrogance, the beast, and behind him

the dragon, will venture to enter into battle with the Lamb. After the kings' gathering together at Armageddon (Rev. 16:16), the Lamb will appear. They will turn against him, but the Lamb will destroy them. His name, "Lord of lords and King of kings," indicates the outcome of the battle right away. The Lamb descends from heaven, together with the heavenly saints, who in Revelation 19:14 are described as an army. These are the believers who at that time will dwell in heaven and will descend with Christ from heaven.

> And I saw heaven opened, and behold, a white horse, and he who sat on it is called Faithful and True, and he judges and makes war in righteousness. And his eyes are like a flame of fire, and on his head are many crowns, and he has a written name that no one knows except he himself. And he is clothed with a garment dipped in blood, and his name is called The Word of God. (...) And out of his mouth comes a sharp sword, that with it he should strike the nations. And he will rule them with an iron rod, and he treads the winepress of the wine of the fierceness of the wrath of God Almighty. And he has on his garment and on his hip a written name: King of kings and Lord of lords. (...) And I saw the beast and the kings of the earth and their armies, gathered together to make war against him who sat on the horse and against his army. And the beast was seized, and with him the false prophet (...) Alive these two were cast into the lake of fire burning with sulfur (Rev. 19:11-13, 15-16, 19-20).

There is here, particularly in verses 11-16, a certain parallel with a Roman triumphal procession, in which the chief commander who had gained a great victory rode through Rome, sitting on a white horse, at the head of his army. The striking difference is that here the triumphal tour already begins before the actual victory has been gained. The humble and meek Jesus of Nazareth, who brought grace, is the same as the Christ triumphing in glory, who brings judgment. The weak, insignificant Lamb, destined for the slaughter (cf. 5:6), is in Revelation always *arnion*, a diminutive of *arèn* (related with Latin *aries*, "ram"), and as such is the great counterpart of *Ares*, or Mars, the god of war. According to Greek mythology, the rash Ares was often forced to bite the dust in spite of his enormous strength. Christ is Aries, the Lamb, that makes war with wisdom and forethought, and throughout the many centuries of the eight world-empires in endless patience finally strikes the eighth king, and in him all previous empires. He is the Stone coming down from the mountain and, by hitting the ten toes of iron and clay, strikes and destroys the whole image.

The notion of a Messiah coming again and making war is found elsewhere in the New Testament too,[1] and is also well-known in Jewish literature.[2] The objection of some expositors that a belligerent Messiah would be contrary to Christianity has therefore no basis. That is not to say that the "war" implied here would be a real battle lasting for an extended period of time, in which the fortunes of war would be turned time and again and the outcome would remain uncertain until the very end. Such a long-lasting eschatological battle is found indeed in the Dead Sea Scrolls,[3] but not in the Bible. There is in Revelation 17 and 19 a threat of war, but the matter is decided immediately. The power of the Lamb is so great that there is no question of any real resistance. One could almost speak of a fire breathing Lamb against a dragon (2 Thess. 2:8; cf. Isa. 11:4)!

The battle is depicted in quite a realistic way for that matter. There is a call to arms and a battlefield (16:13-16), there is a going to war (17:14; 19:19), there is a mighty War Lord with battle-horse, sword and rod (19:11, 15), and after the battle there is even a field bestrewn with the dead and wounded

1. Matt. 24:27-28; 25:31, 46; 2 Thess. 2:8.
2. 1 Enoch 60:2; 90:13-19; 2 Baruch 39:7-40:4; 72; 4 Ezra 12:32; 13:1-13; Ass. Mos. 10; Ps.Sal. 17:23-51; Test.Dan. 5:13; Sib.Or. 5:108-110; Pal.Targ.Gen. 49:11.
3. 1QM; 1QH6:25-26.

falling a prey to the birds (19:17f.). Striking is also the bloodstained garment of Christ. People have thought of the martyrs' blood or of Christ's own blood, but especially the apparent parallel with 14:17-20 and Isaiah 63 show that the blood is that of Christ's enemies. It is a symbolism indicating beforehand the certainty of Christ's victory in the coming battle (cf. Isa. 59:17-18).

The Lamb is accompanied with mighty heavenly armies. But that does not mean that they come to carry out judgment, or that the Lamb would need them. He executes judgment alone (Isa. 63:3; cf. Rev. 19:13a, 15b):

> I have trodden the winepress alone,
> and from the nations no one was with me;
> And I have trodden them in my anger
> and trampled them in my fury,
> and their blood sprinkled on my clothes
> and all my garment I have stained.

> The Father judges no one,
> but has given all judgment to the Son (John 5:22, 27).

The heavenly saints are only there to accompany him. It is the "wrath of the Lamb" descending here on his enemies (cf. 6:16-17). It is said of him alone, not of the armies, that a sword goes out of his mouth. If we notice the parallelism between Revelation 19 and Isaiah 63 just quoted, it will strike us that the latter passage speaks of Edom, the hereditary enemy of Jacob. The greatest adversary of the Lamb is the dragon, the angelic prince of Rome, but he is none other than the angelic prince of Edom. Jerusalem asks,

> Who is this, coming from Edom,
> bright-red [his] clothes, from Bozrah?
> [Who is] this, shining in his garment,
> striding in the greatness of his strength?

And the Messiah replies (Isa. 63:1),

> It is I, who speak in righteousness,
> mighty to save.[4]

In Isaiah 34 this judgment over "Edom" (= Rome) is described extensively too, here and there in identical terms.

10.2. The Last Redemption

10.2.1. The Thousand Years

Beside a sword the Lamb has a rod. He not only comes to rule as a Judge, but also to reign as a King. At the same moment when the four world-empires are brought to a definitive and complete end—and not before—the empire is set up

> that in eternity shall not be destroyed and that shall not be left to other people,
> [the empire that] shall shatter and consume [all previous empires],
> [but that itself] shall stand in eternity (Dan. 2:44).

When the Son of Man will come with the clouds of heaven he will be given "authority, glory and sovereignty," and

> all peoples, nations and languages will worship Him;
> his dominion is an everlasting dominion, which shall not pass away,
> and his kingdom shall never be destroyed (Dan. 7:14; cf. v. 18, 27).

In Revelation 19:15 the reign of the King is presented by the term "tending" or "herding." This word (Gr. *poimaino*) is related to "shepherd" (*poimèn*) and "flock" (*poimnè* or *poimnion*), and thus means that the Messiah will tend his subjects as a

4. In the Talmud (Makkot 12a), Resh Lakhish applies Isa. 63:1 ("Who is this who comes from Edom…") to the angelic prince of Edom (= Rome), namely, at the time when Rome's cruelty and the murdering of many innocent people will be punished. According to this rabbi, the prince in this passage looks for a hiding-place in Botzrah to escape judgment. To us it seems evident from the context that YHWH himself is intended here.

shepherd tends his flock.[5]

> The Lamb who is in the midst of the throne will shepherd them
> and lead them to fountains of living waters,
> and God will wipe away every tear from their eyes (7:17).

Whereas the Lamb executes judgment all alone, the heavenly saints will reign with him as kings (cf. 5:10; 20:6; 22:5).

> He who overcomes (...) to him I will give power over the nations;
> and he shall rule them with an iron rod,

is said of the faithful believer as well (2:26-27; cf. Ps. 2:9). In verses 17-18, the armies of the beast and the false prophet are left to the birds of prey that (as it is literally said) fly "in mid-heaven," that is the zenith, the highest point of the ecliptic. That point lies "in mid-heaven," for it is reached at midday. There is a connection here with the angel calling the birds of prey and standing himself "in the sun," that is, surrounded by the sunlight. From the domain of the highest power and the most brilliant glory—in paganism that is the domain of the sun god!—the (symbolic) birds of prey are called forth to throw themselves upon the armies gathered together in Armageddon. But they do not touch the beast and the false prophet; these the Lamb reserves for himself. With the breath of his mouth he himself consumes the "man of sin," the "son of perdition," the "lawless one," and destroys him with the mere brightness of his coming (2 Thess. 2:8; cf. Isa. 11:4). In Revelation 13:4 the bragging question was still heard,

> Who is like the beast,
> and who is able to make war with him?

Who is like Zeus, like Jupiter, the supreme god? Here we learn the answer. Not even a word is lost about some possible colli-

5. Matt. 2:6; cf. 1 Chron. 11:2; Micah 7:14 LXX. The word can also have a negative meaning ("destroy tendingly"; e.g., Jer. 22:22), and some want to read this into Rev. 19:15 too, in my opinion wrongly so.

sion, some clash of arms, or even some skirmish only. The text immediately jumps to the outcome of the battle. The beast and the false prophet are simply seized by the collar and, without first undergoing physical death, are directly thrown into the lake of fire, that is, hell.

> And I saw an angel descending from heaven, having the key to the abyss and a great chain in his hand. And he seized the dragon, the old serpent, that is the Devil and Satan, and bound him [for] a thousand years; and he cast him into the abyss, and closed and sealed it above him, that he should deceive the nations no more till the thousand years were finished (...) and [the deceased saints] became alive and reigned with Christ a thousand years (...) they shall be priests of God and of Christ, and shall reign with him the thousand years (Rev. 20:1-3,4c,6b).

This is not the place to enter into discussions about the precise nature of the "millennial" reign of Christ; to this end see extensively what I have written elsewhere.[6] Yet I cannot withstand pointing to the great church father, Jerome (c. 347-420), who in his commentary on Malachi refers to the Jewish view of the Messianic kingdom. Malachi 1:4-5 speaks of Edom's destruction and the glorification of YHWH beyond the boundaries of Israel. With a certain disdain Jerome mentions that the Jews see in Edom the Romans, and that they indulge the hope that, when the Roman empire will have been destroyed, the rule of the world will come to the Jews.[7] And in his commentary on Daniel, with regard to Daniel 2:34-35, 45, he again

6. See especially Ouweneel (2012).
7. *Judaei falso sibi blandiuntur, Edom Romanos et Israel in consummatione mundi se prophetari: quod destructo Romano imperio, hoc est Idumaeo, regnum orbis veniat ad Judaeos* (quoted by Kocken 1935:7). See for this Jewish interpretation, implying that with the fall of the "Edomite" (= Roman) empire an Israelite world-empire arrives, Flavius Josephus (*Jewish Antiquities*), 4 Ezra, 2 Baruch (see Kocken 1935:6-7; Adamek 1938:27-28). Kocken (1935:6) ventures to write that this Jewish interpretation is "totally different from the Christian view in this connection"! Here the Augustinian view is simply called "the Christian" one; apparently, there is no room for other Christian views.

mentions in a negative way that according to the Jewish expositors the Messianic kingdom will be a *Jewish* kingdom.[8]

Well, this is exactly what I, with many other Christian theologians, believe too. Like the rest of the Augustinian expositors, Jerome did not see that the "people of the saints of the Most High" (Dan. 7:27), which in the Messianic kingdom will form the center of the world,[9] can be nothing but what Daniel necessarily understood by them, namely Israel. In their turn, the Jewish expositors in the Christian era did not see that this "Israelite world-empire" would be headed by Jesus of Nazareth. He is the Son of Man, to whom at his coming again will be entrusted the dominion of the world (v. 13-14). Therefore, it is the kingdom of the Son of Man.[10] But at the same time it certainly is also an *Israelite* world-empire: the kingdom (or, kingship, royal power) is given to the Son of Man, but it is also given to "(the people of) the saints of the Most High" (v. 18, 22): "all powers shall serve and obey *it* [= God's chosen nation][11]" (v. 27).

Like almost all pre-Augustinian church fathers as well as the Jewish expositors, I thus believe that the Messianic kingdom is an infra-temporal kingdom (that is, embedded in common time and history), and is to be distinguished from the eternal state of the new heavens and the new earth. The kingdom of the Son of Man is erected after his second coming, and not at his birth or his ascension. The foundation of that kingdom will imply the destruction of all diabolical powers that throughout the centuries have dominated the world-empires, and particularly have threatened Israel. This is the empire of the Ninth King. He was there all the time, and behind the

8. *(...) quod Judaei (...) male ad populum referunt Israel, quem in fine saeculorum* [nl. after the destruction of the Roman empire] *volunt esse fortissimum, et omnia regna conterere, et regnare in aeternum* (Kocken (1935:7).
9. See Isa. 2:2-3 (= Micah 4:1-2); 56:1-8; 60:8-16; Zech. 8:23.
10. Thus also Matt. 13:41, "the Son of Man... his kingdom."
11. This seems to me the proper translation; others believe that the word rendered "it," although it literally is in the singular, to refer back to the plural word for "Most High."

scenes of world history he continuously had all the threads in his hands. Therefore, this whole book deals in fact with the Ninth King, not just this last (briefest) chapter. But at the end he *manifests* himself in power and majesty, and establishes his kingdom in a *visible* way on earth, as an *infra-temporal* kingdom, with *Israel* as its center. Concerning these evident facts there should in fact be no discussion among conservative expositors anymore today.

The dragon had inspired the campaign against the Lamb (Rev. 16:13-16). Like unclean frogs his ghostly companions had hopped through the earth to drive the kings of the earth to the ultimate war. Now an angel from heaven (perhaps Michael again?) descends to seize the dragon that before had been cast on the earth by the archangel. He is bound with a chain and thrown into the abyss. We have seen in Revelation 9 that this is perhaps the underworld, the realm of the spirits, *hades*. In chapter 9 a key was needed to release evil powers from the abyss; here a key is needed to shut up the most evil power in the abyss. The aim of this is that during the Messianic reign of the Lamb he will not deceive the people any longer. At the end of the thousand years he is released for a short time to bring to light that even the most blessed circumstances as such cannot change the heart of man (20:7-10). He unleashes a rebellion, which is suppressed immediately. Then the devil himself is also cast into the lake of fire, where he, as the beast and the false prophet, is to be tormented in all eternity.

This book has referred already several times to the Messianic kingdom of peace, in which Christ reigns for a thousand years as the Son of Man (Rev. 20:4c). Revelation 11:15 announces:

> The kingdom of the world of our Lord [YHWH] and of his Christ [Messiah] has come.

It is the time when it will become fully manifest that Christ is "the ruler over the kings of the earth" (1:5). It is the time when Christ will sit on his throne, the throne of David (Luke

1:32-33), as he now with his Father is still sitting in heaven on the Father's throne (Rev. 3:21). The saints *shall* "reign over the earth" (5:10); that is no present reality yet, as the manifest reign of the Son of Man is not either. The New Jerusalem, in whose light the nations will walk, and into which the kings of the earth will bring their glory (21:24), is still a blueprint for the future.

10.2.2. The Restoration of Israel

The dragon, the angelic prince of the Roman Empire, is the angelic prince of "Edom." After centuries of conflict and oppression, in the ultimate victory of the Messiah over the dragon, Jacob will finally prevail over Edom. Jacob is not every Jew as such, but "a remnant will return" (Isa. 10:21), "a remnant according to the election of grace" (Rom. 11:5). When the wicked of Israel as well as the nominal Christians and the ungodly gentiles will have been judged, the new Israel of the Messianic kingdom will be built from the "rest" of Israel. Therefore, Romans 11:25-26 can say that, when the Deliverer will come out of Zion, *all* Israel will be saved. Israel will be the center of the Messianic kingdom of peace on earth:

> And it shall come to pass in the latter days,
> then the mountain of the house of YHWH shall be firm as the highest of the mountains,
> and it shall be exalted above the hills.
> And peoples shall flow to it,
> and many nations shall come up and say,
> Come, let us go up to the mountain of YHWH,
> to the house of the God of Jacob (!),
> that he will teach us concerning his ways,
> and that we walk in his paths.
> For out of Zion the law shall go forth,
> and the word of YHWH from Jerusalem.
> And he shall judge between many peoples,
> and administer justice over mighty nations even in far countries.

> Then they shall beat their swords into plowshares,
> and their spears into pruning knives;
> no nation shall lift up sword against another nation,
> and they shall learn war no more.
> But they shall sit, everyone under his vine and under his fig tree,
> without any one frightening them;
> for the mouth of YHWH of hosts has spoken.
> For all peoples walk each in the name of his god,
> but we will walk in the name of YHWH, our God,
> forever and ever (Micah 4:1-5; cf. Isa. 2:2b-5).

Notice this remarkable last verse: the nations, the empires, all had followed their own god, that is, their own angelic prince. But Israel walks in the name of the God of gods, who in the person of the Messiah will prevail one day over all angelic princes. It has not always been like this; often Israel too has been in the power of foreign angelic princes. Therefore, it says at its conversion (Isa. 26:13),

> YHWH, our God, other masters besides you have ruled over us;
> [now] your name alone we honor.

Nowhere is this metahistorical restoration of Israel from the claws of the diabolical powers depicted in a more beautiful and acute way than in the book of Zechariah. Already in the first chapter, the prophet pictures a man on a red horse, standing between the myrtle trees in the deep places, and behind him red, sorrel, and white horses (v. 8). This "man" is either the angel of YHWH himself, that is, the pre-incarnate Christ, or he is another angel reporting to the angel of YHWH (v. 11).[12] The color red seems to point again to war and death (cf. Isa. 63:1-2; Rev. 19:13). The myrtle trees are presumably a

---

12. Rabbi Berekhiah (c. 340) sees in him the angelic prince of Rome (Aggad. Beresh. 56 [40a]): "Hard/bad (or: The hardest/worst) is the angelic prince of Edom [= Rome], for thus Zechariah has seen him" (1:8). The three kinds of horses would then represent the Roman emperors, led by their angelic prince, the man on the red horse.

foreboding of the Messianic blessing (cf. Neh. 8:15; Isa. 41:19; 55:13). Here they are standing in the "deep places," which possibly refers to the Kidron valley (at the foot of the Mount of Olives), where indeed myrtle trees grow. This ravine is possibly a picture of Israel's low state at the time of Zechariah, and the myrtle trees thus form a ray of hope for better times. Behind the horseman apparently other angels are coming (cf. v. 10).

The mission of the group of heavenly messengers is "to range the earth" and to size up the situation there (v. 10-11). They report to the angel of YHWH and announce that all the "earth," that is here, the Persian Empire, is resting quietly, but that Judah is still sighing under foreign dominion and is oppressed. The angel of YHWH intercedes for the tormented people, and YHWH answers with "good words, comforting words" (v. 12-17). He announces that Jerusalem and the temple will be restored, and that he will bless Zion. In the prophecies, such a promise always has an eschatological "depth-layer," that is to say, finds its final fulfillment in the Messianic kingdom of peace to be founded after the second coming of Christ.[13] The promise therefore goes much further than the rebuilding of the temple in the days of Zechariah, and points toward the Messianic era, as especially chapter 14 makes clear.

That which is described in this Scripture has a universal, significant bearing: while the world is busy with its own affairs and only works for its own economic, political and military interests, God is concerned with the miserable state of Israel.

In the light of Zechariah 6:1-8 (see below), one may wonder if the "horsemen" in verse 8 might not be the angelic princes of the three world-empires left: the Persian, the Macedonian, and the Roman angelic prince. This the more so because verses 18-21, too, clearly seem to refer to the four world-empires, as was taught already by Jerome.[14] The empires are

13. See extensively Ouweneel (1991), especially ch. 6.

14. *Commentary on Zechariah* (cf. Kocken 1935:52-53).

compared to four "horns," which have each pushed and scattered Israel, but which each in its turn are broken by a "craftsman." If the four "horns" represent the angelic princes of the four world-empires, the "craftsmen" are the angelic powers that successively broke the power of the empires. The striking point here is that the first three empires were each broken by the very next empire. It was the angelic prince of Persia who struck the one of Babylon, the angelic prince of Greece–Macedonia who struck the one of Persia, etcetera. If this reasoning is correct, each "craftsman" himself becomes a "horn." But the last "craftsman," breaking the Roman Empire, is no common angelic prince, but the angel of YHWH, the Messiah, the Lamb.

10.2.3 Horses and Horsemen

In Zechariah 3 we see that the miserable state of Israel had not been caused by the gentiles only, but basically was the consequence of its own sins. Even the priesthood, which mediated between YHWH and his people, was unclean. Israel's future was therefore not just a political affair; behind the scenes of its earthly history a heavenly conflict took place, as in Job 1 and 2. The high priest, Joshua, clothed with filthy garments, who represented Jerusalem (cf. v. 2), stood before the heavenly judgment seat; Satan was the accuser, and the angel of YHWH was the defender. The outcome of this law suit is the mercy of the Judge: the sins are not glossed over, but blotted out by God's electing grace. Angels carried out this cleansing (v. 4), and the high priest received access among these heavenly beings (v. 7c).

Here again the lines are drawn toward the Messianic era: Joshua and his priestly companions are "wondrous signs," pointing forward to the time of God's Servant, the Branch, when the Israelites will invite each other under the vine and under the fig tree (v. 8-10). Then again Israel will be like a brand plucked from the fire, as at the time it had been plucked from the fire of Babylon (cf. v. 2). The restoration of the priesthood depicted here looks forward to the Messianic kingdom of peace, when Israel in the full sense will be a priestly kingdom and a holy nation (cf. Exod. 19:6; Isa. 61:6).

In Zech. 6:1-8 we find a vision similar to the two in chapter 1. Here again angelic powers are presented as horses and horsemen, and here again one of the four powers seems to execute judgment upon the other, as in the case of the horns and the craftsmen. The angelic powers make use here of chariots, as we known them from the sun god, for instance among the Assyrians (cf. the "chariots of the sun" in 2 Kings 23:11) and the Greeks. Possibly the "mountains of bronze" in verse 1 are like the brazen pillars before the temple in Jerusalem, thus marking the entrance to God's heavenly palace. "Your righteousness is like the mountains of God," says Psalm 36:7, and the bronze underscores this. It is a symbol of divine righteousness, testing man according to his responsibility (compare the brazen altar), and is thus connected with judgment.

In this Scripture, something of the movements of the four angelic princes in their relation to Israel is revealed to us. From the heavenly palace, "their station before the Lord of all the earth" (v. 5b), the four chariots sprawl to the four winds of heaven. Thus they are themselves like "winds," that is, spirits, or angels. As the angelic princes believe, they act according to their own power and intelligence, but in reality they are only rods, staffs, axes, saws, hammers, and clubs in the hand of the God of gods (cf. Isa. 10:5, 15; Jer. 50:23; 51:20). Let us now look at verses 6-8:

> As to the [chariot] at which are the black horses, [these] go out to the north country.
> And the white go out after them [or, backward from them, i.e., to the west].[15]

15. Our maps are oriented towards the north, but those of antiquity are oriented (! orient = east!) to the east. Standing with the face turned eastward one has the west behind the back. Therefore, if one goes westward, one goes as it were "backward."

And the dappled go to the south country.
And the strong horses went out, and they insisted to go ranging the earth.
And he said, "Go, range the earth."
And they ranged the earth.
And he called me, and spoke to me saying,
"See, those who have gone out to the north country
have given rest to my Spirit in the north country."

Mysterious words, often too easily passed over by the expositors. Thus, many have not recognized in the number "four" a hint to the four world-empires.[16] The north country is, as so often in Scripture, Babylon. The first chariot, the one with the red horses, is not mentioned in verse 6. This is the angelic prince, Bel, who founded there a mighty empire, that of Nebuchadrezzar. It is an empire, however, that brought "unrest" to the Spirit of YHWH (v. 8), and the book of Daniel makes it sufficiently clear in what sense this is to be understood. Therefore, judgment comes upon this angelic prince, namely, by means of the second angelic prince, the chariot with the black horses. This prince, the one of Medo-Persia (Dan. 10:13, 20), brings judgment upon Babylon, thus giving rest to the Spirit of YHWH. Jeremiah 51:11b says,

YHWH has raised up the spirit of the kings of Media,
for against Babylon is his plan to destroy it;
for this is the revenge of YHWH.[17]

But then we see a third power coming up. Two translations are possible here, which both give a good meaning. If we translate that the white horses go out "after" the black ones, the idea is that Alexander the Great in his turn put an end to the Medo-Persian Empire and conquered its territory (cf. Dan. 8:20-21; 11:1-3). If we translate that the white horses go out to the "west," the idea is that the Greek angelic prince

16. This was recognized by Cyrillus of Alexandria and Jerome, for instance (see Kocken 1935:5, 36-37, 52-54).
17. Cf. Isa. 13:17-19; 21:1-2; Jer. 25:12-14; 27:6-8; 51:28.

rather founded an empire in the West, namely, on European soil. It is striking that Daniel 8 so strongly emphasizes these wind-directions. The Medo-Persian "ram" pushes westward, northward, and southward, the chief directions of his power. But then from the very West the Greek-Macedonian "male goat" comes rushing along, overthrowing and trampling the "ram." The third empire is therefore explicitly a Western power.

The fourth angelic prince has a chariot with dappled, strong horses. Of course, Rome is also a Western power, but it has also stretched out its hand to the south country. According to Daniel 11, this is Egypt, which in verse 30 is visited by the "ships of the Kittim," a first reference to the Romans, who eventually conquered the Ptolemaic empire. But the Roman Empire is not a typically "Western" or "Southern" power; with the permission from Above it ranges the whole earth (v. 7).

10.3. The Last Empire

10.3.1. Shepherd and King

It is remarkable that Zechariah 6 does not yet digress on the destiny of the fourth, Roman angelic prince. His decline and that of all nations that have oppressed Israel is depicted in chapter 12-14. All peoples of the earth will gather together at Jerusalem (12:3, 9; 14:2). But YHWH himself, in the person of the Messiah, will appear on the Mount of Olives. It can hardly be doubted that the literal Mount of Olives is intended here; this also seems to be implied in the words of the angels to the apostles (Acts 1:11-12). We have to do here with the destruction of all nations marching against Jerusalem and with the deliverance of the city and its inhabitants. The converts in Israel will confess their sins and look on him whom they have pierced (12:10). There will be a fountain opened for them in view of sin and the cleansing from it (13:1).

It is peculiarly striking that this very Scripture draws all attention to the *suffering* Messiah again. His sorrows are the foundation for Israel's final redemption. He is the Pierced One and the Firstborn in 12:10. He is the humble Man tilling the ground, acquired to this end through the sins of the first Adam, the Man in whose hands the wounds have been inflicted and who has been beaten in the house of his friends (13:5-6).[18] He is God's Shepherd, the Man who is his Companion, and against whom the sword of God has awaked, the Shepherd who has been stricken that "the little ones" may be saved (13:7). And he is the very same as YHWH, who will gather all nations to battle against Jerusalem (14:2). Once more he will even allow that during the great tribulation of Israel, the "time of Jacob's trouble" (Jer. 30:7; cf. Dan. 12:1), the city is taken, the houses are rifled, the women ravished, and half of the inhabitants go into captivity. But

> then YHWH will go forth to fight against those nations,
> as he fought before, in the day of battle;
> in that day his feet will stand on the Mount of Olives...
> and YHWH, my God, will come, all the saints with you (14:2-5).

That is the appearance of the Man on the white horse in Revelation 19, with his heavenly armies, making war against the dragon, the beast, and the false prophet. But the importance of Zechariah 14 and related Scriptures is that this final battle is immediately connected with the restoration of Jerusalem. In Revelation 19, too, Armageddon is related with Israel, possibly (as explained before) even with Zion or Jerusalem; but Zechariah 14 deals far more clearly with the restoration of Jacob. When YHWH/Christ will become King over all the earth, Jerusalem will have been gloriously restored and rebuilt, and have become a safe place (14:9-11). This *restoration* of the *ancient* Jerusalem is in no way to be confused with the *New* Jerusalem. The restored Jerusalem is the earthly, the New Jerusalem the heavenly capital of the Messianic kingdom of peace.

The wealth of all the surrounding nations will be gathered

18. See for this interpretation of Zech. 13:5-6 Ouweneel (1995).

together in Jerusalem, and all those who survive the final battle will go up from year to year to worship the King, YHWH of hosts, and to keep the feast of tabernacles (14:14, 16). This is not the state of the new heavens and the new earth, for there it will be impossible that, for instance, the Egyptians withdraw from the command by not turning up at the feast of tabernacles in Jerusalem (14:17-19). Neither is the present situation in the Church of God described here, for then the whole presentation has to be spiritualized away, apart from the fact that the fulfillment of this blessed state is strictly linked with the second coming of Christ. No serious expositor can "explain" Zechariah 14:8-21 in such a way that these verses could be fulfilled before the second coming of verses 1-7.

There is another striking point in the very last words of Zechariah:

> and there shall no longer be a Canaanite
> in the house of YHWH of hosts in that day.

For "Canaanite" one could also read "merchant." We find the same word in the same ambiguous meaning in Hosea 12:8 (compare the various translations and marginal notes), where the "Canaanite/merchant" holds "deceitful scales" in his hand: "he loves to extort." *The* Canaanite pre-eminently is the god Baal, the "lord" of the land of Canaan, the same as the Babylonian god Bel. As we have seen, this is the same as the Greek god Hermes, who is identical with the Roman god Mercury, the god of commerce, and the god of thieves as well. Hermes/Mercury comes "as a thief in the night," while gods and men are asleep. Hardly born he already begins stealing. This deceitful god, who in many regards is also the same as Osiris/Apollo, is looming up once more at the end of Zechariah in a mysterious way. When one day Christ will be King over people, city, and temple, there will be no room anymore for the greatest deceiver of all times (John 8:44).

10.3.2. Again: Horses and Horsemen

It is striking to see how some expositors try to discredit the literal interpretation of these and similar prophecies by emphasizing that Zechariah 12:4 and 14:15, 20 only speak of horsemen and horses, whereas present-day armies dispose of the most advanced weapons. Of course, even if the eschatological armies would dispose of tanks and missiles, it is hardly to be expected that Zechariah would mention them in his description. But there might be a deeper reason. In Zechariah 1 and 6, too, we found horses and horsemen, but there they turned out to be a symbolic reference to angelic powers. Why could this not be the case particularly in Zechariah 12:4 (not so much in 14:20), too? Is YHWH only concerned with earthly nations and rulers? Not rather with the spiritual powers behind them? In Exodus 15:1, rabbinical tradition refers "the horse and its rider" not to Pharaoh, but to the angelic prince of Egypt. Why could in Zechariah 12:4, too, the "horses and riders" not primarily imply that the spiritual powers will be stricken with confusion and madness?

There are two interesting examples of such horsemen and horses representing spiritual powers in the life of Elijah and Elisha. First, I think of the chariots of fire and the horses of fire that took Elijah to heaven (2 Kings 2:11). Elisha connected this right away with the spiritual power of Elijah himself, as if Elijah represented in his person the whole army of Israel: "The chariots of Israel and its horsemen" (v. 12). Secondly, even clearer is 2 Kings 6:15-17, where Elisha tells his servant, who was scared by the horses and chariots of the enemy:

> "Do not be afraid, for those who are with us are more than those who are with them." And Elisha prayed and said, "YHWH, please open his eyes that he may see." And YHWH opened the eyes of the young man, and he saw, and behold, the mountain was full of horses and chariots of fire all around Elisha.

The literal, visible horses and chariots of the enemy found their counterpart in the—normally—invisible "fiery" horses and chariots of the angelic powers that protected Elisha. These powers remind us of the "seraphs" in Isaiah 6:2, 6, a group of angelic beings whose name means something like "fiery beings." Also notice the link between God's angelic servants and "flaming fire" in Psalm 104:4.

10.3.3. Once More: Jacob and Esau

The most important adversary of Jacob is the angelic prince of Esau. One day "the Star will rise out of Jacob, the Scepter out of Israel," which refers to the coming of the Messiah and the arrival of the kingdom of God:

> and Edom, Israel's enemy, shall have been conquered;
> and Israel shall act valiantly,
> and he will rule out of Jacob,

as Balaam already prophesied (Num. 24:17-19). We saw that, according to a Jewish tradition, the "Edomite" empire fights with Israel "till dawn," that is, till the end of Israels' exile, which terminates at the coming of Messiah's kingdom.[19]

I have argued before that Jacob/Israel has never given up Esau/Edom. It has never forsaken Western culture, particularly Europe, on the contrary, it occupies crucial posts in that culture, and later also the other Western parts of the world (think of the enormous significance of the Jews in American culture). Jacob/Israel grasps Esau and will not let him go "until the day breaks," no matter how much it has been smitten by Esau. It does not do so in order to destroy Edom, but precisely that Edom will own Israel's birthright and will convert to the God of Israel. "Salvation is out of the Jews" (John 4:22).

For the angelic prince of Rome there is no hope; his end is in the lake of fire and sulfur (Rev. 20:10). For Western culture as such, by and large, there is no hope either; the beast undergoes the same destiny as the dragon who deceived him. But the blessing that the angel gave to Jacob does imply that *within* Western culture there are those who in the end time

19. Tankh.wayyishlach 40b.

will own Israel as God's people, and own God as the God of Israel (Zech. 8:23):

> In those days [it will be] that ten men from all languages of the nations shall grasp,
> even grasp the sleeve of a Jewish man, saying,
> "Let us go with you, for we have heard [that] God [is] with you."

In the end, it will turn out to be impossible to believe in the God of Israel and the Messiah of Israel without blessing Israel itself. There will be no blessing for the *goyyim* without blessing Abraham and his seed (Gen. 12:3; 27:29).

When the angelic prince of Edom/Rome will be judged, it will be peace for all "Edomites" who have put their trust in the God of Jacob and his Anointed. Both in the Bible and in rabbinical tradition the restoration of Israel is connected with the fall of the angelic prince of Edom/Rome as well as with the coming of the Messiah and the erection of his kingdom, in which the restored Israel will take up the central place.

> God will begin with driving out the angelic prince of the "great city" from his [heavenly] dwelling-place.[20]

This great city is either "Babylon," that is Rome (cf. Rev. 16:19), or it is the heavenly city. It is the Messiah who will destroy Edom/Rome, and who subsequently will reign from sea to sea (Ps. 72:8); the wicked Edom will therefore remain in power until the Messiah comes.[21] God will return to his temple at Jerusalem, as Ezekiel 40-48 describes extensively, when he will have brought retribution on wicked Edom.[22] The Messiah will come when Rome will fall into the thorns, that is, will be torn apart.[23]

Edom will fall through the hand of him who has been

20. Pesiqta R. 14,15.
21. Pesiqta R. 13,2 (on Num. 24:18-19).
22. Pesiqta K. Suppl. 5,3.
23. SoS.R. 2:17 (§1) (rabbi Levi).

anointed for war, the descendant of Joseph.[24] According to Jewish tradition, Messiah ben Joseph is the great fighter of the end time and the forerunner of the actual Messiah, Messiah ben David. Thus, also in Jewish tradition there is the vivid notion that one day it will be the Messiah who will defeat the angelic prince of Edom/Rome, will destroy the hostile powers, will restore Israel in its land, will rebuild the temple in which again the glory of YHWH will come and dwell, and will establish his blessed reign of peace and righteousness from sea to sea.

Seven world-empires have successively oppressed Israel. The Pharaoh of Egypt committed the first holocaust by putting the people to slavery and by massively killing their sons. Adolf Hitler carried out the seventh oppression, the last and most horrible holocaust that Israel has ever experienced so far. But the end is not yet. There still has to come the eighth empire, the revival of the empire of Edom/Rome, that is the empire of the Antichrist, the dragon, the beast. And that empire, too, will once more bring a great tribulation on the so terribly tormented Jacob. Once more, Edom will try to smash Jacob. We saw how in this eighth empire the features of Egypt become visible, how Assyria seems to revive in it, how characteristics of each of the four great world-empires become manifest in it, how the beast will even appear to be a new and greater Napoleon and Hitler. But then the end will be. Then comes the ninth and last King; there will be no tenth anymore. One day Jacob's trouble will have come to an end.

> The people that walk in darkness
> see a great light;
> those who dwell in the land of the shadow of death,
> upon them dawns a light.
> You have multiplied the nation,
> You have increased its joy;
> they rejoice before you [Lord]

24. Gen.R. 99,2.

as men are glad about the harvest,
as men jubilate when dividing the spoil.
For the yoke of his burden,
and the staff on his shoulder,
the rod of his oppressor,
You have broken as in the day of Midian.[25]
For every sandal of the warrior in the battle,
and [each] garment rolled in blood,
will be [used] for burning,
fuel for the fire.
For unto us a Child is born,
unto us a Son is given,
and the government is upon his shoulder,
and his name is called
Wonderful Counselor,[26]
Mighty God,
Everlasting Father,
Prince of Peace.
Of the increase of [his] government
and of the peace [there will be] no end
upon the throne of David and over his kingdom,
because he founds and maintains it
with judgment and justice,
from now on into eternity.
The zeal of YHWH of hosts will do this.[27]

---

25. This is the day when Gideon defeated the Midianites (Judg. 7). Just as he, with a handful of men, slew an army "as numerous as locusts" with their leaders (cf. Judg. 7:12, 25; Isa. 10:26), thus the Messiah, all on his own, defeats both the "locusts" of Rev. 9 and their leader, Abaddon/Apollyon, the dragon and all his powers.
26. Or, "Wonderful, Counselor."
27. Isa. 9:1-6.

Appendix 1: Angels and Demons

IN THE FRAMEWORK OF THIS STUDY, it is useful to make some general remarks about angels and demons. The Hebrew *malakh* comes from the verb (not occurring in the Bible) *la'akh*, "to send (with a mission)," and thus means literally "[someone] sent (with a mission)," that is, "messenger, ambassador." In the Septuagint, this word is represented by the Greek word, *angelos*, derived from the verb *angello*, "to announce, to send a message" (John 20:18). In classical Greek, *angelos* refers to a (human) "herald," but in the Septuagint, and later in the New Testament, the word could also refer to a celestial messenger. In the meaning, "messenger," *mal'akh* and *angelos* can simply be used for humans too.[1]

Even where "messengers of God" are intended, these are sometimes humans: the prophet, the priest, or even the whole nation of Israel.[2] In cases where no humans are intended the terms refer to celestial messengers or servants of God. In the Vulgate, the Latin version of the Bible, the human *mal'akh* or *angelos* was represented by the Latin word, *nuntius*, but the celestial messenger was referred to as *angelus*, which so far in Latin had been an unknown word. Through Latin, the word landed in a corrupt form in modern languages: *engel* (Dutch and German), *angel* (Eng.), *ängel* (Swedish), *ángel* (Span.), *ange*

1. See, for instance, Gen. 32:3; Num. 20:14; Judg. 9:31; Luke 7:24; 9:52; James 2:25..
2. Eccl. 5:5; Isa. 42:19; Hagg. 1:13; Mal. 2:7; 3:1; Matt. 11:10.

(Fr.), *angelo* (Ital.), etcetera.

They are not eternal but created beings.[3] They are "spiritual," that is, immaterial creatures, or perhaps more accurately, "material" in a different way than we are.[4] They are beings with their own personality, will, understanding and feeling. This is shown, for instance, by their outstanding character, their benevolence towards humans, and their obedience to God.[5] The angels' lofty character is shown particularly by the nature of the missions which they receive from God. They are sent to humans as messengers with very different missions: bringing messages;[6] executing judgment and chastisement;[7] bringing deliverance, benefits, blessing;[8] guiding, and assisting at, human tasks;[9] giving interpretation,[10] etcetera. Their task as heavenly servants of God comes to light, among other things, in the fact that they form his heavenly household, surrounding his throne, and his retinue when he marches out.[11] As servants, they are even referred to as "slaves."[12] They bring those fallen asleep into the bliss with God (Luke 16:22). They themselves are clothed with the splendor of heaven.[13]

The honor and the service that the angels render to God, are also rendered to Christ on earth. The angels served him, were at his disposal in numerous numbers, and even strength-

3. Col. 1:16; cf. John 1:3; Ezek. 28:15.
4. Heb. 1:13-14; cf. Luke 24:39.
5. Cf. 1 Sam. 29:9; 2 Sam. 14:17, 20; 19:27; Luke 15:10.
6. See, for instance, Gen. 18; 22:19-23; Matt. 1:20; 2:13, 19; Luke 1:11-20, 26-38; Acts 8:26; 10:3-7, 30-32; 11:13-14; 27:23-24; cf. Acts 7:53; Gal. 3:19; Heb. 2:2.
7. See, for instance, Gen. 19; 2 Sam. 24:16-17; 2 Kings 19:35; Matt. 16:27; 24:30-31; 25:31; 2 Thess. 1:7-8.
8. See, for instance, 1 Kings 19:5-7; Luke 22:43.
9. See, for instance, Gen. 32:1-2; 2 Kings 6:17; Ps. 91:11; Acts 5:19-20; 12:7-10.
10. See, for instance, Ezek. 40:3-4; Zech. 1:9, 19; 2:1-3; 4:1, 5; 5:5, 10; 6:4.
11. See, for instance, Deut. 33:2; Dan. 7:10; Ps. 68:18; Heb. 12:22; Rev. 5:11.
12. Rev. 19:10; 22:8-9.
13. Isa. 6:1-4; Ezek. 1 and 10; Matt. 28:2-3; Luke 2:9; 24:4; Acts 1:10; 6:15.

ened him in his suffering.[14]

Particularly due to a tradition nourished by the visual arts, angels are imagined as effeminate young men in white garments and with large birds' wings. As to the wings, we only know these in Scripture in the case of the cherubs and seraphs.[15] The cherubs (Heb. *kherub*, "he who blesses, prays [for someone]") are the bearers of the "theophany," the manifestation of God.[16] In Gen. 3:24, they are the guardians of the garden of Eden, and in Ezek. 28:14, 16, we hear of a protecting cherub on God's holy mount (cf. Appendix 10). Seraphs are literally something like "fiery beings," fire-angels, and only occur in Isa. 6.

The actual *mal'akh* is, when appearing to humans, never a winged being. He looks like an earthly being, and cannot be distinguished from a common man.[17] Please note: this concerns appearances. Of themselves, angels are spiritual, or possibly other-material beings, who, when appearing to humans, apparently have to assume an earthly form for the time being. When appearing to humans in visions, of course, the case is different again. Then they sometimes appear in a radiant, supra-earthly form (see, for instance, Dan. 10:5-6).

I leave out the peculiar figure of the "Angel of YHWH," because a study of this fascinating figure would carry us too far.[18]

We now come to the subject of "demons." These too are beings with their own will and feelings.[19] They are very intelligent too; Plato derived the word *daimôn* from a word meaning "knowing" or "intelligent," although not all interpreters agree with this. Scripture emphasizes time and again the demons' cunningness and understanding: they know Jesus,

14. Matt. 4:11; 26:53; Luke 22:43.
15. Exod. 25:20; 1 Kings 6:24; Ezek. 1:6; 10:2, 5, 20-21; Isa. 6:2.
16. 2 Sam. 22:11; Ps. 18:11; 99:1; Ezek. 9:3; 10:1-9, 15-20; 11:22.
17. Cf. Gen. 18:2 with 19:1; see Judg. 6:11, 21-22; 13:3, 6, 8-11, 21.
18. See extensively Ouweneel (2007:§7.3).
19. Mark 5:10; Luke 4:34.

bow down before him, and own him as the Son of the Most High God,[20] they recognize that there can be no communion between him and them, and ask favors of him,[21] obey him, and are aware of their eternal destination,[22] they are active in corrupting the truth and spreading falsehood.[23] It is even said of them that they believe in God, but they do so trembling; they cast themselves down before Christ, but they do so with hatred, not out of love.[24]

Very often, the demons are called "unclean."[25] Their corrupted nature is illustrated in the behavior of the demonically possessed, who sometimes manifest the desire to live naked, and that in such unclean places as graves, or to enter such unclean animals as pigs.[26] In the possessed, they can unchain terrible diseases and also a devilish strength.[27] Their power is indeed enormous. They can make direct use of the forces of nature to immerge humans into suffering.[28] This is often ascribed to Satan personally, but since Satan is neither omnipresent, nor omnipotent, nor omniscient, as God is, no doubt the execution of his actions usually takes place through his servants. If we read in 1 Peter 5:8 that he walks about like a "roaring lion, seeking whom he may devour," it is obvious that he walks about with a host of demons, for he is "the prince of the power of the air" (Eph. 2:2).

Since the demons serve and follow Satan as their king, like him they are adversaries of God. This comes to light in a special way in the life of Christ, God's Son: in the beginning of his service, Satan personally tries to seduce him,[29] afterwards

20. Mark 1:24; 5:6-7.
21. Luke 8:28, 31.
22. Matt. 8:16, 29.
23. 1 Tim. 4:1-3; 1 John 4:1-3.
24. James 2:19; Mark 3:11.
25. Matt. 10:1; Mark 1:27; 3:11; Luke 4:36; Acts 8:7; Rev. 16:3.
26. Luke 8:27; Mark 5:12.
27. Matt. 9:32-33; 12:22; Mark 9:18, 22; Luke 8:26-36; 13:11-17.
28. Job 1:12, 16, 19; 2:7; also cf. Mark 4:39.
29. Matt. 4:1-11; Mark 1:12-13; Luke 4:1-13.

he personally enters Judas, so that the latter will betray his Lord, and he manages to make Peter deny his Lord.[30] In spite of their hatred towards God and his Anointed, however, they are limited in their power, they can never go any further than God allows them to go, and in many ways they are even instruments in God's hand to help carry out his plans, whether this regards unbelievers,[31] or believers.[32]

30. Luke 22:3, 31; John 13:2, 27.
31. 1 Kings 22:19-23; Ps. 78:49; Rev. 16:13-16.
32. Job 42:5-6; Luke 22:31; 1 Cor. 5:5; 1 Tim. 1:20.

Appendix 2: The "Gods" As God's Household

THE INTERPRETATION OF PSALM 82 given in this study—the "gods" are angelic powers, is strongly supported by other psalms, which give a similar picture. In Psalm 97:7b, 9, the call is heard,

> bow down before him, all [you] gods...
> For you, YHWH, [are the] Most High over all the earth,
> you are exalted far above all gods.

In Psalm 29, we see God in his "palace" (cf. 11:4), where all say, "Glory!" (v. 9), where all surround the throne of YHWH (v. 10), and where the call is heard (v. 1),

> Ascribe to YHWH, [you] sons of God,
> ascribe to YHWH glory and strength.

The Hebrew expression for "sons of God" is here *bené elim*. *Elim* is the plural of *el*, "god" or "God," not to be confused with *elohim*, which is the plural of *eloah* (a form which occurs particularly in the book of Job), and which means "gods," or God (in the latter case the plural form refers to a bundling of forces in God, or it is a majestic plural). In the expression, *bené elim*, the expression *ben*, "son," is of importance too. Here, "son of" does not mean "begotten by," but "belonging to," as so often in Hebrew.[1] "Sons of the *elim*" are therefore beings with the quality *el* (= lit. "strong, mighty"? "chief, principal"?). Such a being was beheld by Nebuchadrezzar in Daniel 3:25, and such "sons of God" (*bené ha-elohim*) are also found in the remarkable passage in Genesis 6:2, 4, and a few times in the book of Job.[2] They are beings belonging to the community of the *elohim*, that is, "sons of the gods," "divine beings," or simply, "deities, divinities," as "sons of man" according to Hebrew idiom simply means "humans," and "sons of Israel" simply means Israelites.

It is striking that the Septuagint in the Scriptures mentioned often translates "angels."[3] In Deuteronomy 32:43, the Septuagint reads a longer verse than the Masoretic text; in this longer text we find, "all sons of God," and in the parallel line, "all angels of God." Also, *elohim* in Psalm 8:6 ("made a little lower than the *elohim*") is read by the Septuagint as "angels," a translation sanctioned in Heb. 2:7, 9, which is an important confirmation of the fact that *elohim* in many places means "angels."

In Psalm 58:2, the Masoretic text reads: "Indeed *elem* righteousness do you speak?" Here, the word *elem* is very hard to understand. Some ancient versions apparently read *ulam* ("thus, still, in any case") or *illem* ("dumb, silent"). It seems the most likely that we should read *elim*, that is, "gods"; not "men," because with this the word is contrasted (v. 1b),[4] if at least this latter part is to be translated, "[in] justice do you judge [the] son of men?" rather than "[in] justice do you judge, [you] son of men?" Also, the expression, "on earth" in verse

1. For instance, "sons of Babylon" = Babylonians (Ezek. 23:15); "son of a cow" = a piece of cattle, or a cow (Gen. 18:7); "son of man" = a human, or in this case, the man pre-eminently (Messiah, the Son of Man).
2. Job 1:6; 2:1 (here, the heavenly beings appear before God); 38:7 (here they shout at the foundation of the earth).
3. Thus, for instance, in Ps. 97:7 ("all his angels"); Job 1:6 ("angels of God"); 38:7 ("all my angels"). In Ps. 82, however, the Greek word for "god" is used.
4. See a similar contrast between *el* and *adam* in Isa. 31:3; Ezek. 28:2; *el* and *ish* ("man") in Num. 23:9; Hos. 11:9.

3, because of the contrast, seems to suggest celestial beings in verse 1. If this reading is correct, we can compare this psalm directly with Psalm 82; here again we hear God's reproaches to the "gods" because of their unrighteous judgment.

Another picture of the heavenly household is found in Psalm 89:6-8. In verse 7, it is asked,

> For who in the sky can equal YHWH,
> [who] is like YHWH under the *bené elim*?

Here again we hear of the "sons of the gods," or "heavenly beings." In the two adjacent verses, we find two other descriptions of these heavenly beings (v. 6, 8):

> And the heavens [read, heavenly beings] praise your wonder[power], YHWH,
> yes, your faithfulness in the congregation of [the] holy ones.
>
> God [*El*] is feared in the council of [the] holy ones—greatly—
> and awesome above all around him.

These "holy ones," or "saints," are not the believers on earth, as follows from the poetic parallelism, "heavens" and "all around him." The latter expression may refer to humans (Ps. 76:12), but, in my opinion, because of the parallelism it refers here to heavenly beings. The "congregation of [the] holy ones," or the "council of [the] saints," is apparently again the heavenly household around God's throne. The name "holy ones" is not unusual for the heavenly beings. Apparently, Elifaz too refers to heavenly beings in Job 5:1, as is also clear from Job 4:18. In Job 15:15, the notion, "holy ones," again is parallel with "heavens" (read, "heavenly beings"). Also, Daniel 8:13 and Zechariah 14:5 clearly seem to refer to "heavenly beings."[5] In Ugaritic, the consonant group *bn qds* simply means "gods." This corresponds with the Hebrew *bené qodeshim*, "sons of the holy ones," in short, "holy ones." There can be no doubt that "holy ones" sometimes refers to holy

5. Also cf. the apocryphal books Sir. 42:17; Tob. 8:15.

(lofty and pure) "heavenly beings."

Well known, beautiful pictures of the heavenly household are offered in Job 1:6 and 2:1, where we find the "sons of God," that is, the "gods" or heavenly beings, before the throne of God, and in Daniel 7:9-10:[6]

> ... an Ancient of Days sat down...
> his throne [was] flames of fire...
> thousand [times] thousands served him,
> and ten thousand [times] ten thousands stood before him.

In particular, we must mention 1 Kings 22:19-22 (= 2 Chron. 18:18-21):

> I saw YHWH sitting on his throne,
> and all the host of the heavens [or, heavenly beings] standing at his right hand and his left,

with whom YHWH consults, and from whom a "spirit" comes forward to seduce Ahab.

6. Cf. Isa. 6:1-4; Rev. 5:11.

Appendix 3: The Essence of Mythology

(a) Mythology and Theology

A MYTH IS A STORY in which certain spiritual (religious, divine, demonic, angelic) powers are represented as concrete figures and forms, adopted from the existing or an imaginary reality. For instance, in the mythologies of all antique nations, but also in the Bible, all kinds of monsters occur which are symbolic pictures of spiritual powers. Invisible angels and angelic princes in the invisible world are depicted as concrete monsters from the visible world, whether such monsters in our world really exist or not. These monsters are not "true" in the sense of "literally existing" – there are no literal dragons – but they are "true" in the sense of referring to real spiritual powers.

Obviously, historical criticism within theology sees in the occurrence of such mythical monsters (representing divine powers) in the Bible a "proof" that mythology is not foreign to the Bible. They believe that the points in which the Bible positively differs from the ancient writings of the pagan nations are only relative, and that therefore not everything in the Bible can be taken historically and scientifically seriously. In many ways, modern science and historiography have allegedly unmasked the Bible as an outdated book. Conservative theologians reject this interpretation; they hold to the trustworthiness of Scripture, also in historical respect. But consequently, they often do not know very well how to handle those "mythical elements" in the Bible. Usually, conservative exegetes do rightly point out that Scripture, when using names of water monsters that are also found among pagan nations, makes its own, independent use of these names. Scripture never adopts pagan-mythological *ideas* and *contents* from the pagans, so that it never binds itself to the pagan *meanings*, but gives to these mythical names and figures their own functions, in a new way and with a new purpose and meaning.

A striking example of this entirely new use is that the monsters in the Bible are never *independent* divine powers standing over against (some supreme) God, but powers created by the Most High God, and thus depending on him, after that departed from him, but again subdued by him. They are therefore powers that never prevail, or could possibly prevail over him. The Bible does not know any dualism of two independent powers of good and evil, standing over against one another, as many pagan religions do know it. For instance, Satan is a very high power, a "god" (2 Cor. 4:4), but after all, that means nothing but an angel created by God and afterwards fallen into sin (cf. Col. 1:16; Ezek. 28:13, 15).

So far, there is no problem. But then, conservative theologians often aim too high by trying too easily to get rid of the mythical elements mentioned. For instance, they claim that we only have to do here with adoptions of certain elements from the mythology of pagan nations around Israel. For instance, the Bible allegedly only calls Egypt with the names Leviathan, Rahab and Tannin ("dragon") according to Egypt's own religious-mythological views, in order to symbolically characterize the Egyptian world-power with its Pharaoh as a monster, placing itself over against YHWH and his people. Supposedly, God only makes *use* here of mythologically colored names, according to the pagans' *own* views of the world-powers, in order to characterize the latter in their self-deification (self-adopted form of deity).[1]

Apparently, those arguing in this way do not (sufficiently) realize that the Bible itself knows very well about spiritual powers and angelic princes. These are demonic beings that in the invisible world may certainly look like monsters, and that are associated with natural elements such as sea, water, fire, and wind (see below). If we recognize this, we do not need to claim anymore that we necessarily have to do here with an *adoption* of pagan motives. True, it is alleged that this adoption occurs in order to characterize the pagans according to their own views, and also that the adopted mythical elements in the Bible have been divested of their original mythological-polytheistic context. But the matter is much simpler. We find no adoption here, but rather Scripture's own thought-content, divine revelation concerning the invisible, spiritual powers hiding behind world history. The names of the mythical monsters are the proper names of the relevant angelic princes. The message is that God is mightier than all pagan angelic princes who intend to devour his people.

Those who do want to see here something of adoptions, no matter how "orthodox" the explanation further may be, still move on the shaky ground of the historical-critical school. According to this school, Israel adopted its views of creation and nature from pagan mythology, and subsequently demythologized them. That is, it divested them of mythical, for instance, polytheistic elements, and reconstructed them into history. Over against this, conservative theologians, including myself, believe that in Scripture we have to do with *inspired historiography*. Israel did not *adopt* its creational belief from the pagans, but *received* it of God through revelation. Not the Biblical creational belief comes from the pagans, but the pagan mythology in its kernel goes back upon a historical reality, which among them has been strongly corrupted and embellished, and has been purely handed down in Scripture alone.[2]

1. As I myself still asserted in Ouweneel (1986:26) in reply to Francke (1970).
2. Loonstra (1994:130) encounters this "corruption theory" with Bavinck

However, after having stated this, I now claim that, in contrast with that which conservative theologians usually do, we have to be consistent by accepting that also figures such as Rahab and Leviathan do *not* stem from religious imagination, and have not been adopted by Scripture from the pagans to defeat them with their own weapons. We have to do here not with pious fantasy, but with concretely existing angelic powers. And we have not to do here with adoptions, for Scripture itself knows very well the names of the relevant angelic princes. The fact that the pagan nations often know these names, too, does not necessarily indicate that Israel adopted these names from them, even if it could be demonstrated that the Jewish writings are much younger than the pagan sources. Rather, this fact indicates that the Jewish and pagan writings concerned go back upon the same concrete experiences of reality.

The advantage of such a view is that we do not have to make a great distinction between the "revelational history" of the historical Bible books—not allowed to contain any mythical elements—on the one hand, and Israel's subjective

---

(1928:439) and Kroeze (1962:19), and states "that the Old Testament unmistakably makes use of mythological motifs, which cannot be reckoned to Israel's own faith contents. In these cases, it is only possible that some adoption from the pagan world is involved" (1994:131). However, it is impossible to establish *a priori*, through objective arguments, what "motifs" did or did not belong to Israel's "own faith contents." Therefore, I claim that, as long as the contrary has not been objectively demonstrated, *everything* that occurs in the Bible can definitely be reckoned to Israel's own faith contents. Loonstra (1994:131-132) also claims, "If we, with regard to these mythological elements, want to maintain the corruption theory, we have to view these memories of the realm of pagan mythology as literary metaphors, and thus as picturesque poetic embellishments. For only then, they do not contain any real claim of truth." However, according to the corruption theory, by definition the Bible never contains "memories of the world of the pagan mythology," for this theory implies that the Biblical view of things does definitely have a "real claim of truth," and that the same things have been corrupted by the pagans. In brief, Loonstra speaks of the corruption theory, but means the adoption theory. This strange error is probably due to the fact that he apparently cannot imagine what Rahab or Leviathan (meta)historically might mean.

"experience of faith" in the Psalms and its "preaching of faith" in the prophetic books on the other hand, which are allowed to contain mythical adoptions. Whether we have to do with the historical or with the poetic and prophetic books, most of what is referred to there as mythical elements in reality goes back upon concretely existing spiritual realities, sometimes described in symbolic language. Such mythical elements do not prove some historical and scientific untrustworthiness of the Bible, but rather point to a concrete, spiritual world of angels and demons revealed by God and hiding behind the natural phenomena. Only such a view saves us from the urge of spasmodically arguing away all that historical-critical theology indicates as mythical elements in the historical books.

A concrete example can do here more than a long argument. For instance, historical criticism sees in Genesis 7:11, which speaks of the "fountains of the great deep" (*tehôm*)"[3] and the "sluices of heaven," a clear example of mythical elements. Over against this assertion, at least three attitudes are possible:

(a) Acceptance of this assertion, namely, in the sense that, because of the mythical character of these elements, one immediately gets rid of their historical significance. In modern theology, the distinction of mythical elements in the Old Testament, particularly in Genesis 1-11, went hand in hand with the denial of the historical trustworthiness of the relevant Bible stories.

(b) Strict rejection of the idea that we have to do with any mythical elements at all. Even more strongly, people emphasize the historical trustworthiness of these Scriptural data so forcefully that they are only prepared to read descriptions of certain astronomical and geological phenomena in the expressions mentioned.[4]

(c) Acceptance of the elements mentioned as mythical (in

3. Cf. what was said in § 3.1.2 about Tiamat or Tehom, the angelic prince of the primordial ocean.
4. I have myself done the same thing in Ouweneel (1977).

the sense of representing metahistorical realities), but without diminishing in any sense the historical trustworthiness of the relevant Bible story but, on the contrary, seeing in these elements references to invisible spiritual powers (chaos angels) which, under God's guidance, played a role in causing Noah's flood.

Obviously, I prefer explanation (c). This one has the advantage of taking into account, along with explanation (a), the reference to higher spiritual powers enclosed in the expressions mentioned, as well as holding, together with explanation (b), to the concrete (meta)historical reality to which these expressions, and the whole story of the flood, refer. With its "insights," historical criticism has tripped the Bible up and bereft the simple of their faith in the Bible's trustworthiness. Over against this, we should not fall into another, equally scientistic approach of the mentioned and other Scriptural data by degrading them to statements of a geological or geophysical nature. We should use the discoveries of the critical school, especially of form criticism, in order to deepen our own understanding of the higher realities described in Scripture, on a standpoint that honors the Bible's own self-understanding.

We have now briefly paid attention to one type of mythical elements, namely, dragons and such monsters. Another type is dealt with in this study several times (see § 2.1.2 and Appendix 4). It involves the fact that Scripture sees behind the natural phenomena the activities of spiritual beings, which act at God's commands, and also sometimes act against his commands, in disobedience to him. These so-called "natural angels" are sometimes also called "elementary spirits." Thus, the Bible knows water-, sea-, fire-, and wind-angels. The relevant Scriptural data turn out to represent within Jewish tradition a thoroughly familiar notion. At many places, it assumes that, as a Midrash formulates it, "over everything an angel was placed."[5] To start with some pseudepigraphic

5. Midr.Ps. 104 §3 (220b).

places, Jubilees 2:2 tells us that God on the first day created the heavens, the earth and the waters, and all the spirits who serve him: the angels of the spirit of fire, of winds, of clouds, of darkness, of snow, of hail, of rime, of voices, of thunder, of lightning, of coldness, of heat, and of the four seasons. 1 Enoch 60:12-22 also mentions the spirit of fog, of dew, and of rain; it is remarkable, by the way, that "spirits" are distinguished here from "angels." 1 Enoch 66:2 speaks of angels of judgment dominating the subterranean waters.[6]

1 Enoch 20:1-7 sums up the "holy angels who watch."[7] These are the seven throne-angels, to whom Revelation 8:2 presumably refers: "the seven angels standing before God." The enumeration is as follows. Uriel is over the world and the tartarus,[8] Raphael is over the spirits of men, Raguel over the world of the celestial bodies, Michael is over the best part of mankind, that is, the nation [of Israel], Saraqael is over the spirits sinning in the spirit,[9] Gabriel is over paradise, the serpents, and the cherubs (cf. Gen. 3), and Remiel over those who rise from the dead.

Talmud and Midrash speak of the angel of rain called Ridyah,[10] and of the angel of hail, called Yurqemi.[11] To Gabriel many functions are ascribed; apart from those mentioned, Gabriel, among other things, turns out to be placed over the ripening of the fruits.[12] According to 1 Enoch 40:9, this is understandable: Gabriel is simply "placed over all

6. Also see 1 Enoch 40:9; 66:2; 69:22; 75:3; 2 Enoch 4-6; 11:4f.; 19:1-4 (which speaks, among other things, of angels over seasons and years, over rivers and seas, over the fruits and the grass). Yalk.Shim. 1 § 739 (on Num. 12:7) distinguishes the spirit of fire, of hail, and of locusts.
7. Cf. § 2.1.2, which further speaks of these angel-"watchers."
8. See 2 Pet. 2:4, which speaks of the *tartarus* as the place where angels who have sinned are kept.
9. Or, against the spirit? Or, against the spirit (of the other angels)? The expression is not clear.
10. Taanith 25b.
11. Midr.Ps. 117 § 3 (240b).
12. Sanhedrin 95b.

[natural] forces." One Midrash[13] speaks of the angels of water, of fire, and of iron, and connects this with Isaiah 43:28, where we literally find: "and I profane princes [*saré*] of holiness [or, the sanctuary]," or, holy princes. The Midrash thinks here of angelic princes; *sar* ("prince") is the usual word for angelic prince, as we have seen.

We now come to a third type of mythical elements which are sometimes pointed out, namely, the so-called anthropomorphisms with regard to nature in the Bible, especially in the poetic books. We have to do here with a reference to rivers, mountains, trees, as if they were humans, or wider, rational beings. Some examples may illustrate this:

> [the] north and [the] south, You have created them;
> Tabor and Hermon, in your name they rejoice (Ps. 89:13).

Note that this follows directly upon the mentioning of Rahab (v. 11; see § 3.1); the notion of angelic powers is therefore not remote.

> Let the heavens rejoice,
> let the earth be glad,
> let the sea roar, and its fullness,
> let the field shout, and all that is in it;
> then all the trees of the wood will jubilate before YHWH (Ps. 96:11-13).

Verse 4 had already stated that YHWH "is awesome above all gods";[14] here too, therefore, the notion of angelic powers lies enclosed in the context. The fact that the heavens and the earth rejoice might mean that the inhabitants of the heavens and earth rejoice.[15] But the sea, the field, and the trees rather seem to suggest the idea of natural angels, the "gods" of the sea, the field, and the wood.

13. Midr.Lam. 2,2 (65a).
14. Cf. Ps. 95:3-5, where the "gods" also seem to be connected with the earth and the mountains, the sea and the dry land. Thus, too, in Ps. 97:9, and cf. vs.2-5!
15. Cf. Ps. 96:1-3, 9-10; 97:1; 98:3-4; 99:1; 100:1.

> Let the sea roar, and its fullness,
> the world and those who dwell in it;
> let the streams [or, rivers] clap the hands,
> let the mountains jubilate together before YHWH (Ps. 98:7-9).

These mountains are very similar to those found in Psalm 96. The "clapping of hands" by the rivers is considered to be an even stronger anthropomorphism than "jubilating." To me, this suggests even more strongly that we have to think of spiritual powers here. In the light of our previous investigation, it is not difficult anymore to see here elementary spirits of rivers and mountains. Rivers and mountains do not have hands; angels do.

> [the] wilderness and [the] wasteland shall be glad,
> and the desert shall rejoice...;
> it shall rejoice,
> even [with] joy and jubilation (Isa. 35:1-2).

This Scripture speaks for itself.

> Jubilate, heavens, for YHWH has done [it];
> shout, [you] lower parts of [the] earth,
> break forth, mountains, [into] jubilation,
> forest, and every tree in it (Isa. 44:23).

Of interest here is particularly the call to the lower parts of the earth, reminding us immediately of Ephesians 4:9. We have to do here with dark powers of *hades*, which once had to give back Christ from death, and who now also are forced to shout over Israel's deliverance. It reminds us also of Philippians 2:10, where Christ is honored by those who are in heaven and on earth, and by those who are "subterranean," that is, the powers of death and darkness. But if these "lower parts" are linked with angelic powers, it is conceivable to connect the latter also with the mountains and the trees. This must also be true, then, for the mountains and trees in Isaiah 49:13 and 55:12.

These Scriptures, too, seem to clearly support the existence of "elementary spirits" in Scripture. This does not mean that nowhere can there be a question of anthropomorphisms. Even if it is difficult to draw a borderline, one might say that Isaiah 24:7—"the new wine mourns, the vine languishes"—is an example of such an anthropomorphism. But in the light of what we meanwhile have found concerning natural angels it is far too cheap to interpret all relevant Scriptures in the sense of anthropomorphisms.

(b) Mythology and Depth-Psychology

I add here a few remarks about the depth-psychological view regarding "the mythical." In our time, it seems hardly conceivable to deal scientifically with the mythical without referring to the very influential depth-psychological school of Carl G. Jung (1875-1961) in particular. Sigmund Freud (1856-1939) reduces the mythical, and also "religion" in the wider sense, entirely to subjective projections of the unconscious. Jung, however, does not do that; he leaves much more room for the objective-religious. As a psychologist, he limits himself strictly scientifically to the psychological aspects of the human "image of god" (German, *Gottesbilder*). He rightly places the question as to whether "images of god" refer to an objective-transcendent "Godhead" outside the domain of (secular) psychology. Jung argues,[16]

> ... [it] is (...) clear that for instance the image of god corresponds with a certain psychological factual complex, and thus means a certain magnitude with which can be worked. The question what God is in himself lies entirely outside the domain of psychology.

And in his *Gegenwart und Zukunft* ("The Present and the Future") he says,[17]

16. Jung (1994:73).
17. Quoted by Jaffé (1967:37). Also cf. Jung (1984:15): "it is a misunderstanding when people blame me (...) for having created an 'immanent' God, and thus a 'surrogate of God.' I am an empiricist, and as such I can show, empirically

> ... With this it is said in no way that that which is called the unconscious is so to say identical with God, or is put in the place of God. It is the medium from which for us religious experience seems to sprout. The question as to what the deeper cause of that experience is cannot be answered by human knowing-ability. Knowing God is a transcendental problem.

This distinction by Jung is of tremendous importance for doing justice to his depth-psychology. This is true especially for his doctrine of the collective unconscious, which, in his opinion, is distinct from the personal unconscious and proper to all humans, and the doctrine of the so-called "archetypes" (primitive images) that he supposes to exist in it. If for instance he speaks of the archetype "God," he emphatically refers to the unconscious "image of god," not of God in the objective sense:[18]

> If therefore as a psychologist I say that God is an archetype, I refer to the form, the type, in the soul, a notion that, as is known, comes from tupos, which means blow or im-pression. The word "archetype" itself already presupposes something that puts its stamp.

Jung often says that we cannot know for sure whether our archetypical images of god refer to "God" (or "gods"! WJO) in the objective-transcendent sense of the term. Yet, he also

---

show, the existence of a totality that surpasses the conscious [called by Jung the "self" and compared with Atman and Tao]. By the conscious, this superior totality is experienced as numinous, as a *tremendum* [something awesome] and *fascinosum* [something fascinating]. As an empiricist, I am only interested in the experiential character of this superior totality, which in itself, viewed ontically, is something indescribable. This 'self' never takes the place of God whatsoever, but perhaps it is a vessel for divine grace."

18. In *Psychologie und Alchemie*; quoted by Jaffé (1967:40). In 1952 he wrote to a critic, "I in no way combat the existence of a metaphysical God. But I take the liberty of examining human statements" (Ibid. 45f.); that is, his psychological criticism refers to the psychological images of god/God, not to God himself. And in his *Antwort auf Hiob* ("Answer to Job") he says, "I am fully conscious of the fact that none of my considerations [for instance, regarding images of God. WJO] concern the unknowable [read, God. WJO]" (Ibid. 46).

has a *psychological* argument that not only subjective "images of god" are involved but also the objective-transcendent itself. He finds this argument in the phenomenon of paranormal observations such as clairvoyance, proscopy (here in the sense of foreknowledge of the future), for instance, proscopic (predicting) dreams, etcetera.[19] Purely inner-psychological events, in which no sensory observation is involved, turn out to refer to objective events, which as such are open to sensory observation. It is not *a priori* inconceivable that inner experiences in an analogous way refer to objective events which as such are not open to sensory observation, that is, which are transcendent.

The reason why I refer to Jung's views is that he assumes psychological contents to be present in the "collective unconscious" which are entirely parallel with—according to Jung: projected in!—many myths, fairy tales, and primitive religions throughout the world. For instance, Jung likes to depict the confrontation with the numinous (= mysterious-awesome-religious) forces in the unconscious as a battle with a mythical dragon.[20] In my study, this "dragon" plays a central role. What I want to emphasize now is two things. On the one hand, in spite of all subjective fantasies and distorted notions, the mythologies of the pagan nations in a certain sense and measure do definitely refer to the objective world of the transcendent powers. Jung does not deny this (although strictly as a scientist he does not wish to confirm it either). On the other hand, according to Jung, these same mythologies go back upon the deepest unconscious of individual man and of mankind as a whole. This means that many pagan (as well as many so-called "Christian"!) notions of "god/God" might in fact be nothing but projection, but that does not mean that everything in those "images of god/God" is *only* projection.

The question which presents itself to me is whether there could be a connection between, on the one hand, the religious

19. Jaffé (1967:31).
20. Jaffé (1967:58).

archetypes in the Jungian sense and, on the other hand, that which Thomas Aquinas (thirteenth century) has called a *cognitio Dei naturalis* ("natural knowledge of God"),[21] and John Calvin (sixteenth century) a *sensus divinitatis* ('sense of the godhead," or, "of the divine") and a *semen religionis* ('seed [or, germ] of religion").[22] It seems to me possible to interpret this "natural knowledge of God" especially as an unconscious "knowing." I have no difficulty in maintaining here the seeming paradox of the "unknown knowing" as an approximation of this complex matter. At the bottom of his heart, man "knows" of God's existence, and because of this "knowledge" he recognizes God's eternal power and divinity (Rom. 1:20), even if this "knowledge" subsequently manifests itself in all degeneration of paganism with its multiple idolatry (v. 21-23).

This *sensus divinitatis* is no rational-conscious "knowledge" of God, but only an inescapable "impression," in a sense analogous with the way Jung's "archetype" is an impression (*tupos*) (see before). Where Jung confesses his ignorance with regard to the relationship between the subjective-psychological "impression" (German, *Ab-druck*) and the possible objective-transcendent "printer" (German, *Drucker*), the Christian confesses that the "knowledge of God" is brought about by the "impressiveness" of God's revelation in man's heart. It seems justified to speak here of a "knowing," because this "knowledge of God" is closely related with the "conscience" (literally a "knowing-with") in Romans 2:15. On the other hand, earlier theologians have already sensed the "unconscious" nature of this "knowledge." Thus, Johannes Musaeus (seventeenth century) prefers to speak of a *dispositio* ("disposition") to the knowledge of God, an *instinctus naturalis* ("natural instinct [urge]"), not a *cognitio actualis* ("actual knowledge").[23]

---

21. *Summa Theologiae* II,2,2 a 3 ad 1.
22. *Institutio* I.3.1; cf. I.3.3 and I.4.1.
23. *Introductio in Theologiam* (1697); quoted by Pannenberg (1988:124). Also see his further discussion of this matter (128-132); he distinguishes between

Now, my suggestion is that this *instinctus naturalis* is closely related to the Jungian archetype of "God," but also to all kinds of other archetypes, which according to Jung are parallel with many mythical views among primitive nations, if not with all archetypes in general. At least, Jung writes,[24]

> the appearance of the archetypes has (...) an outspoken *numinous* character, which one has to call, if not "magical," then at least "spiritual." Therefore, this phenomenon is of the greatest importance for the psychology of religion. (...) It is (...) not uncommon that the archetype appears in the form of a *spirit* in dreams or in fantasy shapes, or even behaves like a phantom. Its numinosity often has a mystical quality and a corresponding effect upon the mind. It mobilizes philosophical and religious considerations (...)

And further down,[25]

> Usually one is not able to see that religious ideas are actually not only founded upon tradition and faith, but have been derived from the archetypes. The "careful observation" (*religere* = to observe!) of this forms the essence of religion.

Now my point is not to further discuss the views of Jung. With regard to the archetypes, on at least two points the Christian view differs thoroughly from Jung's. First, Christians would argue that on the basis of God's revelation the subjective "knowledge of God" refers to an objective-transcendent spiritual realm; Jung only ventures to express a conjecture here. Secondly, a point not yet mentioned is that the Christian view implies a dualism in the spiritual realm, and thus in the human unconscious. This is the antithesis between the (personal) Most High God and the (personal) "gods." The accepta-

---

a *notitia acquisita* ("acquired knowledge"), linked with the experience of the world and acquired through this experience, and founded in a *notitia innata* ("innate knowledge"), which becomes a consciousness of God through the observation of his creational works (131).

24. Jung (1987:49).
25. Jung (1987:65).

tion of such an antithesis would be unthinkable in the Jungian perspective.[26] Jung only owns "the divine," which is identical with "the demonic."[27] Insofar as there is an antithesis, this is a *complexio oppositorum* ("intertwining of opposites") within the "divine/demonic" as such.[28]

The most important inspiration I got from Jung's thinking is the conjecture that in the human unconscious we do not only have to do with a *sensus Dei* ('sense of God"), but also with a *sensus deorum* ('sense of the gods"). Only in this way, it seems to me, we can explain why in paganism such striking parallels with certain Christian truths can occur, whereas these pagans did not have the Word revelation and the knowledge of Christ at their disposal. Jung explains these parallels on the basis of the archetypes that the pagans carried along in their collective unconscious. In analogy with this, I explain these parallels on the basis of the natural, innate "knowledge" of God (in the sense of Rom. 1) as well as of the "gods," with their misleading imitations of the true God of gods. That which is involved in these imitations is more extensively dealt with elsewhere in this study. It involves primordial ideas such as those of the god-son, the virgin birth, death and resurrection of the divine hero, redemption, world consummation, etcetera. The *sensus deorum* of the pagans, linked with the realm of the gods, made the gentiles a prey of these demonic imitations, whereas in Christianity these primordial ideas, divested of all demonic corruption, found their *historical* fulfillment in the person and the work of Christ.

In this respect, even more things can be learnt from Jung, as long as we consistently reinterpret his syncretistic, at times anti-Christian, thought within a Christian framework of

---

26. Cf. Jung (1984:50): "a childish spirit views the gods as 'metaphysical' entities existing by themselves, or else as a playful or superstitious fabrication"; apparently, I myself belong to the first type, and the naturalistic-positivistic theologians to the second type of "childish spirits."
27. In *Erinnerungen* von C.G. Jung, quoted by Jaffé (1967:36-37).
28. See, for instance, Jung (1987:86) and particularly his *Mysterium Coniunctionis* (1957); cf. Ouweneel (1988a:65-66).

thought. For instance, Jung points out that, with regard to the "image of God" (*imago Dei*) in man, already Philo (first century) speaks of an "archetypus," and that this archetype, as for instance Irenaeus (second century) and Pseudo-Dionysius (c. 500?) taught too, corresponds with the Platonic "idea."[29] I add that this is the more remarkable because Philo personifies these ideas, or archetypes, into "angels," to which the "gods" belong too. Thus, his view implies a relationship between the subjective images of God as archetype and the objective ideas or angelic powers. Again, in these subjective "images" of God, and particularly of the gods, no doubt many misrepresentations will occur, such as projections of, for instance, people's own fears, reflections of the pious imagination, reinterpretations from people's own (sinful) inclinations, visualizations inspired by the empirical reality (for instance, the presentation of spiritual powers as monstrous animals). But this fact does not alter their basic reference to the objective-transcendent world of the spiritual powers.

29. Jung (1987:80).

Appendix 4: The Chaos Powers

THE SUBJECT OF THE CHAOS POWERS, which first seem to play a role at the origin of the world, and subsequently at Israel's exodus out of Egypt, is important enough to be given some special attention. As in the case of creation and the exodus (see § 3.1), we find in the New Testament a divine victory over the waters, or water powers. In the story of the storm on the lake, Jesus, walking on the water, comes to the disciples in their little boat.[1] There is still another story of a storm on the lake, in which from the outset Jesus is in the boat, fast asleep.[2] For our investigation of the spirits' realm, this other story is important because it contains a significant clue. After the disciples in their distress had awakened Jesus, he blamed them for their fears, stood up, and "rebuked the winds and the sea," says Matthew. Mark says, "he rebuked the wind, and said to the sea, 'Peace! Be still!'" And Luke says, "he rebuked the wind and the raging of the water." The winds and the sea immediately obey him and it becomes stock-still.

Usually, people overlook this remarkable fact of Christ addressing the winds and the sea in a commanding way, and even "rebuking" them.[3] The same word is used in Jude 9, where Michael does not venture to "rebuke" the devil; only

1. Matt. 14:22-33; Mark 6:45-52; John 6:16-21. This story is dealt with by De Graaff (1987:291-292; 1989:247-252), who also thinks of the chaos powers.
2. Matt. 8:23-27; Mark 4:35-41; Luke 8:22-25 (cf. De Graaff 1989:157-160).
3. The verb *epitimaô* means, "to rebuke, scold, blame."

the Lord can do so (cf. Zech. 3:2). Now, who is "rebuked" in the present story? Is it only a matter of symbolism, or of reality? In § 3.1, enough has been said of the chaos powers to suggest that here again we may have to do with the dark powers of wind and water, rebuked by Jesus. Elsewhere in this study, we already met an angelic prince of the lake of Tiberias.[4] It is again the malicious chaos powers trying to destroy Jesus and his disciples, but put to silence at his word. They have to submit themselves just as we find this everywhere in the Gospels with regard to the demons.[5] It is striking that the same word for "rebuking" occurs in the Septuagint, namely, in Psalm 105:9 (Masoretic text, 106:9):

> And he rebuked the Red Sea, and it dried up;
> and he led them through the depths (*tehomot*) as [through] the wilderness.

Here again we find exactly the same rebuking of the chaos powers, as we discussed this in § 3.1. Another striking Scripture is Psalm 18:16:

> And the vallies of the waters became visible,
> and the foundations of the world were exposed
> at your rebuke, YHWH!

This psalm, too, supplies us with all kinds of references to the realm of the spirits. YHWH rides on a cherub (clearly a celestial being) and hovers on the wings of a *ruach* (v. 11), he is surrounded by dark water powers (v. 12), from the splendor of his presence cloud-, hail-, and lightning-angels pass (v. 13). A third important psalm is Psalm 104. Verses 4 and 6 speak of wind- and fire-angels, and of the *tehôm*, that is, the primordial ocean, of which verse 7 says,

> At your rebuke they [i.e., the waters] fled;
> at the voice of your thunder they hasted away.

4. Pal. Sanhedrin 7,25d,18.28.43.
5. See, for instance, Mark 5:7-13; 9:25-26; especially with "rebuking": Matt. 17:18; Luke 4:39; 9:42 (cf. v. 55).

A fourth important psalm is Psalm 77, which may refer to both creation and the crossing of the Red Sea (v. 17; cf. v. 20-21):

> The waters saw you, God,
> the waters saw you, they trembled,
> yes, the *tehomot* were troubled.

"Trembling" here means, "trembling of fear."[6] Is this speaking of waters "trembling of fear" only an anthropomorphic or poetic saying? Is it not more obvious to think of the trembling water *powers*, the chaos powers, the *tehomot*, which have to give way before God's power? "Your way [is] in the sea" (v. 20), that is, your way is prevailing amidst the sea powers. Also see, in this context, Nahum 1:3b, 4, where we might read,

> Amidst (the angelic powers of the) whirlwind and of the storm [is] his way,
> and (angelic powers of) the clouds [are] the dust of his feet.
> [He is] rebuking the (angelic powers of the) sea,
> and makes it dry...

In this respect, one of the most interesting passages in Jewish tradition is the Targum (Aramaic paraphrase) of 1 Kings 19:11-12, where YHWH says to the prophet Elijah:

> "Go out and stand upon the mount before YHWH!" And, behold, YHWH revealed himself. And before him was a host of the angels of the height, rending the mountains and breaking the rocks before YHWH; but the *Shekhina* of YHWH was not in the host of the angels of the wind. And after the host of the angels of the wind was the host of the angels of the earthquake; but the *Shekhina* of YHWH was not in the host of the angels of the earthquake. And after the host of the angels of the earthquake was fire; but the *Shekhina* of YHWH was not in the host of the angels of the fire. And after the host of the angels of the fire, there was the voice of those who softly praised him.

6. Cf. Deut. 2:25; 1 Sam. 31:3; Ps. 97:4; Isa. 23:5; Jer. 51:29; Ezek. 30:16; Joel 2:6; Hab. 3:10 (mountains!); Zech. 9:5.

Here we see how self-evident it was for the Jewish reader to see behind the natural phenomena no "natural laws" in the modern scientific sense, but the activity of angels. That this is not just founded in some ancient popular faith of the Jews is shown by the fact that the inspired Word of God, too, is clearly aware of these "elementary spirits." To the Jewish mind, "YHWH was not in the wind (the earthquake, the fire)" means, YHWH was not in the company of the wind-, earthquake-, and fire-angels, respectively. His *Shekhina* (presence) was in "the low whisper," that is, in the company of angels who praised him in a gentle, lovely tone.

When speaking of storms on the sea, what to make of Jonah 1:4?

> YHWH sent a great *ruach* on the sea, and a great storm came on the sea.

God leads all natural phenomena; he "prepares" a fish, a gourd, a worm, and a vehement east wind (1:17; 4:6-8). In our verse we find that he even fully disposes of the water powers. Therefore, the mariners, realizing that spiritual powers were behind this storm, called to their "gods" (1:5-6) hoping that these would be able to subdue the water powers. When Jonah was finally cast overboard, "the sea ceased from its raging" (v. 15); the water powers came to rest, as in the Gospel story. By the way, Jonah is quite conscious of the power into which he has gotten. It is the power of the *sheol*, yes, of the *tehôm*, the primordial chaos (2:2, 5). YHWH alone is capable of delivering from that.

Let us go back to the Gospels. The story of the rebuking of the winds may have made it clear how we have to take this rebuking, and thus how we have to view the raging winds and the sea. Armed with this insight, we now turn to the story in which Christ walks on the waters of the raging lake. We might imagine three explanations here:

(a) Of course, the historical-critical explanation takes this story in the mythological sense, and thus, in its urge for demythologizing, unequivocally denies the historical trustworthiness of the story (see further Appendix 3). According to the "modern worldview," it is simply impossible to walk on water, and that is it.

(b) The fundamentalist explanation argues that Christ, through his divine power, temporarily "lifted the gravitation force," or "altered the surface tension of the water," or something similar. It needs no argument that such a manner of explanation is entirely foreign to Scripture. The background of this exegesis is the very same overestimation of science ("scientism") as the one that led the liberal exegetes to the denial of the historical trustworthiness of the story.

(c) In my opinion, we have to look in a different direction. Demythologizing theology is right in saying that mythical elements (read, spiritual powers; see again Appendix 3) play a main role here; fundamentalist theology is right in saying that the story is historically fully trustworthy, that is, really happened. What we find here is a tug-of-war between the chaos powers and the Son of God. Again, the chaos powers of sea and wind[7] try to destroy the disciples; again, they rise against God's people, as once at the Red Sea. This time, Christ does not "rebuke" them, this time he does not command them to become quiet, but defies them in another way: he walks on them. He forces them to carry him, and thus triumphs over them.[8]

The striking point is that, when Christ has entered the ship where the disciples were, we are literally told that "the

7. Cf. the "power of the air" in Eph. 2:2.
8. Cf. Job 9:8b: "he [is] treading on [the] heights of [the] sea," where many exegetes also see a subdual of the chaos powers and compare this with *Yam* (Heb., "sea"), the sea god of the Canaanites (Albright 1969:121; cf. Hartley 1988:168, 171). Of interest is also Job 7:12, where "sea" and tannin ("[sea] dragon") are mentioned in one breath, that is, the sea as well as the angelic prince of the sea (the "sea god"). We have to do here with a "monster" that is fought, or around which a watch is set. Job asks as it were, Am I such a dangerous monster, such an awesome angelic power, that you, God, take such strong action against me? (Cf. Wakeman 1973:55-82; see Hartley 1988:149).

wind became tired." Thus it is said in Mark 6:51, but equally in Mark 4:39. We find here the verb *kopazo*, which actually means "slacken, become weary, or tired,"[9] but is commonly used for the "dropping" of the wind. But how striking is the original meaning: the wind became tired! In Mark 4 this is due to the rebuking by Christ, but in Mark 6 this is not necessary. The powers stood up to Christ, they willy-nilly had to carry him, they succumbed against him, and at last they wearily lie down. Again, Christ, the One through whom God created and sustains the world, has prevailed over the chaos powers.

9. Cf. *kopos*, "weariness," and *kopiaô*, "become weary, fatigue oneself."

Appendix 5: Which Are the Four Empires of Daniel 2 and 7?

THE AGE-OLD JEWISH as well as Christian view is that the four empires in Daniel 2 and 7 are the Babylonian, the Medo-Persian, the Greek-Macedonian, and the Roman Empire. In rabbinical tradition, when referring to the Romans, the fourth empire was consistently that of "Edom" (see extensively Appendix 7). Also church fathers such as Irenaeus, Hippolytus, Augustine and Jerome (in his commentary on Daniel) gave the traditional summary of the four empires. Until modern time, this interpretation was accepted by all Catholic and Protestant exegetes. In particular, I refer to the very extensive survey of the four-empires interpretation by Edmund Kocken.[1] However, the present-day historical-critical view only wishes to find entirely fulfilled prophecy in the book of Daniel, and to this end places the book in the second century BC. It thus breaks with the traditional interpretation, and usually asserts that the four empires are the Babylonian, the Median, the Persian, and the

1. Kocken (1935), part 1: "the theory of the four world-empires," p. 1-119. Among the host of the church fathers, Kocken only mentions three deviating opinions. According to Orosius, the four empires are the Babylonian/Medo-Persian, the Macedonian, the Carthaginian, and the Roman Empire (ibid. 3, 62). According to Primasius, the four empires are the Assyrian, the Median, the Persian, and the Roman Empire (ibid. 3, 69). In both cases, the fourth empire is still the Roman one. Only Ephraem of Syria mentions the Macedonian as the fourth empire (ibid. 3).

Greek-Macedonian empire. In my opinion, this view has to be rejected for the following reasons:

(a) There never existed a separate Median empire between the Babylonian and the Persian empire. To be sure, there had been a distinct Median rule, but for Daniel this was not interesting because the Medes never ruled over Israel. Moreover, this earlier Median Empire only lasted until it was absorbed by the Empire of the Persians, which occurred already before the fall of Babylon. It was therefore a united Medo-Persian Empire that conquered Babylon and replaced the Babylonian Empire.

(b) The book of Daniel itself never regards the Medes and the Persians as distinct empires. On the contrary, in Daniel 5:28 God's servant prophecies to king Belshazzar that the latter's empire was to be given to the Medes as well as the Persians.

(c) In the vision of the ram and the goat (Dan. 8), it is described how the Medo-Persian Empire is destroyed by the Greek Empire. The perished empire is explicitly described as that of the "kings of the Medes and Persians" (v. 20). Here again, therefore, the second empire is seen as a unified Medo-Persian power. It is thus very far-fetched to forcefully introduce a distinct Median and a Persian Empire into Daniel 2 and 7. In Esther 1:19 and Daniel 6:9, 13, 16, too, we find this coupling, "Medes and Persians."

(d) Also in Isaiah 21:2, the Medes and Persians (referred to as Elam) are mentioned in one breath as the conquerors of Babylon.

(e) The idea that the second empire is the Medo-Persian one is supported by the suggestion of a duality in that empire: the breast as well as the (two) arms in Daniel 2:32. The bear in Daniel 7:5 raises itself up on one side, presumably at the expense of the other one, which seems to point to the superiority of the Persians over the Medes (cf. 8:3!).

(f) The idea that the third empire is the Greek-Macedonian

one is supported by the fact that this empire is characterized by the number four, pointing to the division of the empire into four parts after the death of Alexander the Great. The third animal in Daniel 7, the leopard, has four birds' wings on its back, and four heads. Similarly, in the case of the shaggy goat in Daniel 8, which is explicitly called the king of Greece (v. 21), we find how the great horn on its head, that is, Alexander (v. 21), breaks off, and four stand up in its place, which are the four kingdoms into which the whole empire is divided (v. 22).

(g) The main argument which the critics adduce for their view that the fourth empire would be that of Alexander is their contention that the "little horn" of Daniel 7:8, 20-26 would be the same as the "little horn" of Daniel 8:9-12, 23-25. The arguments that are adduced for this identification, however, are quite superficial. The little horn in Daniel 7 comes up between the ten horns on the head of the fourth, terrible animal, and drives out three other horns. The little horn in Daniel 8, on the contrary, arises on the head of the shaggy goat, after its large horn is broken and four others have come in its place. No further correspondence between the two horns can be pointed out other than that both are "little." Taking everything together, it is obvious that the little horn in Daniel 7 comes out of the fourth, and the little horn in Daniel 8 out of the third empire. At most a typological connection might be pointed out: the little horn of Daniel 8 (Antiochus Epiphanes) is a forerunner of the cruel world-leader who will come forth from the Roman Empire.

Now there are authors who do accept that the third empire is that of Alexander, but who interpret the fourth empire as that of the Seleucids. But this is not acceptable either. For, in the first place, this would imply that the third empire would only have lasted eleven or twelve years, plus the twelve years in which Perdiccas and Antigonus tried in vain to preserve the unity of the empire (fourth century BC). Secondly, we would have to assume that the fourth (Seleucid) empire at the same time would be one of the four parts of the third, Greek-Macedonian Empire (cf. Dan. 7:6; 8:22). Thirdly, in this way, the other three parts of the third empire would be totally ignored, whereas Palestine has also belonged to the Ptolemaic kingdom. As the kingdom of the "king of the south," it plays a great role in Daniel 11. Fourthly, I fail to see how the fourth empire could be called more dreadful and terrible than the previous empires (7:7), whereas in fact it would only be a limited part of the third empire. The fourth empire can only be that empire which ultimately has swallowed the entire previous empire of Alexander.

The view that the fourth empire of Daniel is the Roman Empire is not only the traditional Christian view, but also the common view in the pseudepigraphic books.[2] It is equally the unanimous view in the entire rabbinical literature. The Rabbis frequently find "the" four great world-empires in quite unexpected Scriptures, for instance, in the four rivers in Genesis 2, the four unclean animals in Leviticus 11, the four animals at the making of the covenant in Genesis 15, etcetera. Of these four empires, the Roman Empire is consistently the fourth and last one. The examples of this are numerous, too many to be summed up here. At many places, we find more direct references to Daniel 2 and 7, in which the fourth part of the image, or the fourth animal, is interpreted as the Roman Empire.[3]

In summing up, we can state that it cannot be reasonably denied that the fourth empire in Daniel 2 and 7 is the Roman Empire. Of course, in this study this identification is of the greatest importance.

---

2. 4 Ezra 12:11-12; 2 Baruch 39:3.
3. For instance, in Aboda Zara 2b,4; Pesiqta K. 4,9; 5,18; 17,4; Pesiqta R. 14,15; 15,25; 33,6; Gen.R. 76,6; 99,2; Exod.R. 15,6; 25,8; 35,5; Lev.R. 7,6; 13,5; 15,9; Num.R. 11,1; Est.R. Intr. 5; SoS.R. 6:10 (§1).

Appendix 6: Who is the Man in Genesis 32:24?

IT CANNOT BE DENIED that not only in Christian, but also in Jewish tradition people have often thought of a good angel, and we will therefore have to keep this possible interpretation open. According to the rabbis, the angel would then be Michael,[1] or more generally, an angel of God. On the whole, however, Jewish exegesis sees in this angel rather the angelic prince of Esau (that is, Rome). The great expositor, Rashi, says that, according to the (Jewish) scholars, the "man" of verse 24 was the guardian angel of Esau. According to one passage in Tanchuma, this man was Samael, the angel of evil, but this Samael is, as we saw before, none other than Satan,[2] or, the angelic prince of Esau/Edom = Rome. Many Christians have thought here of a (good) angel of God for at least two reasons:

(a) In verse 28, the angel says that Jacob has fought with *elohim*, and this is then, without further ado, taken in the sense of "God," as in verse 30, where Jacob says, "I have seen *elohim* from face to face." The parallelism of Hosea 12:4b and 5a clearly shows, however, that the *elohim* is not "God," but an angel, that is, "a god," a son of God (or, of the gods), a celestial being, as we saw in chapter 2 of this book. Whether this is

1. See, e.g., Tankhuma, Yalk.Shim., Yalk.chad., Targ.Jonathan, according to Lueken (1898:16); thus also rabbi Chelbo in Gen.R. 78,1.
2. E.g., Asc.Isa. 2:1; 3 Baruch 4 and 9.

a good or an evil angel is to be seen next.

(b) On the other hand, precisely Hosea 12 seems to indicate that this *elohim* is a good angel, but below I will try to show that this idea is founded upon a wrong reading, or translation, of verses 4-6, an interpretation that equals the *elohim* of verse 4 with YHWH, the *elohim* of hosts in verse 6. Quite a different, and I think better, translation is possible, as I will try to show.

Over against these two exegetical arguments that, as people believe, can be adduced for thinking of a good angel, there are two grounds to be mentioned why, in my opinion, we should rather think of an evil angel:

(a) People do not account for the fact that this *elohim* comes in the very night to fight with Jacob. It is a spirit of darkness. This is corroborated by the fact that, when the night is over, the *elohim* begs Jacob to let him go because the day breaks (v. 26). If he were really an angel of God, an angel of light, why would he come at night to Jacob, and so clearly shun the daylight?

(b) If he were really an angel sent by YHWH, how then is it conceivable that Jacob gained the victory?[3] In that case, Jacob would have been overcome himself by this angel. But one of the essentials of the story is this very fact that not the *elohim* but Jacob gains the victory, be it at the high price of his disjointed hip (v. 25, 31-32). Rabbi Shimeon has pointed out that the words of the angel, "Let me go" (literally, "send me away"), demonstrate that the sender is greater than the sent one, as Jacob is greater than the angel.[4]

In my opinion, these considerations not only suggest that we have to do here with an evil angel, but there is a third consideration to be made which teaches us something about the identity of this evil angel. This is because, as Jewish tradition does, this passage can be connected with Genesis 33:10. This verse, dealt with in this study, can be read in such a way that

3. Cf. v. 28: "you [Jacob] have prevailed"; also see Hos. 12:5.
4. Gen.R. 78,1; cf. Midr.Ps. 91,§6 (199b), 104,§3 (220b).

Jacob alludes here to his wrestling at the Jabbok: the face of the *elohim* with whom he fought was the face of Esau himself. That is only to be understood if we see that this *elohim* was the angelic prince of Esau, and this is exactly what the majority of the Jewish rabbis and expositors assumed.

For a careful exegesis of Genesis 32, the wrestling of Jacob with *elohim*, it is necessary to enter into Hosea 12:4-6 as well. We read here in a translation as literal as possible,

> In the womb he held the heel of his brother,
> and in his [male] strength he fought with[5] *elohim;*
> and [or, yes] he fought with the angel and prevailed;
> he wept, and begged him for grace;
> [at] Bethel he will find him,
> and there he will speak with us,
> namely, [lit., and] YHWH, the God of hosts;
> YHWH [is] his memorial.

First, we notice here the poetic parallelism in verse 4: in the womb he held the heel of Esau, and in his adult strength he fought with *elohim*. The parallelism clearly suggests here a connection between Esau and *elohim*, therefore we think here of the *elohim* of Esau. But there is more. As a man, Jacob acts princely toward Esau, or the latter's guardian angel, but with the baby this may not be so evident. The holding of the heel can be taken positively, as I have argued before. In any case it implies, as we saw, that in the youngest day the kingdom of God will replace the empire of Esau/Edom/Rome.

But then the great question comes up, Who is the "he" of verse 5, second line: "he wept, and begged him for grace"? In Genesis 32, Jacob does beg the angel to bless him, but that is quite another matter than begging for grace. Such a weeping supplication does fit the loser, but not the overcomer. It is rather the angel, having been overcome after all and shunning the daybreak, who exclaims, "Let me go!" Therefore,

---

5. Or, acted princely toward.

together with Jewish sources,[6] I think that it is the angel who weeps and begs Jacob for grace. Perhaps this becomes even clearer when we consider the rest of the verse. It is striking that literally we find here imperfects with a present or future sense. Hosea regards the situation here from the angel's viewpoint, who in this story weeps and begs for grace, and then continues, "At Bethel he [= the angel] will find him [= Jacob]," that is, there they will appear together before YHWH, in order that he will judge between them, or, as the verse continues, "There he [= YHWH, see v. 6] will speak with us [= the angel and Jacob]." In fact, we are to take these last words as words of the angel himself. The latter begs Jacob for grace, counts upon appearing together with him before YHWH, and then says beggingly, "There he will certainly judge between us—please, not here!"

Jewish tradition points out that, according to Genesis 28:12, 17, 19, Bethel is the "gate of heaven," where angels ascend to heaven and descend from heaven. Perhaps in Bethel the angel hopes to be able to escape from Jacob's dominion by fleeing into heaven. According to the Talmud,[7] the angel says, "Let me go, for the day breaks," and when Jacob asks him, "Are you a thief or a scoundrel that you are afraid of the morning?" his adversary replies,

> I am an angel, and from the day when I was created
> my time to sing praises [to the Lord] has not come until now.

According to rabbi Berekhiah (c. 340), in a corresponding Midrash,[8] the angel said to Jacob,

> Let me go, for the dawn has come;
> that is, my time has come to sing a song.

And according to another Midrash,[9] the angel said, "Let me

6. E.g., Rashi and Chullin 92a (on Hos. 12:5).
7. Chullin 91b.
8. Gen.R. 78,1.
9. Hgl.R. 3:6 (§3).

go, for my turn has come to sing praises," at which rabbi Levi notes that the angel saw the *Shekhina* standing above Jacob, and understood from this that he would not be able to overcome him. Other expositors give another motivation why the angel would say, "At Bethel... He will speak with us." According to Mitzrakhi, the angel only predicts here what God himself would do later on. Thus also Rashi (rendered freely): later, God will reveal himself to you at Bethel [Gen. 35:10]. There, he will change your name and bless you. I will be there too, and own your title to the blessing. The angel's begging would then imply, Please wait until he will speak with us; then I will bless you, that is, own your title to your father's blessing. But Jacob did not want to wait that long, and already there at Penuel forced the angel to own this title; thence the emphasis upon the word, "there," in Genesis 32:29: the angel blessed him already there, and not only at Bethel.

Appendix 7: Jewish Tradition about Esau/Edom/Rome

THE PRESENT BOOK CLAIMS that Jacob holding Esau's heel at his birth implies that after divine right he will take Esau's place. In this connection, there is a striking passage in 4 Ezra 6:8-10:

> Abraham... of him descend Jacob and Esau;
> the hand of Jacob, however, held in the beginning the heel of Esau.
> The heel of the first era is Esau, the hand of the second is Jacob.
> The beginning of man is the hand, his end the heel.
> Between heel and hand further nothing. -
> Consider this, Ezra! [or, Between heel and hand seek further nothing, Ezra!].

In the light of Jewish tradition, the edition Kautzsch explains this mysterious text as follows (rendered freely). Man's "beginning" (fore part) is his hand, his "end" (rear part) is the heel.[1] Thus the "hand" of an era is its beginning, and the "heel" is the end of that era. The present era is that of Esau's world dominion, that is, Rome, and the coming era is that of Jacob's world dominion, that is, Israel (or, the empire of the

1. Heb. *ᶜaqav*, "take by the heel," and thence also, "deceive," or, "take the place of" (§ 4.2, note 2). In a derived sense, the word *ᶜaqev* can therefore also mean "end"; see Josh. 8:13: the "end" of an army, that is, the rear-guard (thus also Gen. 49:17, "heels"). The related *ᶜeqev* can mean "end" (Ps. 119:33, 112).

Messiah). Now the whole point of the text in 4 Ezra is that, as Jacob's hand held Esau's heel, so that his hand followed directly, without interruption, upon Esau's heel, thus the era of Jacob (that is, of the Messiah) will follow immediately upon the era of Esau. Jacob is "he who steps into Esau's place," and this so immediately as at his birth he followed upon Esau. In other words, there is but one way in which there will come an end to the Roman Empire, or Western culture, namely, *in that it is replaced by the empire of Jacob, that is, the empire of the Messiah*. This is exactly the message of Daniel 2 and 7 too.

In Genesis 32 we see how the angelic prince of Esau comes to fight with Jacob. In the solitude of the night Jacob is attacked. But Jacob is strong, for a whole army of *elohim*, given to accompany and protect him (32:2-3), is with him; yes, the *Shekhina* itself is with him, as a Jewish tradition tells us (see Appendix 6). According to a Midrash,[2] rabbi Chanina ben Yitzchaq (c. 325) said that God spoke to the angelic prince of Esau wrestling with Jacob:

> "How do you want to stand? He [Jacob] comes against you and five amulets[3] are in his hand: his own merit, and the merit of his father [Isaac], and the merit of his mother [Rebecca], and the merit of his grandfather [Abraham], and the merit of his grandmother [Sara]. Measure yourself with him, even against his own merit you cannot stand up!" Rabbi Chanina continued, "Immediately he [the angel] saw that he did not prevail over him [Jacob]."[4]

The guardian angel of Esau sees that he will not manage to throw off Jacob's yoke, leave alone that he could totally overcome him. Therefore, he inflicts a terrible injury upon him by hitting the socket of his hip. According to a Midrash,[5] the fact that Jacob's "loins" are wounded here means that

2. SoS.R. 3:6 (§3).
3. Means of defense against evil powers.
4. See Gen. 32:26; cf. Gen.R. 77,3; 78,3.
5. Gen.R. 77,3.

Jacob's descendants are struck, which is then associated with the persecutions of the Jews under the Romans. According to the *Baal HaTurim* (Jacob ben Asher, ca. 1300), Esau's guardian angel only wanted to mutilate Jacob, so that he would not be able anymore to offer sacrifices, for that is one of the privileges connected with the right of the firstborn.[6] The history ends with the sun rising on Jacob (v. 31). On behalf of rabbi Acha (c. 320), rabbi Chuna (c. 350) said about this important expression "on Jacob,"[7]

> It was indeed thus: the sun healed our father Jacob, but burnt Esau and his princes. The Holy One—praised be he—spoke to him [Jacob], "You are a pledge for your children: as the sun heals you and burns Esau and his princes, thus the sun will heal your children and burn the gentiles,"

with a reference to Malachi 4:1-2. Here the Midrash no doubt implies by the "gentiles" the Romans in particular. In the rabbinical writings, where Edom (the national name for Esau's descendants) is the common name for Rome, this can be corroborated time and again in the Targums, the Midrashim, and the Talmud (also cf. Num. 24:17-19). In the light of Daniel 2 and 7 it can be understood how the dispersed Jews when hearing the name "Edom" thought of the fourth, Roman Empire, for this would be destroyed at the coming of the Messiah (the "sun of righteousness" in Malachi 4:2). A Jewish tradition[8] holds that the angel represents the Edomite Empire, which fights with Israel "until daybreak," that is, till the end of Israel's exile, for this ends at the coming of the Messiah's kingdom.[9]

Interesting is also another tradition,[10] according to which

---

6. Cf. Lev. 21:16-24.
7. Gen.R. 78,5.
8 Tankh.wayyishlach 40b.
9. Cf. to this end also 4 Ezra 11:1-12:39, especially 12:31-34; 2 Baruch 36:1-11; 39:1-40:4.
10. Yalk.chad. 46,4/47,1; cf. Yalk.Rub. 169,2.

Michael, the *epitropos*[11] of Israel, tries to bring about for his people the deliverance out of the "Edomite exile," that is, the dispersion in the Roman Empire. To this end he has to fight with Samael, the *epitropos* of Edom/Rome. Samael, pointing to Israel's impenitence, is chased away by God because he speaks evil against the people. But when Michael prays God to have mercy on Israel, although it does not deserve it, he receives the answer that first the people have to repent to God for at least as much as a needle's point.

Another reference to Edom/Rome is found in a tradition[12] in which rabbi Berekhiah (c. 340) says,

> Hard[13] is the angelic prince of Edom [= Rome], for thus Zechariah has seen him: "behold, a man, sitting on a red horse, and standing between the myrtle trees in the deep places, and behind him red, sorrel, and white horses" [Zech. 1:8].

These three kinds of horses supposedly represent the Roman emperors, led by their angelic prince, the man on the red horse. He is seen "in the deep places," for there the Israelites, represented by the myrtle trees, are found, namely, in the misery of the exile. Before and at the time of Zechariah, that was the exile in Babylon, at the time of rabbi Berekhiah it was the exile in the Roman Empire. Elsewhere[14] we encounter the view that the materials mentioned in Exod. 25:4-5 in view of the tabernacle represent the four world-empires: the gold, the silver and the bronze represent the Babylonian, the Medo-Persian, and the Greek Empire, respectively, but the rams' skins dyed red represent "Edom" (= Rome), for Esau was red and hairy (Gen. 25:25). One Midrash[15] says in connection with Psalm 57:9 ("Awake, my soul..."),

> Against Babylonia awoke Hananiah, Mishael and Azariah

11. That is, ruler, overseer; it is a Greek loanword in Hebrew.
12. Aggad. Beresh. 56 (40a).
13. Or, Bad; or, The hardest/worst (among the enemies of Israel).
14. Tankh.B. theruma §6 (46a).
15. Midr.Ps. 22 §9 (93a).

> [Dan. 3], against the Medo-Persian Empire awoke Mordecai and Esther, against Greece awoke the house of the Hasmonaeans [= the Maccabaeans], and against Edom [= Rome] the king, the Messiah himself.

This idea, that Rome is the actual adversary of the Messiah, is found frequently in the Jewish sources.[16] In the Talmud,[17] rabbi Jochanan translates and interprets Isaiah 21:11-12 as follows:

> The burden of (the angel) Dumah (who is placed over the souls). He [= each of the souls] calls to me (= the angel) out of Seir [= Edom = Rome], "What [says] the Watchman [= God] of the night?"

That is, how long is the exile of Israel in Edom/Rome still going to last? Dumah is presumably a word play on Edom and means, "silence, keeping silent." It is therefore at times a reference to the land of the dead (Ps. 94:17; 115:17). Rabbi Jochanan seems thus to imply that the souls of the dead call to the angelic prince of Edom/Rome, How long will YHWH still continue our exile under your (Rome's) power? It is worthwhile to compare this interpretation, which rather deviates from the usual interpretation (according to which it is the Edomites calling here to the prophet), with Rashi's four possible explanations of verse 12. The watchman says,

(a) "Is the morning already coming? No, rather the night," that is, it is not yet the time of the deliverance, that is, the end of Israel's exile in the Roman Empire.

(b) "The morning comes," that is, deliverance will certainly come, "but also [still first] the night," that is, the rest of the night of the exile.

(c) "The morning comes," that is, the end of the Babylonian exile, "but also night [again]," that is, a new exile,

16. 2 Baruch 39:5-7; 4 Ezra 11:36-46; 12:10f.,31-33; Pesiqta K. 5,9 (on SoS. 2:10ff.; cf. SoS.R. 2:13 [§4]); Pesiqta R. 15,14/15.
17. Sanhedrin 94a.

namely, in Edom/Rome.

(d) "The morning comes," that is, the deliverance of the righteous, "but also night," that is, the judgment over the wicked (this is also the interpretation of the Targum).

Interesting is Isaiah 63:1, which says,

> Who is this, coming from Edom,
> bright-red [his] clothes, from Botzrah?
> [Who is] this, shining in his garment,
> striding in the greatness of his strength?

In the Talmud,[18] this verse is applied by Resh Lakhish to the angelic prince of Edom/Rome, namely, to the time that Rome's cruelty and the murdering of many innocents will be punished. According to this rabbi, the prince looks for a hiding-place here in Botzrah to escape from judgment. To us this interpretation is strange because from the context it seems so evident that YHWH himself is intended here. But the point that matters right now is this continually returning notion of the existence of this angelic prince of Edom/Rome, oppressing the people of God until the time of the end. In the end time, the Messiah will destroy the angelic prince, a victory which at times is ascribed to God himself. According to a Midrash,[19] God will one day chase the angelic prince of Edom/Rome out of his heavenly dwelling-place. In another Midrash,[20] we find something similar. The famous commentary of Hermann L. Strack & Paul Billerbeck translates it as follows:

> God will drive out the angelic prince of the "great city," namely, Babylon, that is, Rome [cf. Rev. 16:19], from his [heavenly] dwelling-place.

The edition Braude/Kapstein translates:

> God will begin with driving out Edom's prince from the "great

18. Makkot 12a.
19. Pesiqta K. 4,9 (on Num. 19:3); cf. Yalk.Shim. on Num.19:2-3.
20. Pesiqta R. 14,15.

city" [of heaven].

In this passage,[21] we also encounter the interpretation by rabbi Berekhiah, who applies Isaiah 34:1 to the angelic prince of Edom/Rome, and verse 6 to God's slaughtering the angelic prince of Edom/Rome in heaven. Very important is here the notion returning time and again in both Scripture and rabbinical literature that the government of the Messiah directly follows upon the Roman Empire. We already found several indications for this, and now add some more:

* The Messiah will destroy Edom/Rome, and subsequently reign from sea to sea (Ps. 72:8); the wicked Edom/Rome will therefore remain in power until the Messiah comes.[22]

* God will return to his temple [cf. Ezek. 40-48] when he will have requited wicked Edom.[23]

* The Messiah will come when Rome will fall into the thorns, that is, will be torn apart.[24]

* Edom will fall through the hand of him who has been anointed for war, the descendant of Joseph[25] (according to tradition, Messiah ben Joseph is the great fighter of the end time and the forerunner of the actual Messiah, Messiah ben David).

* According to a Midrash,[26] God will strike the wicked empire, Edom/Rome, with leprosy, just like its angelic prince, as it is written in Jeremiah 46:15: "Why is your valiant one stricken?" In line with the context, the word "valiant" is taken here as "angelic prince," analogous to Psalm 78:25.[27] The word for "stricken," *niskhaph*, is taken here, with metathesis of two consonants, as *nispakh*, "made scabby (leprous)." The text continues,

21. Also see Pesiqta R. 15,25.
22. Pesiqta R. 13,2 (on Num.24:18-19).
23. Pesiqta K. Suppl. 5,3.
24. SoS.R. 2:17 (§1) (rabbi Levi).
25. Gen.R. 99,2.
26. Tankh.B. thizria §16 (21b).
27. The LXX reads *angelos*, "angel," in this verse.

> In the future world, God will sit in judgment over the wicked [= Roman] empire; he will say to it, "Why did you enslave my children?" It will reply, "You did that, for you delivered them into my hands!" God will say to it, "Because I delivered them into your hand, you did not show mercy to them, but made your yoke weigh heavy on the old man"[28] (...) God will say, "(...) I will punish your angelic prince and strike him with leprosy, and afterwards I will punish you."

28. Cf. Isa. 47:6, referring to Babylon, which in Rev. stands for Rome.

Appendix 8: The Birth of Moses and Jesus

AT THE BEGINNING OF THE HISTORY of the old covenant stands the birth of Moses. At the beginning of the history of the new covenant stands the birth of Jesus Christ. It is therefore understandable that Scripture sees various parallels between Moses and Jesus.[1] For our study, this is of importance because after the eight world-empires the Ninth King, Jesus Christ, appears, whereas Moses as a miraculous deliverer stands at the very beginning of the history of the world-empires. The God-sent opponent of the "first king" (the Pharaoh) is thus a type of the last, Ninth King, who is the opponent of all the eight diabolical predecessors.

The New Testament mentions, for instance, the following correspondences and contrasts.

(1) Moses lifted up the serpent in the wilderness, thus also the Son of Man was lifted up (John 3:14).

(2) Moses gave the bread from heaven, the Father gave his Son as the bread from heaven (John 6:32).

(3) Moses is a prophet, Jesus is one too (Acts 3:22).

(4) Moses was rejected by his people, Jesus was too (Acts 7:20-28, 51-52).

(5) Israel was baptized unto Moses, we are unto Christ

1. Also see Ouweneel (2001:§6.3.3).

(1 Cor. 10:2).

(6) Jannes and Jambres resisted Moses, the heretics of today resist (the truth of) Christ (2 Tim. 3:8).

(7) The song of Moses is parallel with the song of the Lamb (Rev. 15:3).

(8) Those who do not listen to Moses will listen even less to one rising from the dead (especially, Jesus) (Luke 16:31).

(9) The law was given through Moses, grace and truth came through Jesus Christ (John 1:17).

(10) Those who do not listen to the writings of Moses, will listen even less to the Lord (John 5:45-47).

(11) Moses brought the old covenant (the ministry of death), Jesus brought the new one (the ministry of the Spirit in glory) (2 Cor. 3:7-8).

(12) Moses was a servant in the house of God, Jesus is Son over his house (Heb. 3:1-6).

(13) The covenant of Moses was consecrated with the blood of animals, that of Jesus with his own blood (Heb. 9:18-23).

(14) Moses is connected with mount Sinai (mountain of judgement), Jesus with mount Zion (mountain of grace) (Heb. 12:18-22).

If we now consider the birth of Moses and that of Jesus, we again discover several parallels:

(a) The book of Exodus begins with a genealogy before the circumstances of Israel and the birth of Moses are described (Exod. 1:1-5). Amram was a grandson of Levi, and a great-grandson of Jacob (Exod. 6:15-19). – The gospel of Matthew also begins with a genealogy before the birth of Jesus is described (Matt. 1:1-17). Joseph was a son of Jacob (Matt. 1:16), and a great-grandson of Levi (Luke 3:24).

(b) At the time of Moses, Israel suffered under foreign oppression; it was a nation of slaves under the power of Egypt, with Pharaoh at its head, who promulgated despotic decrees:

heavy forced labor (Exod. 1:11, 14; 5:6-9). - At the time of Jesus, Israel suffered again under foreign dominion; it was a nation of slaves (cf. Ezra 9:8-9; Neh. 9:36-37) under the power of the Romans, with the emperor at their head (emphasized by Luke) as well as the Edomite king, Herod (emphasized by Matthew). Israel was submitted to the despotic decrees of Augustus: the "registration" involved a census and a valuation in view of heavy taxes (Luke 2:1).

(c) Against the background of Moses' birth, we hear of a terrible massacre of little boys (Exod. 1:16, 22): the Pharaoh had all the newborn boys thrown into the Nile. Moses, however, was kept hidden by his parents. - Against the background of Jesus's birth, we also hear of a terrible massacre of little boys (Matt. 2:16): king Herod had all the boys from zero to two years slaughtered at Bethlehem. The child Jesus, however, was taken by his parents and escaped.

(d) Jochebed saw that her child was "beautiful" (Exod. 2:2; Heb. 11:23), that is, "beautiful to God" (Acts 7:20), and hid it for three months. - Mary during her pregnancy spent three months in quietness with Elizabeth (Luke 1:56); after the birth, others honored her child, and she herself "kept all these things and pondered them in her heart" (Luke 2:19, 51).

(e) Jochebed put her child into an exceptional "cradle," an ark of bulrushes, because there was no room for the boy in society; a young woman stayed near the basket: Miriam (Greek, *Maria[m]*) (Exod.2:3v.). - Mary (Greek, *Maria[m]*) put her child into an exceptional "cradle": a manger, that is, a food-trough for animals, because there was no room for the boy in the inn; the young Mary sat at the manger (Luke 2:7, 16).

(f) Strangers came to see the child of Jochebed in its queer "cradle": the daughter of Pharaoh with her servants discovered little Moses (Exod. 2:5). - Strangers came to see the child of Mary in its queer "cradle": the shepherds came to the child, the manger functioning as one of the signs (Luke 2:12, 16); later the wise men from the East came as well (Matt. 2:1-12).

(9) Moses spent the first years of his life in Egypt. - The striking fact is that Jesus, too, spent the first years of his life in Egypt (Matt. 2:13-15).

I add to this that Flavius Josephus[2] supplies us with several other details about the birth of Moses, which are not mentioned in the Old Testament, but which Matthew, and his Jewish readers as well, will probably have been familiar with:

(1) An Egyptian astrologer predicted the birth of a Hebrew boy, who would defeat Egypt and deliver Israel. Because of this, Pharaoh decreed that all Hebrew boys were to be killed. - "Wise men" (*magoi*, that is, astrologers) from the East predicted the birth of a Jewish boy, who would be king over Israel (which also implied that he would deliver his people from the Romans). Because of this, Herod decreed the massacre of the innocents at Bethlehem (Matt. 2:1-18).

(2) Amram was a distinguished man among his people. - Joseph was of the house of David (Matt. 1:20; Luke 2:4).

(3) God appeared to Amram in a dream to enlighten him about the significance of the child that his wife expected, including the words, "He will deliver his people from slavery." - An angel of the Lord appeared to Joseph in a dream to enlighten him about the significance of the child that his wife expected (Matt. 1:20-23), including the words, "He will deliver his people from their sins" (v. 21).

(4) Josephus calls Moses the greatest personality who there has ever been among the Hebrews. - Jesus is the greatest personality of the New Testament, even of the whole Bible, even of all mankind.

2. *Jewish Antiquities* 2,5.

Appendix 9: Apollo and Jesus

There are important differences between the Greek-Roman god Apollo and the person of Jesus, between the false angelic prince and the true Son of God, between the women's deceiver and the women's redeemer, etcetera. Yet the correspondences between them are striking too:

(1) Apollo is considered to be the son of the chief god, Zeus. - Jesus is the Son of God, of the God of gods.

(2) Apollo, who among the Romans is often called Phoebus (the "Radiant One"), is the *sun god*. When he appears to the Argonauts, whom he assists, his rays are so glaring that they do not dare to lift their eyes. - Jesus appears on the mount of transfiguration, as well as to Saul of Tarsus, as well as to John on Patmos, shining as the *sun*, in Saul's case even in a blinding way (Matt. 17:2; Acts 26:13; Rev. 1:16; cf. 10:1).

(3) When Apollo is born, he is threatened by the goddess Hera. When he has arrived at male maturity, he kills the great dragon, Python. He also kills the Cyclops and the giant Tityus. - When Jesus is born, he is threatened by the great red dragon, that is, Satan. At the cross he defeated the dragon, and at the end he throws him into hell, just like the beast and the false prophet (Rev. 12, 19 and 20).[1]

(4) Apollo twice assumes the form of a man (as a

1. Collins (1976) considers the myth of Apollo and his mother, Leto, as the one exhibiting most parallels with Rev. 12.

punishment for that matter!) to serve men as a slave and as a shepherd. - Jesus has himself voluntarily sent to the earth, becomes a man, even assumes the form of a slave, and serves as the good shepherd (Phil. 2:6-8; Matt. 20:28; John 10:11; cf. Zech. 13:5-7).

(5) Apollo is the great healer, as his son Asclepius (or, Aesculapius). He heals the sick, raises the dead, delivers people from evil spirits. He understands all, sees all, and knows the most hidden thoughts. - That is the same as what the Gospels tell us about Jesus.

(6) Plato tells us about the righteous Apollo that he "enacted the most important, the most beautiful, the first laws."[2] All Greece goes to Delphi to learn there Apollo's counsel in political and religious matters. - Jesus gives to his disciples his righteous commandments (e.g., Matt 5-7; the "law of Christ," Gal. 6:2), and commissions them to carry these throughout the world (Matt. 28:19).

(7) In the Orphic religion, Apollo promises salvation and everlasting life to his followers; he also rules over paradise. - Jesus, too, promises to his followers salvation and everlasting life (John 10:27-29), and a portion with him in paradise (Luke 23:43).

Twice the New Testament reports an event that we might describe as a kind of confrontation between Apollo and Jesus. The first event is the testimony of the Roman centurion at the death of Jesus. Matthew 27:54 renders this testimony as follows: "Truly, this was God's Son"; Mark 15:39: "Truly, this Man was God's Son"; and Luke 23:47: "Certainly, this Man was righteous." What crossed a Roman centurion's mind when calling Jesus "God's Son" as well as "righteous," and when considering the latter's blessing of the repenting crucified criminal, as well as the return of the sunlight, as well as Jesus's triumph over death and the accompanying phenomena in nature? As a Roman he cannot but have thought inad-

2. Plato, *Politeia* 4, 427.

vertently of Apollo. Or does he rather see the *contrast* with Apollo? Here it is not the young, handsome, radiant Apollo, but a tormented figure (cf. Isa. 52:14) fighting and wailing in darkness who gained the victory! Apollo is in fact never interested in people; he only helps them if he is forced to do it. But Jesus at the cross is, even in his gravest sufferings, still a blessing for his environment: he asks for forgiveness on behalf of the soldiers (Luke 24:34), entrusts his mother to his beloved disciple (John 19:26-27), has mercy on the repenting criminal at the cross (Luke 23:43). Apollo is proud and reckless; Jesus is gentle and lowly of heart (Matt. 11:29).

The second confrontation is even more striking. Paul and his companions walking through Philippi are followed by a poor, possessed woman. The text literally says that she had a "Python spirit" (Acts 16:16). We saw that Python was the name of the serpent or dragon that Apollo had defeated. This dragon dwelt at Delphi, where he guarded the oracle of Themis, the goddess of justice, but also harassed the neighborhood. Apollo killed the dragon, instituted the Pythian games, consecrated the sanctuary and the Pythia, the priestess, through whom he would henceforth deliver the oracles. Later, the name was also applied to other fortune-tellers considered to be inspired by Apollo.

The woman following Paul in Philippi was a "fortune-teller." Luke uses here the word *manteuomenè*, which does not occur elsewhere in the New Testament and implies that a "deity" (here, Apollo) delivered oracles through her, as in Pythia's case at Delphi. It is the more striking to notice what she exclaims here: *Apollo* witnesses through her that Paul and his companions were "slaves of the Most High God," and that they proclaimed the "way of salvation." These are impressive words on behalf of a "deity" who himself has several times been "slave" of the chief god, and is considered to be the great savior of mankind! Here Apollo has to own up. He who outwardly resembles Jesus so much must own in him his superior here. At Paul's command, "in the name of Jesus Christ," the evil spirit, this servant of Apollo, has even to depart from the possessed woman, so that she is delivered (v. 18).

Appendix 10: Rome, Babylon, Tyre, Egypt

NOT ONLY EDOM (see Appendix 6 and 7) but sometimes also Babylon is a symbol for Rome, as in the book of Revelation (see § 4.1.3). This is understandable insofar as the Babylonian and the Roman Empire, the first and the last of the four world-empires, are directly correlated. Also see 1 Peter 5:13, where many believe that Peter means by "Babylon" the city of Rome. This connection between Babylon and Rome is quite important for the understanding of Isaiah 14:4-21. This Scripture deals with the king of Babylon, but in verses 12-15 we very clearly see a higher, spiritual power rising, which because of its identification with the king of Babylon can be none other than the angelic prince of Babylon (see § 3.3.3). Already church fathers such as Tertullian and Jerome saw in the "morning star" and the "son of the dawn" (v. 12) a reference to Satan, whom we identified as the one who is in particular the angelic prince of Rome. Here again we therefore find a direct connection between (the angelic prince of) Babylon and (the angelic prince of) Rome, the dragon of the book of Revelation.

Far less obvious than this connection is the fact that Scriptures about Tyre are sometimes applied to the Roman Empire as well, and this for a striking reason. The normal Hebrew word for Tyre is *tsor*, written with the consonants *ts-w-r*, but usually more shortly ("defectively") written as *ts-r*, that is, with the omission of the letter *waw* pronounced as *o*. However, this shorter word can, with other vocalization, also be read as *tsar*, which means "enemy." There is a rabbinical tradition that wants to read *ts-w-r* always in the common way as "Tyre," but *ts-r* as "enemy," and wants to apply this to the Roman Empire.[1] This yields some surprising results. Thus, we are immediately struck by some connections between Isaiah 23 (speaking of *ts-r*) and Revelation 17 and 18, dealing with the great Babylon/Rome. For instance, one may compare Isaiah 23:8 with Revelation 18:23, and Isaiah 23:17 with Revelation 18:3.[2] Thus, Revelation seems to sanction this rabbinical application of prophecies concerning Tyre to Rome.[3]

As a consequence of this, especially Ezekiel 27 and 28 are lightening up in a striking way (be it that we find here alternately *ts-r* and *ts-w-r*). In a Midrash,[4] Ezekiel 27:27 is indeed applied to Rome. We are now particularly concerned with 28:11-19, where we find a lamentation about the king of Tyre but, as in Isaiah 14, behind the earthly prince clearly an angelic prince is looming up: a "covering (protecting) cherub... on the holy mountain of the gods [or, of God]" (v. 14, 16). Also, in this case some expositors have thought of the fall of Satan, especially in verses 14-17, entirely parallel with Isaiah 14:12-15. We cannot enter here into the many exegetical problems of this Scripture. It suffices at present to point to the interesting suggestion that, if the rabbinical parallel between Babylon or Tyre on the one hand and Rome on the other is correct, both Isaiah 14 and Ezekiel 28 supply us with a striking description

1. See Gen.R. 61,7; Exod.R. 9,13; Pesiqta R. 17,8; 49,9.
2. Interesting here is that Eccl.R. 1:7 (§9) applies Isa. 23:18 to Edom [= Rome], and concludes that the wealth of Edom will be dispersed in the days of the Messiah.
3. The identification, Edom = Rome, as well as Tyre = Rome, is supported if it is true that the Tyrians were Edomites, as Rashi says in his comment on Gen. 25:23: "Tyre was colonized by Esau"; also compare the close relationship suggested in Amos 1:9-10 between Tyre and Edom (Martin 1993:165).
4. Pesiqta R. 14,15.

of the satanic angelic prince of Rome.

Jewish tradition also sees a connection between Rome and Egypt, but not in the sense of identification but of a parallelism (see § 4.1.3). In total, Israel has known six exiles,[5] namely, in the Egyptian, the Assyrian, the Babylonian, the Medo-Persian, the Greek, and the Edomite (= Roman) Empire. Therefore, a parallelism between the first (Egypt) and the last empire (Rome) is just as obvious as the connection between the first (Babylon) and the last (Rome) of the four world-empires in the book of Daniel.

I point to three striking parallels between the redemption out of Egypt and the redemption out of the Roman exile. These parallels are primarily based upon the book of Revelation. The redemption out of Egypt and that out of the Roman exile are connected with the same plagues. That is to say, just before the days of the Messiah the ten plagues of Egypt will come over the Roman Empire as well, as direct forebodings of the second coming of the Son of Man:[6]

- First plague (blood): Revelation 8:8; especially 16:4, 6 (second and third bowl),
- Second plague (frogs): Revelation 16:13 (sixth bowl),
- Third plague (sores): Revelation 16:2 (first bowl),
- Fourth plague (hail): Revelation 9:18; 11:19; 16:21 (second trumpet/seventh bowl),
- Eighth plague (locusts): Revelation 9:3 (fifth trumpet = first woe),
- Ninth plague (darkened sun): Revelation 16:10 (fourth and fifth bowl).

The second parallelism is that both the exodus out of Egypt and the exodus out of Israel's last exile are accompanied by a similar song, as indicated in Revelation 15:3,

> And they sing the song of Moses, the servant of God,
> and the song of the Lamb.

5. Num.R. 10,2.
6. Cf. Pesiqta K. 7,11 and Pesiqta B. 17,8.

The third parallelism is even more remarkable. Just as, at the exodus out of Egypt, Moses, the deliverer of Israel, emerges out of Egypt itself, thus, according to a Jewish tradition, the Messiah emerges out of Rome itself. One Midrash[7] says that the daughter of Pharaoh raised the one who was going to take revenge on her father, and also that the king, the Messiah, who will take revenge on Edom [= Rome], is sitting with them in the city [= Rome]. As evidence for this Isaiah 27:10 is quoted:

> there [in the "fortified city" = Rome] the calf[8] feeds,
> and there it lies down and consumes its branches.[9]

The most astonishing passage about this present hidden sojourn of the Messiah in Rome we find in the following Talmudic story:[10]

> R[abbi] Joshua b. Levi [c. 250] met Elijah standing by the entrance of R. Simeon b. Jochai's [c. 150] tomb. He asked him: "Have I a portion in the world to come[11]?" He replied, "If this Master desires it."[12] R. Joshua b. Levi said, "I saw two [viz., himself and Elijah], but heard the voice of a third [viz., the Shekhina]." He then asked him, "When will the Messiah come?" "Go and ask him himself," was his reply. "Where is he sitting?" – "At the entrance [gate] of Rome[13]." – "And by what sign may I recognize him?" – "He is sitting among the poor lepers:[14] all of them untie [their wounds] all at once, and rebandage them together,[15] whereas he [= the Messiah] unties and rebandages

7. Exod.R. 1,26.
8. Lit. singular! According to the Midrash a picture of the Messiah.
9. Cf. Tankh.shemot 61b; Tankh.B. thizria 65.
10. Sanhedrin 98a.
11. Cf. Matt. 12:32; Mark 10:30; Eph. 1:21; Heb. 2:5; 6:5.
12. Rashi: he referred to the Shekhina that was with him.
13. Current editions read, "of the city'; the Vilna Gaon reads, "of Rome."
14. Rashi: ...those who are struck with leprosy, and he [= the Messiah] too is leprous, for it says in Isa. 53:5, "He was pierced for our transgressions," etc., and further v. 4, "He himself took our diseases," etc.
15. That is, they first take off all the bandages, attend to each diseased spot, and then rebandage them all again.

> each separately,[16] thinking, should I be wanted [by God],[17] I must not be delayed."[18] So he [= R. Joshua] went to him [at Rome] and greeted him, saying, "Peace upon you, Master and Teacher!" "Peace upon you, O son of Levi," he replied. "When will you come, Master?" asked he, "To-day!", was his answer. On his returning to Elijah, the latter enquired, "What did he say to you?" – "Peace upon you, O son of Levi," he answered. Elijah said, "Therewith he assured you and your father [a share in] the coming world." He answered him, "Deceitfully he dealt with me, for he said to me, 'Today I come,' and he has not come." Thereupon he [= Elijah] observed, "He thereby assured you and your father of [a portion in] the world to come." "He spoke falsely to me," he rejoined, "stating that he would come to-day, but has not." He [= Elijah] answered him, "This is what he said to thee, *To-day, if you will hear his voice*" [Ps. 95:7].

Of course, such a haggadic story does not intend to be taken in a historically literal sense. Its concern is rather the deep spiritual principles that are, as it were in the form of a parable, illustrated in it, such as:

(a) the application of Isaiah 53 to the Messiah: he is the One who bears the sins of his people;

(b) the Messiah waits for God's time to appear for the redemption of his people;

(c) the coming of the Messiah depends on the conversion of Israel;

(d) and particularly, in the meantime the Messiah sojourns in Rome.

We certainly are not to generalize this Jewish tradition, but it does represent a certain important view. It is the tradition that the Messiah sojourns today in the Roman Empire, that is, in the *imperium christianum*, Western Christendom. This quite remarkable notion apparently implies that in the

16. That is, before attending to the next diseased spot.
17. That is, to appear as Messiah for the people's redemption.
18. That is, in having still first to rebandage many spots.

Roman-Christian West there are people who know a vivid connection with the true Messiah of Israel, in that he granted them, the miserable "leprous" of the Roman West, healing from their sins.

Bibliography

Aalders, G.J.D., *Mensen en machten: De rol van de grote mannen in de geschiedenis* (Kampen 1954).

Aalders, G.J.D., *Julianus de Afvallige: Het leven van een verbitter-de keizer* (Kampen 1983).

Adamek, J., *Vom römischen Endreich der mittelalterlichen Bibel-erklärung* (Würzburg 1938).

Adams, P.C.B., *America's Economic Supremacy* (New York 1900).

Albright, W.F., *Yahweh and the Gods of Canaan* (Garden City 1968).

Bailey, G., *The Germans* (New York 1972).

Barth, K., *Kirchliche Dogmatik*, Vol. I/1 (Zollikon-Zürich 1932; Eng: *Church Dogmatics*, Edinburgh 1969).

Bavinck, H., *Gereformeerde dogmatiek*, Vol. 2 (Kampen 1928; Eng.: *Reformed Dogmatics*, Grand Rapids 2004).

Binion, R., *Hitler Among the Germans* (Dekalb 1984).

Blauw, J., *Gezanten van de hemel: Het bijbels getuigenis aangaan-de de engelen* (Baarn n.y.).

Bondt, A. de, *De Satan* (Baarn n.y.).

Bousset, W./H. Gressmann (eds.), *Die Religion des Judentums im späthellenistischen Zeitalter* (Tübingen 1926).

Braude, W.G. (ed.), *Pesikta Rabbati*, Yale Judaica Series XVIII (New Haven 1968).

Broadbent, E.H., *The Pilgrim Church* (London 1931).

Bruce, F.F., *The Epistles to the Colossians, to Philemon, and to the Ephesians*, New Intern. Comm. NT (Grand Rapids 1984).

Brugmans , H. & Frank, A., *Geschiedenis der Joden in Nederland*, Vol. 1 (Amsterdam 1940).

Buber, M., 'Recht und Unrecht: Deutung einiger Psalmen', in: *Werke II: Schriften zur Bibel* (1964), p. 951-990.

---, 'Die Götter der Völker und Gott', in: *Ibid.*, p. 1067-1083.

Buber, S. (ed.), *Aggadat Beresit* (Krakau 1902).

Buber, S. & J.T. Townsend (eds.), *Midrash Tanhuma* (Hoboken, N.J. 1989).

Burden, H.T., *The Nuremberg Party Rallies* (New York 1967).

Burton, A.H., *The Apocalypse Expounded* (London 1932).

Bury, R. de, *Philobiblon* (ed. Oxford 1960).

Cameron, N. & Stevens, R.H. (eds.), *Hitler's Conversations 1940-44* (New York 1976).

Charlesworth, J.H. (ed.)., *The Old Testament Pseudepigrapha*, Vol. I, II (Garden City 1983-85).

Chater, E.H., *The Revelation of Jesus Christ* (London 1914).

Collins, A. Yarbro, *The Combat Myth in the Book of Revelation* (Harvard Diss. in Rel. 9, 1976).

Comte, F., *De grote mythologische figuren* (Utrecht 1994; cf. Eng.: *Dictionary of Mythology*, Ware 1997).

Cross, F.M., *Canaanite Myth and Hebrew Epic* (Cambridge, MA 1973).

Cumont, F., *Oriental Religions in Roman Paganism* (1911; repr. New York 1956).

Cumont, F., *Astrology and Religion Among the Greeks and Romans* (1912; repr. New York 1960).

Dalman, G., *Der leidende Messias nach der Lehre der Synagoge im ersten nachchristlichen Jahrtausend* (Karlsruhe 1887).

Darby, J.N., *Collected Writings* (Stow Hill-ed.) (Kingston-on-Thames n.y.).

Delling, G., Stoicheion, *Theological Dictionary of the New Testament*, Vol. VII (Grand Rapids 1971), p. 670-686.

Dennett, E., *The Vision of John in Patmos* (repr. Oak Park, Ill. n.y. [written before 1914]).

Dhorme, E., *Les Religions de Babylonie et d'Assyrie* (series 'Mana', Vol. I,2) (Paris 1949).

Dibelius, M., *Die Geisterwelt im Glauben des Paulus* (Göttingen 1909).

Epstein, I. (ed.), *Taanith* (London 1984).

Fijnvandraat, J.G., *Babylon, beeld & beest: Bijbelstudies over de profetie van Daniël*, Vol. II (Vaassen 1990).

Francke, J., *Veelkoppige monsters: Mythologische figuren in bijbelteksten* (Goes 1970).

Frankfort, H., *Kingship and the Gods* (Chicago 1948).

Fung, R.Y.K., *The Epistle to the Galatians*, New Intern. Comm. NT (Grand Rapids 1988).

Gibson, J.C.L., *Canaanite Myths and Legends* (Edinburgh 1978).

Gispen, W.H., *Genesis*, Vol. 1 (Kampen 1974).

Goebbels, J., *The Goebbels Diaries 1942-43* (Garden City 1948).

Goldberg, M.H., *The Jewish Connection* (New York 1976).

Graaff, F. de, *Anno Domini 1000, Anno Domini 2000: De duizend jaren bij de gratie van de dode god* (Kampen n.y.).

---, *Het geheim van de wereldgeschiedenis* (Kampen 1982).

---, *Jezus de Verborgene*, Vol. I, II (Kampen 1987/1989).

Graetz, H., *Volkstümliche Geschichte der Juden*, Vol. I-VI (1853-1875; repr. Munich 1985; Eng.: *History of the Jews*, Eugene, OR 2002).

Grant, F.W., *The Numerical Bible: Hebrews to Revelation* (Neptune, N.J. 1902).

Groen van Prinsterer, G. (ed. and trans. H. Van Dyke), *Groen van Prinsterer's Lectures on Unbelief and Revolution* (Jordan Station, Ont., 1989 (orig.: *Ongeloof en revolutie*, Amsterdam 1940[4]).

Grote Mysteries: Mysteries van de droom (Lekturama Rotterdam 1978a).

Grote Mysteries: Toekomstvoorspellingen (Lekturama Rotterdam 1978b).

Grundmann, H. 'Die Grundzüge der mittelalterlichen Geschichtsanschauungen', in: Lammers, W. (ed.), *Geschichtsdenken und Geschichtsbild im Mittelalter* (Darmstadt 1984), p. 418-429.

Harmsen, G., *Inleiding tot de geschiedenis* (Baarn 1968).

Hartley, J.E., *The Book of Job*, New Intern. Comm. OT (Grand Rapids 1988).

Hartvelt, G.P., *Het gebinte van de tijd: Een historische studie over constructies van de geschiedenis, met name in de tijd der Reformatie* (Kampen 1977).

Hendriksen, W., *Visioenen der voleinding* (Kampen 1952, 1988[2]; Eng: *More than Conquerers*, Grand Rapids repr. 1998).

Hengel, M. (Hrsg.), *Uebersetzung des Talmud Yerushalmi* (Tübingen 1983 etc.).

Hengstenberg, E.W., *Christology of the Old Testament and a Commentary on the Messianic Predictions*, Vol. I-IV (Edinburgh 1854-58).

Herodotus, *The History* (Chicago 1987).

Hesemann, M., *Hitlers religie: De fatale heilsleer van het nationaal-socialisme* (Soesterberg 2007; orig.: *Hitlers Religion: Das Wahngebäude des Führers*, München 2004).

Hislop, A., *The Two Babylons* (Neptune, N.J. 1916, 1959).

Hitler, A., *Mein Kampf* (München 1925-27).

Hohne, H., *The Order of the Death's Head* (New York 1983).

Holland, T. *In the Shadow of the Sword* (London 2012).

Ironside, H.A., *Lectures on Daniel the Prophet* (New York n.y. [1940-50?]).

Jaffé, A., *Jung over de zin van het leven* (Rotterdam 1967; cf. Eng.: *The Myth of Meaning in the Work of C.G. Jung*, Einsiedeln 1984).

Jennings, F.C., 'The Boundaries of the Revived Roman Empire', *Our Hope* 47 (Dec. 1940).

Jones, A.H.M., *Constantine and the Conversion of Europe* (repr. Toronto 1978).

Jung, C.G., *Goed en kwaad in de westerse wereld* (Rotterdam 1984).

Jung, C.G., *Archetypen* (Utrecht/Antwerpen 1987; Eng.: *The Archetypes and the Collective Unconscious*, Princeton, NJ 1934-54).

Jung, C.G., *Dromen* (Rotterdam 1994[4]; Eng.: *Dreams*, Princeton, NJ 1974).

Kakes, H., *Waar zijn de engelen nu?* (Kampen n.y.).

Karsawin, L.P., 'Der Geist des russischen Christentums', in: N. von Bubnoff & H. Ehrenberg (eds.), *Östliches Christentum: Dokumente*, Vol. 2: Philosophie (Munich 1925), p. 307-377.

Kaufman, Y., *The Religion of Israel* (New York 1972).

Keller, W., ... *En zij werden verstrooid onder alle volken* (Zwolle n.y.; Eng.: *Diaspora: The Post-Biblical History of the Jews*, San Diego 1969).

Kelly, W., 'Remarks on the Book of Daniel', *The Bible Treasury* 3 (1860), p. 2 etc.; repr.: *Notes on the Book of Daniel* (New York 1902, 1952).

Kelly, W., *The Revelation* (London 1904).

Kittel, R., *Die hellenistische Mysterienreligion und das Alte Testament* (1924).

Kittel, R./Bromiley, G., *Theological Dictionary of the New Testament* (Grand Rapids 1964 etc.).

Kocken, E., *De theorie van de vier wereldrijken en van de overdracht der wereldheerschappij tot op Innocentius III* (Nijmegen 1935).

Kramer, G.H., *Ambrosius van Milaan en de geschiedenis* (Amsterdam 1983).

Kroeze, J.H., *Strijd bij de schepping* (The Hague 1962).

Kümmel, W.G. (ed.), *Jüdische Schriften aus hellenistisch-römischer Zeit* (Gütersloh 1973 etc.).

Kurze, G., *Der Engels- und Teufelsglaube des Apostels Paulus* (Freiburg 1905).

Kuyper, A., *Calvinism: Six Stone-Lectures* (Grand Rapids 1943).

Kuyper, H.S.S., *Een half jaar in Amerika* (Rotterdam 1907).

Langer, W.C., *The Mind of Adolf Hitler* (New York 1972).

Loonstra, B., *De geloofwaardigheid van de Bijbel* (Zoetermeer 1994).

Luckenbill, D.D., *Ancient Records of Assyria and Babylonia* (New York 1927).

Lueken, M., *Michael: Eine Darstellung und Vergleichung der jüdischen und der morgenländisch-christlichen Tradition vom Erzengel Michael* (Göttingen 1898).

McRae, H., *De wereld in 2020* (Haarlem 1994; Eng.: *The Word in 2020*, Cambridge, MA 1996).

Madelin, L., *Histoire du Consulat et de l'Empire*, Vol. 1-16 (1937-1954).

Martin, E.L., *The People That History Forgot: The Mysterious People Who Originated the World's Religions* (Portland 1993).

Medema, H.P., *Europa 1992: De nachtmerrie van een supermarkt* (Vaassen 1992).

Mehrtens, G.F., *De Nieuwe Romeinen: Een cultuurfilosofische verkenning* (Houten 1987).

Mellen, P.J., *The Third Reich Examined As the Dramatic Illusion of Ritual Performance* (dissertation, UMI 1988).

Moore, G.F., *Judaism in the First Centuries of the Christian Era: The Age of the Tannaim*, Vol. I-III (1927-1930; repr. Cambridge, MA 1970-71).

Mosse, G., *Nazi Culture* (New York 1981).

Murphy, R.E., Roland, J., Stevens, F. & Trivers, H., *'National Socialism', Readings on Fascism and National-Socialism* (Denver n.y.).

Neusner, J. (ed.), *Pesiqta deRab Kahana: An Analytical Translation* (Atlanta 1987).

Nitschke, A., 'Opkomst en bloei van de christelijke rijken in West-Europa', *Universele Wereldgeschiedenis* Vol. 5 (The Hague/Hasselt 1975).

Ouweneel, W.J., *De ark in de branding* (Amsterdam 1977).

Ouweneel, W.J., Nogmaals over draken, *Bijbel & Wetenschap* 92 (1986), p. 26v.

Ouweneel, W.J., *Het domein van de slang* (Amsterdam 1988a).

Ouweneel, W.J., *De Openbaring van Jezus Christus* (Vaassen 1988b/90).

Ouweneel, W.J., *Israël en de Kerk* (Vaassen 1991).

Ouweneel, W.J., *Godsverlichting: De evocatie van de verduisterde God: Een weg tot spiritualiteit en gemeenteopbouw* (Amsterdam 1994).

Ouweneel, W.J., Valse profeet of Gods dienstknecht?, *Bode van het Heil in Christus* (1995).

Ouweneel, W.J., *De zevende koningin: Het eeuwig vrouwelijke en de raad van God* (Metahistorische trilogie, Vol. 2) (Heerenveen 1998).

Ouweneel, W.J., *F.M. Dostojevski: De groot-inquisiteur: Christus door de Kerk verworpen* (geredigeerd en becommentarieerd door Willem J. Ouweneel) (Soesterberg 2003).

Ouweneel, W.J., *De Christus van God: Ontwerp van een christologie* (Vaassen 2007).

Ouweneel, W.J., *De Kerk van God (I): Ontwerp van een elementaire ecclesiologie* (Heerenveen 2010).

Ouweneel, W.J., *De Kerk van God (II): Ontwerp van een historische en praktische ecclesiologie* (Heerenveen 2011).

Ouweneel, W.J., *De toekomst van God: Ontwerp van een eschatology* (Heerenveen 2012).

Ouweneel, W.J., De glorie van God: Ontwerp van een godsleer en van een theologische vakfilosofie (Heerenveen 2013).

Ouweneel, W.J., *Een dubbelsnoer van licht: Honderd grootse joodse en christelijke godsmannen door de geschiedenis heen –*

en hun moeizame relaties (Soesterberg 2014a).

Ouweneel, W.J., *Wisdom for Thinkers: An Introduction to Christian Philosophy* (St. Catherines, Can. 2014b).

Ouweneel, W.J., *Power in Service: An Introduction to Christian Political Thought* (St. Catherines, Can. 2014c).

Ouweneel, W.J., *Thinking God's Thoughts: An Introduction to Christian Theology* (St. Catherines, Can. 2014d).

Pentecost, J.D., *Things to Come: A Study in Biblical Eschatology* (Grand Rapids 1964).

Picker, H., *Hitlers Tischgespräche* (München 2003).

Ploeg, J.P.M. van der, *Psalmen*, Vol. 2 (Roermond 1974).

Pomian, Kr., *Europa en de Europese naties* (Amsterdam 1993).

Popma, K.J., *Calvinistische geschiedenisbeschouwing* (Franeker 1945).

Pot, J.H.J. van der, *De periodisering van de geschiedenis* (The Hague 1951).

Presser, J., Napoleon: *Historie en legende* (Amsterdam 1978).

Prinz, J., *Popes from the Ghetto* (New York 1966).

Quinn, C., *Adolf Hitler* (New York 1978).

Robertson, O.P., *The Books of Nahum, Habakkuk, and Zephaniah,* New Intern. Comm. OT (Grand Rapids 1990).

Rashie, *Commentaar op de Pentateuch* (ed. A.S. Onderwijzer) (Amsterdam 1895, repr. 1977).

Rauschning, H., *Revolution of Nihilism* (New York 1939).

Rauschning, H., *Voice of Destruction* (New York 1940).

Sale-Harrison, L., *The Resurrection of the Old Roman Empire* (London 1928, [1939]).

Schoonwater, H., 'Keizer Otto III, de grote Nijmegenaar', *Valkhofnieuws* 8 (1986), nr. 2.

Schopen, E., *Geschichte des Judentums im Morgenland* (Bern 1960).

Schulte Nordholt, J.W., *De mythe van het Westen: Amerika als het laatste wereldrijk* (Amsterdam 1992).

Schürer, E., *Geschichte des jüdischen Volkes im Zeitalter Jesu Christi*, Vol. I-IV (Leipzig 1901-1911).

Scott, W., *Exposition of the Revelation of Jesus Christ* (London 1920).

Seppelt, F.X. & K. Löffler, *De geschiedenis der pausen* (Maastricht 1939; Eng.: *A Short History of the Popes*, London 1932).

Shirer, W., *Nightmare Years* (Boston 1984).

Sneller, Z.W., *et al.*, *De zin der geschiedenis* (Wageningen 1944).

Soncino Hebrew-English Edition of the Babylonian Talmud (London 1980 etc.).

Speer, A., *Inside the Third Reich* (New York 1971).

Speer, A., *Spandau Diary* (New York 1976).

Spengler, O., *The Decline of the West* (Oxford 1991; orig.: 1923).

Strack, H.L., *Einleitung in Talmud und Midras* (Munich 1887, 1921).

---/P. Billerbeck, *Kommentar zum Neuen Testament aus Talmud und Midrasch* (Munich 1922-1928).

Tarn, W.W., *Alexander the Great*, Vol. I, II (Cambridge 1948).

Tarn, W.W., *Hellenistic Civilization* (London 19523, repr. 1974).

Toland, J., *Adolf Hitler* (Garden City 1976).

Tuveson, E.L., *Millennium and Utopia: A Study in the Background of the Idea of Progress* (New York 1949, 1964).

Van Campen, M., *Gans Israël: Voetiaanse en coccejaanse visies op de joden gedurende de 17e en 18e eeuw* (Zoetermeer 2006).

Van de Kamp, H.R., *Israël in Openbaring* (Kampen 1990).

Van Ryn, A., *Notes on the Book of Revelation* (Kansas City [ca. 1960]).

Visser, J.Th. de, *Kerk en staat*, Vol. 1: *Buitenland* (Leiden 1926).

Volz, P., *Die Eschatologie der jüdischen Gemeinde im neutestamentlichen Zeitalter* (Tübingen 1934; repr. Hildesheim 1966).

Voorhoeve, H.C., *De toekomst onzes Heeren Jezus Christus* (The Hague 1866, 1922).

Vries, J. de (vert.), *Edda* (Deventer 1980).

Wagner, R., 'Was ist deutsch?', *Gesammelte Schriften und Dichtungen* 10 (Leipzig n.y.3), p. 36-53.

Wakeman, M., *God's Battle with the Monster* (Leiden 1973).

Weber, F., *Jüdische Theologie auf Grund des Talmud und verwandter Schriften* (Leipzig 1897; repr. Hildesheim 1975).

Weiler, A.G., *Willibrords m*issie (Hilversum 1989).

Wilson, J., *Parsi Religion* (Bombay 1843; online ed. 2003).

Yates, F.A., *Astraea: The Imperial Theme in the Sixteenth Century* (London 1975).

Zijlstra, A., *De wereldpolitiek in het licht van de Schrift* (Goes 1950).

Zlotowitz, M. & Scherman, N., *Bereishis*, Vol. I, II (New York 1986).

Quoted Apocryphal and Pseudepigraphic Writings

I) Apocryphal writings

1 Ezra (= 3 Ezra)
(Jesus) Sir(ach)
Wisd(om of Solomon)
1 Baruch (= often shortly: Baruch)
Ep(istola) Jer(emiae) (= Epistle of Jeremiah)
Tob(it)

II) Pseudepigraphic Writings

Jub(ilees)
Asc(ensio) Jes(aiae) (= Ascension of Isaiah)
Ass(umptio) Mos(is) (= Assumption of Moses)
1 Enoch (= the Ethiopian book of Enoch)
2 Henoch (= the Slavic book of Enoch = Book of the Secrets of Enoch)
2 Baruch (= the Syrian Apocalypse of Baruch)
3 Baruch (= the Greek Apocalypse of Baruch)
4 Ezra

Test(ament of) Benj(amin)
Test(ament of) Levi
Hebr(ew) Test(ament of) Napht(ali)

See Charlesworth (1983-85; and similar editions by R.H. Charles, Oxford, and E. Kautzsch, Tübingen) and the series *Jüdische Schriften* (Kümmel, 1973 etc.) for the apocryphal and pseudepigraphic writings.

Quoted Rabbinical Literature

(for extensive information see Strack 1921) (where no further bibliographic circumscription is given see the relevant edition of The Soncino Press at London)

I) Midrash (= exegesis of Scripture)

- a) the Targums (= Aramaic paraphrase)
  - 1) Targum Onkelos
  - 2) Targum Jonathan
  - 3) Targum Yerushalmi (= T. Pseudo-Jonathan = Palestinian or Jerusalem-Targum)
- b) Midrashim in the stricter sense
  - A) the old-Palestinian halakhic(-haggadic) [= legislative-(narrative)] commentaries]
    - 1) Mechilta (on Exod.)
    - 2) Sifra (on Lev.)
    - 3) Sifre (on Num. and Deut.)
  - B) the haggadic-homiletic commentaries (quoted with chapter and paragraph)
    - 1) oldest: Pesiqta [deRab Kahana] (old-Palest.) (ed. Neusner 1987)
    - 2) Shemot Rabba (= Exod.R.), Wayyiqra R. (= Lev.R.), Bemidbar R. (= Num.R.) and Debarim R. (= Deut.R.) (Soncino-ed.)
    - 3) Tankhuma (oldest known coherent Midrash on the Pentateuch; haggadic) (Tankh.B. = ed.

Buber & Townsend 1989)
4) Pesiqta Rabbati (9th cent.) (ed. Braude 1968)
5) smaller, e.g., Aggadat Bereshit (ed. Buber 1902).

C) the expository Midrashim
1) Bereshit Rabba (= Gen.R.) (Soncino-ed.)
2) Midrashim on the five 'scrolls' (Megillot): Lam.R., SoS.R., Ruth R., Eccl.R., Est.R. (Soncino-ed.)
3) other Bible books: Jonah, Ps., Prov., Job

D) other haggadic works, e.g., Megillat Taanit (ed. Epstein 1984)

E) Midrashic collections
1) Yalkut Shimeoni (often briefly: Yalkut)
2) Yalkut Rubeni
3) Yalkut chadash

II) Actual halakhic [= legislative] literature

a) Mishna (commentary on the laws of Sinai; N.B.: e.g. Pirke Abot strongly haggadic)
b) Tosephta (N.B.: many chapters entirely haggadic)
c) Talmud (= Gemara, commentary on the Mishna) (names of tracts usually quoted in full with chapter and paragraph)

A) Palestinian or Jerusalem Talmud (e.g., tract Aboda Zara strongly haggadic) (tracts from this T. indicated by the prefix pal.) (ed. Hengel 1983 etc.)

B) Babylonian Talmud (mixed halakhic-haggadic) (Hebrew-English ed., Soncino 1980 etc.) Some tracts according to their divisions:
1) Zeraim: e.g., Berakhot, Pea
2) Mo'ed: e.g., Shabbat, Yoma, Khagiga, Pesakhim, Taanith
3) Nashim: e.g., Sota
4) Neziqin: e.g., Sanhedrin, Makkot, Aboda Zara, (Pirke) Abot, Baba Bathra
5) Qodashim: e.g., Khullin, Tamid, Arachin

6) Toharot: e.g., Para, Nidda

www.ingramcontent.com/pod-product-compliance
Lightning Source LLC
Chambersburg PA
CBHW020427130626
46549CB00001B/24

* 9 7 8 1 9 9 8 7 1 1 0 7 9 *